THE BRITISH POLITICAL ELITE

STUDIES IN SOCIET

General Editors: Ruth and David Glass

W. L. GUTTSMAN

The British Political Elite

LONDON
MACGIBBON & KEE
1968

FIRST PUBLISHED 1963 BY MACGIBBON & KEE LTD
3 UPPER JAMES STREET, GOLDEN SQUARE, LONDON W.1
SECOND IMPRESSION 1964
THIRD (REVISED) IMPRESSION 1965
FOURTH IMPRESSION 1968
COPYRIGHT © W. L. GUTTSMAN, 1963
PRINTED IN GREAT BRITAIN BY
COX & WYMAN LIMITED
LONDON, READING AND FAKENHAM
SBN: 261.61535.1

For Valerie who helped and for Janet who distracted

CONTENTS

CONTENTS

TABLES IN THE TEXT

TABLES IN THE TEXT

DIAGRAMS

PREFACE

THIS book deals with the evolution of the British Political Elite and its changing social composition since the first Reform Act in 1832. Against this historical background I have attempted to analyse the political leadership within the two major parties as well as within the wider group of those who occupy positions of power and influence in our Society. In doing so I was led beyond a formal sociological analysis of concrete groups of politicians to a consideration of selection processes in the field of politics and to an assessment of the distribution of power in British Society today.

My interest in the theme of this book arose during post-graduate studies at the London School of Economics. Some of the material contained in Chapter IV, VI and VII was first presented in a thesis submitted to the University of London for the degree of M.Sc. (Econ.) and elaborated in articles which appeared in the British Journal of Sociology in June 1951 and March 1954. Chapter IX is based on a contribution to *Political Decision— Makers: Recruitment and Performance* edited by Dwaine Marwick and published by the Free Press, Glencoe, Illinois., whom I should like to thank for their permission to reproduce parts of it. The quotations from W. B. Yeats are taken from the *Collected Poems* published by Macmillan.

My debt to the London School of Economics has grown over the years; its Library formed in more senses than one the 'operational basis' for this work. I am grateful for the grant of a period of sabbatical leave during the summer of 1961 which enabled me to devote myself for a few months wholly to work on this book. I should also like to thank the Sociological Research Division of the School for a grant which enabled me to obtain some assistance in connection with biographical researches into the membership of some contemporary élite groups and to Mr C. Robertson for carrying out this laborious task.

It is however to many friends and former colleagues at the London

School of Economics that I am particularly indebted. To Alan Stuart and John Hajnal for advice on points of statistical techniques, to Anne Martin for elucidating some points in connection with the discussion of land ownership and agricultural rent, and to Basil Yamey for his comments on some of the issues raised in Chapter XI. Above all, I have greatly benefited from the criticism and suggestions made by those who at various stages read the manuscript or parts of it: Geoffrey Allen, Gerald Curzon, David Lockwood, Donald MacRae, Ralph Miliband, and Richard Pear. To David Glass I owe a debt, not only for this but also for his general encouragement and helpful prodding in the writing of this book. I am very grateful to Miss Dorothy West for the helpful and efficient way in which she typed the manuscript and to Lloyd Warburton for assistance with the proof reading. My greatest debt I have sought to acknowledge in the dedication.

December 1962   W.L.G.

CHAPTER I

Politicians in British Society

'It is not names that constitute governments but the use and exercise of those powers that were intended to accompany them.'—JOHN LOCKE.

'Men make their own history but they do not make it just as they please; they do not make it under circumstances as chosen by themselves but under circumstances directly found, given and transmitted from the past. The tradition of all the dead generations weigh like a nightmare on the brain of the living'.—KARL MARX.

ALL men make politics, particularly in a democratic society where the right to participate in decisions affecting public and private welfare is widely shared. Yet at the same time immediate and effective power in the sphere of government is vested in a very small number. Given the complexity of the modern state and the size of the social and economic units within which decisions must be taken this is probably inevitable: politics cannot be conducted on the basis of daily referendums. Democracy can only ensure that those who wield great power shall hold their positions on trust and that, if they abuse their trust or fail in their policies, their fall shall be swift and sure. A democratic political system cannot make élites superfluous, though it may ensure their rapid and regular circulation. Hence our interest in the wielders of power.

Among students of politics this interest is of comparatively recent growth. When thirty years ago the late Sir Lewis Namier set out to analyse the British political scene in the eighteenth century he broke new ground. Eschewing considerations of parties and policies, he concentrated on the men who got into Parliament and on why and how they got there, and he likened his approach to that of non-euclidean geometry.[1] Since Namier wrote *The*

---

[1] *cf.* the preface to the first edition of *The Structure of Politics at the Accession of George III*, 1929.

Structure of Politics at the Accession of George III there have been repeated attempts to study the social background of policies and politicians and we have become familiar with sociological analyses of political institutions.[1] Today few will argue that to look at politics through the lives of politicians is to use the wrong end of the telescope. I think that the few hundred or few thousand who in the past exercised considerable power, or who do so today, merit study in their own right. A knowledge of their character and of the formative influences of their lives helps us to understand their policies.

Moreover, politics—like medicine or painting—is a craft as well as a profession. The background of those who exercise it and the talents and experiences which they can bring to bear on it, affect the quality of the political dialogue and the wisdom and efficiency of the acts of governing. Our centralized and highly complex system of government, which has gradually become responsible for an ever-widening area of life, demands different qualities from the politician than did the 'nightwatchman state' of a hundred and twenty years ago. Furthermore, if we observe British politicians within the context of their society and see their rise under the influence of new social forces and in changing social conditions we may also gain some understanding of structural changes in British society.

These, however, are the recurrent themes of this study and I shall take them up throughout this book. This chapter will only give a broad outline of the development during the past two centuries and pose some of the principal questions which arise in the study of the British Political Elite.

In the eighteenth century, the elected representatives and others who devoted much of their time to politics were part of a much smaller population of those who were at all eligible for a political career than they are today, so that 'very few among those who

---

[1] The number of relevant studies is by now too large for listing. The majority have, however, been concerned with electoral behaviour rather than with the social background of politicians. The pioneer study in the latter field is H. J. Laski's *The Personnel of the British Cabinet, 1832–1924*, published originally in 1928. For a summary of relevant studies see D. R. Matthews: *The Social Background of Political Decision-Makers*, 1954.

desired to enter the House of Commons failed to get a chance'.[1]
The eighteenth-century M.P. did not enter politics either to
press certain policies or to enjoy the thrill of being a cog in the
wheel of the legislative and deliberative machine. We rarely find
men like the private Labour M.P., without hope or desire of office,
who 'after he lost his seat in 1931 never once walked down Whitehall until he was re-elected for fear of suffering the pang which the
sight of Palace Yard would give him'.[2] To be an M.P. was, above
all, a means to an end, and the end was 'non-political' and could be
defined in terms of material advantages, or non-material satisfaction. For the aristocracy a career in the House of Commons was
almost a natural stepping-stone to the House of Lords; for the
country gentleman, Parliament enhanced his prestige in the
county. For the Civil Servant it could mean more sinecure offices,
and Officers in the Army and the Navy hoped for promotion via
the House of Commons. Merchants and Bankers could seek and
receive valuable contracts. In 1761 twenty-one out of thirty Admirals, Vice-Admirals and Rear Admirals either were M.P.s, or
had sat in Parliament, and of twenty-two leading City Men fifteen
had sat in Parliament at one time or another.

Some men hoped for places, others desired only to escape their
creditors. Social climbers would find the possession of a seat in the
House of Commons almost essential for their goals, but on the
whole, a parliamentary career tended to be firmly rooted in an
established social position. The political and the social élite were thus
closely identical. Esteem was enhanced by attendance at Westminster, while the purchase of a seat was an investment conducted
for the sake of material gain or emotional satisfaction. Worldly
success went hand in hand with the exercise of political power and
it was the very venality of the system which made it so. Members
bought or bribed the electorate, and ministers, in turn, if necessary bought members' votes.

A hundred years later, all this had changed. A succession of
legislative measures had removed from Parliament all men holding

---

[1] Namier, *op. cit.*, 2nd ed., p. 2. On the average fifty men entered the House of
Commons annually and the educated and sufficiently wealthy formed only a
small fraction of the 70,000 men who each year came of age.

[2] Related by R. H. S. Crossman: *The Charm of Politics*, 1958, p. 3.

an office under the Crown.[1] Sinecure offices were being abolished and contracts and places at the disposal of the Government were not given in recompense for political loyalty, or at least not obviously so.[2] With a greater earnestness the standards of parliamentary conduct had improved. Politicians were no longer like jousting knights seeking fame and fortune in and through parliamentary life. The changes in the electoral system destroyed one of the fundamental bases of the eighteenth-century parliamentary system: boroughs ceased to be just commodities sold to the highest bidder.[3] Electoral corruption was of course still widespread, but bribery implies competition. In 1761 only 48 constituencies out of 315 went to a poll. In 1865 there were 204 contests out of a total of 401 possible ones, and the figure was to rise steadily in the second half of the nineteenth century. Among the contestants the 'inevitable Parliament men' still loomed large and in the counties and the small boroughs aristocratic influence was especially strong. In 1761 'not more than a dozen M.P.s could be described as of obscure origin'; over 50 per cent belonged to families with roots in the Peerage and the Baronetage.

A century later this had not changed greatly; complete newcomers without family or personal position were still rather rare and lack of prestige, social influence or economic power weighed the scales heavily against them. *The Economist* wrote in 1864 that, unless the conditions under which men entered Parliament were changed 'England would be governed by Peers' sons and by men with £20,000 a year'.

By the middle of the Victorian era the price of politics was on the whole greater than at any time previously. The cost of elections had risen with the increase of the electorate; attendance in the House of Commons entailed more financial sacrifice than earlier, without bringing any rewards. At the same time there were more people whose incomes, possessions and social standing made them eligible for a political career. This is not just the result of the enormous

---

[1] Ministers could overcome this by seeking re-election.
[2] On this see W. B. Gwyn: *Democracy and the Cost of Politics in Britain*, 1962, ch. I.
[3] Namier noted that in the eighteenth century not all constituencies were venal. There were 'faithful wives, kept mistresses and prostitutes ready to receive any adventure'.

increase of population since the previous century. The middle class had grown in numbers and in importance. The transformation of Britain from an agricultural and trading nation to a vast manufacturing one had brought new professions and new men forward.

In 1851 nearly one-fifth of the population belonged to what may very roughly be described as 'Middle Class'.[1] The bulk of these were clerks, shop assistants, farmers and the like, men who would hardly look towards a political career. But it also included over 11,000 'Masters' employing more than ten men; 12,500 men whom we would now describe as members of the leading professions; 20,000 landed proprietors and finally 10,856 who are listed as 'independent Gentlemen'.[2]

The last-named groups, which contained undoubtedly the bulk of the members of the aristocracy and the gentry, furnished candidates for most of the county seats and the small borough constituencies. M.P.s there owed their election almost invariably to the pre-eminent position which they occupied in the constituency. Even if they were not men of great property, the selectors, who were, would choose men of their own social stamp, 'a candidate for the county is selected by the leading men of the county, and no man who had not the endorsement of their approval would have the slightest chance whatever'.[3] It is only in the larger borough constituencies that we find the self-made men without a substantial family background. In the 1850's the large Yorkshire borough constituencies all approach the character of popular constituencies. The smallest, Halifax, had just under 1,500 electors while Sheffield, the largest, contained over 7,000 men eligible to vote. The nineteen candidates who sought election in 1859 were similar in type to a great number of their constituents. All but two were members of the great middle class, richer no doubt than the average, but mostly men who for a great part of

---

[1] i.e. 1,214,000 or 18·3 per cent of all occupied males. These figures are the result of calculations made by Dr Charlotte Erickson. See her British Industrialists: Steel and Hosiery, 1850–1950, 1960, p. 234.

[2] These figures are taken from The Census of Great Britain in 1851: An Analytical index condensed from official reports and tables, 1854. The figure for 'Masters' refers to England and Wales only.

[3] Philip Rose (Conservative Chief Agent) in evidence before the House of Lords Select Committee on the Elective Franchise (BPP 1860, vol. XII).

their lives had followed careers in commerce, industry and the professions.[1] Men like them manned the committees of local political associations and these proud citizens of the new manufacturing centres chose others from their own midst.

The new M.P.s generally had roots in the local community, in the dissenting churches and occasionally in political reform movements. Although strictly speaking only a third of the candidates for the Yorkshire cities stood for the constituencies in which they lived, a number resided in neighbouring towns or in the county, and had strong ties with the constituency which they sought to represent. The Liberals in York tried, albeit unsuccessfully, to find 'a man of standing and position . . . and if possible a resident in this county as every exertion should be made to return men who would oppose everything calculated to lead to centralization'.[2] In the selection of these men local prestige and political conviction mingle. Indeed, in some respects selection of the candidates and the conduct of that election strike us as decidedly modern. Sabbatarians and Temperance men sought assurances from the candidates, 'non-electors' met to draw attention to their plight. Pledges about franchise Reform and about the ballot were given and refused. Meetings were held in wards and at factory gates; canvassers tried to convince, cajole or occasionally to corrupt. Politicians became at least for a time part of a local quasi-party machine.[3]

These happenings are important in themselves and as portents of things to come; they show how new patterns of political behaviour arise when new and generally suppressed social groups seek entry into the arena of politics. Unable to influence the selection or the political conduct of politicians of the traditional stamp, they use voice and vote to exert pressure whenever the numbers and weight of their organization gave them a chance.

Until Victorian times those who entered on a parliamentary career did so on the whole as unconnected individuals, each seeking

---

[1] Halévy noted that in the years before the first Reform Act the *nouveaux riches* did generally represent the larger open boroughs. See his *England in 1815*, p. 118.

[2] According to the *York Herald*, the local Liberal paper.

[3] *cf.* W. L. Guttsman: 'The General Election in the Cities of Yorkshire in 1859', *International Review of Social History*, Autumn 1957, pp. 231–58.

election for a borough or a county constituency. They generally subscribed to a 'colour' and expressed their loyalty to one leader or another. If elected to Parliament they would swell the ranks of one of the parties, or the groupings which went by that name, and would give it general but far from unquestioning support. But in the whys and hows of their parliamentary conduct they felt little responsibility to anyone. From the 1840's onwards, powerful pressure groups attempted to whip up nation-wide enthusiasm for specific policies and to secure the election of men pledged to advocate them in Parliament, and their success leavened the lump of parliamentary representation. The Anti-Corn Law League is the most vigorous and successful example of this type of organization. Nonconformity constituted the basis of another pressure group. Labouring under the social and religious disadvantages of their denominations, its members sought redress through parliamentary activity. And as dissent was largely a religion of the lower orders, or of those who had sprung from them, its endeavours tended to bring men of the middle classes into Parliament.

The third popular movement and the only one which was genuinely thrusting from below, was Chartism. Its radical programme, violent language, poor resources and the general lack of working-class franchise made it practically impossible for Chartists to secure the election of their leaders. From 1837 onwards a number of them stood for Parliament, but of the small band who then and in the 1840's sought election only Feargus O'Connor was successful. He and the majority of the defeated Chartist candidates belonged to the middle-class section of the movement; throughout all these years only a handful of them were actual workingmen. How they would have managed to carry out their parliamentary duties had they been elected is difficult to see. In 1841 Francis Place, who had by now become disillusioned with Chartism, sought to dissuade Henry Vincent from pursuing his candidature for Banbury. Francis Place thought that Vincent could not possibly find the money necessary to being an M.P. He advised him to 'follow his trade'—he was a compositor—and become a man of business for the next ten years. 'You may perhaps, at the end of that time, be in a condition to do some public service.'[1] To Place this seemed the

---

[1] *cf.* G. Wallas: *Life of Francis Place*, 1918 ed., p. 381.

only way in which a man without an independent income could become a politician. Essentially it remained so until the organized Labour movement became convinced of the necessity of sending its representatives into Parliament at its own expense. The first stirrings in this direction took place after the second Reform Act. In 1874 the Labour Representation League sponsored 13 candidates, only two of whom were elected. Alexander MacDonald gained a seat for Stafford, where he stood under the auspices of the local Working Men's Radical Association, and Thomas Burt, whose candidature was sponsored by the Northumberland Miners, was elected for Morpeth. They were the first two working-class candidates.

In 1880 Broadhurst, the Secretary of the Labour Representation League and Parliamentary Secretary of the T.U.C., followed them. Broadhurst's income at the time was £150 per annum and he found it extremely difficult to carry out his duties with such slender resources. He was now 'face to face with an entirely new situation, imposing new responsibilities and requiring larger means'. He met this 'by maintaining the same habits at home as before my election, with the exception of such changes as were unavoidable when Parliament was sitting. For years past all my clothes had been made at home by my wife, and for several years of my parliamentary life my wife remained my only tailor'.[1]

From then on a growing number of working men sought election and after 1885 nearly a dozen actually sat in the House of Commons at one time.[2] The majority of them were officials of the Miners' Federation returned for constituencies where the working class had been enfranchised for the first time by the third Reform Act. If the number of working-class M.P.s remained small this was not due to insurmountable electoral obstacles, but to the internal logic of the Labour representation. From the beginning, the rôle of the 'Lib–Lab' M.P.s—as they became known—was strictly circumscribed. They were spokesmen of the Trade Union Movement, not the representatives of the working class which by now

[1] cf. H. Broadhurst: *Henry Broadhurst, M.P. The story of his Life from a Stonemason's Bench to the Treasury Bench.* 1901, pp. 101–2, and also pp. 286–93.

[2] For a detailed list of Labour and Radical M.P.s during this period see Appendix I of G. D. H. Cole: *British Working Class Politics, 1832–1914*, 1941.

formed the overwhelming majority of the electorate in many constituencies. Working-class M.P.s were elected with Liberal support and they were Liberals at heart, as was the majority of the Trade Union leadership and probably the bulk of the British workingmen.

It needed the independent, politically organized Labour Movement, expressed in the Labour Representation Committee, which in 1906 became the Labour Party, to push a large number of men of their own kind into Parliament. From 1918 onwards a growing minority of the membership of the House of Commons consisted of men born in working-class homes. But apart from the Trade Union officials and a number of men who were still following manual occupations and whose political roots were firmly planted in local Labour parties or socialist organizations, few members of the working class have entered politics. For a skilled worker to make a political career within the ranks of the Conservative party has always been practically unknown and, of the M.P.s who have risen into the middle class from below, only comparatively few can be found on the Conservative side of the House of Commons.

This seems to me significant. It probably reflects the social bias of Conservative selection committees, but it may also be a symptom of more deep-seated traits. It may be based on the acceptance by the working class of one of the underlying assumptions of our social system, namely that higher social status implies greater ability. For even in the Labour Party the fortunes of Trade-Union sponsored M.P.s are declining and following on this the strength of the working-class politicians is diminishing. The unions tended generally to support candidates in safe constituencies and with the growth of Labour Party representation and the capture of marginal seats their influence in the Parliamentary Labour Party was bound to decline. Today the parliamentary succession in Trade Union held seats is often competed for by men from outside the Trade Union Movement, former M.P.s perhaps, with greater experience and ability than the ageing Trade Union organizer who may be able to make a financial contribution but not much else.[1] Likewise in the upper levels of the Labour Party leadership the

---

[1] cf. M. Harrison: *Trade Unions and the Labour Party since 1945*, 1960, pp. 262–279.

importance of the Trade Union leader has decreased. They have generally found real industrial power preferable to possibly spurious and generally limited political power. The history of the Labour Party, especially since 1945, has thus falsified Beatrice Webb's assertion that 'the Trade Union Movement has become, like the hereditary Peerage, an avenue of political power through which stupid, untrained persons may pass to the highest office if only they have secured the suffrage of the members of a large union'.[1]

Beatrice Webb's strictures fail to take the career element in politics into account. The British aristocracy accepted quite naturally, and without much heart-searching, positions in the political élite which men below them coveted for that very reason. Status-seeking has been endemic for a long time and in all classes, and a parliamentary career has always had a place in the general upward social mobility. At a time when the House of Commons was largely the preserve of the landed classes, members of the prosperous middle class sought to gain status and secure social acceptance through parliamentary activity. The long entrenched positions of the members of the traditional ruling strata, buttressed by their economic independence and by the influence of family ties, was thus actually reinforced by men from the groups below them who clamoured for admission but who, in aping their 'betters', acquiesced in their power and prominence.

Working-class representatives were in a sense immunized against the siren-calls of personal social salvation. In the Labour Party the desire for personal advancement was held to be in conflict with established thinking and socialist ideology. The Labour leadership as a whole was expected to subordinate individual social mobility to the raising of the standards of all the lowly and suppressed. Workingmen, it was thought, should move with their class, not out of it. In practice many of the skilled workers and Trade Union officials who were elected to Parliament became silently assimilated into the upper and middle-class society which manifests itself strongly in the House of Commons even in this century.

The character and composition of the political leadership and especially that part of it which is represented in the House of

---

[1] Beatrice Webb: *Diaries, 1912–24*, 1952, p. 89.

Commons and in the Cabinet has followed, albeit slowly, the general changes in British social structure. The *contemporary* political élite, unlike its predecessor a century or two ago, is no longer anchored so firmly in a particular stratum of British society, and its members can much less justly be called the natural leaders of their society than at any time before.

A gradually disappearing landowner class has long taken a back-seat on the political stage and with its decline the hereditary legislator has made his last bow. A hundred years ago Bagehot could write that 'the counties not only elect landowners, which is natural, but also elect landowners from their own county...there is no Free Trade in the agricultural mind; each county prohibits the import of able men from other counties'.[1] Since then the character of the counties has changed throughout the greater part of the country and even the remaining county families are not as influential as they used to be. And with the decline in local 'inbreeding' and the rise of new groups and new political influences[2] the continuity of parliamentary representation, found so frequently among landed families in the eighteenth and nineteenth centuries, has disappeared. I think the decline of political families is one of the fundamental features in the evolution of the British Political Elite and one which has not yet been sufficiently appreciated. Its effects were not merely social but extended to the character of political activity and parliamentary performance itself. Even if the House of Commons still contains more sons and grandsons of M.P.s than we would expect to find there on the basis of a purely random selection, the loss of political family tradition which used to extend over several generations, is a real loss and I shall return to this point later.

The basis of urban parliamentary representation has undergone parallel changes. During the nineteenth century the representative of a large or medium-sized borough was frequently a man who had already exercised positions of leadership in the community and he could generally be found at the apex of local society. He might be a local merchant or industrialist and his constituents were

---

[1] Walter Bagehot: *The English Constitution*, 1919 ed., p. 164.
[2] Notably the inroads made by the Labour Party in the representation of rural constituencies.

sometimes economically dependent on him as the principal employer.[1] Such men not only served their town in Parliament but through their economic and social position, their membership of many leading organizations and committees and, last but not least, through their private munificence, they could exercise great influence over local affairs. This type of M.P. has not disappeared completely but he is less common today than a hundred or even fifty years ago. His decline is partly due to the fact that, where at one time the representative of a sizeable borough was a Liberal or even a Conservative, his modern counterpart is frequently a Labour M.P., who for obvious reasons is unlikely to come from the same social group as his predecessor.

Moreover, the very importance of this group of leading citizens who had strong economic and family ties in the town is declining. Today there are comparatively fewer individual entrepreneurs who own an enterprise and direct it personally. Firms grow or amalgamate and the patriarchal owner of yesterday is replaced by the more impersonal manager. The manager, moreover, is frequently an 'outsider', a man who has come into the locality to take up his post, but who was brought up elsewhere. And whether outsiders or native-born, those who direct enterprises have tended increasingly to reside outside the urban areas in which their factory is situated.

Geographical mobility affects the urban leadership also in another way. The local élite contains today a much greater number of professional men, officials, teachers, doctors, accountants, engineers—men who, by the nature of their profession tend to migrate and who often settle in a place in which they have no roots. Their prominence may be great and the result of their social or political activity may be very beneficial, but their influence over local affairs is unlikely to be as significant as that of the men who could base their status on great wealth, economic power and a connection with the town extending perhaps over several generations.

All these changes are strengthened by the growing importance

---

[1] Sir Josiah Guest, owner of the Dowlais Iron Works, sat for Merthyr from its enfranchisement until his death.

[2] cf. A. H. Birch, Small Town Politics, 1959, pp. 22–33 and 184–191; M. Stacey, Tradition and Change. A Study of Banbury, 1960, ch. I and VIII.

of the democratic selection process for office and the influence of local party organizations on the choice of the men who will sit in the Council chamber or on other representative bodies. The local political oligarchs who hold positions of power, honour and trust as councillors, magistrates, governors of schools and hospitals, reach their eminence largely through the party organizations. They, like the national political leaders, are recruited mainly from the middle class. This is clearly so in the Conservative Party, but even the representation of the Labour Party on local elected bodies contains a considerably larger proportion of men and women from groups above the manual working class than we find in the population as a whole, let alone in the group of Labour voters.[1] Activity on elected local authorities, especially on the top-tier authorities, can under present conditions be undertaken only by those whose job gives them a modicum of independence, a regular and sufficient income and, above all, a fair amount of spare time. All these requirements favour the middle class.

If we ascend the political hierarchy, from the voters upwards, we find that at each level—the membership of political parties, party activists, local political leaders, M.P.s, National Leaders— the social character of the group is slightly less 'representative' and slightly more tilted in favour of those who belong to the middle and upper levels of our society.[2] Ability and availability, deference and assumed superiority contribute to this pattern at each level.[3] For major politicians are initially made by minor politicians and the 'political leaders in miniature' who man the local party Executives and Management Committees tend to choose as candidates men who are like themselves or who are socially above them.

Entry into the arena of full-time politics is thus governed by the democratic rules of the game as they are interpreted by the two or

---

[1] cf. A. H. Birch: op. cit., ch. IV and V passim; T. Brennan and others: Social Change in South West Wales, 1954. The fullest study to date of the social background of local councillors is L. J. Sharpe: 'Elected Representatives in Local Government', British Journal of Sociology, September 1962.

[2] cf. Stacey, op. cit., pp. 43-44.

[3] This is not meant to imply that those near the top of the social scale have better intellectual endowment than those at the bottom; but education and experience do normally give members of the middle class advantages as organizers and speakers over those in the groups below them.

three political parties who regularly send men into Parliament. And today only those candidates who bear party labels will be elected. Independents may occasionally put up a good fight but their chances of success are practically nil. A quasi-democratic process also decides who is to occupy the position of party leader in the two major parties, even if the outcome of a particular choice will often be a foregone conclusion. The positions which lie between the rank and file M.P. and the Leader are filled by less formal methods of selection. Here office and function are more important than personality or political wisdom. Leadership is increasingly linked with ministerial status or with the position of shadow-minister. Their fixed rôle in the Government or in the procedure of the House of Commons bring individual parliamentarians to positions of public prominence. Ministers gain a place in the forefront of public attention and the official spokesmen of the opposition are similarly placed in the limelight. And like the planets in two opposing solar systems they circle around the party leaders.[1]

That the selection will reflect performance and ability as shown in the House of Commons is obvious, yet it is seldom the only element in the choice. At a time when party ties were less constraining, and when the appeal of personal loyalty was stronger, rank and station exerted their influence and aristocratic leaders tended to choose men of their own class. Today orthodoxy and expertise are possibly of greater import.

Of the posts which the Prime Minister has to fill those that have Cabinet rank are clearly the most important. For 'the Cabinet is the mainspring of the mechanism of government: its constitution and its methods of procedure must depend to a large extent on the circumstances of the time, the personality of the Prime Minister and the capacities of his principal colleagues'.[2] To be in the Cabinet is the goal of ministerial ambition. Cabinet office confers leadership and those who are near the centre of power in their party will generally get there when their party obtains power. The personnel

---

[1] The Leader of the Labour Party when in opposition does, however, give major responsibility to the members of the elected Committee of the Parliamentary Party.

[2] Report of the Machinery of Government Committee, 1918, BPP, vol. XII, para. 5.

of the Cabinet is thus not only the political élite par excellence, it also reflects the wider group from which its members are selected. The story of its changing composition, to which I shall return, manifests the persistence of aristocratic influences at a time when in the lower echelons of politics new social groups had gained ascendancy. Their continued political ascendancy was probably connected with their social prestige, for 'the British nation is a deferential nation' and there is no reason to exclude the rank and file politicians from the working of Bagehot's dictum. Yet more important still, I think, are some features of their political career which facilitated advancement on the ladder of office: independence, youth, training and family ties all worked in their favour. Their ethos, as we shall see, predestined them for the public life and the nature of the services demanded made it possible for them to combine political activity with the life of a gentleman.

For politics was regarded as an amateur's pursuit, one which neither demanded a man's entire energies nor aroused so much partisanship as to interfere with the easy social relationship with men of the same class, regardless of their politics. By now the duties of politicians have greatly increased and the scope and issues of political action demand much greater attention and wider knowledge; yet old concepts die hard. Writing from the background of patronage and pressure group politics of the American Congress, Roland Young sees the essence of Parliament in its *non-professionalism*. 'The concept of amateurism is kept in the foreground, providing for the members a standard for their actions and prescribing their proper rôle.'[1] Many M.P.s will agree with him even if their conduct might belie their convictions.

Some aspects of 'professionalism' have existed in parliamentary politics for almost as long as the belief in their mutual incompatibility. Even when Parliament was the only regular pursuit of an M.P.—and by the end of the nineteenth century this might still have applied to half the membership of the House—he did not necessarily devote a great part of his time and energies to it. 'Some members with large connections in the Metropolis, moving by old associations in London Society, having social avocations of great variety and extent, attend the House for performance of such duties

[1] R. Young: *The British Parliament*, 1962, p. 54.

as may be imperatively necessary, but do not otherwise take an onerous or active share in the work.' But for others, 'who regard their service with the utmost seriousness . . . the work is harassing, fatiguing and, in the long run, exhausting'.[1] According to Temple, this group comprised over one quarter of the private members of the House of Commons.[2] These men were the regular attenders, who manned the committees and enabled in other ways the business of the House to be carried out.

Judged in terms of regular full-time attendance on the affairs of the House of Commons the number of professional M.P.s in the 1960's may not be any larger than at the end of the last century. But this estimate disregards the growing volume of extra-parliamentary duties which fall on an M.P. today. His public performances in the House of Commons may only be the part of the political iceberg which is visible. Less obvious is his work for his constituents who write to him or whom he sees in his 'surgeries' in his constituency at the week-ends. He is equally the subject of attempts at persuasion by organized pressure groups or interested individuals and he is unlikely to be free from all non-party political partisanship for himself. He will thus foster some cause and if he is an independent-minded man he may well lend his support to a number of them.[3]

M.P.s have always acted for constituents and have sponsored 'good causes' of various kinds but their activities in this respect have increased greatly over the years. This work is intimately connected with the widening of governmental action which now impinges directly and daily on the life of the majority of citizens in a number of ways. The men and women who are aroused, aggrieved or directly involved in the actions of public authority will turn to their M.P. if and when personal representation appears of no avail.[4]

---

[1] Sir R. Temple: *The House of Commons*, 1899, p. 74. Temple was M.P. for Evesham and for Kingston from 1885 to 1895.

[2] *ibid.*, p. 76.

[3] On the relation of M.P.s to pressure groups see J. D. Stewart: *British Pressure Groups: their rôle in relation to the House of Commons*, 1958, and A. Potter: *Organized Groups in British National Politics*, 1961, especially part 5.

[4] Lord Attlee, however, has denied that this is a task which M.P.s should perform. See his article in *Fabian Journal*, November, 1958.

The politician acting in this fashion has been called by the Americans a 'fixer' and, in the context of British political institutions he has been referred to as an 'adjuster of interests, the point of contact with public opinion'.[1] He mediates between the electorate and the Government, between the party organization and the organized supporters among his constituents. In all this he uses, and in its use perfects, those techniques of suasion and manipulation of opinion and men which have become increasingly important throughout the world of business and mass-communication.[2]

To the 'arcana' of techniques in this field must be added others which, in their turn, make the politician into a professional even against his will. The complexity of the public issues which confront him in home affairs and in the world at large make it impossible for him to keep abreast in all but a limited number of fields. To make a mark as a politician he must be an expert and expertise demands specialization and study. The leading politicians of the Victorian era regarded the whole field of government as their province. They tended without much hesitation to take up any issue which presented itself to them on the Government front bench or in opposition, and speaking largely on their own brief would express their views unabashed. If necessary, they would seek to master by study an unfamiliar subject, whatever its complexity. In this way Gladstone tackled the Irish land problem when he prepared a Bill in 1869. A letter to the Duke of Argyll shows his approach: 'For the last three months, I have worked daily, I think, upon the question, and so I shall continue to do. The literature of it is large, larger than I can master, but *I feel the benefit of continued reading upon it.*'[3]

The modern government demands greater expertise and relies on more relevant past experience. While much of this is supplied by a larger and more specialized Civil Service and by a host of specialist advisory committees, the widening functions of the state have influenced the selection of men for office. As we shall see, men with specialist experience outside the political arena have

---

[1] J. D. B. Miller: *Politicians* (Inaugural Lecture, University of Leicester) 1958, p. 5.

[2] See also below, p. 298 n. 1 and pp. 315–317.

[3] John Morley: *Life of Gladstone*, 3 vols., vol. II, p. 288 (my italics). Note their belief in the efficacy of a purely theoretical approach to the problem.

increasingly been brought into the sphere of government. The new talents, enlisted by Prime Ministers since Lloyd George, demonstrate another aspect of the professionalization of the political career.

The changes in the rôle and function of politicians which have gone on over the past half century do, in turn, influence the social character of the British political élite. The particular skills which are demanded of M.P.s and of ministers today favour intellectuals or administrators, the specialists or the captains of industry. They give scope to the professional man rather than the agitator, the entrepreneur rather than the rentier. Such qualifications and experiences are found in the middle classes but to a lesser extent in the landed aristocracy or the skilled working class. If at one time high social rank and great landed possessions were frequently linked to positions of political eminence we can in the twentieth century trace the movement from positions of power and command in business, industry, the armed forces or public administration into the political élite and equally so, the journey in the opposite direction. Like the great nobleman of old, the expert or administrator of today may be chosen for political office merely for the sake of his illustrious name, but this does not invalidate the crucial importance of the general trend.

The British political élite is, however, linked to other élite groups not only through direct movement of personnel. Nowadays Government more frequently gives power over important areas of public affairs to quasi-political bodies whose members are appointed and not elected. It relies on the formal or informal advice of those who occupy key positions in the economic, social or cultural field. We must therefore seek to understand the background of other élite groups and discuss the relationship between the group of leading politicians and other powerful sections of British society.

This raises again the question of the relationship of élite rule and political democracy and of the efficiency of the process by which men and women are selected as representatives and chosen for positions of power and influence. Because I analyse the political leadership against the background of changes in society and in relation to the rôle and function of government I do not wish to imply that the character of a particular group of politicians is, in

effect, ideally suited to the task which they are asked to perform.
I don't think that all talents in the community present themselves
at the bar of politics and I am sure that the judges who sit there
and select the candidates are not all full of wisdom and free
from prejudice. Indeed, I am more than doubtful whether the
working of the political system gives full scope for the exercise of
all skills of those who take part in it.

To this the wise may retort that men and the machinery of
government are full of imperfections and the rash may suggest that
all that is needed is a change of institutions. The student of political
élites ought perhaps be content to measure and compare without
asking questions which require judgment and qualification. However, having raised the problem of the quality and representativeness of the political élite I propose to return to it in the last
chapter.

CHAPTER II

A Traditional Elite in Power

'The august wiggery of state craft.'—TROLLOPE.

'The aristocracy ... still ... administers public affairs; and it is a great error to suppose, as many persons in England suppose, that it administers but does not govern. He who administers governs, because he infixes his own mark and stamps his own character on all public affairs as they pass through his hands; and, therefore, so long as the English aristocracy administers the commonwealth, it still governs it.' —MATTHEW ARNOLD, 1861.

THE events which culminated in the first Reform Act were of a similar significance to those of 1689. Both brought about fundamental changes in the legal basis of political power which gradually changed the political reality. Yet the effect of neither was cataclysmic or immediately apparent. They were revolutions in a formal sense only. Unlike earlier or later events given that name, the changes of 1832 did not bring a new class into power with a magic constitutional wand. It is strange to recall today Croker's statement that the reform would produce: 'No kings, no lords, no inequalities; all will be levelled to the plane of the petty shop-keepers and small farmers; this perhaps not without bloodshed but certainly by confiscation and persecution.'[1] Without a reform of electoral practices the extension of the franchise and the changes in the system of parliamentary representation could hardly have produced a decisive increase of the political power of the middle class. In any case no such increase took place immediately. The Parliaments which were elected in the years following on the Reform Act did not differ in any way from those under the unre-formed franchise. The accession of the middle class to political power proceeded only slowly in the 1840's and 1850's. It owed as

[1] *Croker Papers* (ed. by L. J. Jennings), 3 vols., 1885, vol. II, p. 113.

much to the enlarged electorate and to extra-constitutional changes, as to the initial provisions of 1832.[1] In some ways, indeed, these were retrograde. The extension of the suffrage, unaccompanied by any control of the conduct of elections, raised the costs of many parliamentary contests to hitherto unknown heights. At the same time it reduced the power of nomination which had enabled wealthy patrons to present a seat—like a living—to the impecunious man of talent. Yet middle-class *influence* over legislation increased despite the smallness of its representation in the legislature. This happened partly through the pressure of public opinion and partly as the outcome of an alliance of men of radical sentiment and advanced opinion with a section of the aristocratic leadership—a marked and fascinating phenomenon in the ideological-political development of European society since the eighteenth century.

But at the centre of power an oligarchy persisted which was not very different from that of the eighteenth century. In order to understand fully the strength of the country's ruling class we must see it against the background of a changing society, which had acquired a new political constitution and had employed new methods of political expression.[2]

THE ANATOMY OF THE POLITICAL ELITE

The government which passed the Reform Bill was paradoxically enough one of the most aristocratic the country had ever seen. Grey is reputed to have boasted that its members owned jointly more acres than any previous administration. Indeed, only two of

---

[1] On the increase of the electorate in the period between the First and the Second Reform Act see W. Newmarch: 'On the Electoral Statistics of the counties and boroughs of England and Wales, 1832–57,' *Journal of the Royal Statistical Society*, 1857 and 1859.

[2] Some of the most fundamental changes were in the field of communication. To summon Peel from Rome to London to take over the Premiership in 1834 took nearly a month. Thirty years later the country and large parts of Europe were connected by railways and telegraphs. During the same period the cheapening of the printed word through the abolition of stamp duties, newspaper taxes and improved printing processes helped political agitation and education. The relationship between the revolution in communication and politics has so far, however, remained largely unexplored.

the members of the cabinet—Lord Brougham and Charles Grant, later Lord Glenelg—were not substantial landowners. The fact that at its formation nine of its thirteen members sat in the House of Lords reflects the character of the Whig oligarchy as well as the practice of the times. The distribution of office between the two houses was governed by law as well as custom. An Act of 1789[1] laid down that not more than two Secretaries of State should sit in the House of Commons, but the general predominance of the House of Lords during the eighteenth century and the emergence of the Cabinet from the King's Council are of more decisive influence. During the fifty years which preceded the first Reform Act, the membership of the Cabinet was drawn predominantly from the House of Lords. Pitt was for many years the only commoner in his Cabinet, and the number of Cabinet Ministers who sat in the lower house was, on the average, less than half of those in the Lords.[2]

TABLE I

Distribution of Cabinet Office between the two Houses of Parliament:

Cabinet (at Formation)	Commons	Lords	Total
Grey, 1830	4	9	13
Melbourne, 1834	9	7	16
Peel, 1834	5	7	12
Melbourne, 1835	7	5	12
Peel, 1841	6	8	14
Russell, 1846	7	9	16
Derby, 1852	6	7	13
Aberdeen, 1852	7	6	13
Palmerston, 1855	7	7	14
Derby, 1858	7	6	13
Palmerston, 1859	9	6	15
Russell, 1865	7	8	15
Derby, 1866	10	5	15

With the Reform Act the power of the House of Commons began

[1] George III, 22, c. 82.
[2] cf. A. Aspinall: The Cabinet Council, 1783–1835 (Raleigh Lectures) in Proceedings of the British Academy, vol. XXXVIII, pp. 145–52.

to increase. This and the growth of governmental activity (with a consequent increase in Cabinet size), brought about a larger share in the representation of members of the lower house in the Cabinet.

Throughout most of the period the two houses were fairly evenly balanced with Conservative administrations containing slightly more Peers than Liberal ones.[1] But despite the growing ascendancy of the House of Commons in the political leadership we find little change in the class composition of cabinet membership.[2] Even at its most 'democratic' the cabinet contained only a minority of 'non-aristocrats' (*i.e.* 5 out of 13) and in none of the governments were the landed interests in a minority. Of Derby's ten Cabinet Ministers in the House of Commons (1866), five were heirs to long-established peerages or baronetcies.

Aristocracy, conceived as a group whose membership is based on descent is, of course, only a partly illuminating and significant concept for the purpose of social analysis. As this chapter seeks to highlight broad trends rather than present a detailed investigation, less definite categories based on subjective evaluation of the individual politician's social origin may be used with some justification.[3] Within the broad group of landed proprietors, which comprises both nobility and untitled squirearchy, we can attempt to draw a dividing line between the large territorial lords—Burke's *Broad Oaks of the Commonwealth*—and the lesser county families. Those outside that class are, however, far from forming a homogeneous group. Among them were men who came economically and socially largely within the sphere of the landed classes, although they were neither large landowners nor did they belong to landed families. These were the members of the commercial and financial élite, sons or grandsons of men who had frequently amassed great, and even enormous, fortunes in banking or perhaps

---

[1] The distribution of portfolios in the last Conservative administration is hardly typical. Its strong representation in the House of Commons was due more to the accident of party and personality than to democratic principles and the Government was actually worried about its weak position in the Upper House. *cf.* Disraeli to Derby, 20.2.1868, Moneypenny and Buckle: *The Life of Disraeli* (2 vol. ed., 1929), vol. II, p. 319.

[2] For a definition of the categories used in the social analysis of the political élite see note on p. 77.

[3] For the analysis of the social structure of the élite in the period 1868–1955 it was, however, necessary to use more definite socio-economic categories.

in the East India trade, as well as the members of military families with the unquestionable right to be regarded as 'gentlemen'. It is outside this group that we find the real *hommes nouveaux* who had only just 'arrived' and whose political career was a move in the process of their upward mobility and not the result of it.

TABLE II

The Social Structure of Cabinet Membership, 1830–68:

Large territorial Lords and their sons	56
Country Gentlemen (lesser landowners)	12
Mercantile and Administrative Upper Class (mainly rentiers)	21
Hommes nouveaux of no 'family' (mostly lawyers)	14
TOTAL	103

Addington was one of the first ministers to reach great political heights from obscure origins. Many thought that it was hardly proper for the son of a country surgeon to become a Prime Minister. Lord Liverpool wrote that:

'nobility, joined to talent, produces a wonderful effect upon the minds of men and talents where there is no nobility must be very conspicuous to be compensated for the want of it. This is exactly the state of Mr Addington.'[1]

Other politicians who came from outside the circle of landed proprietors had also to encounter opposition on their way to office and political leadership. Huskisson, who reached the Chancellorship of the Exchequer and whose ability was generally recognized, thought that he could not aspire to the Premiership as the country required a man of 'rank, property and consideration at the head'.[2] However, comparative newcomers, whether aristocrats or mere men of wealth, reached high office and some even the highest of all. The fortunes of Grey and Melbourne were of recent origin, while Peel and Gladstone came from outside the aristocratic sphere

---

[1] B.M. add MSS., 38236 f. 269, quoted in Aspinall, *loc. cit.*, p. 205.
[2] *ibid.*, p. 200, quoting Welbeck MSS.

altogether and represented the group of mercantile and industrial interest which had gained access to the polite and political society. 'There stands his Grace (*i.e.* the Duke of Wellington) between two bank-directors' was Russell's comment on Peel's government of 1834 which was somewhat less aristocratic than its predecessor.[1] Wellington was the last Duke to hold the premiership—and he was hardly a territorial magnate. His political precept—uttered conveniently at a time when he was no longer in power or had hope of again attaining it—that henceforth the Prime Minister ought to be in the House of Commons was realized only during twenty out of the thirty-eight years between 1830 and 1868—but in general an increasing number of the great offices of state were held by men of lesser rank. Nine Dukes held Cabinet office during the period, yet apart from Wellington's tenure of the Foreign Office during Peel's 'hundred days' they tended to occupy sinecures or held minor offices, rising occasionally to Admiralty, Colonies or War.

Important as these tendencies are, they should not blind us to the fact that the power of the old-established ruling-class remained largely unimpaired. Within that class the balance of power had shifted somewhat in favour of newer wealth and away from mere landed property and this process had not gone on without some tension and conflict. But the rumblings which led to the reform of 1832 were only very slowly affecting the councils of state. Gladstone and Peel, although regarded by some as parvenus, had yet received the traditional upbringing of members of the upper class. Indeed of the fourteen 'new men' in the thirteen cabinets of the period only three can be regarded as middle-class politicians, representing the specific aspirations of their class. Disraeli, who belongs to this group, is really a political phenomenon, *sui generis*, and as such not classifiable. The rest are career politicians, mainly lawyers.[2] Thomas Erskine May had held various offices in the administration of Parliament; he was thus well placed to observe the decline of aristocratic influence in the constituencies which followed—albeit much more slowly than had been hoped or feared—the extension of the franchise and the abolition of the proprietory boroughs. But he also saw that:

[1] Speech in Totnes, 2.12.1834, quoted in Halévy, *History of the English People, 1830–41*, p. 180.
[2] *cf.* pp. 57–58 below.

'Notwithstanding the more democratic tendencies of later times, rank and station still retained the respect and confidence of the people. When the aristocracy enjoyed too exclusive an influence in the government, they aroused hostility and jealousy; but when duly sharing power with other classes and admitting the just claims of talent, they prevailed over every rival and adverse interest and—whatever party was in power—were still rulers of the state.'[1]

If that share was exceedingly small in the Cabinet it was not much larger among the country's elected representatives. This was obvious to the men at the time and later investigations have not changed the picture. The territorial classes represented well over half the interests of the unreformed House of Commons; they continued to do so in the 1840's and also in the 1860's. Before 1832 one-third of all M.P.s were aristocrats in the most restricted sense of the word and this proportion had not declined by 1865. The commercial and industrial interests did probably account for not more than a quarter in either period. Whatever the formal distinction, the modern historian of the early Victorian House of Commons was 'impressed by the comparative homogeneity of this Parliament by any of the ordinary standards of social measurement. These were for the most part wealthy persons of consequence in their own community, an élite who in their general character and composition differed profoundly from the population of England as a whole.'[2]

The failure of the newly enfranchised middle class to gain parliamentary leadership and, above all, governmental office, extends far beyond the Reform Act of 1868 and will be dealt with in subsequent sections of this book. For the period between the two Reform Acts, which is studied in this chapter, we gain greater insight into the character and functioning of the political élite if we study the processes of cohesion and conflict within the group of leading politicians. Against that background the rest of the chapter will deal with the activities of predominantly middle-class pressure groups and their influence on the composition of the cabinets and finally the emergence of the 'new men' themselves.

[1] T. E. May Constitutional History of England, 1760–1860, 7th ed., vol. I, p. 165.
[2] W. H. Aydelotte: 'The House of Commons of the 1840's', History, 1954, pp. 248–62 at p. 258.

TABLE III

The Social Character of the House of Commons, 1831–65:

	Period		
	1831	*1841–47*	*1865*
	In percentages:		
'Aristocrats' (Baronets, Irish Peers, Sons of Peers and Baronets)	33	38	31
Gentry (by descent) and other relations of Aristocrats	..	34	45*
Etonians	20	..	16
Harrovians	11	..	8
Rugby, Westminster, Winchester, Shrewsbury	13	..	8
All Public Schools	..	46	..
Manufacturers, Merchants, Bankers	24	15†–22‡	23§

Sources:

1831 According to G. P. Judd: *Members of Parliament, 1734–1832.*

1841–47 Derived from W. H. Aydelotte: 'The House of Commons of the 1840's' *History*, 1954, pp. 248–62.

1865 (*circa*). Derived from B. Cacroft: 'An analysis of the House of Commons, or Indirect Representation' in *Essays in Reform*, 1867, pp. 155–90.

Notes:

* *i.e.* all county members and those borough members who were known to have territorial interests. According to Cacroft only few *county* members lacked territorial connections.

† Excluding 122 Directors of Insurance Companies and 145 Railway Directors.

‡ The total of 'those actively engaged in the operation and control of major business enterprises . . . but not including those who were only incidentally concerned'. (Aydelotte.)

§ *i.e.* those of the total of 200 (30 per cent) engaged in Industry, Commerce or Banking who were without territorial interests.

COHESION AND CONFLICT

Not the least reason for the remarkable staying-power of the ruling oligarchy, and its resilience in times of change, lay in its inherent cohesion and unity in the period under discussion. The total size of the group from which the country's leading statesmen were drawn remained comparatively small. The number of those meeting in the circle of London Society was even smaller in view of the fact that a large section of the country gentlemen were not drawn into the social life of the metropolis. The ties of party alignments were thus further strengthened by those of friendship and kinship. In 1845, when charged with the formation of a government, Russell wrote to his wife: 'Can I do such a wild thing? For this purpose, and to know whether it is wild, I must consult my friends, especially Lansdowne; here ends politics.'[1]

Nothing makes the fundamental social exclusiveness of the Cabinets clearer than the custom of regular Cabinet dinners. At first held weekly, they provided a vehicle for the transaction of Cabinet business, like the more formal Cabinet meetings. When Viscount Howick entered the Cabinet he and his wife prepared for their first 'Cabinet Dinner' by holding a 'dress rehearsal' (which in the event preceded the actual dinner by four months), for which they took out their new dinner service and plate and also borrowed Lord Francis Egerton's cook.[2] Cabinet dinners were not formally abolished until some time after the second Reform Act.

Genealogical ramifications, which turn the whole of the aristocracy into a web of cousinhoods, can obviously be disregarded here but the application of more obvious kinship ties in the formation of an administration should be considered. In forming his government, Grey provided places for eight of his nearest relatives and friends. One son-in-law, Lord Durham, was made Lord Privy Seal, another became his Private Secretary.[3] E. Ellice, his brother-in-law, became Patronage Secretary, another brother-in-law, George Ponsonby, was appointed a Junior Commissioner of the Conference of London to the Belgian Provisional government. His son, Viscount Howick, was made Under Secretary at the Colonial Office. Duncannon, related to him through his wife, became a Government whip, and his old friend Lord Holland, received the sinecure office of Chancellor of the Duchy of Lancaster, an appointment which was severely criticized.[4] Derby sat in the same Cabinet as his son, who became Secretary of State for the Colonies in 1858

---

[1] Sir S. Walpole, *Life of Lord John Russell*, 2nd ed., 2 vols., 1892. vol. I, p. 410.
[2] Aspinall, *loc. cit.*, p. 184.
[3] *i.e.* Sir Charles Wood, 1st Earl of Halifax.
[4] Aspinall, *loc. cit.*, p. 156.

and Foreign Secretary in 1866, and Russell appointed his father-in-law ('universally considered a detriment and a disgrace to the Government. A man whom all would repudiate')[1] as Lord Privy Seal.[2] His Cabinet also contained two pairs of brothers-in-law (the third Lord Grey and Sir Charles Wood; Henry Labardiere and Sir Francis Baring) who were also related through the Home Secretary Sir George Grey.

Few were as forthright as Peel in resisting the clamour for office from those who thought that the ties of family and friendship or the service to the Party, let alone mere need, constituted a claim to office. His own father-in-law interceded for his brother and was refused and the argument that he had turned down an application from his own brother served in refusing applications from others. Reading his correspondence we may well believe what he told Greville, that 'nobody could form any idea of what he had to go through in the disposal of places, the adjustment of conflicting claims'.[3] At the same time these practices imply more than mere nepotism. The promise of loyalty from a subordinate, who is also a relative, is a double bond. It may well influence the choice of colleagues by a Prime Minister, especially when we bear in mind that the absence of clear-cut party alignments and policies strained loyalty within the Cabinet to breaking point.

Friendship is equally important as a force which knits together members of the same administration. Even in the days when the burden of official business was considerably lighter than fifty years later, Ministers were tied to their political duties more than private members. Thus Palmerston wrote to his brother on the occasion of the secession of Stanley, Graham and Ripon from Grey's government:

'To me personally it is a great loss. Stanley, Graham and Ripon were three of my most intimate friends and though I am equally intimate with many who remain and very well with all who came in, yet I hate these sudden changes of private intercourse, especially when the necessary course of official life makes one's official colleagues

---

[1] Greville: *Memoirs*, vol. V, p. 257.

[2] When the 'Woburn Bench' was attacked in the House of Commons, Russell defended his selections on the ground that 'his ancestors had such a quiverful of daughters' that he was related to members on all the benches of the House.

[3] *cf.* C. S. Parker: *Sir Robert Peel*, vol. II, pp. 271–4 and 482–9.

so much one's private companions. I regret to be thrown out of inter-course with men I like and esteem so much.'[1]

The influence of personality and the existence of factions based on personal allegiance enhanced the power of individuals in the bargaining process which went on at the time of Cabinet forma-tion, especially as, in addition to the comparative weakness of party allegiances, the strength of both Whigs and Tories was for most of the time fairly evenly balanced. After 1835, no party could command a decisive majority, hence the need for support from those groups, often minute, which were not clearly committed or whose allegiance the leaders hoped to gain by adroit manoeuvring. Lord Grey's government was really a coalition; apart from those Whigs who were committed to Reform, it contained representatives of the Stafford interest (Graham and Stanley), Canningites in the persons of Melbourne, Goderich, Grant and Palmerston, as well as the Duke of Richmond, who was really a Tory. After the secession of the High Church party over the use of the surplus rev-enue of the Irish Church and the consequent dismissal of Mel-bourne by the King, Peel attempted to induce the same group to join forces with him. Stanley and Graham refused and Peel could only land a small fish in the person of Lord Wharncliffe, who accepted office as Lord Privy Seal on receiving an assurance that he could remain a Liberal.[2]

Sir James Graham and Lord Stanley (later Lord Derby) did, however, accept office under Peel in 1841. Yet while Stanley be-came a Conservative proper, the 'Right Honourable Baronet', one of the largest landowners in the country, who had started his political career as a near-radical but an upholder of the Corn Laws, became in turn a Conservative, a Peelite and, towards the end of his life, again a Liberal. No wonder *Punch* referred to him as a 'Ministerial top who was suffering from severe fits of vertigo by his extraordinary propensity for turning around'. At the time of the Whig–Peelite coalition under Aberdeen the need to secure as wide a support as possible was even more obvious. Lord John Russell was prepared to be extremely broadminded. He thought that 'if a man is really a Liberal and has always, or of late years, professed

---

[1] W. H. (Sir Henry Lytton) Bulwer: *Life of Palmerston*, vol. II, p. 195.
[2] *cf.* Greville: *Memoirs*, vol. III, p. 122.

Liberal opinions, he ought not to be barred from office or promotion, though for a few months he may have given his adhesion to
Lord Derby'.[1]

After the split of the Conservative party and the emergence of a
fairly cohesive group of Peelites the scope for coalition became even
greater and the need for it paramount, at least for the Conservative
rump. The Protectionists failed to win new allies or regain old
ones and in consequence the Conservative administrations after
1846 were to be short and unsuccessful. Had the Conservatives
been successful in winning Whig or Peelite support in 1852 or
1858, or the allegiance of either Clarendon or the Adullamites in
1865, the political kaleidoscope of the period would have resembled
even more strongly the picture of a stage army arrayed continuously in battle under a variety of colours.[2] The Tory leaders were
in consequence forced to mobilize all the support they could get
from within their own ranks. In 1858 Lord Derby felt himself
constrained to write to the Queen in the following terms:

'With regard to the filling up of particular offices, Lord Derby would
humbly beg your Majesty to bear in mind that, although among his own
personal friends there will be every desire to make individual convenience subservient to the public interest, yet among those who are
not now politically connected with him there may be some whose
co-operation or refusal might be greatly influenced by the office which
it was proposed that they should hold . . .'[3]

Six years later he spoke to the Queen of the necessity of asking
'Lord Lansdowne and Lord Elcho—though foolish and vain men
—to join the government'.[4]

Individual politicians and their ambitions were obviously a
constant source of conflict in the process of Cabinet formation and

---

[1] Letter to Lord Murray quoted in G. P. Gooch (ed.): *The Later Correspondence
of Lord Russell*, vol. II, p. 121.

[2] Clarendon was invited to continue at the Foreign Office and to name two
of his colleagues to join the administration. The 'Adullamites' were similarly
promised a number of posts but refused. In view of the subsequent developments this was obviously wise for the inhabitants of the 'cave' who had seceded
from the Liberal Party in protest against its comparatively mild proposals for
electoral reform.

[3] *Letters of Queen Victoria*, First series, vol. III, p. 269.

[4] *Letters of Queen Victoria*, Second series, vol. I, p. 346.

the quality of Cabinets was to suffer in consequence in political as well as in administrative terms. On the occasion of Russell's attempts at Cabinet formation in December 1845, Grey, the son of the Prime Minister and one of the leaders of the advanced Liberals, wrote to him:

> 'To press upon you the extreme importance of the utmost caution in the step you take ... you cannot afford to lose any strength by not filling your offices as well as you can. You therefore really owe it to the cause, to yourself and to your friends to allow no deference for the personal objects of others to interfere with your making the arrangements best calculated to secure for your government the largest possible measure of public confidence and support ... you ought, above all things, to guard against giving the public an impression that your administration is a mere revival with as little alteration as possible of the last Whig government.'[1]

The issues on which Grey sought an unequivocal commitment from the future administration related to free trade, and the establishment of 'complete religious equality in Ireland'. In addition, Grey was resolutely opposed to the return of Palmerston to the Foreign Office. He remained adamant about the latter condition, and, as Palmerston was equally unwilling to take another post, the decision to form an administration had to be abandoned at the last minute when the portfolios had already been distributed.

Throughout this period we can observe how political differences and personal conflicts reinforce each other to create tensions inside the political élite. This is especially marked on the Liberal side. The formation of Grey's administration was already greatly encumbered by the question of how to place Brougham. It was hardly possible to exclude from the Cabinet the most vigorous of the Reformers who had just won a spectacular political success, by his election for the West Riding, one of the few popular constituencies in the country. On the other hand it seemed equally dangerous to leave this temperamentally unstable and highly volatile personality as a government spokesman in the House of Commons. Whether officially the Leader of the House, or in any other capacity, he would usurp the leadership. He eventually accepted the

---

[1] Walpole, vol. I, p. 412.

office of Lord Chancellor after having declared that 'he would drop on the Woolsack as on his political deathbed'. As a matter of fact it proved the means of his political extinction.

Melbourne was equally anxious to be rid of Palmerston or at least to force him to take another office. For him 'the questions of Brougham and Palmerston are of the utmost importance, fully as much as any question of principle can be', and Ellice wrote to his brother-in-law, Durham, in a similar vein (in 1834) 'We did all we could to throw over both worthies . . . at least to oblige them to change character for the unpopularity of the one and indolence of the other were admitted on all sides and they have not hitherto changed their habits'.[1]

Melbourne was unsuccessful in his second attempt to remove causes of friction from his Cabinet. The conflict between Russell and Palmerston was to dominate the Liberal benches and to influence decisively the formation and fate of Liberal administrations. It had prevented Cabinet-formation in 1845, and made things difficult in the following year. 'There is no cordiality between Lord John and Lord Palmerston, who, if he had to make a choice would even forget what passed December last and join the Grey Party in preference to Lord John personally', wrote the Prince.[2] Their position *vis-à-vis* each other and as representatives of the two wings of the Liberal Party emerges clearly from the process of government formation in 1859. The Queen had originally charged Granville with this task. Palmerston, whose return to the Foreign Office was clearly out of the question, would have demanded the Leadership of the House of Commons but Russell was unwilling to serve under him. He put his point frankly to Granville.[3]

'With Palmerston as a possible Prime Minister I could only have to consider who is to have the first and who the second office in the state. With you I could only occupy the third and should not feel that I had sufficient security either on Foreign Affairs or on Reform.'

---

[1] S. J. Reid: *Life of Durham*, vol. I, p. 111 (quoted in Halévy, *op. cit.*, p. 188).
[2] Memo of Prince Albert in *Letters of Queen Victoria*, First series, vol. II, p. 86.
[3] E. G. Fitzmaurice: *Life of Earl Granville*, vol. I, p. 337. See also Granville's explanatory letter to Palmerston and Russell, *ibid.*, p. 340.

If Palmerston and Russell are thus prima ballerinas on the political stage, Gladstone is cast in the rôle of a first dancer. He epitomises perhaps more than anyone else the extreme fluidity of the group alignments and the pragmatic approach of individuals to political decisions which determined the political scene. In his own career he was to cover almost the whole width of the political stage. He entered politics as an ardent protectionist and a stout defender of the privileges of the established Church, and ended the period as a firm believer in Free Trade, an advocate of household franchise and of a liberal policy with regard to religion. In 1855 Palmerston rightly regarded Gladstone's participation as crucial for the success of the administration. 'You are one of the first persons with whom I wish to communicate on this matter', (*i.e.* the Cabinet formation) he wrote. Gladstone was, however, apprehensive, worried by what Palmerston termed 'the shadow of a shadow', namely the possibility of Russell being excluded and a belligerent foreign policy being pursued. Gladstone had been equally pressingly approached by Derby, Lansdowne and Russell, who at various stages during the interregnum had been charged with the formation of a government. This is not surprising; what is important from our point of view is that while Gladstone refused his support to each of them he was nevertheless not completely adverse to joining any. Each step seemed possible provided certain conditions as to the composition of the Government and its policy could be fulfilled.[1] In a similar way he did not regard his adhesion to Palmerston in 1859 to be a complete break with his political past. He had not voted against Derby in the division which led to the latter's defeat in June 1859. A year earlier he had even considered joining his administration. Now he favoured a juncture— Palmerston and Derby to form jointly a strong government. Yet when asked by the man whom he had bitterly opposed for many years, to join his Cabinet in his old post of Chancellor of the Exchequer, he accepted without much hesitation. War was raging in Europe and the need for the intervention of the British Government to bring it to an end was great; there was still useful work to be done in the field of finance so he wondered whether he 'could have looked anyone in the face had he refused his aid at such time

[1] cf. Morley: *Life of Gladstone*, vol. I, pp. 525–36 *passim*.

and under such circumstances'.[1] Yet in many ways Gladstone had, by this step, crossed the watershed. He had always had a strange, almost uncanny instinct to identify himself with what were to be the popular causes of the future. As he had once refused a chance to be the likely successor to Derby as Leader so he was now on the road to the leadership of the Liberal Party. The wide support for the new government would hardly have been possible had it not been for the 'Willis Rooms Agreement' reached after the election when the two wings of the Liberal Party agreed to seek a £6 franchise in the boroughs and a £10 franchise in the counties. Words were, however, not immediately followed by deeds. Palmerston was little amenable to radical pressure and the advanced Liberals formed a weak element in the new administration. Bright did not accept office but, as Greville noted, he was 'displeased that he has not been more consulted and probably office not having been more pressed upon him'.[2]

At this stage we must examine the position of radicals and other minority groups in the House of Commons *vis-à-vis* the old political élite.

PRESSURE GROUPS AND GOVERNMENT PERSONNEL

It has been said that Lord Grey, when returned to power in 1831 with an overwhelming majority, was the first British Prime Minister to hold office as the clear choice of the electorate.[3] When Sir Robert Peel dissolved Parliament four years later, the electorate had for the first time in British politics a platform on the basis of which it was invited to return the Government.[4] The effectiveness of such an appeal to an electorate, still strongly influenced by corruption and intimidation, must be doubted; its importance is solely that of a portent of things to come. For the time being, Whig or Tory Prime Ministers, when forming their administrations, were not influenced greatly by public opinion, extra-parliamentary

---

[1] *cf*. Morley: *Gladstone*, vol. I, p. 627.

[2] *op. cit.*, vol. VI, p. 525.

[3] J. R. M. Butler, *The Passing of the Great Reform Bill*, 1914, p. 288.

[4] *i.e.* the letter of Sir Robert Peel to his constituents which has become known as the 'Tamworth Manifesto'. *cf*. Ivor Jennings: *Cabinet Government*, 2nd ed., 1951, p. 15.

organization or by minority groups in the House of Commons. Conservative governments were, for obvious reasons, not to any great extent subject to extra-parliamentary pressure. Yet even Whig and Liberal administrations were little concerned to reward their radical followers with office. While the activities of radicals inside, and outside, Parliament have been widely studied, the influence of the extreme wing of the Liberal leaders on Liberal administrations has received little attention. To give it attention seems essential, not only in order to understand the process of government formation, but also to account in part for the prevalence of aristocratic personnel in the Cabinet. Only strong pressure by the new electorate, working through a greatly changed House of Commons, could have brought about substantial changes in the composition of the political élite. Yet we must not go too far in drawing our analogy between ineffective radical pressure and the persistence of aristocracy in the political leadership. The representation of radicals is not equivalent to middle-class representation, nor is middle-class representation in the Government identical with the representation of radicals. The rôle of Lord Durham is a case in point. Radicals looked up to him as a possible leader, and in Lord Grey's Cabinet he clearly represented the radical point of view. His identification with the rising middle class, from which his family had but recently emerged, as well as his irascible temper, led to his exclusion from Melbourne's administration in 1835.[1] His political extinction was clearly a blow to the radicals.[2] For reasons of prestige, if no other, they valued the support which men of the established order could give to their cause. 'It is of great importance in this wealth loving aristocratic country to have among [the radical spokesmen] men of good standing and rank', Roebuck wrote in a letter welcoming the adherence of Molesworth to the radical cause.[3] On the other hand, the Whigs sought to reward the Irish Roman Catholics for their support of the Reform Bill, and Russell even wished to offer the post of Irish Attorney General to O'Con-

---

[1] Lord Lansdowne declared quite categorically that 'he would not sit in the Cabinet with him', J. C. Hobhouse (Lord Broughton): *Recollections of a Long Life*, vol. IV, p. 357.

[2] 'The radicals will be very angry that Durham is not brought in', wrote Palmerston to his brother.

[3] R. E. Leader: *Life and Letters of J. A. Roebuck*, 1897, p. 81.

nell. The King and Russell's colleagues in the Cabinet objected to this and he had to content himself with giving this office, and that of Solicitor General for Ireland, to two of O'Connell's followers. It was in an attempt to pacify Irish opinion that Lord Melbourne appointed Lord Morpeth to the post of Irish Secretary on his return to office in 1836. Lord Morpeth sympathized with Irish aspirations and had just been triumphantly elected for the West Riding.[1] The presence of the Marquess of Clanricarde in the Government of Lord John Russell in 1846 and in that of Palmerston in 1855, has been similarly explained as due to the fact that he was *persona grata* with the Irish. Lord John Russell himself had partly the confidence of the reform-minded middle class. 'Mr Milner Gibson', wrote Lord Granville to the Queen in 1859, when charged with the formation of an administration, 'considered it a *sine qua non* condition of support that Lord John should be a member of the Government.'[2] The Whig leaders obviously preferred to allow the expression of radical sentiment and interest in the Government by men of the same mould as the leaders of the majority group; aristocrats who identified themselves with the radical cause or were at least sympathetic towards it. Attempts to reverse the process and to bring middle-class radicals into the Government through aristocratic pressure were less successful. Lord Grey strove vigorously to bring Cobden into the Cabinet in 1846 and so did Mr Horsman who wrote to Lord John Russell that 'Mr Cobden represents great interests, who feel that when Sir J. Graham pronounced him the most remarkable man who had entered Parliament for thirty years, he signed his passport to the Cabinet, and it would be a source of regret to many who care nothing personally for Mr Cobden, but are sincerely attached by their principle to you, if you were to enter on power without the full confidence and support of the commercial interests which it is yet in your power to command'.[3] But Russell demurred. 'The only thing he could offer (to Cobden) would be a Cabinet Office. Now this would affront a great many people whom he had to conciliate and create even possible dissension in the Cabinet', he wrote to the Queen.[4] In the end Russell

---

[1] W. T. McCullagh Torrens: *Melbourne, 1890* (new ed.) p. 385.
[2] *Letters of Queen Victoria*, First series, vol. II, p. 345.
[3] Walpole, *op. cit.*, vol. I, p. 425.
[4] *op. cit.*, Second series, vol. II, p. 84.

found an excuse in the fact that Cobden had earlier declined office
and that he was about to go abroad, and wrote to him, that
although he regarded him entitled to Cabinet rank, he felt that
Cobden would be disinclined to accept.[1]

Twelve years later Palmerston did actually offer office to Cobden, and Russell wrote strongly supporting acceptance. The offer
was refused. Cobden thought that having opposed Palmerston's
policy for so many years he could not all of a sudden take office. A
conversation with the Prime Minister failed to persuade him but
it resulted in an invitation to one of Lady Palmerston's receptions.
At his first visit to Cambridge House the *bête noire* of the aristocracy was, in his own words 'the lion of the party. The women
came and stared with their glasses at me and then brought their
friends to stare also.'[2]

Gladstone wrote to his brother that he was 'exceedingly sorry to
find that Cobden (did) not take office. It was in his person that
there seemed to be the best chance of a favourable trial of the
experiment of connecting his friends with the practical administration of the country.'[3] Others, probably including Palmerston,
were less disappointed. He had, as Cobden relates, offered him
office not from any desire to change his colleagues. Left to himself,
he would have preferred to go on as before with his old friends. 'I
offer you the seat because you have a right to it.'[4] The admission
of radicals into successive administrations is clearly linked to the
general relationship between aristocracy and middle class inside
the political élite and must be investigated.

---

[1] J. Morley: *Cobden*, p. 403. See also *Letters of Queen Victoria*, First series,
vol. II, p. 60. The antagonism to Cobden was most probably social as much as
political. The fact that after Cobden's failure in business his friends were just
then collecting money as a testimonial to him was probably regarded by many
as an obstacle to his obtaining office and Morley himself comments that 'the
ground of omission was not unreasonable'. To the modern observer the distinction between the monies given by a grateful nation to a successful military
commander (Wellington) thirty years earlier and the much smaller sum collected
for the man who more than anyone fought the battle for the repeal of the
Corn Laws and neglected his own business in the course of it seems somewhat
artificial.
[2] J. Morley: *op. cit.* p. 697.
[3] *ibid.*, p. 626.
[4] *ibid.*, p. 695.

THE ENTRY OF NEW MEN

In order to understand the lack of middle-class representation in the political élite, we shall have to consider not only the legal and economic obstacles but even more the social tensions existing between the landowning class with its immediate entourage and the new commercial and industrial middle class. The Hammonds have made an illuminating comparison between the English ruling class, at the end of the eighteenth and the beginning of the nineteenth century, and the Roman senatorial order. Each claimed office on the basis of descent, 'a Cavendish being as inevitable as a Claudius and an Aemilius as a Gower'. The manufacturers, on the other hand, corresponded to the *equites*. And as an *eques* could become a senator by holding the quaestorship so 'an English manufacturer could pass into the governing class by buying an estate'. But neither group was welcomed with open arms and 'even a Cicero or a Canning might complain of the freezing welcome of the old nobles'.[1]

The Hammonds might have added that the political arena also provided an opening for the advance into the ruling class. But even here we shall see that a brilliant talent and a fluent tongue were by no means a guarantee of success and acceptance. Formally at least, entry into politics was conditional on the possession of landed property as laid down by the Disqualification Act of 1710, which remained in force until 1838.[2] However, the provisions of the act were widely evaded through fictitious transfers of titles to land, either as a personal favour or as a *pro forma* transaction carried out by lawyers against payment.[3]

The cost of elections was a much more effective obstacle to a political career. An expenditure of tens of thousands of pounds was by no means uncommon and it was rare to get away with less

---

[1] J. L. and B. Hammond: *The Village Labourer*, Guild Edition, vol. II, p. 135.

[2] It is interesting to observe that this Act clearly recognized the *a priori* claim of the aristocracy to representation by exempting the sons of Peers and those qualified to be Knights of the Shire. Cf. E. & A. Porritt: *The Unreformed House of Commons*, 2 vols. 1909, vol. I, p. 169 ff.

[3] Hansard, 3rd series, vol. XXXVI, p. 526. The recourse to this ruse may, in part, have been due to the shortage of suitable land for purchase.

than £1,000.[1] The Reform Act increased costs considerably and it also led, at first, to a large number of electoral contests. Middle-class candidates for Parliament were frequently forced into a fight. They usually stood for the larger boroughs where personal influence was less pronounced, contests more common and results less certain.[2]

Once the 'new men' had entered the political arena the obstacles to their successful political career were hardly diminished, although less easily definable. The resentment against representatives of the new strata can already be observed in the debate on the Reform. It was then feared that the abolition of the proprietary borough, and the widening of the franchise, would open the House of Commons to demagogues and 'dangerous revolutionaries' in place of the quiet country squires and 'shining men of talent' who had been enabled to come into the House through the generosity of enlightened borough patrons. 'The new men, speaking the dialects of Lancashire and the West Riding—with the rough manners of the Mill and the counting-house—were not congenial associates for the high-bred politicians who sought their votes but not their company.'[3] The Whigs were as much afraid of the new forces as the Tories. What was feared was not so much radical or unorthodox views but the non-observance of all or of some of the minutiae of gentlemanly conduct. Thus O'Connell, although a small landowner himself, had lost their confidence through the violence of his speeches and actions. His support for the Liberals, after 1835, became for many of them a source of social embarrassment. 'Mr Thomas Granville, with whom I had been most intimate for many years, wrote to me saying that he regretted he could no longer visit my house, as he could not go anywhere where he incurred the risk of meeting O'Connell . . .'

---

[1] The average expenditure for all contested county and borough elections in 1859 was £1,466 (Select Committee of the House of Lords on the Elective Franchise, BPP 1860, vol. XII). On the financial aspects of a parliamentary career in general see W. B. Gwyn, *op. cit.*

[2] Between 1832 and 1859 the small boroughs of Yorkshire held only 46 out of a possible total of 88 contests—General Elections only—while in the large boroughs 51 out of 56 elections were contested.

[3] T. E. May: *Constitutional History*, 7th ed., vol. II, pp. 407–10, 418.

[4] Lansdowne to W. M. Torrens quoted in Torrens' *Melbourne*, p. 363.

On the Conservative side, the position of Peel was socially rather ambiguous in spite of his political eminence. According to Ellenborough there was need 'to conciliate Peel to the Aristocracy and this the Duke might manage by asking him to meet Peers who will ask him to dinner . . .'[1] Peel himself referred to his position in a speech made after his resignation in April 1835. 'Will you allow me to recall to your recollection what was the great charge against myself? That the King had sent for the son of a cotton-spinner to Rome to make him Prime Minister of England. Did I feel that by any means a reflection on me? Did that make me at all discontented with the laws and institutions of the country? No, but does it not make me, and ought it not to make you gentlemen, do all you can to reserve to other sons of other cotton-spinners the same opportunity by the same system of laws under which this country has so long flourished, of arriving by the same honourable means at the same distinction?'

What were the difficulties which faced the 'sons of cotton-spinners' and men who were themselves merchants or manufacturers in their political career? Speaking to his constituents in Sheffield at the General Election of 1859, Roebuck recalled a conversation with Lord Stanley about a celebrated man in the House of Commons. 'Know you, my Lord,' Roebuck told the heir to an estate with a rent roll of over £150,000, 'his case and yours are very different. Such a man's goal is your starting point, where other men end you begin. You step right into the business of government; he has to conquer his way up to that. By the time he has conquered his way to where you start from, old age comes upon him and he is unfitted for his office.'[2]

The careers of some of the new men illustrate the position of the middle class vis-à-vis the aristocracy in the House of Commons and in the political élite.

Charles Poulett Thomson, later Lord Sydenham, was born in 1799 the son of a Russia Merchant. At the age of sixteen he entered his father's Trading House in St Petersburg and after a successful career there he returned to England in 1824. In 1826 he entered

---

[1] Diary, 28.1.1831, in *Three Early Nineteenth Century Diaries* (ed. by A. Aspinall), 1952, p. 43.
[2] *The Times*, 9.4.1859.

Parliament with the help of the Philosophical Radicals. Bowring was instrumental in finding a constituency for him and Bentham assisted in his campaign. On the other hand his family was strongly opposed to his political venture, thinking that it would deflect his interests from his business. His brother Andrew even threatened to dissolve their partnership. He was elected—at a cost of £3,000—and became a not very vocal collaborator of Hume in his endeavours to repeal the Corn Laws and to effect reforms. Without much formal education and lacking in oratorical talent he attempted to impress the house with 'facts with which the majority are unacquainted' and he achieved a reputation as an expert on commercial and financial measures. As such he advised Althorp, and as the latter's protégé he was offered the Vice-Presidency of the Board of Trade in 1830. His appointment created considerable consternation. Mrs Arbuthnot noted that 'the same Gazette which announced their appointments notified the dissolution of their partnership with houses in the City. This is all *quite new*,'[1] and according to Croker, Thomson was 'exposed to mortifying sneers when—a plain merchant—he took his seat on the Treasury Bench'.[2]

J. C. Herries was another merchant's son who became a Cabinet minister. His slow but steady advancement was largely the result of the happy connection, which his father had formed when he was Colonel of a regiment of Light Horse Volunteers in the City of London. His charges included many men of wealth and influence. On his bankruptcy they purchased for him an annuity of £1,000, and they helped the son in his career in the Civil Service and in politics. When Spencer Perceval, one of his subordinates, succeeded to the office of Chancellor of the Exchequer he appointed young Herries, then twenty-nine, as his Private Secretary. From then onwards Herries advanced from one lucrative Civil Service appointment and sinecure to another, until in 1823 he became Financial Secretary to the Treasury. A seat was found for him through government influence at Harwich. He stayed in office when the bulk of the Conservatives seceded on the accession of Canning. After Canning's death, Goderich offered him the post of Chancel-

---

[1] *Journal*, vol. II, p. 405.
[2] Croker in his diary, *cf. Papers*, vol. II, p. 78.

lor of the Exchequer. The choice was really the King's, and the unhappy Prime Minister had to accept it, despite protests from his Whig colleagues.

In a letter to Canning, Herries described himself as 'belonging to the working class of politicians'[1], and his significance does not lie in any qualifications of character or intellect, but rather in his rôle as a financial and administrative expert and a manipulator behind the scenes. It is significant, that he was one of the originators of the Carlton Club. For him, being in Parliament meant being in office. In 1834 Peel made him Secretary at War with a seat in the Cabinet, but in 1841, when Herries failed to secure election, he did not receive office via a Peerage. Peel merely expressed a hope that Herries would come back into the House of Commons, but received the reply that his ability to do so would 'depend a good deal on the position which he might happen to occupy with relation to the Government', and even the offer of a seat did not shake his determination not to be a back-bencher. In a memorandum to Goulburn he put his position unequivocally. 'On the occasion of this great change every individual, so far as I know having any fair claims to office, has derived some advantage from it, excepting self . . . The assurance which I should have given to everybody, that it was only because the vacancy did not actually exist at the very moment when my former fellow-labourers were called into employment again, would, if urged under such circumstances as an explanation of my exclusion, rather have tended, I think, to create than to remove, any unfavourable doubts.'[2]

Most of the 'new men' who reached the Cabinet did so, however, as occupants of the Woolsack. Victorian Lord Chancellors and other legal luminaries provide some of the little explored success stories of the period; indeed they have done so ever since. The men who presided over the House of Lords for most of those years were anything but aristocratic in origin. Among their fathers we can find a not very successful Royal Academician, an attorney, a hairdresser, a minor Colonial Civil Servant, a Presbyterian Minister, an army captain and a physician. Only three can claim descent from families distinguished by landowning, legal or political

---

[1] E. Herries: *J. C. Herries, A Memoir*, 1880, vol. II, p. 87.
[2] *ibid.*, vol. II, p. 194.

eminence. This ought not to surprise us. Law Officers are all 'working class politicians'. They are appointed for their experience and forensic skill, and their political life is in no way an interruption of their professional career; if anything it may heighten it. Their earnings rose rather than fell when they took office, and if the fall of an administration should throw them out of office there was generally a judicial appointment or, in the case of the Lord Chancellor, a substantial pension available for them. While in office their earnings, of course, exceeded those of other Ministers and unlike them they were not debarred from private legal practice.[1] One cannot help suspecting that there were among them quite a few who entered Parliament with an eye on the main chance. If we reflect on the large number of barrister M.P.s who were raised to the bench during the nineteenth century, this is hardly surprising.[2] The costs have, of course, to be weighed against the likely advantages. Lord Campbell was a son of the Manse. He succeeded at the Bar through an outstanding legal talent and the wealth which he thus acquired enabled him to enter politics. He was 'inclined to think that since we lost our estates in the county of Angus, my election at Brooks' is the greatest distinction our house has met with'.[3] Yet Parliament seemed barred by the excessively high costs of obtaining a seat. In 1825 he received an invitation to contest Stafford but was forced to decline owing to the high cost of the contest, estimated at £5–6,000. He eventually consented to stand for the borough in 1830 and was elected. His victory, however, was 'dearly bought' and he was only consoled by the fact that 'other lawyers were worse off than he . . . Slaney is supposed to have spent £8,000 . . .'[4]

It is not surprising that *la carrière ouverte aux talents* was in Britain most marked where 'know-how' and expertise were greatly in demand: in industry and in the professions. Napoleon had applied it to his generals and later to the men who were to govern the provinces of his centralized state. In England, where vast economic and technological changes were the counterpart of the social

---

[1] The right to private practice did not, of course, apply to the Lord Chancellor.
[2] *cf.* H. J. Laski: *Studies in Law and Politics*, 1932, p. 168–9.
[3] Letter to father quoted in Hardcastle: *Life of Lord Campbell*, 2 vols., 1881, vol. I, p. 409.
[4] *ibid.*, p. 475.

and political upheavals which transformed the *ancien régime*, the doctrine was first preached and practised in the entrepreneurial field.[1] Fifty years after its introduction into French Public Administration, it began to be applied in the Civil Service; at first informally, in the staffing of the new Inspectorate in the 1850's and 1860's and, following on the Northcote-Trevelyan report on Civil Service recruitment of 1853, formally but very gradually throughout the whole of the administrative sphere.[2]

In politics it arrived last of all and, as further analysis will show, progress was slow and the road full of obstacles. In early Victorian England detailed acquaintance with a particular sphere of administration was, as a rule, not required from ministers and was only rarely found. It was held that, if necessary, politicians of really outstanding ability could master the technical problems comparatively quickly. Hence the scope for the 'amateur' and hence, perhaps, the need for Sir Robert Peel as Prime Minister to supervise in detail the administration of all government departments.[3]

Yet the rise of 'new men' owes more to the democratization of politics, which took place during the last thirty years of the 19th and the first thirty years of the present century, than to earlier changes in the function of government. And the power of the traditional ruling class rested as much on the ideology which justified it, as on the political and economic institutions which made their rule possible. We must now turn to the investigation of this ideology.

---

[1] On this see Reinhold Bendix: 'The Self-Legitimation of an Entrepreneurial Class' in the *Zeitschrift für die Gesammte Staatswissenschaft*, vol. 110 (1954), pp. 48–72.

[2] The background of the Inspectorate charged with the administration of the Factory Acts, the Education Acts and similar measures has recently been examined by David Roberts in his book *The Victorian Origins of the Welfare State*, New Haven 1960. On the Civil Service see the discussion in chapter XI below where relevant references will be found.

[3] *cf.* B. E. Carter: *The Office of Prime Minister*, London, 1956.

CHAPTER III

The Self-Legitimation of a Ruling Class

The Fifth: Whence came our thought?
The Sixth: From four great minds that hated Whiggery
The Fifth: Burke was a Whig
The Sixth: Whether they knew it or not,
        Goldsmith and Burke, Swift and the Bishop of Cloyne
        All hated Whiggery; but what is Whiggery?
        A levelling, rancorous, rational sort of mind.
                                    —W. B. YEATS.

'You long for the rule of the ablest man, everywhere, at all times? To find your ablest man and then give him power and obey him—that you should hold to be the highest act of wisdom which a nation can be capable of?'
'Yes, and you know you believe that too, just as firmly as I do.'
'I hope so. But then how about our universal democracy and every man having a share in the government of his country? . . . Will that find our wisest governor for us—letting all the foolishest men in the nation have a say as to who he is to be?'
        —THOMAS HUGHES: *Tom Brown at Oxford.*

THE persistence of aristocratic rule in a country which, thanks largely to its entrepreneurial middle class, had reached a position of economic and industrial eminence in Europe, is an extraordinary historical phenomenon. Neither revolutionary thoughts nor the famine and misery brought about by the wars in Europe had succeeded in shaking it. The Bastilles of the new Poor Law were not stormed by an angry population incited by radicals and reformers. Despite the panic of the well-to-do citizens, who enlisted as special constables in order to meet the dangerous columns marching on London from Kennington Common, there was never any real threat to the established order.

This largely undisturbed enjoyment of political power by the traditional ruling class cannot be explained solely in terms of political institutions and the parliamentary situation. It is doubtful whether the aristocracy would have been so successful if it had not on the whole been convinced of the justification of its own exercise of power and, in addition, had managed to persuade a large section of the population of the righteousness of its claim. Max Weber regarded the self-legitimation of rule and the ruler as one of the most essential attributes of successful government. 'All experience points to the fact that rulers are unwilling to rest the continued exercise of power on material or emotional factors or even on a recognition of the value which that rule confers. All seek to instil in the ruled a lasting belief in their legitimacy.'[1] Individual noblemen might seek the destruction of the old order and propagate measures to bring about the rule of the middle class, but the majority of the landed proprietors clearly believed that in holding positions of political power they and the group closely allied to them, were acting in the best interests of the nation.

Lord Grey, that 'coronated Necker, the worn-out Machiavel', who was considered by many of his contemporaries to be the destroyer of the old order, thought that his Reform Bill would increase rather than diminish the power of the aristocracy. 'The more the Bill is considered,' he wrote to Lord Somers, 'the less it will be found to prejudice the real interests of the aristocracy.'[2]

In any case, the conflict between Whigs and Tories was, with the exception of a few extremists on either side, not carried out on the basis of irreconcilable differences of principle. Each side was eager to preserve the aristocracy in power. The Duke of Wellington may have firmly believed that the British Constitution, 1829-model, was devised by Providence, but many of his followers thought that they should bring in a Reform Bill of their own. They paid for their faintheartedness with ten years of opposition.

---

[1] Max Weber: *Wirtschaft und Gesellschaft*, 1921, p. 122. Lenin thought that the conditions of the rule of a minority over millions was that they must possess control of the army, the police, and have the mythos of official orthodoxy.

[2] 26.9.1831, *Howick Papers*, quoted in J. R. M. Butler: *The Passing of the Great Reform Bill*, 1914, p. 255.

It is illuminating to trace some of the ideological concepts which formed the basis of the aristocracy's justification of its rule. In this we are concerned with attitudes pertaining to a class rather than a political party; the conflict between Whigs and Tories is only incidental to our theme. Practical as well as more fundamental methodological considerations suggest a limitation of the period to be covered. Burke's defence of the established order against the ideological threat contained in the French Revolution is a convenient starting point; Bagehot's ideas on politics and government, maturing in a period of widespread clamour for a further extension of the franchise, forms a suitable place to halt.

The mere existence of such ideologies developed by philosophers and political propagandists cannot, of course, tell us anything about their immediate effectiveness. In the short run the character of the *hommes politiques moyens intellectuels* appears more determined by precept and prejudice which each man absorbs in the process of growing up. The ideas of economists and political philosophers seem most effective in the *middle* distance of time.[1] Yet the attitudes proclaimed from pulpit or lectern, or often from a judge's dais, are really part and parcel of the ideology which more astute and lucid minds have proclaimed. Moreover, it is in this watered-down form that they reach wider circles.

Three distinct but naturally related chains of reasoning and argumentation emerge as convenient guiding lines for an analysis of contemporary thought. One is the hypothesis of class representation according to which the formal division of power in the constitution corresponded to the natural order of society. A second is the belief in the beneficial effects of the maintenance of tradition and of the established hierarchy. A third may be termed the 'rabble' hypothesis and the theory of an 'élite'. Each of these will be examined in turn.

THE HYPOTHESIS OF 'CLASS' REPRESENTATION

The young Disraeli, in his journalistic writings during the 1830's, is probably the best exponent of the view that the power enjoyed by the British aristocracy was justly enjoyed because of their

---

[1] How the attitudes to politics of members of the traditional ruling class were formed is discussed in Chapter VI below.

talents and their services. His defence of the hereditary legislator is singular and convincing within its given premises. The *arriviste* intellectual, seeking place and power for himself, could hardly deny the shortcomings of the traditional holders of power. Disraeli agrees that they are no innovators, nor do they initiate new constitutions or inaugurate new political systems. But, for the ordinary ruling of the state, genius is not necessary. It is sufficient to find in the legislator 'a somewhat more moderate portion of sagacity and science'.[1] Now these qualities are to be found most happily united in the general body of the aristocracy.

The virtues and excellencies which are the peculiar qualifications of the hereditary branch of the legislature have been the main causes of the stability of British political institutions, and 'of the order and prosperous security which that stability has produced'. It follows that the aristocratic component of the constitution, far from being expendable, is an essential part of it. Indeed, compared with the relative obscurity of the members of the House of Commons, the Peers are 'known, and seen and marked'. Because of their limited numbers they can meet in person and, in consequence, cannot devolve their responsibility on others. Contrasted with the 'elevation of thought and feeling, learning and eloquence' and 'that mastery of detail and management of complicated commonplace which we style in this country "Businesslike habits" ', and in which the hereditary legislators excel, is the evil genius of the mob. Men—though apparently not aristocrats—are ruled by 'passion and interest'. Echoing Hobbes, Disraeli exclaims that 'life is short, man is imaginative, our means are limited, our passion high' and, in consequence, 'the leaders of the mob will become the oppressors of the people'. The hereditary legislators, on the other hand, far from being swayed by narrow selfish motives, bestow general benefits on society, not only directly through their services to state and community, but also more indirectly through the example and precept which they set through the 'sustained splendour of their stately lives'. Virtue, pomp and circumstance make the hereditary principle justly extendable to parliamentary

---

[1] Benjamin Disraeli: 'The spirit of Whiggism' in *Whigs and Whiggism: Political Writings* ed. by Wm. Hutcheson, London 1913. All subsequent quotations are taken from this.

representation through the House of Commons. 'The representative of a county is selected from one of the first families of the shire, and ten years after, the son of this member, a candidate for the same honour, adduces the very circumstances of his succession as an increased claim upon the confidence of the constituency.' This is another proof that the talents required for rule are not of the kind which demand more than the 'average human capacity' which 'may descend from father to son'.

The basic idea underlying the colourful exposition of the *littérateur-politicien* is the thought that the landowning class is the best representative of the general interest of the nation and that the rule of this class alone guarantees security and stability. The debate of 1831 and 1832 is curiously lacking in references to general principles, especially on the part of those who opposed the Bill.[1] There were repeated appeals to the 'spirit' of the constitution, but the discussion was befogged by such issues as the value of the nominee-member and the 'rights' of existing voters, let alone the motives behind the disfranchisement of boroughs. Only occasionally do we find that the supremacy of the old ruling class is voiced. 'The present constitution' we are told by Sir H. Inglis 'admits all classes, represents all talents' but 'in the proportion as you increase the popular will in this house you risk the existence of the sovereign and of the House of Peers.'[2] Mr Twiss was strongly opposed to a Bill which 'swept away all the fixed landmarks between the ancient estates of the kingdom; an expanded system of representation would only lead to the representation of "classes" [*i.e.* narrow material interests] as opposed to the interest of the whole'.[3] Another member of the middle class who made the interest of the aristocracy his own was Alexander Baring. He thought that there was grave danger if the theory of popular representation was followed to its logical conclusion. It was 'upon the practical violation of this principle' that Britain's power 'to conciliate the existence of a monarchy and an aristocracy with the greatest degree of real

---

[1] *cf.* Butler, *op cit.*, p. 235.
[2] Speech in the House of Commons on March 1, 1831. Reprinted in *The Speeches in both Houses of Parliament on the Question of Reform*, London, 1832, p. 43 ff.
[3] *ibid.*, p. 58.

substantial liberty that the people of any country ever enjoyed' depended.[1]

Even among those who supported the extension of the franchise in principle many held that in giving the vote to the *middle class* they would do nothing to abrogate the powers of the aristocracy. Lord Palmerston thought in 1831 that the Reform Bill would maintain for 'property, rank and respectability the same influence in the representation . . . it is the possession of those qualities, united with rank and station which now command admiration and respect'.[2] If anything, reform could only strengthen the position of the aristocracy unless the latter deliberately alienated middle-class support. 'The Aristocracy must maintain their influence by other means than merely looking to parliamentary patronage . . . if (it) will bring to the support of high rank and station in society corresponding personal conduct, virtue and influence; if they will endeavour to attach themselves to the middle classes by offices of kindness and conciliation . . . they may then safely throw themselves on that class for support, who have never yet known to refuse acknowledging the claim of rank and influence, when coupled with qualities which they have been taught to respect and esteem.'[3]

When we examine the public status of the members of the British aristocracy we realize that their rôle in the world at large was as much the product of their economic position as of the political eminence which they occupied as 'hereditary legislators'. Without it we could hardly speak of the 'sustained splendour of their stately lives'. The pattern of aristocratic conduct in the Victorian age was, however, rapidly abandoning the quasi-feudal pattern which still characterized it during the eighteenth century. The cost of maintaining an establishment rose without any corresponding increase in income from many estates. The introduction of railways brought to an end the lordly retinue in travelling which, in the eyes of the mass of the people, had been one of the conspicuous features of the aristocratic way of life. Parliament alone preserved in full the hierarchical order of a dying age.

[1] *ibid.*, p. 190.
[2] *ibid.*, p. 205.
[3] *ibid.*, p. 337. (Sir J. Johnstone.)

In the panoply of its state occasions, the ceremonials of a feudal Court were re-enacted. Its members—formally all equal—did yet show deference to the rank of a representative and the antiquity and prestige of a Constituency. The standing orders of the House of Lords still provided for the seating of Peers according to rank, men could still vote by proxy, and in the division lists each rank was separately listed.[1] In seeking to maintain the old order, Disraeli and other of its advocates based their arguments not just on a fairly rationally constructed model of a political system but equally on affective, even aesthetic factors.

Such considerations loom large in the general scheme of conservative thought, the appeal of a stable, well-ordered and externally magnificent system of government is strong.[2] Similar views were to the fore in the political thought of the German romantics who reacted against the dissolution of traditional social ties which resulted from the enlightenment, and looked back longingly to the stable system of human relationship, which had existed under feudalism.[3]

In England the feudal heritage was fortunately a matter of a more distant past than in Germany. English romantic thought accepted the basic tenets of the Enlightenment: freedom of thought, equality before the law, but it reacted against the libertarian and egalitarian views of the French revolution. This thought has a direct bearing on the legitimation of the ruling class and must, in consequence, be examined at some length.

THE DEFENCE OF HIERARCHY AND TRADITION

Burke, as we know, described the nobility as 'the Corinthian capital of polished society', but his views were not based on an

---

[1] The Duke of Richmond: 'I rise to order. Noble Lords are not in their places, and I beg that the Standing Order No. 1 be read, which renders it necessary that noble Lords should sit in their proper places. I rise to suggest this, because I see a noble Earl sitting next to one of the junior Barons.' From the debate of the House of Lords, April 22, 1831.

[2] Conservatism is conceived here in the general and not in the party-political sense unless specially mentioned.

[3] For a general discussion of this aspect of conservative political thought see Karl Mannheim: 'Conservative Thought', Ch. II of his *Essays in Sociology and Social Psychology*, 1953 especially pp. 89–90, 104.

exaggerated belief in the virtues and wisdom of its individual members. He could be critical of these; he referred to the Duke of Bedford, who had opposed his pension, as one who was 'swaddled and rocked and dandled into a legislator'[1] but in the main he saw in the traditional ruling class the 'embodiment of tradition', 'the chain that connects the ages of the nation'. Its members were 'the great oaks that shade a country and perpetuate [their] benefits from generation to generation', while he and his kind 'creep on the ground, belly into melons that are exquisite for size and flavour yet . . . are but annual plants that perish with their season . . .'[2] His belief in the right of the aristocracy to exercise power was thus a matter of prudence rather than abstract principle. Any system of representation must allow for the principle of selection and leadership. What better leadership could there be than a natural aristocracy which is not a separate interest in the state nor separable from it but 'an essential integral part of any large body rightly constituted'. Burke, like Disraeli, does not fail to recognize the existence of natural talent and the ability found in other, independent strata of society, but his belief in the beneficent power of tradition and 'the collective wisdom of the ages' made him single out the aristocracy as the natural repository of tradition. Equally important to him is the sense of security which results from the hierarchical organization of society. Its historical antecedents are to be found in the ties of family and neighbourhood first sustained and supported by unified hierarchy of ranks, which engenders affection and loyalty towards those in authority.[3] 'We fear God, we look up with awe to Kings, with affection to Parliaments, with duty to Magistrates, with reverence to priests and with respect to nobility.' It will be obvious that for Burke this feeling is a positive good, providing a cement for society. Social inequalities are justified, if they entail deference and obligation and thus make for stable social relationship. Property imposes obligations on its owner, especially landed property which 'in its nature is the firm base of every stable property'. It is therefore both natural

---

[1] *Letter to a Noble Lord*, 1796, p. 29.
[2] Letter to the Duke of Richmond, 1772, quoted in J. L. and B. Hammond: *The Village Labourer*, Guild Edition, 1948, vol. I, p. 18.
[3] *cf.* C. Parkin: *The Moral Basis of Burke's Thought*, 1956, pp 33-34.

and right that those with more property should be at the head of society.[1]

The owners of landed property are also identified more closely with the general well-being of society and with the security of property as such. For Burke 'the argument for the connection of political power with property is more than just a claim for the ascendancy of *the propertied*, those with the largest stake in the country. They are important but still a partial interest. It is a belief that property, in all its gradations, represents the stable rational self-interest from which the good of the community is to be elicited.'[2]

Coleridge was similarly convinced of the great power attaching to *landed* property. He regarded land as a synonym for country, and he attached to both a feeling of stability. 'The notion of superior dignity,' he said, 'will always be attached in the minds of men to that kind of property with which they have most associated the idea of permanence.' Only property had a right to representation; the working masses 'are not sought for in public counsel, nor need they be found when politic sentences are spoken. It is enough if every one is wise in the working of his own craft, so best *will they maintain* the state of the world.'[3] In his 'Lay Sermon addressed to the Higher and Middle Classes on the existing Distress and Discontent' Coleridge refers to the general impoverishment occasioned by the return of peace and ascribed it to an 'overbalance of the commercial spirit'. To this the natural counter-force is the 'ancient feeling of rank and ancestry', for the ancient families 'acted as a counterpoise to the grosser superstitions of wealth'. 'Like the stars in heaven their influence was wider and more general because for the mass of mankind there was no hope of reaching and therefore no desire to appropriate them.'[4]

Subordination to the leadership of the landowning nobility was

---

[1] In a judgment delivered in 1794 Clarke, L. J., referred to the landed interest: 'who alone had a right to be represented in Parliament not the rabble who have nothing but personal property' quoted in J. A. Spender: *Public Life*, vol. I, p. 37.

[2] Parkin: *op. cit.*, p. 46.

[3] S. T. Coleridge: *Lay Sermons* (1852) edition by Derwent Coleridge, pp. 6–7.

[4] *ibid.*, p. 190. (Coleridge makes it clear, however, that he was aware of the evils following from that state of affairs in the past.)

not only a matter of enlightened self-interest and a foundation of social harmony; it also provided the only acceptable basis for firm and effective national government. 'To enable men to act with the weight and character of a people . . . we must suppose them to be in that stage of habitual social discipline in which the wise, the more expert and the more opulent conduct the less knowing and the less provided with the goods of fortune.'[1]

Property was the basis of all claims to political representation; on this the ministerialists and the opposition of 1832 were fully agreed. They were only divided on the implications of this fundamental principle. The opposition thought that if representation is by virtue of property and if property is unequally distributed, there must be a corresponding inequality of influence. The existing constitution embodied just the right distribution of power between the various forms of property. If you destroy it, Sadler asserted, you will 'prepare in some form or other, for those agrarian struggles which long disturbed and at length destroyed Rome; for similar spoliations which have recently been witnessed in a neighbouring country where property, bereft of its political influence, lost its right, and only served to mark out its possessors to certain destruction'.[2]

The Whigs, on the other hand, believed that only by enfranchising the commercial, manufacturing and professional middle class, would they be able to prevent a union of that class with the lower orders and link its interests fairly and squarely to those of the old ruling strata. It was, as one of them put it, 'of the utmost importance to associate the middle with the higher orders of society in the love and support of the institutions and government of the country'.[3]

THE 'RABBLE' AND THE 'ELITE'

The defenders of the established order at the time of the first Reform Bill thought that even the moderate extensions of the

---

[1] Burke: *Works* (Rivington Ed.), vol. VI, p. 216, quoted in Parkin, *op. cit.*, p. 45.

[2] Hansard, Third Series, vol. 3, col. 1536.

[3] From a memorandum of T. F. Kenneday, M.P. for Ayr, submitted to Lord John Russell. Quoted in N. Gash: *Politics in the Age of Peel*, 1953, p. 15.

franchise would 'open the floodgates'. There could be no equality in political society, Coleridge asserted. To let all have a say in the Government would shift power from the 'people', that is the responsible members of society, to the population which included the mob. Instead of democracy you would have 'fool and knaveocracy'.

Nothing of the sort happened after 1832, yet when Bagehot contemplated the likely outcome of a further and, admittedly, more radical extension of the franchise a generation later he raised a similar spectre. He thought that social and political collapse would inevitably follow on the granting of urban household franchise. He was 'exceedingly afraid' of the ignorant multitude of the new constituencies. Their numerical electoral superiority would mean 'the supremacy of ignorance over instruction and of numbers over knowledge'.[1] He called on the leading statesmen to give the masses a responsible political programme. He went further, he appealed to the aristocracy and the plutocracy to set aside their differences and to unite. Bagehot thought that in this fusion the aristocracy should—and could—take the position of leadership.

Carlyle stood equally aghast at the torrents which male adult suffrage was about to let loose. The Reform measure would 'call in new supplies of blockheadism, gullibility, bribability, amenability to beer and balderdash'.[2] The nobility, with all its shortcomings, was to him still 'intrinsically (more) valuable and recommendable than any other class'. If the aristocracy of birth would only unite with the aristocracy of talent—industrial and intellectual—it could achieve great things for the country.[3] For Bagehot this primary position of the aristocracy 'as the head of the plutocracy' was based on the still general admiration of birth by wealth and on the fact that there had never been a country 'in which all old families, and all titled families received more ready observance from those who were their equals, perhaps their superiors in wealth; their equals in culture and their inferiors only in descent and rank'.[4]

---

[1] *The English Constitution*, 2nd. ed., Preface p. xxiii (in 1904 ed.).
[2] Carlyle: *Shooting Niagara*, 1867, p. 10.
[3] *ibid.*, p. 52.
[4] *British Constitution*, 2nd ed., Introduction pp. xxx. Bagehot recognized at the same time that on the purely formal, *i.e.* the electoral, plane the plutocracy was more powerful than the aristocracy.

Bagehot, the astute observer of the political scene, was thus induced by practical considerations to stress the importance of élite rule. The principal bases for his political standpoint, however, were his views of the laws governing the political system which lie at the back of his examination of the working of the British constitution. The theories expressed in *Physics and Politics* arose out of the spirit of scientific inquiry into social phenomena, conceived under the influence of Comte, Darwin and Spencer.[1]

Bagehot saw the basis of social action and motivation in the (biological) phenomenon of imitation. 'Unconscious imitation and encouragement of appreciated character ... is the main force which moulds and fashions men in society as we see it.'[2] In the evolutionary process of mankind advance depended on the breaking of the 'cake of custom'. The institutions of a stable society were transformed through the widening of the primitive family. At first man was uncertain of the fact of paternity. Knowledge of it led to the recognition of the right of the *patria potesta* and eventually widened the area of free discussion. In the latter process the more inventive and morally refined persons are the most influential. This rise of free discussion had brought Britain to her present state of eminence and within the nation, the same process had enhanced the development of the higher classes. According to Bagehot, the lower classes, 'are clearly wanting in the nicer part of those feelings which, taken together—we call the sense of morality'.

Imitation as such is ethically neutral, it may fix on anything, primitive superstition or exhortation to altruistic conduct. This consideration in turn reinforces the need for the right leadership. 'We are most of us earnest with Mr Gladstone', Bagehot tells us, 'we are most of us *not* so earnest in the time of Lord Palmerston ... each predominant mind calls out a corresponding sentiment.' Thus considerations based on the causes of social progress lead the author to postulate—implicitly more than explicitly—the importance of an intellectual and moral élite. 'Nature is like a schoolmaster, she gives her finest prizes to her high and most instructed

----

[1] Its significant subtitle, rarely quoted, is 'Thoughts on the application of the principle of "natural selection" and "inheritance" to Political Society'. Originally published in the *Fortnightly* in 1867, it appeared in book-form only in 1873.

[2] *Physics and Politics*, p. 97.

classes. Still, even in the earliest society, nature helps those who help themselves and helps them very much.'[1]

Bagehot's concept of Society is delicately poised between recognition of the evils of a static social system and abhorrence of mass democracy. He recognized the claims of talent and the fact that in Britain it is possible to cross removable social barriers which segregated classes, without confining them completely.[2] 'The principle of popular government is that the supreme power, the determining efficiency in matters political, resides in the people, not necessarily or commonly in the whole people *but in a chosen people, a picked and selected people.*'[3] At the same time, he saw in the deep-rooted desire for deference in all but a few not just an historical accident but the very cement of British Society. It is this deference which had so far allowed the élite to rule.

Much of this discussion centred around the demands for a more popular franchise which culminated in the Act of 1867. Had the Reform of that year been fought over with the same bitterness which earlier reform measures had encountered, the protagonists of the established order would have mustered much more support. As we know, the quirks of parliamentary tactics made the party, which most clearly represented the 'Gentlemen of England', the advocates of household suffrage. Their conversion to this principle had been swift. In the debate on Lord Russell's Bill of 1866, Sir Hugh Cairns spoke of the House of Commons as 'representative of every class not according to numbers but according to everything which gives weight and importance to the world without'.[4] Speaking as Lord Chancellor in the House of Lords, less than a year later, he proclaimed that it was 'utterly impossible for the country to be governed by any party otherwise than in accordance with the opinion of the great majority of householders in the country'.[5]

---

[1] *Physics and Politics*, p. 211.

[2] *cf.* his 'Essay on Sterne and Thackeray', in *Works*, vol. IV, pp. 229–66, at p. 261. The British social system is a system of *'removable inequalities* where many people are inferior and worse off than others, but in which each may in theory hope to be on level with the highest below the throne' (Bagehot's italics).

[3] *English Constitution*, pp. 28–29 (my italics).

[4] Hansard, 3rd Series, vol. 182, col. 1463.

[5] Hansard, 3rd Series, vol. 188, col. 2007.

The minority of dissident Whigs and Tories who opposed the
Bill in its passage through Parliament based their opposition on
two major arguments: The power of ignorance and the prostitu-
tion of politics. They were afraid that the large new electorate
would return new kinds of representatives, rich men and demagogues, who would ingratiate themselves with the electorate, or
appeal to their baser passions. And 'when you have made [the
House of Commons] irksome to men of cultivation and refinement'
a dissident Tory told the House of Lords, 'you will find that your
educated classes will first feel themselves powerless and then,
before long, will become silent'.[1] Even Russell was afraid on that
score and thought that the Household suffrage, now to be introduced, would eventually lower the quality of the House of Commons. Neither he, nor his successor in office, had any doubt that
the character of the elected representation which had emerged
from the 1832 reforms could not be bettered by any kind of electoral devices imaginable. The two Earls thought that the men who
had been returned to Parliament in the past thirty-five years, had
always considered the interests of all classes of the community and
had acted throughout in a thoroughly enlightened and selfless
manner.[2]

Many Liberals and Conservatives would have agreed with this
view. They would undoubtedly have shrunk from such radical
changes, if considerations of party-loyalty and party-advantage
had not dictated otherwise. Russell and Shaftesbury were both
afraid of what the latter termed 'the residuum', the lowest strata
of the population, whose voting would be inconsidered and irresponsible. It would take ten years 'to bring up the residuum by
education; but it would not take six months for them, through
their representatives, to destroy everything before them'.[3]

Salisbury's fear went further. He did not disguise his fundamental opposition to any attempt to tilt the balance of political power in
favour of the working class. He accepted a dichotomy of interests
between Labour and Capital, between wealth and want. Whoever
the parliamentary representatives of the working class might be,

---

[1] *ibid.*, vol. 188.

[2] See their speeches on the second Reading of the Reform Bill in the House
of Lords.

[3] Hansard, 3rd Series, vol. 188, col. 1931.

however strong the feeling of deference shown to them by the lower orders, their political action would be dictated by the character of the electorate which they represented. 'If ever you come to a question between class and class . . . where the interests of one class are pitted against those of another,' he said in the debates on the third reading of the Reform Bill in the House of Commons, 'you will find that all those securities of rank, wealth and influence, in which you trust, are mere feathers in the balance against the solid interest and the real genuine passion of mankind.'[1]

The development of the political system during the next sixty years shows that these prophecies remained largely unfulfilled. A long time was to elapse, and another two reform bills were to reach the statute book, before a democratic electorate could bring forth the political representation of the working class which would be in a position to present such a challenge. The second Reform Act is nevertheless a greater landmark in British politics than its predecessor; and the 'fears' expressed on this occasion had more force behind them than those which accompanied the events of 1832. Even if they do not presage the future, the discussions which accompanied the advent of democracy help us to understand the basis of the belief in the old order.

[1] Hansard, 3rd Series, vol. 188, col. 1532.

CHAPTER IV

The Changing Social Structure of The British Political Elite: 1868-1955

'It is in the nature of things that a man's self should be nearer to him than his constituency. There is a homely saying, that a man's skin sits closer to him than his shirt. And without any imputation on their good faith, so it is with Members of Parliament. Single individuals are no doubt capable of preferring the interests of others to their own. But in the case of classes, dealing with class interests, it is the law of their being that they should consider thesmslves paramount and necessary to the public welfare.'—BENJAMIN CACROFT in 'Essays in Reform', 1867.

'In the course of the nineteenth century England adopted peacefully and without violent shocks almost all the basic civil and political reforms that France paid so heavily to achieve through the great revolution. Undeniably, the great advantage of England lay in the greater energy, the greater practical wisdom, the better political training that her ruling class possessed . . .'—GAETANO MOSCA in 1923.

FOR the more detailed analysis of the British political élite, the year 1868 is a more convenient and appropriate starting point than 1832. It is now generally recognized that the second Reform Act, which introduced suffrage in the boroughs, affected the British political system more decisively than earlier or later measures of parliamentary or constitutional reform. To increase the electorate of England and Wales from 1,057,000 in 1865 to 1,995,000 in 1869 entailed a shift in the distribution of electoral strength, which was potentially far more revolutionary than the conferment of political power on the middle classes in 1832.[1]

The introduction of a household franchise in the boroughs was

---

[1] Expressed in percentages the 1832 Act resulted in an increase of the electorate of 49 per cent, the 1867 Act led to an increase of 88 per cent and of 140 per cent in the boroughs only.

bound to lead to changes in the character of political representation, but the effects were to be felt only gradually. However, another factor was equally at work in influencing the composition of the political élite: the decline of a political generation and the emergence of a new one. In 1865, Palmerston died, still holding the reins of power. His political career had spanned half a century. He had held office for most of the fifty years he had sat in the House of Commons; 'at his death all at once a new generation started into life, the pre-1832 all at once died out'.[1]

Seven years later men were saying that there was 'not a brick of the Palmerston House standing'. Palmerston's contemporaries felt that with his death an epoch had come to an end and that the mental climate was changing. Dean Church commented on it in a letter to an American scholar: 'as you know, we have lost Palmerston. While he lived there was a tacit understanding that no internal battles of consequence were to be fought or great issues raised. He was like a great-grandpapa to the English political world whose age was to be respected.'[2] Beginning with Gladstone's administration, new and previously untried men were coming to the fore. It is the coincidence of new men, carrying out new measures, under a new set of constitutional provisions, which makes the year 1868 such a decisive milestone in the development of the British political system.

The factor of a 'political generation', like the generational concept as such, is inevitably somewhat loose and imprecise but it should not be neglected in a social analysis of politics and we shall return to it later. Politicians fall into groups which are divided not only by loyalties to parties and programmes, but also by the period during which they become Members of Parliament and by the events which cause them to form political attitudes. Particularly violent inter-party conflict, electoral landslides and events which decisively influence the life of the community, such as wars, put their stamp on certain groups of men and turn them into a political generation.[3]

---

[1] Bagehot: *The English Constitution*, 2nd ed. p. xi.

[2] Mary C. Church (ed.): *Life and Letters of Dean Church*, 1894, p. 171.

[3] On the concept of the generation in general *cf*. Karl Mannheim: 'The concept of the generation' in *Essays in the Sociology of Culture* and B. M. Berger: 'How long is a generation', *British Journal of Sociology*, March 1960.

The Cabinets of the period 1832–68 were, as we saw, still predominantly aristocratic in character, and even Radical pressure did not change this fundamentally. Palmerston's last government was still a most august body, although it was formed as the result of the avowed collaboration of the two factions of the Liberal Party. It contained three dukes, two Earls and six other aristocrats out of a total of fifteen members.[1] Only five of these fifteen served under Gladstone in 1868 and we shall see that, beginning with his first administration, men of middle-class background form at first a significant and later a predominant part in the personnel of the top layer of the British political élite.[2]

The entry of the middle-class representatives in the Cabinet is paralleled by a process of diffusion of office-holding among a widening range of political functions. Governments have their own hierarchy of posts, and the representatives of the *new* middle class tended, at first, to hold offices with less prestige, such as the Presidency of the Board of Trade, the Chancellorship of the Duchy of Lancaster, the Poor Law Board or, later, Local Government Board. Men of affairs tended to be put at the head of departments, which had large administrative functions, while the sinecure posts

[1] At the meeting in Willis Rooms which cemented the alliance, Bright had asked that in the formation of the Government some attention should be paid to members below the gangway. As a result Milner Gibson was appointed President of the Poor Law Board (with a seat in the Cabinet). Bright was angered at this cavalier treatment of the radicals, 'the chief offices are to be given to the old place-men and the crumbs to the representatives of the independent Liberals' he wrote in his diary. (*Diaries*, p. 241.)

[2] For the class-breakdown of politicians of the nineteenth and twentieth centuries the following criteria were used. *Aristocracy*: All those who were descended from a holder of a hereditary title in the grandparent generation, thus excluding the sons of the newly ennobled or those who had received hereditary titles themselves. *Working Class*: All those whose fathers at the time of the subjects' childhood were manual workers, clerks, tradesmen or who belonged to the ranks of the armed forces. The *Middle Class* lies between these two. In nearly all cases this meant the sons of businessmen, professional men, managers, administrators and the like. The group of Cabinet Ministers and political leaders here analysed presented few 'borderline' problems; the men studied could almost invariably be easily arranged into one of the three above categories. The members of gentry families, discussed below, form the only general exception to this. The class background presented here must, of course, be seen in conjunction with the educational and occupational analysis which is given in later tables.

TABLE I

Class Structure of Cabinets, 1868–1955:*

Administration	Year	Aristocrats	Middle Class	Working Class	Total
1. Gladstone	1868	7	8	—	15
2. Disraeli	1874	7	5	—	12
3. Gladstone	1880	8	6	—	14
4. Salisbury	1885	11	5	—	16
5. Gladstone	1886	9	6	—	15
6. Salisbury	1886	10	5	—	15
7. Gladstone	1892	9	8	—	17
8. Salisbury	1895	8	11	—	19
9. Balfour	1902	9	10	—	19
10. Campbell-Bannerman	1906	7	11	1	19
11. Asquith	1914	6	12	1	19
12. Lloyd George	1919	3	17	1	21
13. Bonar Law	1922	8	8	—	16
14. MacDonald	1924	3	5	11	19
15. Baldwin	1925	9	12	—	21
16. MacDonald	1929	2	4	12	18
17. National Ministry	1935	6	10	2	18
18. Baldwin	1935	9	11	2	22
19. Chamberlain	1937	8	13	—	21
20. Churchill	1945	6	9	1	16
21. Attlee	1945	—	8	12	20
22. Churchill	1951	5	11	—	16

* Churchill's wartime government has been left out as the War Cabinet was a very small body.

in the Government went almost invariably to elderly politicians of long aristocratic lineage. Foreign and empire affairs were likewise the prerogatives of the traditional politicians from the aristocracy. The first non-aristocrat to hold the office of Foreign Secretary was James Ramsay MacDonald who combined it with the Premiership in 1923.

Beginning with 1906 the aristocratic group in the Cabinet has occupied a minority position, albeit a powerful one. Labour administrations apart, this has continued to the present day.

TABLE II

Class Structure of Cabinet Personnel, 1868–1955:

	1868–86	1886–1916	1916–35	1935–55	1868–1955
Aristocracy	27	49	25	21	93
Middle Class	22	49	62	57	159
Working Class	—	3	21	21	42
TOTAL	49	101	108	99	294

Each of the three great parties which shared the political representation and governmental power during this period, have contributed, in varying degrees, to the composition of the political élite. The Cabinets of each have their specific social profile. The Conservative administrations were, until recently, composed almost entirely of men of aristocratic or upper middle-class origin, and they contained among the former, representatives of some of the largest landed magnates in the country. After 1886 the centre of gravity of the Liberal leadership, always more decidedly middle class, lost the adherence of most of the old Whig families and consequently became increasingly dependent on its new leader-cadre, many of whose members were of new middle-class and even of lower middle-class origins. The Labour Party, the alternative government since 1923, was a governing élite composed almost equally of members of the middle class and of the working class, with only a sprinkling of aristocrats.

TABLE III[1]

Class Structure of Cabinets, 1868–1955, according to Party:

	1868–86		1886–1916		1916–35		1935–55		1868–1955		
	Cons.	Lib.	Cons.	Lib.	Cons.	Lab.	Cons.	Lab.	Cons.	Lib.	Lab.
Aristocracy	13	15	26	23	19	3	20	1	60	32	4
Middle Class	8	14	21	28	33	12	40	14	86	54	25
Working Class	—	—	—	2	1	19	2	19	3	3	36
TOTAL	21	29	47	53	53	34	62	34	149	89	65

[1] This breakdown concentrates on the two major governmental parties. It leaves out one Labour Cabinet Minister for the period 1886–1916 and all Liberal Ministers since 1916. Owing to the fact that 9 ministers sat in Cabinets of two different parties the total for the three parties adds up to 303 and not 294.

In order to assess the significance of changes in the social origin of Cabinet Ministers at various periods and of various parties, we must view it against the background of parliamentary representation as such. Throughout this period the Cabinet was predominantly recruited from the House of Commons, and the selection process by which the party leadership emerges, took place largely in the House. Its membership is the foil against which the ruling group must be set. Yet the character of the House of Commons reflects, in turn, not only the changes in the composition of the electorate but also more subtle changes in the social structure, and the opportunities which the different groups in the community enjoy.

1868–86: THE BREAK-THROUGH OF NEW MEN

Whilst the second Reform Act inaugurated the era of the middle-class politician, its effects were strengthened by later measures, the Ballot Act of 1872 and the Corrupt Practices Act of 1883. Finally the entry of men from other ranks and occupations than those which had been traditionally associated with the political career could not have taken place if the growth of local party associations, although limited in scope and uncertain of their powers at first, had not brought new voices and methods into the process by which candidates, and consequently M.P.s, were selected. All these developments helped to reduce the powers of the local landowners and local party managers to impose a candidate of their own choosing on the constituencies.

In spite of all this, the institutional and economic obstacles to the entry into the House of Commons remained considerable, and this fact must be borne in mind in assessing the extent of the change in the character of Parliamentary representation.

The road into Parliament was often long and nearly always extremely costly. It was thus an effective obstacle to the political aspirations of any but the wealthy.[1] For the three elections, 1868, 1874 and 1880, the average cost of a county contest was about £3,000 and for the boroughs it ranged from £742 (in 1874) to £1,212 (in 1880).[2] To this figure we must add other expenses,

---

[1] *The Economist* estimated in 1864 that the career of politics was effectively open to only about 5,000 men (p. 480).

[2] *cf.* H. J. Hanham: *Elections and Party Management*, 1959, p. 251.

which an M.P. was bound to incur, such as the cost of keeping up the electoral register, and subscriptions to local associations and charities. Taking these into account, it has been estimated that the cost of being an M.P. or even a candidate could not average less than £500 per annum in the case of boroughs, and £1,100 in the case of counties.[1]

While the ability to pay continued to be at the root of all political careers, the financial standing of candidates was even more decisive in the boroughs in which bribery could still be practised. In 1865 there were still 64 constituencies, returning 113 M.P.s, which could be termed 'corrupt'. By 1885, more as the result of the redistribution of seats in 1884, than as the result of the 1883 Act, the number had been reduced to 34 constituencies with 46 M.P.s. After that date the effects of the Corrupt Practices Act made themselves felt, and the numbers fell still further. By the turn of the century there were perhaps 15 seats where corruption could still influence the outcome of an election.[2] In addition, there remained in England and Wales a number of boroughs and a few counties which, as the result of the strong influences of one or two landowners or manufacturers, were still virtual nomination boroughs.[3] The middle-sized towns were particularly suitable for the exercise of entrepreneurial pressure on working-class voting. Large employers of labour were often returned for boroughs which were economically dependent on them. Politically, such men tended to be Liberals rather than Conservatives, and the boroughs which they represented 'illustrate one of the main features of late Victorian politics; the association of political emancipation with dependence on the great employer'.[4]

---

[1] *ibid.*, p. 258. We can gain some indication of the relative costs of general elections by relating the total amount involved to the size of the electorate and to the National Income. Both figures show a remarkable decline over the years. In 1880, when the total cost of the election was around £2,000,000 the expenditure amounted to 15/– per head and formed about one-500th of the National Income. By 1900 expenditure per vote polled had fallen to 4/4d. and the amount formed less than a 2,000th part of the National Income. Although absolute costs began to rise again—until checked by further legislation—the expenditure per voter has fallen further. In recent elections the costs per elector have been below one shilling.

[2] *cf.* Hanham, *op. cit.*, ch. XIII.   [3] *ibid.*, pp. 40–51 and Appendix III.

[4] Hanham, *op. cit.*, p. 68.

Thus even after the introduction of household franchise in the boroughs, a total of at least 108 M.P.s still owed their seats to the combined power of influence and long purses.

It is essential to know the conditions governing entry into the House of Commons in order to appreciate the changing social composition of the membership of the House of Commons. Among the M.P.s elected in 1868, the members of landed families still predominated and accounted for nearly two-thirds of all members. By 1886 that figure had declined to 50 per cent.[1] Not all these men actually owned land, and others combined landownership with industrial or professional careers. The figures are quoted rather as illustrations of the prevalence and decline of the traditional strata from which politicians were recruited, than as exact measurements of M.P.s' occupations. Unfortunately, all existing analyses of the membership of the House c f Commons (which are not based on detailed biographies and on an identical system of classification for all Parliaments) suffer from similar faults. The figures given below can therefore reveal only certain general configurations and trends.

TABLE IV

Occupations of M.P.s:

	1874		1880		1885	
Landowning, Rentiers	209	32%	125	19%	78	16%
Army and Navy	116	18%	86	13%	58	12%
Civil Service	11	2%	8	1%	—	—
Professions	157	24%	167	26%	154	32%
Commerce-Industry	157	24%	259	40%	186	38%
Other	2	—	7	1%	11	2%
No. analysed	652	100%	652	100%	487	100%
Total No. of M.P.s	652	—	652	—	670	—

1874 and 1880. From the table on p. 222 of Saunders: *The New Parliament* (for 'Landowning', 'Rentier' read there: Country Squires, Magistrates, Sons of Peers, Baronets, etc.).

1885. From the *Pall Mall Gazette*, Extra. No. 21, December 1885.

[1] *ibid.*, p. xv. Figures based on Bateman: *The great Landowners of Great Britain*, 4th ed., 1883.

In interpreting these figures we must, of course, bear in mind that of the three elections which were analysed, the first resulted in a Conservative majority while the second and the third resulted in Liberal victories. And in the ranks of the latter it was the Radical or advanced wing which gained ascendancy over the Whigs.

By contrast the 49 men, who held Cabinet office during the period belonged to a much greater extent to old established aristocratic families, and the traditional ruling strata, than the membership of the House of Commons. If we use a combination of class and parental occupation as a criterion, we find a group, which is not only largely aristocratic but in which even the non-aristocrats are often recruited from landowning, rentier or clergymen's families. Less than one-third of the Cabinet Ministers, who held office in the period, which saw the effects of household suffrage, were the sons of entrepreneurs or professional men. The lower orders did not even approach the threshold of the governing élite, nor did they, with one or two exceptions, even gain a foothold in the House of Commons.

TABLE V

Cabinet Membership 1868–86: Socio-Occupational Background:*

Father's Occupation	Aristocrats	Non-Aristocrats	Total
Landowning	21 (8)	1 (1)	22 (9)
Rentiers	1 (1)	1 (1)	2 (2)
Services, Diplomacy	3 (2)	1 (—)	4 (2)
Clergymen (C. of E.)	2 (2)	3 (2)	5 (4)
Manufacturers, Merchants, etc.	—	9 (6)	9 (6)
Upper Professionals†	—	5 (4)	5 (4)
Lower Professionals‡	—	2 (2)	2 (2)
TOTAL	27 (13)	22 (16)	49 (29)

* Figures of those who entered Cabinets for the first time during this period in parentheses.
† e.g. Barristers, Physicians.
‡ e.g. Teachers, Ministers of Religion.

The occupational career of the Cabinet Ministers naturally reflects their social background. The members of landowning families became in turn landowners almost without exception. Those sons of entrepreneurs, who followed in their father's footsteps, had severed all connections with their parental enterprises by the time they entered politics; others had followed a profession or had from the beginning lived the life of rentiers. If we compare the group of those of the Cabinet Ministers of this period, who had already held Cabinet office before 1868, with the new recruits of the period after 1868 we can observe the changes in the structure of the political élite.

TABLE VI

Occupations of Cabinet Ministers, 1868–86:

Occupation	Pre-1868 Cabinet Ministers	Entrants 1868–86	Total
Landowning	12	9	21
Rentier	3	3	6
Civil Service	2	2	4
Professions	2	10	12
Entrepreneurs	1	5	6
TOTAL	20	29	49

Who were the 'new men' on the ministerial front bench? The two party leaders of the period came into this category, although by the time they emerged into national prominence they were fairly well assimilated into the ruling group. They were fundamentally strangers to aristocratic England and each was occasionally to feel —or made to feel—his existence as an outsider. They were, however, reacting and adjusting to their ambivalent class position in different ways. Disraeli showed throughout his life a romantic attachment to the values, institutions and the individual representatives of aristocratic England. Gladstone on the other hand was gradually discarding some of the values and precepts of traditional political rule. Although he had become integrated into 'Society', it is well to remember that its values had not been his originally. Coningsby's Mr Millbank was aware of the distance between himself and the British aristocracy. 'People call Lord Lincoln my friend and he acts as such,' Gladstone noted, 'but it is well to remind myself of the difference of rank between us.'[1] Some thought that through-out his life there clung to him something of the parvenu 'something in his tone of voice and his way of coming into a room that is not aristocratic'.[2]

The administrations, which 'the people's William' formed, showed only a minority of the 'broad oaks of the Commonwealth' and of the descendants of ennobled financiers. Instead we find rep-resentatives of the new Liberalism: Bright, Forster, Stansfield and Chamberlain who came into the political élite as spokesmen of new social groups and a new segment of the 'body politic'. Their power and influence at Westminster often derived from the fact that they were the leaders and spokesmen of the new party organ-ization, both on the local and on the national level.

They were also men who had experience of business and local administration. Moreover, their emergence into national eminence followed from a prominent position in municipal or regional leadership. Lancashire, Yorkshire, Wales and Scotland furnished their contingent of local politicians for the national leadership, and men might receive office not just because of their own ability or pressure but also as a reward for 'loyal' parts of the kingdom. This applied not only to the Liberal Party. The appointment of R. A. Cross as Home Secretary by Disraeli in 1874 was, so Disraeli's biographer wrote, 'the natural outcome of the substantial support given by his native Lancashire, to the Conservative cause'.[3] Between the second Reform Act and the Great War the voice of regional opinion was probably heard more loudly in the central government than before or since.

The spokesmen of the new interests, who derived their income from industry and trade, or were dependent on their professional activity, were bound to come into conflict with representatives of the traditional political views inside the Liberal Party. The Duke of Argyll was a prominent spokesman of the older, traditional and landed interests. His approach to the Irish question had frequently

---

[1] Millbank is generally thought to be modelled on Gladstone. This reference to Lord Lincoln was made when Gladstone had been appointed a junior Lord of the Treasury with Lord Lincoln as one of his colleagues. *cf.* Sir Philip Magnus, *Gladstone*, 1954, p. 21.

[2] Emily Eden quoted in Magnus, *op. cit.*, p. 142.

[3] Moneypenny and Buckle: *Disraeli*, vol. II, p. 629 (two vol. edition).

been opposed to that of Gladstone. This, and strong interests outside the political sphere, led him repeatedly to contemplate resignation 'I wish and long to be out' he wrote to the Earl of Dufferin in
1880 'but I have to consider the political position and the certainty
that Gladstone may be driven to extremes'.[1] This he sought to
prevent; he did resign a year later but continued, until after the
proposal of Home Rule for Ireland, to be an outspoken critic of
Gladstone *inside* the Liberal party. Writing to the latter about the
proposal to create agricultural allotments he gave expression to
more fundamental objections to the policy of the Liberal leadership. 'The Parliamentary prominence which you give to a mere
nostrum of the radicals, distinctly outside your own programme,
marks a decided patronage on your part of the radical section
against the reasonable Liberals. I do not deny that the nostrum may
be squeezed into reasonable dimensions, but that is not the question. There is not one of the Peers whom I would trust to stand out
for any principle of politics inconsistent with unity of the party. It
is quite impossible to sympathize with this state of mind. I have
seen what it leads to. It leads to the triumph of inferior men who
become the real leaders and movers of Liberal opinion.'[2]

There was, of course, something rather artificial about the proposal of the 'Three acres and a cow', which had figured with some
prominence in the General Election of 1885. It was clearly more
of a vote-catcher than a realistic plan to improve the lot of the
agricultural labourer. The point of issue between Gladstone and
his critics inside the Liberal Party went deeper than this. It brought
into the ranks of the party in Parliament the battle of the platform
which had been fought by Chamberlain and his supporters during
the election campaign. In the critical vote which brought down
Salisbury's government, eighteen Liberals voted with the Conservatives and 76 were absent.[3]

This split was to widen in the discussion on the Government's
Home Rule Bill which now faced the opposition not only of the

---

[1] *Autobiography*, 2 vols, 1906, vol. II, p. 354.

[2] Gladstone Papers, (MSS. 44, 106), 29.1.1886, quoted in W. G. H. Armytage: 'The Railway Question and the Fall of the third Gladstone Ministry',
English Historical Review, 1956, p. 19. See also Argyll's letter to Gladstone
quoted in the former's *Autobiography*, vol. II, p. 399.

[3] *cf.* Morley: *Gladstone*, vol. III, p. 288–9.

Whigs, but also of a section of the Radicals. The mixed character of the opposition, the fact that Chamberlain found himself in the same lobby as the Marquis of Hartington, and that religious, *i.e.* strong anti-Catholic, sentiments entered into the Home Rule issue have tended to mask the social significance of the defection of nearly one-third of the Liberal M.P.s and of over half of the Liberal Peers.[1]

The numerical decline in the Liberal representation in the House of Lords is important in absolute terms, but it is even more significant with regard to the social character of the Party's representation in the Upper House. The Whigs had deserted the Liberal Party, and the representation of the latter in the Peerage was increasingly composed of members of the plutocratic section of society and of a few ennobled Liberal politicians and lawyers. Landowners were almost completely absent from the peerage creations of the Liberal administrations of 1892–95 and 1906–15; and the creations are themselves largely responsible for the remaining Liberal strength in the House of Lords. Of the 104 Liberal Peers in 1913, 59 had been created since 1892. No wonder the list of government supporters in the final reading of the Parliament Bill of 1911 read (largely) 'like the Directory of Directors or a Lloyd George Honour's List. For the first time in the advance to political democracy in this country there was hardly a patrician who would aid the process.'[2]

1886–1916: THE BREAKDOWN OF THE 'VICTORIAN COMPROMISE'

It is widely accepted today that major political parties are in themselves coalitions of diverse elements. This applies especially to those

---

[1] Composition of the House of Lords according to Party:

	Conservatives	Liberal Unionists	Liberals	Other	Total
1884	..	—	198	..	507
1891	333	91	77	41	542
1904	..	—	61*	..	591
1913	..	—	104†	..	650
1922	..	—	131‡	..	738
1936	543	—	56	247	846

* 11 created since 1892. † 48 created since 1904. ‡ 30 created since 1913.

[2] R. Jenkins: *Mr Balfour's Poodle*, 1954, p. 183.

which operate in a two-party state. This idea, however, is not so very new. Empirically minded writers on politics, and those mid-Victorian politicians, who did think more deeply about the system of political representation, conceived each party as reflecting vital interests in the community. Just because the classes were represented in almost the same proportion in each of the two parliamentary groupings, which went by the name of Liberals and Conservatives, oscillation of power, without acute conflict, was possible, and political decisions often bore the imprint of compromise. For the period 1832–68, Bagehot's dictum that England was governed alternatively by the left centre and the right centre is remarkably accurate.

After 1868, the two parties became more clearly crystallized, yet each remained an amalgam of social forces. It was thought that any deliberate attempt on the part of groups of politicians, or their leaders, to change the party structure through an alignment of Whig and moderate Conservatives would cause a dangerous imbalance of political forces, and would lead to 'greater violence in party warfare and the loss of that tacit understanding between the leaders of both sides which has more to do with the smooth working of our complex political system than superficial observers, who only see the outside of public affairs, imagine'.[1]

Such a situation was about to emerge with the change in the character of the Liberal Party, which resulted from the secession of the Liberal Unionists. The Liberal Party remained to some extent an alliance; it still counted among its numbers members of the old established political families, but the size and importance of the representation of new strata, of non-conformist businessmen from the Midlands and the North and of carpet-bagging lawyers from London, grew. The local party organizations, especially the caucuses of the large towns, which furnished such a large share of Liberal parliamentary representation, were often favourably disposed towards new men. Even comparatively impecunious candidates were sometimes helped to a seat in Parliament.

The difference in the character of Liberal and Conservative Parliamentary representation can be gauged from the distribution

---

[1] Lord Kimberley: 'Journal of events during the Gladstone Ministry (1868)', in *Camden Miscellany*, vol. XXI, 1958, p. 1.

of economic interests among M.P.s, which is given below. J. A. Thomas's analysis, used for this purpose, is valuable in so far as it gives an account of the economic strata, which were at different times represented in the House of Commons, and allows an assessment of the economic pressure exercised through the House.[1] On the one hand it duplicates entries, as it counts a landowner, who is also a Railway Director, under both categories, without distinguishing between principal occupation and part-time occupations or minor interests. Some facts stand out nevertheless. First of all we can observe the progressive decline in the number of landowning M.P.s. This is marked in each party, yet it is decidedly more significant on the Liberal than on the Conservative side. Lawyers, and other professional men, on the other hand, tend to be more prominent on the Liberal than on the Conservative benches.

In 1868, when 379 Liberals were elected, they could still count just under 200 men with landowning interests in their midst. Among the 279 Conservative M.P.s the figure was higher (219). The commercial and industrial interests were nearly twice as marked among the Liberals than among the opposition, and this holds good also for the representatives of law and of the professions. By 1902, when the two parties were actually more evenly balanced, the Liberals, with 274 seats, could only muster a comparatively small section of landowners. The Conservatives, who with their supporters numbered over 300, could still count 163 men with landed interest amongst them. Business interests as well as those of the Law and of the Professions, on the other hand, are more strongly represented in the party of the left than on the right.

The series of figures for all General Elections between 1868 and 1910 have been placed at the end of this chapter. (See Table XIII, on page 104.) They show the changes which occurred in broad outline. The real difference in the social character of the representation of the two parties can be seen more clearly through an analysis into more definite socio-occupational categories. Such a breakdown for the Parliament elected in 1906 is given below.[2]

[1] cf. J. A. Thomas: The House of Commons, 1832–1901; a study of its economic and functional character. Cardiff, 1939, and his The House of Commons, 1906–11, an analysis of its economic and social character. Cardiff, 1958.

[2] Derived from Jenkins, op. cit., p. 7.

TABLE VII

Education and Occupation of M.P.s, 1906:*

	Liberals†		Conservatives‡	
	Nos.	Per cent	Nos.	Per cent
At Public School other than Eton	93	25	37	24
At Eton	32	8	42	27
At Oxford or Cambridge	135	36	56	36
'Gentlemen'	69	18	48	31
Armed Forces§	22	6	32	20
Businessmen, Upper‖	80	21	26	17
Businessmen, Lower¶	74	20	31	8
Barristers (practising)	64	17	21	13
Solicitors	21	6	5	3
Writers and Journalists	25	7	6	4
Teachers**	9	2	3	2
Doctors	5	1	2	1
Trade Unionists	8	2	—	—
Others	—	—	1	1
TOTAL	377	100	157	100

* Applying to the two major parties only, excluding Irish Nationalists and Labour M.P.s.
† Excluding Lib.-Lab. M.P.s.
‡ Including Liberal Unionists.
§ With more than ten years' service.
‖ Those who started life in well-to-do circumstances.
¶ Those of comparatively humble origin.
** Mostly University Dons.

If we turn from the membership of the House of Commons to that of the Cabinet a similar picture emerges. The background of those politicians, who achieve high office and by virtue of it make the vital political decisions, widens during this period, but the character of Cabinet membership is still much more predominantly aristocratic and upper class than that of the House of Commons from which it is drawn. Moreover, as in the House of Commons, the difference between Conservative and Liberal Cabinets is significant. The Liberal élite, like the whole body of Liberal Parliamentarians, contains a much larger proportion of new men than we find in the Conservative ranks. Parliament and the political career-ladder often proved to be a step in a process of upward movement in the social hierarchy. No similar movement can be discerned in the Conservative ranks, and although the middle-class politician who reached office and eventually the Cabinet is not absent, his rôle is generally a minor one. If we leave out Disraeli, whose career is unparalleled, there were only a few Conservative leaders, who lacked a distinguished family background and who succeeded in politics largely through their own efforts. And the new men in the ranks of the Conservative leadership of this period did not reach positions of particular eminence. W. H. Smith, the owner of the newspaper and bookselling business, a Wesleyan and a man who had started work at sixteen, is the only exception to this; he was for six years Leader of the House of Commons. Contrast this with the part which typical middle-class politicians, men like Campbell-Bannerman, Asquith, Morley, Lloyd George, Haldane, Birrell and McKenna played in the Liberal leadership. Indeed middle-class politicians formed the backbone of the Liberal administrations between 1906 and 1915; with the exception of Sir Edward Grey, aristocrats like Crewe and Ripon performed largely honorific, representative functions.

Taking the period 1886–1916 as a whole we find, that among the 101 men who held Cabinet office during those thirty years, the aristocratic and the middle-class element are evenly balanced. Beside them the three Cabinet Ministers of working-class origin are numerically insignificant. There were still 41 landed proprietors mostly owning estates of considerable size. Nearly two in three of all the politicians in this group had been educated at one of twenty major Public Schools; indeed, Eton and Harrow alone could claim nearly half of the total Cabinet membership of the period.[1] Compared with the body of men who held office during the previous twenty years this group contains a larger proportion of professional men, mostly lawyers. They often entered politics via the Party organization; the Liberal caucuses especially had been kind to

---

[1] *i.e.* Eton, Harrow, Rugby and Winchester as well as sixteen other schools listed in a footnote to Table XII.

carpet-baggers, who had to combine a legal or professional career in London with the representation of a constituency in the provinces. The significant differences in the character of the two parties are given in detail in Table XII on page 102.

1916–55: NEW ALIGNMENTS AND OLD BASES

The Liberal leadership at the onset of the twentieth century was beginning to be fairly broadly based. The membership of the Liberal cabinets which held office between 1906 and 1915 was recruited from a wider field than any non-Labour cabinet since. And the party, as a whole, was during this period, more than ever before, open to democratic pressure and to the claims of talent for a political career and for office.

Yet the edifice was about to collapse. In the House of Commons, which acquiesced in the transfer of power from Asquith to Lloyd George, the Liberals had 254 seats. Within five years Liberal representation declined to 115; by 1924 it was 40 and, although there was an upsurge in 1929, the fall continued. After 1945 Liberal M.P.s numbered less than 10.[1] The place of the Liberal Party on the political stage was taken by the Labour Party, which emerged as a mass party and which, in 1922, became the official opposition. Although in 1918 the Labour Party only barely increased its parliamentary representation, it polled two and a quarter million votes—one-fifth of the total. The growing Labour vote took much of its strength from the Liberal sector of the electorate, or at least from that section of the working class which had supported the Liberal Party in the past.

We now know that Labour's electoral success before 1914 owed much to tacit agreements with the Liberals. This had led to voluntary restrictions on Labour's electoral activities, and among Liberal voters there were probably many who would have supported a Labour candidate had there been one. In the 1920's, after the disintegration of the Liberal Party, support for the Labour Party widened socially as well as numerically. The party began to contest an ever-growing number of constituencies, and

---

[1] For figures of election results and also for the evidence of the decline in Liberal votes and M.P.s see David Butler: *The Electoral System in Britain 1918–51*, p. 173.

not only those which had a predominantly working-class population. Its candidates were also no longer exclusively of working-
class origin. Increasingly members of the middle class stood as
Labour candidates and with the growing success at the polls more
of them sat on the Labour benches in the House of Commons.

The changing composition of the Parliamentary Labour Party,
which followed on the development of the whole party from the
representation of more specific working class interests to a national
party, will be discussed in Chapter IX. Its *embourgeoisement*
and the changing character and functions of its leadership, which
now regarded itself as the alternative government, will then become
more evident. Here an analysis of the social structure of the
political élite will have to base itself on the fact that, since 1918,
the Labour representation in the House of Commons has varied
between 10 per cent and 60 per cent, but that the share of the
working-class man in the House has fluctuated within much
narrower limits. Except for the years when Labour representation
was abnormally low, the number of ex-working-class M.P.s in the
House of Commons has never been below 100, nor above 200.

The social composition of the House of Commons changed
almost entirely as the result of the fluctuating political fortunes
of the Labour Party, for throughout these years the character of
the Conservative *Homo politicus* has not changed much. The new
political allegiances of a section of the middle class have left their
mark on the character and composition of the Labour Party leadership, but the changes in social structure produced by two world
wars have failed to make an impact on the type of men whom local
Conservative Parties selected as their representatives in Parliament.
Although the party depends for its electoral success on working-
class voters it has rarely recruited its officers from their ranks.[1]

If we now look at the social class composition of the House of
Commons since 1918, the following picture emerges. At the bottom of the social pyramid of Westminster we find a group of men
of working-class origin who sit almost exclusively on the Labour
benches. Next we observe a surprisingly small group of men of
lower middle-class origin who, again, are found largely in the
Parliamentary Labour Party. The middle class proper, especially the

[1] The character and ethos of the Conservative Party leadership is discussed
in Chapter X below.

professional element, is divided between the main parties tending to the right rather than to the left. At the top of the pyramid we find a strong upper-class element, representatives of the landed aristocracy and of big business. They sit predominantly on the Conservative benches, but there is a sprinkling in the Labour and the Liberal ranks.

A detailed social analysis of the Parliamentary representation between 1918 and 1955 is given in Table XIV on page 105. Although subject to the obvious errors of enumeration and vagaries of classification, this shows the changes in the social background of Labour M.P.s, and the largely unchanged composition of the Conservative benches. Yet the figures may well mask certain other changes. Educational opportunity has undoubtedly brought a number of working-class men into the House of Commons via a professional career. Indeed, in some cases, the very choice of a particular professional career may itself have been the result of political ambition. The numerical significance of the careers which led into politics via extra-mural teaching and adult education point in this direction. On the Conservative side too, other more subtle changes are left unrecorded in Table XIV. While by all accounts the upper-class element has remained steady (throughout this period Etonians and Harrovians have accounted for one third, or slightly more, of Conservative M.P.s) we can observe a definite and marked decline of the aristocratic element. In 1928 the House of Commons still contained 58 sons of Peers and Baronets; in 1955 there were only 12.

The 'inevitable Parliament men' have largely disappeared from the House of Commons and the connection between local land-ownership and Parliamentary candidature is much weaker than it was.[1] On the other hand, new groups have absorbed the style of life of the traditional ruling strata and in the course of this development they have entered the political élite. If we look at the background and careers of cabinet ministers during this period we find some amplification and verification of this.

To bring out the full significance of these changes the figures given in Table XV (page 106) should be compared with the analysis of the cabinet membership for the previous period given in Table

---

[1] For the changing character of the aristocracy see Chapter V.

XII. We find that aristocratic politicians form now only one-fifth of all Cabinet Ministers and that landowning is no longer the most prominent economic basis of political activity. Indeed, landed proprietors occupy fourth place in the occupational grouping, a long way behind professional men and following on Trade Union officials and entrepreneurs. The last group is really extraordinarily small, especially if we bear in mind that nearly 60 per cent of all Cabinet Ministers belonged to the middle class. In the House of Commons the proportion of entrepreneurs and businessmen was, during that period, about twice as large as in the Cabinet.

In this, as in earlier periods, we find that the Cabinet Ministers of both parties have a more elevated social background than the larger body of M.P.s whom they lead, but when we study the figures over a long period, we find that the gulf is narrowing. In the Cabinet and in the House of Commons the aristocratic and landed element has steadily declined. Its place has largely been taken by members of the upper class, pure and simple, descendants of entrepreneurial or professional families, or city dynasties, or even just sons of the newly rich.[1]

We can observe this trend very clearly in analysing the leadership of the party which enjoyed undivided power for nearly fifty of the past one hundred years.

TABLE VIII
Conservative Entrants into Cabinets, 1868–1955:

	1868–86	*1886–1916*	*1916–35*	*1935–55*
Aristocrats	5	17	15	12
Fathers-Landowners	5	20	13	10
Etonians and Harrovians	5	21	17	23
Grammar School Pupils	—	3	11	2
Professionals	4	8	21	14
Family without political association	4	12	31	33
Total in each period	10	31	44	47

[1] *cf.* 34 Cabinet Ministers and other ministers of the Crown who held office in 1959 eight were linked by kinship ties to prominent City bankers and Directors of Insurance Companies. *cf.* T. Lupton and C. Shirley Wilson: 'The Social Background and Connections of Top Decision Makers', *Manchester School*, January 1959, pp. 30–51.

The most significant feature which emerges from the above table is the steady proportion of Conservative ministers who were educated at Eton and Harrow. Indeed, compared with the inter-war years, when a quarter of the new entrants into the Conservative Cabinet were grammar-school educated, there followed a resurgence of those who passed through these two establishments on their way into politics. Curiously enough this trend is not restricted to the Conservative Party. Among Labour Cabinet Ministers, too, there has been an increase of public school men. Of those who sat in MacDonald's Cabinet, only four were public school products. Among Mr Attlee's 34 colleagues, 11 passed through these institutions.

But the educational background of the two parties is still very different. At an age when over two-thirds of the Labour M.P.s had effectively finished their schooling, three-quarters of their Conservative opponents entered on the most significant part of their pre-University education. For the two élite groups, the discrepancy is not so great, but is still highly significant. One half of the Conservative Cabinet-Membership of the period had been to Eton or Harrow, compared with 8 per cent on the Labour side. The differences between the two parties and, within each party, between the body of M.P.s and the Cabinet, are given in Diagram A.[1]

DIAGRAM A

Educational Background of M.P.'s and Cabinet Ministers
1918–1955

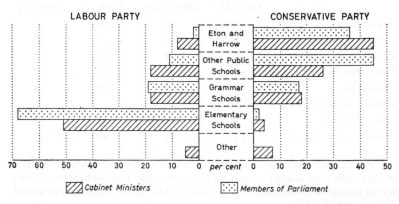

[1] The data for the House of Commons are taken from Table XIV averaged for the whole period.

The Liberals have been left out of the above comparison. They formed in this period a small and rapidly diminishing group. Apart from the members of the Coalition of 1916–22, only few held office in the National Government. The Liberal leadership belongs almost entirely to the middle class and so does its declining representation in the House of Commons. Gone are the remnants of the old Whigs, gone are the members of the new Victorian and Edwardian *haute bourgeoisie*. Instead we find rather minor entrepreneurs, barristers, solicitors and teachers. These men are the products of grammar schools and of the less well known public schools, not of Eton and Harrow. The most significant aspect of the Liberal group of Cabinet Ministers is perhaps the preponderance of those who were not members of the Church of England. Nonconformists, Presbyterians or Jews account for 14 of the 23 Liberal ministers of this period.[1]

POPULAR REPRESENTATION AND POLITICAL ÉLITE

In the discussion on the claims of 'democracy' and on the character of the governing élite, the legitimate interests of the 'classes' for representation were contrasted with the 'irresponsible' claim of the masses to decide the fate of the country. Once it was admitted that political rights ought to accrue no longer solely to those, who had a 'stake in the country', the 'masses' ceased to be clearly defined. They became just another class. And once they had secured representation as a class they also sought entry into the governing group. The gradual broadening of democracy after 1868, although resisted by a vocal minority of the political leadership, did not stop short at the composition of the political élite. But the progress towards a politically more egalitarian society was slow and less effective the higher we advance in the political hierarchy. This chapter describes how the widening of the franchise, and the growing representativeness of the political system, was reflected in the composition of the political leadership over a period of nearly a century. It is time to attempt a synthesis of the evidence.

The social analysis of the political élite was presented in three

---

[1] We are, of course, concerned largely with the Coalition Liberals, *i.e.*, the followers of Lloyd George. Among Asquith's followers the remnants of the patrician element of the Liberal Party could be found.

D

periods. Although these are divided by dates of some political significance, they are yet arbitrary when we look at the social evolution of Britain's political leadership. They are equally meaningless when we consider the changes in the social structure which have taken place in Britain during the past one hundred years. Before 1832 the political leadership was essentially aristocratic and it remained predominantly so during the period between the first and the second Reform Act. Although the political élite was already 'open', this meant only that the aristocracy was in itself absorbing recruits from the middle class below it. Admittedly, after 1868, the tempo of change quickens and the aristocracy begins to lose its pre-eminence. Yet the present analysis does not bear out Bagehot who, after examining the character of the House of Commons elected in 1868, came to the conclusion that the aristocratic element was not very noticeable and that this was particularly so among the most prominent members of either party. 'Considering the power and prestige of the titled aristocracy,' he wrote, 'you will perhaps be astonished at the small degree in which it contributes to the active part of our general assembly. The spirit of the present House of Commons is plutocratic not aristocratic; its most prominent statesmen are not men of ancient descent or of great hereditary estate.'[1] If we substitute 'upper-middle class' for 'plutocracy' we are, however, approaching a fairly accurate description of the political élite in the twentieth century. The aspiring masses achieved political power, if political power is conceived electorally. They achieved political maturity, as manifested in their organizations, but given the weight and strength of these factors, they failed, on the whole, to launch a significant number of their representatives into the political élite. For the place of the aristocracy in the political leadership was only partly filled by entirely 'new men'. Those who succeeded the aristocratic politicians in the Cabinets and elsewhere were frequently their social equals, coming from similar backgrounds, having gone to similar schools. Education is in many ways a better criterion of social status than membership of titled families or economic background, and what is significant here is the extent of public-school membership in the aristocratic as well as the middle-

---

[1] Bagehot: *The English Constitution*, p. xxvi.

class sector of the political élite. Table IX brings this out very clearly.

TABLE IX

Schooling of Cabinet Ministers, 1868–1955:

School	Aristocracy	Middle Class	Working Class	Total
Privately educated	6	8	—	14
Elementary only	—	5	36	41
Grammar School	1	45	6	52
Eton	58	17	—	75
Harrow	16	11	—	27
Rugby	2	10	—	12
Winchester	3	11	—	14
Other Major Public Schools*—		21	—	21
Other Public Schools	5	11	—	16
Boarding School	1	10	—	11
Other and abroad	1	10	—	11
TOTAL	93	159	42	294

* Details for these are as follows: Marlborough 3, Charterhouse 3, Cheltenham 5, Clifton 4 and one each at Shrewsbury, Haileybury, Fettes, Sedbergh, Sherborne and Repton.

Of the aristocratic Cabinet Ministers, over three-quarters went to either Eton or Harrow; even in the middle class the products of these two schools account for nearly 20 per cent. If we consider all the major public schools we find that almost half of all cabinet Ministers, who came neither from the aristocracy nor the working class, went there.

A comparison of parental occupations of the aristocratic and the middle-class group of cabinet ministers presents a like picture: a part of the middle-class group is itself similar in character to the aristocratic section.

The nearer we come to the present, the less meaningful becomes an analysis which singles out members of aristocratic families from the rest, without seeking to refine the analysis of the group which lies between them and the group of politicians who come from the working class. By combining criteria of descent with those of

TABLE X

Occupations of fathers of aristocratic and middle-class Cabinet Ministers, 1868–1955:

Father's Occupation	Aristocracy	Middle Class	Both
Landowning	69	11	80
Rentier	6	7	13
Services, Diplomacy, Civil Service	7	15	22
Clergymen, Church of England	3	11	14
Banking and Commerce	1	22	23
Industrialists (Entrepreneurs)	3	20	23
Managers in Industry	—	3	3
Upper Professions**	4	37	41
Lower Professions**	—	13	13
Other	—	6	6
Not Known	—	14	14
TOTAL	93	159	252

** See notes to table XII on p. 103.

parental occupation and education, we can possibly get nearer to a division of the political élite into those who can be said to belong to the traditional ruling strata and upper-class families on the one hand, and the 'new men' on the other. The former have been defined here as those who were either aristocrats by descent, or were landowners (or the sons of landowners), or men who had been educated at one of the seven principal public schools which were the foremost educational institutions throughout the whole of our period.[1] This group formed 80 per cent of the political élite in the first period (1868–86) and at no period did it form less than 40 per cent of the personnel of the Cabinet. This was during the years 1916–35. Since then, the share of those who belong to the

[1] *i.e.* Eton, Harrow, Winchester, Rugby, Shrewsbury, Charterhouse and Westminster, or in other words, seven of the nine schools investigated by the Public School Commission under Lord Clarendon. The nine 'Clarendon Schools' included also Merchant Taylors' and St Paul's, but the Public Schools Act of 1868 left out the latter two as they were principally Day Schools. Incidentally only one Cabinet Minister was educated at Merchant Taylors' and none at St Paul's.

'traditional ruling class' has grown. Between 1935 and 1955 they comprised nearly one-half of the political élite. Indeed, as the earlier analyses have shown, 'new men' arose largely on the radical wing of the Liberal Party and among Labour politicians.

TABLE XI

Traditional Ruling Class and 'New Men' in the Cabinet Membership, 1868–1955:

	1	*2*	*3*	*4*
Party	*Traditional Ruling Class*	*'New Men'*	*All*	*2 as % of 3*
Conservative	100	49	149	33%
Liberal	44	45	89	50%
Labour	9	56	65	86%
All Cabinet Ministers*	149	145	294	49·5%

  * As nine Ministers sat in Cabinets formed by two different parties the figures for the three parties add up to 303 and not to 294.

No comparative analysis for the membership of the House of Commons exists but the figures given earlier, as well as our general knowledge of the character of the House, suggests that socially it is more broadly based than the personnel of the Cabinet. Between the multitude of private members and the narrow apex of the Cabinet, there lies the plateau of junior office. The analysis of a sample of junior ministers shows that this group has an even greater proportion of members of the traditional ruling class than the Cabinet.[1] The numbers involved are, of course, small, but they are divided into the three main parties in the same proportion as the group of Cabinet Ministers, and within each party the proportion of 'new men' is lower than among the corresponding section of the Cabinet membership.

The figures for this sample are given in Table XVI on page 108

  [1] The sample analysed consists of the holders of the office of Financial and Parliamentary Secretary of the Treasury, and the Parliamentary Under-Secretaries of the Home Office, Foreign Office, Colonial Office, War Office and India Office for the period 1868–1945, with the exception of those who subsequently entered the Cabinet (*i.e.* 107 out of 191). Allowing for the vagaries of human life and of political fortune we are concerned here with a second eleven in political leadership.

which shows that, of the 107 junior ministers, 58 were the descendants of aristocrats. The remarkable strength of the aristocratic element in this group, the fact that 40 per cent were the sons of landowners, while less than one-tenth are known to have been engaged in industry or commerce, again brings out the opportunities enjoyed by those politicians who belonged to old-established families, families in which ancestors had more often than not already been politically active. In the front ranks of the political leadership we find that the push of talent and the pressure of representation bring more men of a middle-class or even working-class background to the fore. Among those who had to remain in the second eleven—and were often content to do so—parentage and social prestige appear to have been more influential.

The persistence of such a career pattern is an important aspect of the British political élite. Its significance is enhanced if we set it against those general trends in British society which caused the aristocracy to lose, over the past eighty years, much of its economic power and social status.

TABLE XII

Cabinet Ministers, 1886–1916: Background and Occupation:

Class	Liberal	Conservative	Total*
Aristocracy	23	26	49
Middle Class	28	21	49
Working Class	2	—	3
Education: School			
Elementary	3	—	4
Grammar	13	4	17
Eton	13	22	35
Harrow	6	7	13
Rugby	1	5	6
Winchester	1	1	2
Other Major Public Schools†	3	2	5
Other Public and Boarding Schools	7	—	7
Privately educated	3	5	8
Not known or abroad	3	1	4

Education: University

Oxford	19	25	44
Cambridge	17	10	27
Other Universities	7	3	10

Father's Occupation

Landowning	16	29	45
Rentier	3	—	3
Services, Diplomacy, Civil Service	4	1	5
Clergymen, C. of E.	2	1	3
Upper Professionals‡	7	6	13
Banking and Commerce	7	5	12
Industry	6	3	9
Lower Professionals§	5	2	7
Manual Workers	2	—	3
Other	1	—	1

Class	*Liberal*	*Conservative*	*Total*

Own Occupation

Landowning	19	22	41
Rentier	5	4	9
Diplomacy, Services, Government	3	2	5
Professions	19	12	31
Commerce and Industry	6	7	13
Other	1	—	2
TOTAL	53	47	101

* The total includes one Labour Minister (Henderson).

† *i.e.* Charterhouse,* Cheltenham,* Clifton,* Fettes,* Haileybury, Loretto, Malvern, Marlborough,* Oundle, Radley, Repton,* Rossall, Sedburgh,* Sherborne,* Shrewsbury,* Uppingham. (The schools visited by cabinet ministers during this period and the period 1916–55 have been marked with an asterisk.) These schools were chosen because they have been used, sometimes with a few additions, in a number of studies on the background of élite groups in contemporary Britain. See the works by Kelsall, Clements, and the Acton Society referred to in Chapter IX.

‡ *e.g.* Barristers, Physicians, University Teachers.

§ *e.g.* Ministers of Religion, Elementary School Teachers.

TABLE XIII*

Economic Interests represented in the House of Commons, 1868–1910:
(in percentages):

	Landowning	Commerce and Industry	Legal and Professional	Others	Total (in Nos.)
Conservatives†					
1868	46	31	9	14	477
1874	36	38	13	13	635
1880	35	42	11	12	446
1885	23	50	16	11	442
1886	23	50	18	9	767
1892	24	49	18	9	679
1895	20	52	19	9	833
1900	20	52	18	10	832
1906	17	64	11	8	377
Jan. 1910	26	53	12	9	644
Liberals					
1868	26	50	17	7	756
1874	21	55	19	5	614
1880	20	55	19	6	786
1885	15	57	23	5	640
1886	13	58	25	4	453
1892	9	60	27	4	565
1895	9	58	29	4	371
1900	9	58	29	4	372
1906	8	65	23	4	766
Jan. 1910	7	66	23	4	541

* Based on J. A. Thomas: *The House of Commons, 1832–1901, a study of its economic and functional character.* Also his: *The House of Commons, 1900–11, an analysis of its economic and social character.*

† Including Liberal-Unionists from 1886–1910.

TABLE XIV

Education and Occupation of M.P.s, 1918–51 (in percentages)*:

	1918–35		1945		1950		1951	
	Cons.	Lab.	Cons.	Lab.	Cons.	Lab.	Cons.	Lab.
(a) Education:								
School—								
Elementary only ..	2·5	75·5	1·5	53·0	2·5	51·0	3·0	51·0
Grammar	19·0	15·5	13·5	24·0	12·5	27·0	14·5	26·0
Eton	27·5	1·5	29·0	2·0	28·0	1·5	25·0	1·5
Harrow	10·0	1·0	7·0	0·5	7·0	0·5	7·5	0·5
Other Public								
Schools	41·0	6·5	49·0	20·5	50·0	20·0	50·0	21·0
Nos. ..	348	153	215	401	299	315	321	296
(b) Education:								
University—								
Oxford ..	45·0	18·0	46·5	26·0	47·5	27·5	48·0	31·0
Cambridge	34·0	23·0	33·0	14·5	33·5	14·0	32·5	14·0
Other ..	21·0	59·0	20·5	59·5	19·0	58·5	19·5	55·0
Nos. ..	503	81	124	129	183	115	202	111
Nos. without a Uni-								
versity Education	500	363	89	272	116	200	119	185
Total Nos.	1,003	444	215	401	299	315	321	296
(c) Occupation—								
Employers and								
Managers ..	32·0	4·0	32·5	9·5	30·5	9·5	32·5	9·0
Rank and file								
workers	4·0	72·0	3·0	41·0	3·0	43·0	4·5	45·0
Professions.. ..	52·0	24·0	61·0	48·5	62·0	46·5	57·5	45·5
Housewives ..	—	—	0·5	1·0	—	1·0	—	0·5
Unoccupied								
(Rentiers) ..	12·0	—	3·0	—	4·5	—	5·5	—

* Figures derived from J. F. S. Ross; *Elections and Electors*, 1955 (section on the Personnel of Parliament) 1918–51 and that author's *Parlimentary Representation*, 1943. The figures for the period 1918–35 refer to the total of all M.P.s except in respect of school education which Ross gives only in respect of the average House of Commons of the inter-war period.

(a) Based on the number of those whose school was *known* to Ross (approximately 80 per cent of all M.P.s).

(b) The percentages refer to the Universities attended and do therefore contain a small number of double entries.

(c) These refer to original occupation; Trade Union officials not given as a separate category. The figures for the inter-war years are 'rough approximations only' (Ross).

TABLE XV

Background and Occupation of Cabinet Ministers, 1916–55:

	Conservative	Labour	Total*
Class Background			
Aristocracy	31	4	38
Middle Class	64	25	108
Working Class	3	36	40
Education: School			
Elementary	4	33	38
Grammar	18	12	37
Eton	32	3	37
Harrow	13	2	15
Rugby	6	—	6
Winchester	3	4	8
Other Major Public Schools†	11	4	9
Other Public Schools	6	4	21
Other	7	3	15
Education: University			
None	30	36	76
Oxford	44	11	59
Cambridge	18	7	28
Other	8	11	23
Father's Occupation			
Landowning	27	1	30
Rentier	6	2	8
Services, Diplomacy, Civil Service	9	4	16
Clergymen, C. of E.	3	3	8
Upper Professionals‡	19	7	27
Industry and Commerce	15	4	26
Managerial	2	2	4
Lower Professionals§	5	1	9
Tradesmen, Clerks	2	5	7
Skilled Workers	1	22	23

	Conservative	Labour	Total
Unskilled Workers	—	6	8
Other	2	3	6
Not known	9	5	16

Occupation

	Conservative	Labour	Total
Landowning	19	2	22
Rentier	16	3	21
Armed Forces	6	1	8
Civil Service, Public Administration	7	3	11
Professions	36	22	69
Commerce and Industry:			
Entrepreneurs	14	4	23
Managers, etc.	2	—	2
Manual Workers	—	2	2
Officials of Trade Unions, etc.	—	28	28
TOTAL	100	65	185

* Including Liberals.
† See relevant note to Table XII.
‡ *e.g.* Barristers, Physicians, University Teachers.
§ *e.g.* Ministers of Religion, Elementary School Teachers.

TABLE XVI

Background of Under-Secretaries, 1868–1945*:

Class		Father's Occupation	
Aristocracy	58	Landowning	42
Middle Class	39	Rentier	1
Working Class	10	Diplomacy, Armed Services	9
		Professions	9
		Entrepreneurs	11
Education: School		Manual Workers	10
Eton	36	Other	5
Harrow	7	Not known	20
Winchester	5		
Rugby	5		
Other Major Public Schools	9	*Occupation*	
Other Public Schools	8	Landowning	21
Grammar School	12	Rentier	13
Elementary School only	7	Armed Services	11
Other Schools, Abroad	8	Civil Service, Diplomacy	9
Not known	11	Entrepreneurs	10
		Managers	1
		Professional Men	25
		Officials of Trade Unions, etc.	8
		Manual Workers	1
		Other	3
		Not known	7

* 1945 rather than 1955 was chosen as the closing date for this analysis because few if any of the junior ministers would be likely to reach Cabinet status after an interval of ten years.

CHAPTER V

The Decline of Aristocracy

'Dukedoms may be abolished by the year 2000 . . . but if they are not, an English dukedom will in that year be a prize beyond all compare . . . such as the throne is now, the ultimate goal of all that is great, or ambitious, or rich.'—*The Great Governing Families of England*, 1865.

'Probably the battle of Waterloo *was* won on the playing fields of Eton but the opening battles of all subsequent wars have been lost there. One of the dominant facts in English life during the past three-quarters of a century has been the decay of ability in the ruling class.' GEORGE ORWELL, 1940.

THE men, who in the nineteenth century followed the favoured twin pursuits of their class, rural sports and the game of politics, the government of the county and the government of the country, are today a dying species. Of the contemporary politicians, who can trace their descent back through generations of 'gentlemen'— whether titled or not—only a few have the full 'appurtenance of gentility'. Among the seventy-six politicians who reached the Cabinet between 1935 and 1955 a mere seven can be described as 'Landowners'. The decline of the aristocratic politician is not just the result of changes in the political system or of the greater importance of the urban over the rural electorate. Other factors have been responsible for it, apart from the rise of the Labour Party or the slow growth of a more democratic party organization in the Conservative Party. All these factors are clearly important, but equally so are the far-reaching changes in the character, economic basis and function of the aristocracy, which have taken place during the past hundred years. These changes contributed greatly to its relative decline in the political sphere.

How, in the period under discussion, the aristocratic strata lost much of their distinctive identity and became absorbed in the wider body of the British upper class is best seen against the background of a brief analysis of their prominent position in the heyday of their power.

BORN SPURRED

The Victorian aristocracy presents a truly unique social pheno-menon. Small in size, but immensely wealthy, economically secure, yet not buttressed by any legal privilege, politically powerful and resting their supremacy on widespread popular consent, leading a society which was in many ways open to the outsider, its members enjoyed a position unrivalled by that of the nobility of any other European power.[1]

The ownership of the greater part of the nation's land was, of course, literally and metaphorically the ground on which the aristocratic mansion was built.[2] But the monopoly of the 'acre-ocracy' in landownership had, by the beginning of the Victorian era, long since ceased to be matched by any claim to legal obliga-tions on the part of the tenants and of the population living on the estate. In other ways, too, landownership did not just follow a dying pattern of the past. As a class, the landowners did not set their minds against the rational conduct of agriculture and, as individuals, many landed proprietors actively helped in the scientific improvement of farming. Nor was there a *deep-seated* economic conflict dividing the recipients of rent and dues from land from the industrial capitalists building up profits by the exploitation of men and machinery. Landowners were not averse to industrial investment and those who had acquired fortunes in manufacture or commerce would frequently seek to 'invest' these in landed property.

The income which owners derived from landed estates was often supplemented, and occasionally even surpassed, by the revenue derived from coal-owning, from investments mainly in railways and to no small extent from the exploitation of urban

---

[1] At least of any country which had destroyed its medieval economic shackles. A comparison with Poland or Spain would be inappropriate. The position of the Prussian 'Junker', although more powerful in some respects, was on the whole—and for the whole of Germany—inferior to that enjoyed by the British Aris-tocracy.

[2] See pp. 127–133 below and especially Table V.

property for residential or industrial purposes. Yet all these activities tended to have one feature in common with landownership: they were predominantly of a rentier character. Some landowners would turn entrepreneurs on their own account—especially in the mining of coal-deposits on their land. Others, like the Dukes of Devonshire, would undertake the development of whole towns such as Buxton and Barrow. The bulk of the landed magnates seems, however, to have regarded their non-agricultural assets as investments promising a higher and often a progressively increasing yield rather than as a means for entrepreneurial activity.[1]

We are, in effect, speaking rather loosely when we use the term 'class' in connection with 'entrepreneurial' or manufacturing as distinct from landed interests. The British aristocracy and the sections of the population within its penumbra, all those who in mid-Victorian parlance were called the 'landed and official classes', are not really quite amenable to an economic definition. The best we can say is that the majority of them derived their livelihood from rents and interest and, occasionally, from sinecures. The mid-Victorian aristocracy and gentry has much more the character of a status group whose members share a distinct way of life and have in common certain patterns of consumption. The criterion of membership was not merely wealth but 'family' and the style of life which one led. The 'characteristic moral distinction' in society, a writer in the *Cornhill Magazine* said in 1862, was that between gentlemen and non-gentlemen, and the word 'gentleman', while implying a degree of social rank, denotes above all a certain form of conduct.[2]

As a group, the nobility and gentry is further characterized by a predominant share in the exercise of political power, accruing to them in their totality, via the House of Lords, and individually through their territorial influence and the patronage which they exercised and obtained. They ruled Great Britain not only through Parliament, but also through their influence over the four pillars on which the canopy of oligarchic power rested: the Military, the Civil Service, the Judiciary and, last but not least, the Church.

The basis of much of this aristocratic influence, as so much else

[1] *cf.* David Spring: 'The English Landed Estate in the Age of Steel and Iron: 1830–80', *Journal of Economic History*, 1951, pp. 3–25.
[2] Article entitled 'Gentlemen' (unsigned), pp. 327–42.

in the England of the Industrial Revolution, was firmly rooted in their wealth. Military rank had its purchase value, and the clerical benefice had its price-tag—although it may not necessarily have been exacted. And as the spiritual so the political 'living'. Parliamentary 'seats themselves tended to become a reality like an advowson, sublime in its ultimate significance, beneficial in practice to its owner'.[1]

The exact nature of the services which the members of the aristocracy rendered are not always easily defined. They might be completely non-existent or be such that could be performed easily by a clerk receiving a fraction of the sum paid to the holder of the office. Political duties were not excessively onerous as yet. What did the officers of an *undermanned* army do in the long stretch of peace between 1815-54? How many livings held in plurality really did amount to an 'occupation'? The questions are rhetorical; it is in the very essence of aristocratic occupational pursuits, that while conferring power, they did not mean a 'job' which would interfere with the style of life of a country gentleman or of his counterpart in the cities. Yet the pattern of life, which the aristocracy followed in the nineteenth century, had in itself elements of public function. In their localities and nationally many of them performed a whole host of unpaid public duties. Justifying the selection of aristocrats for the task of diplomacy, Bagehot pointed out that 'an ambassador is not just an agent he is also a spectacle'.[2] The British aristocracy, acting through the institution of the House of Lords, was an essential element of the dignified part of the British Constitution; its deeds and misdeeds were accepted and applauded by the very section of the population which had least opportunity to emulate them.[3] Whether there is, in any meaningful way, an affinity of interest and sentiment between the aristocracy and the working class, so that the largesse or ostentatiousness of the one finds a sympathetic echo in the amorality of the other cannot be put to a rational test.[4] It may well be that in Britain the admiration of rank had the positive function of eschewing mere wealth as an

---

[1] Sir L. B. Namier: *The Structure of Politics at the Accession of George III* 2nd ed. (1957), p. 126.

[2] Bagehot: *English Constitution*, 2nd ed. (1904 printing), p. 120.

[3] *ibid.*, especially pp. 90–91.

[4] 'Gentlemen', *loc. cit.*

ideal worthy of emulation and that it has prevented the admiration of the 'official' which was so marked in Germany and France.[1]

There was, of course, in England never a territorial 'estate' corresponding to the French *noblesse du pays* or to the Prussian 'Junkerdom'; no legal or quasi-legal restrictions circumscribed the occupational pursuits of descendants of titled men, whether land-owners or otherwise. Nor can we trace anything in the bearing of most members of the British nobility which we could equate easily with the spirit of social selectivity so typical, for example, of the German officer-caste. The great dividing line, as already noted, is between gentlemen and the non-gentlemanly class. At one time this was a division capable of some legal definition, but by the nineteenth century it had become perplexing to foreign observers and English writers alike.[2] Taine thought, that the word ' "Gentleman" expresses all the distinctive features of the English upper class . . . for example a large private fortune, a considerable household of servants, habits of ease and luxury . . . add to them . . . a liberal education, travel, information, good manners and ease in society'.[3] An Englishman, writing at the same time, stressed more subtle distinctions. Gentlemen constitute, above all, 'a body associated together for the sake of pleasure which is to be derived from each others society', and the gentleman ideal implies a seemly and dignified conduct, an abhorrence of the ugly and the caddish. These and not moral considerations are his chief characteristics; if we speak of him 'we do not mean either a good man or a wise man, but a man socially pleasant . . .'[4] Were mere possessions a sufficient criterion, the term would be less selective, but it is of the essence of 'gentility' that it cannot be just acquired. 'There are' the anonymous writer goes on to say 'scores of men in our great manufacturing towns who, having pushed their way to great wealth and influence by mere force of character, would willingly buy the refinement of mind and manner which early education would have given them at the price of half their fortunes, and they would make an excellent bargain if they could do so'.[5] Gentlemanly virtues are

---

[1] Bagehot, *op. cit.*, pp. 92–93.

[2] On the attempts of a legal definition of the 'gentleman' see A. R. Wagner: *English Genealogy*, 1960, pp. 102–21 *passim*.

[3] Taine: *Notes on England*, 1953 ed., p. 1945.

[4] 'Gentlemen', *loc. cit.*, p. 331.   [5] *ibid.*, p. 332.

conceived as the product of breeding and the result of imbibing a tradition which is thought to lie deep in the family and the social setting. The counterpart of the 'gentleman' is the 'upstart' and the 'cad' and against him the social drawbridges were firmly raised. Within that gentlemanly class, social intercourse took place easily and naturally; to move outside it might carry penalties. When in 1793 the King ordered the three daughters of Mr Coutts—the banker—to attend a drawing-room, London Society was enraged. Even Mrs Child, it was suggested, had never gone to Court until she was Lady Ducie.[1] To marry outside the 'gentlemanly' class was rare and generally frowned upon.[2]

ARISTOCRACY PHOENIX

In spite of the tendency towards endogamy inside the 'gentlemanly class' the desire for 'pure' lineage did not permeate the British nobility. The very system which—courtesy titles apart—restricts the outward symbol of aristocratic status to one couple in each generation hardly permits the correct filling in of the 'sixteen quarters'.[3] The almost universal practice of entailing property so that it passed to the heir of the title, who, in turn, only held it in trust for the next generation, also made for considerable differences in wealth within noble and landed families. While younger sons and all daughters might be provided for through small annuities or through dowries charged on the estate, such benefits rarely went further than the immediate descendants of the holder of a title or the owner of an estate. Members of aristocratic families sufficiently far removed from the holders of the title must thus almost by definition shade off into the wider and, alas, formally much less distinct middle-class surroundings, as the ripples on a smooth sheet of water are eventually lost to view. Sir Bernard

---

[1] J. Wake: *The Brudenells of Deene*, 1953, p. 331 (Mrs Child, the wife of the Banker, married in 1791 the third Lord Ducie, thus uniting two banking fortunes).

[2] It is interesting to observe that when Peers married outside the (wider) class to which they belonged they often allied themselves to American and Continental brides.

[3] To be truly 'blue-blooded' a German aristocrat must be able to trace his descent back to sixteen aristocratic members in the great-great grandfather generation.

Burke speaks of the 200,000 'nobles in the Continental sense of the term" who could be found in Britain in the last century, in addition to the 1,630 men with transmissible titles. But those on the very margin of the aristocratic sphere would seek to refer their own status to that of the truly aristocratic members of the family and this, in turn, would strengthen the disappearing boundaries.

Even more important is the fact that the flux on the social mill-pond is such that the waters in that part of it which we term 'aristocratic' are slowly but constantly changing. It is the speed and extent of such changes that have, above all, characterized changes in the aristocracy over the past 130 years. Before the first Reform Bill the number of Peers on the roll of the House of Lords was just under 400, today there are 843 hereditary Peers with a seat in the Upper House. If it had not been for the large and growing number of Peerages which have become extinct, the increase would have been much larger.[1] In addition there are to-day 1,250 Baronetcies in existence, yet of these less than 300 were created before 1800.[2]

TABLE I

U.K. Peerages, created 1830–1957:

Period	Nos.		Annual Average
1830 (Total)*	364		—
1830–68†	151		4
1868–95‡	173	962	6·5
1895–1922§	264		10
1923–57‖	374		11
1957 (Total)*	842		—

* Excluding Royal Dukes, Bishops, Life Peers, Scottish and Irish Representative Peers, Peers who are minors and Peeresses in their own right.
† Grey–Disraeli.
‡ Gladstone–Rosebery.
§ Salisbury–Lloyd George.
‖ Bonar Law–Introduction of Life Peerages.

All aristocracies must renew themselves or die out; it is only a question of the conditions governing new entries which determine whether renewal will spell social change. The very fact that the British aristocracy was for so long a part and parcel of the governing structure made its patronage an important part of government strategy. A knighthood, a Baronetcy and, above all, a Peerage were often bestowed as a reward for help given or in anticipation of favours to be received. The 'Earl de Mowbray' who commanded six votes in the House of Commons received his promotion from mere Baron—the great aim of his life—through the adroit use of his parliamentary powers. His was a comparatively easy road; his father, 'Lord Fitz-Warene' had a steeper climb from the position of waiter in a St James's Street Club. His fortune was made in India. From there John Warren returned:

'purchased a large estate in the north of England, was returned to Parliament one of the representatives of a close borough which he had also purchased: a quiet gentleman-like middle aged man, with no decided political opinions; and, as parties were then getting very equal, of course very much courted. . . . The minister asked the new member to dine with him, found Mr Warren was one of those members who announced their determination to listen to the debates and to be governed by arguments. All complimented him, all spoke to him. Mr Fox declared that he was a most superior man; Mr Burke said that these were the men who alone could save the country. Mrs Crewe asked him to supper; he was caressed by the most brilliant of duchesses.

'At length there arrived one of those fierce trials of strength which precede the fall of a minister. . . . How would Warren vote? was the great question. . . . The day before the debate there was a levee, which Mr Warren attended. The sovereign stopped him, spoke to him, smiled on him . . .

'The debate came off, the division took place, Mr Warren voted for the minister. Burke denounced him, the king made him a baronet.

'Sir John Warren . . . married the daughter of an Irish Earl; became one of the King's friends, supported Lord Shelburne, threw over Lord Shelburne, had the tact early to discover that Mr Pitt was the man to stick to, stuck to him. Sir John Warren bought another estate, and picked up another borough.

'The Nabob, from faithful adherent of Mr Pitt, had become even his personal friend. The wits, indeed, had discovered that he had been a waiter . . . but Mr Pitt cared nothing about the origin of his supporters. On the contrary, Sir John was exactly the individual from whom the minister meant to carve out his plebeian aristocracy; and using his friend as a feeler, the Nabob one morning was transformed into an Irish Baron.

'The new Baron figured in his patent as Lord Fitz-Warene, his Norman origin and descent from the old Barons of this name having been discovered at Herald's College. . . . The new Baron cared nothing for ridicule, for he was working for posterity . . . he lived long enough to realize his most aspiring dream. Two years before his death, the Irish Baron was quietly converted into an English Peer and without exciting any attention . . . the waiter of the St James's Street club took his seat in the most natural manner possible in the House of Lords.'[1]

Yet despite Disraeli's assertions, Pitt's creations were, on the whole, not taken from the *nouveaux riches* or other newly arrived men. In the eighteenth century the 'Peer of unknown social origin was a *rara avis*'.[2] The bulk of the new Peerages went either to men who already held Scottish or Irish titles, or to members of the landed gentry.[3] Nor did the eighty Peers whom the Whigs created during the first decade after their return to power represent in any way the newly enfranchised section of the middle class.[4] In the first fifty years of the Victorian age all but 10 per cent of the newly created Peers were of aristocratic or gentry background. Only seven were, so to speak, 'new men'. Of these C. P. Thompson and E. Cardwell had served in the government, Macaulay, although a man of commercial background, was at the very end of his life rewarded for his public service. Only three bankers and one industrialist received peerages. The latter was Mr Edward Strutt. 'It is as a manufacturer, and to mark the interest which the Queen takes in the manufacturing pursuits of the country that Mr Strutt is metamorphosed into Baron Belper. As such it is a graceful and a prudent

---

[1] Disraeli: *Sybil* (World's Classics ed.), 1926, pp. 79–81 *passim*.

[2] A. S. Turberville: *The House of Lords in the Eighteenth Century*, p. 420.

[3] *cf. Quarterly Review*, vol. 62 (no. 84), p. 321 [Classified table of creations, (1760–1830)].

[4] *cf.* R. E. Pumphrey: The Introduction of Industrialists into the British Peerage. *American Historical Review*, 1959, pp. 1–16.

act. It shows a wise appreciation of the signs of the times. It is
something for those who claim to be regarded as the descendants
of the mailed barons of England to admit into their order, a man
who has not only made but is making his fortune by spindles and
looms.'[1]

At that time and for a considerable period to come it was
thought that large private means and a guarantee of financial
independence for the subject to be honoured and also for his
descendants, was a necessary requisite for the bestowal of hereditary honours. This was one of the reasons for restricting the
entry of new men into the Peerage. Indeed, the repeated attempts
to enable men to sit as life peers were not unconnected with this.
When the proposal to introduce Life Peerages was first discussed
in the House of Lords, the case for it was based on the need for a
stronger legal representation to enable the House to carry out its
judicial functions adequately.[2] Legal luminaries, it was thought,
might not be able to endow their descendants with sufficient
wealth to enable them to maintain their father's status. Then, and
in subsequent discussions of the issue, fear was expressed that
unless Life Peerages were introduced, the granting of hereditary
Peerages to men 'unable to sustain the dignity' would imperil the
independence of the House of Lords. For the men who thought
this, the continuance of noble families was clearly linked to the
existence of transmissible and entailed possessions.

One wonders what size of property was regarded as necessary
for each level of honour? Disraeli wrote to the Queen in 1874
asking whether some recognition might not be given to the arts.
'Mr Disraeli knows of two authors who are especially conspicuous

---

[1] *Manchester Examiner* as quoted in *The Times* and cited by Pumphrey, *loc.
cit.*, p. 11. (Mr Strutt was, however, hardly the typical millowner, he had been
an M.P. for twenty-five years prior to his ennoblement, had been Chancellor of
the Duchy of Lancaster and had married the daughter of the Bishop of Chiches-
ter. His son married the daughter of the second Earl of Leicester.)

[2] The debate of 1856 arose out of the case of the 'Wensleydale Peerage' which
had been limited, by patent, to the Life of the ennobled. As Sir James Parke, the
subject of the controversy, was then seventy-four years of age and childless, the
conferment of a Barony for Life was irrelevant and the government did practically admit that this was a test case. The patent was referred to the Committee
of Privilege which decided that, as the law stood, the Crown had no power to
create Life Peers who would be able to sit in the House of Lords.

at the present moment, Tennyson and Carlyle. . . . He has the impression that Mr Tennyson could sustain a baronetcy and would like it. . . . Mr Carlyle is old and childless and poor; but he is very popular and respected by the Nation. There is no K.C.B. vacant, would a G.C.B. be too much?'[1] Views like these about the relation of financial status and honour die hard. Haig told Lloyd George that 'unless an adequate grant was made to enable a suitable position to be maintained' he would have to decline the offer of a Peerage.[2] The fear of 'parvenu' Peers flooding the House of Lords by the hundreds caused a large number of Conservative Peers to acquiesce in the passage of the Parliament Act of 1911. A group which had already absorbed distillers and brewers was yet afraid of further dilution.

To this process we must now turn.

METAMORPHOSIS OF ARISTOCRACY

The inquiry into the connection between economic position and aristocratic status raises wider issues. Under a feudal system the hierarchy of titles and designations, from Esquire to Duke, did in themselves manifest social and political gradations and, to a lesser extent, differences of wealth and possessions. To some extent these continued into the nineteenth century. Of the twenty-seven Dukes who marched at the head of the Peerage in 1873, four had rentals from landed property of more than £100,000 per annum and thirteen received between £50,000 and £100,000; none received less than £10,000 annually.[3]

The mid-Victorian, who accepted the social order, could only marvel at the magnitude of the nobility's territorial possessions, the number and size of their country mansions, and grandeur of their establishments, their private conspicuousness and their public munificence. An aristocracy not based on substantial landed

---

[1] Moneypenny and Buckle, *op. cit.*, vol. II, p. 696.

[2] P. A. Bromhead: *The House of Lords and Contemporary Politics, 1911–57*, London, 1958, p. 25, quoting R. Blake's edition of Haig's *Diaries* (Haig was given a grant of £100,000 and an Earldom).

[3] The total number of those with income from rentals of over £50,000 was 66 (Bateman, *The Great Landowners of Great Britain and Ireland*, 1883, p. 496).

property, not impressing the population by the 'sustained splend-our of their stately lives' was inconceivable.

Yet as the political system and the social structure of the country changed, the aristocracy was to change with it. Honours which up to the seventeenth century were the rewards given by monarchs to 'needy' kinsmen, personal favourites, useful allies or powerful magnates came during the eighteenth century gradually into the gift of the Prime Minister and the Cabinet.[1] The tie-up of (party) politics and ennoblement has clearly characterized the bulk of the creations of Peers and to a lesser extent of baronetcies ever since that date. When parliamentary activity was clearly linked to wealth and landed possessions, those who held territorial status did naturally think of their reward in terms of honours; others, as we saw, acquired landed wealth to qualify for coronets. When in the course of the nineteenth century the old ties between possessions and political activity disappeared, new ones arose between party-organizations and men of wealth and influence. And the money-hunger of the party machine did eventually put such ties on a purely financial footing.

The virtual sale of honours with a regular scale of fees for rising heights of elevation had, by all accounts, only become more blatant when the scandal came into the open in 1922.[2] The revela-tions of that time did much to hasten the end of the coalition, and led to a change in the system by which the applications for honours are scrutinized, but they did not change the system by which honours are bestowed for political service. Given the institution of honours it was obvious that, in the words of the Royal Commission set up to investigate existing abuses, the practice of rewarding men and women for services to their party 'has been continuously followed since the growth and development of the party system of government' and 'nearly all the witnesses that we have examined proffered the opinion that such a system is right and ought to prevail'.[3]

In a sense, the higher honours have always been bestowed for

---

[1] The *sale* of honours by Charles I must not be forgotten.

[2] *cf.* G. Macmillan: *Honours for Sale*, 1955, and the debate in the House of Commons on 17.7.1922.

[3] BPP, 1923, vol. XI. Owing to the recess the report which had been signed in December was not published until the following February.

what are now called 'public and political services' but while Gladstone, according to his biographer, 'brought to the bestowal of honours the same diligent care as to the branches of public business' and 'especially in the altitudes of the Peerage tried hard to find solid political ground to go upon'; Lloyd George was clearly less scrupulous.[1]

The new Peerage, created since the 1880's, was bound to reflect the changing social composition of the House of Commons but it also mirrored wider changes in economic and social structure. It signifies the social acceptance of 'mere wealth' and reflects changes in the character of entrepreneurship and new forms of industrial organization. And as some positions in the community increase in importance, power and esteem, the field of recruitment of the peerage is widened.[2]

The recipients of peerages have often combined a number of functions and positions in society and are therefore notoriously hard to classify. In interpreting the following tables this must be borne in mind.

Numerically the largest single group of men elevated to the Peerage are former members of the House of Commons. M.P.s are sometimes sent to the Upper House to act as spokesmen or even as officeholders there; they are occasionally 'kicked upstairs' to stifle a critic in the rarefied atmosphere of the upper house, and they are sometimes ennobled to find a seat for a party leader, who was defeated in an election. But in most cases titles are the reward offered either for ministerial service or for faithful but inconspicuous partisanship on the backbenches.

'Political Peerages' of another kind are those which go to men who are not M.P.s but whose presence in the Lords is considered important by the party which elevates them. 'Ministers-to-be' can thus be accommodated in Parliament, as were Professor Lindemann and Mr Leathers when Churchill gave them office in the wartime government—or some of the men whom MacDonald appointed to Cabinet Posts in 1924 and 1929. Yet the majority of such

---

[1] Morley, *op. cit.*, vol. II, p. 428. Robert Blake, in his *Life of Bonar Law* speaks of 'the wholesale traffic in honours with which (Lloyd George) celebrated the closing years of his Premiership'.

[2] We are concerned here only with actual creations. The careers of subsequent generations in the new peerage will be discussed below.

TABLE II

The Background of New Peerages, 1901–57:

(Excluding advancements):

(a) Relation between Peerage Creations and Political Activity:

	Period of Creation						
	1901–1910	1911–1920	1921–1930	1931–1940	1941–1950	1951–1957	Total
M.P.–Backbencher*	30	42	25	33	38	12	180
M.P. and Minister ..	20	20	25	27	21	24	137
'Political Peer'† ..	—	1	8	2	15	1	27
No specific political service	20	46	35	38	53	20	212
Total ..	70	109	93	100	127	57	556

(b) Socio-Economic Background of Peers:

	1901–1910	1911–1920	1921–1930	1931–1940	1941–1950	1951–1957	Total
1. Landowning ..	12	8	13	9	3	1	46
2. Rentier, Company Director	6	6	4	5	13	8	42
3. Banking, Finance, Insurance ..	5	4	5	7	6	—	27
4. Industrialists ..	13	19	24	17	9	9	91
5. Newspaper Proprietor ..	2	4	2	4	—	—	12
6. Merchants ..	4	3	3	1	—	1	12
7. Barrister, Judge	13	15	16	12	9	7	72
8. Other Professions	2	3	4	5	10	4	28
9. Armed Services	2	18	7	7	19	1	54
10. Home Civil Service, Public Administration ..	1	3	1	2	5	2	14
11. Foreign and Colonial Civil Service	5	4	6	2	5	3	25
12. Men of Science and Letters, Academics ..	—	1	—	3	8	3	15
13. Officials of T.U.s etc., Manual Workers ..	—	—	—	1	17	3	21
14. Other	3	4	4	7	12	5	35
15. Unknown ..	2	17	4	18	11	10	62
Total ..	70	109	93	100	127	57	556

appointments were made by Labour leaders to increase Labour representation in the Upper Chamber. They represent the middle-class element among Labour politicians even more than the upper ranks of the party leadership. Apart from a few leaders of the Trade Union and Co-operative Movement, Labour creations have largely been from the ranks of business men and professionals. Whether this has happened by accident or by design is difficult to say.[1]

Numerically small, the group of Diplomats, Civil Servants and Public Administrators who received peerages at the end of their official career is not without significance. Before 1900 such high rank had rarely been given to Public Servants with the exception of British Pro-Consuls in India (invariably bestowed before assumption of duties), or to high-ranking diplomats, all of whom tended, in any case, to come from the traditional group of aristocratic politicians. Slowly, a tradition seems to have emerged by which first the Permanent Secretary of the Foreign Office and later the head of the Civil Service were offered peerages on retirement. Occasionally men who retire from important Colonial Governorships or principal embassies abroad are also elevated. In any case, public servants who have reached the thrones of departmental power rarely sink nowadays into inconspicuous and self-effacing retirement. A seat in the House of Lords may be for some what a seat on the Board is for others.[2]

Lawyers and other professional men constitute a large group

---

[1] Only one Labour Peer in three is ex-working class with only elementary education. One in six has been to Eton.

[2] Some have of course occupied both. Thus Lord Bridges who has presided over the Royal Fine Arts Commission and academic bodies is also a Director of Babcock and Wilcox and of other companies.

---

* Not all the M.P.s had sat in Parliament to a date near their elevation to the Peerage; a few had actually been M.P.s only for short periods and these did sometimes antedate their ennoblement by many years.

† Political Peers: those (mostly Labour Peers) who owed their ennoblement to the apparent needs of increased representation for their Party in the Upper House. A few were ennobled to serve as Ministers.

among the ennobled, but as they are almost invariably former members of the House of Commons, their elevation to the Peerage is not a recognition of their professional services.[1]

Economically and occupationally the largest group in the Peerage creations of the twentieth century are businessmen and industrialists. Here we find both self-made men and those who took over control of well-established family firms; tycoons who left millions, and men of comparatively modest achievement. The type most frequently found, however, is the man who started with a sound fortune, and often with an existing enterprise founded originally by his father, or possibly even earlier, and who expanded it or started a new venture. The father of Lord Furness had begun life as a coal trimmer and had later founded a provisions business. On these foundations the son branched out into sea-transport and shipping. Lord Airedale (J. Kitson) was the son of a successful manufacturer of railway engines who then started other forms of engineering and ironworks. Both Furness and Kitson were M.P.s in the 1890's and during the first decade of this century. Lord Bearsted started with a small fortune and eventually became the founder of Shell. To advance *literally* from rags to riches is probably as rare in the Peerage as in the upper ranks of British entrepreneurs as a whole. A career such as that of Lord Trent (Jesse Boot), who was the son of a herbalist, and who built up a vast chain of chemist shops within a lifetime, is uncommon.

British industrialists and businessmen who were raised to the Peerage were by and large either bankers and financiers, occupations which have always been closely allied with the titled aristocracy and the landed gentry, or the heads of large industrial concerns. It is thus only natural that industries in which large enterprises are the rule should be more strongly represented in the entrepreneurial Peerage than industries in which the typical units are small. We thus find iron and steel Barons, beer Barons and whisky Lords, newspaper Lords, shipping Peers and representatives of the chemicals, oil and tobacco industries. On the other hand there are comparatively few who come from food industries, from textiles or clothing, furniture manufacture or the retail trade.

---

[1] In addition to Barrister M.P.s certain occupants of high judicial positions tend to be rewarded with Peerages; thus the Master of the Rolls and the outgoing Lord Chief Justice are often given hereditary Baronies.

The contrast between such industries as steel and hosiery with regard to hereditary honours is illuminating. In the latter industry, where firms were small, and where many of the entrepreneurs were self-made men, who had started their own enterprises, few honours were awarded. Among the Nottingham hosiers, active since the 1840's, Miss Erickson found only one who was given a Peerage, and he was the son of a Liberal M.P. and the brother of a Liberal Chief Whip and a member of Gladstone's last administration.[1] For the steel industry Peerages, Baronetcies and Knighthoods fell thick and fast. Among steel manufacturers, active between 1905 and 1925, thirty-eight (or 20 per cent) received hereditary honours. Even in the first generation of Steel manufacturers, active in 1865, twelve (or 17 per cent) were ennobled.[2]

Today, as a hundred years ago, some of the very rich are members of the Peerage, but numerically they form a much smaller part of our contemporary 'plutocracy' than the territorial magnates did in the nineteenth century. Even the considerable incomes enjoyed by some Peers today do not enable them to vie with the style of life which that class had led. Nor can the rich of today maintain the large landed establishments which were the characteristic feature of aristocratic life before 1914, and which, at that time, a large number of 'mere' plutocrats sought to emulate. Even the Edwardian millionaires, while building large country mansions, did not as a rule invest their wealth in *large-scale* landownership. Their successors have done so even less frequently. Peers, like other entrepreneurs or successful professional men, tend to acquire a place in the country, but all accounts suggest that this is a country house rather than a landed estate. There is little evidence that they seek to link their peerage with large territorial estates and invest their capital in land, forgoing as a result more than half of the possible return on their investment, and most of the likely capital appreciation on which their standard of living may well depend.

---

[1] *cf.* C. Erickson: *British Industrialists, Steel and Hosiery, 1850–1950*, London 1960, p. 121.

[2] *ibid.*, p. 48 (Table 17). A small number were the sons of Peers or Baronets and their honours may have been hereditary.

TABLE III

Types of Industry and Enterprise represented by newly created Peers, 1901–57:

	1901–1910	1911–1920	1921–1930	1931–1940	1941–1950	1951–1957	Total
1. Banking..	5	3	2	4	5	—	19
2. Trade ..	4	3	3	1	—	—	11
3. Insurance	—	1	—	1	1	—	3
4. Stockbroker	—	—	3	2	—	—	5
5. Coal ..	1	—	—	1	—	—	2
6. Iron and Steel ..	2	3	2	2	1	—	10
7. Engineering	1	1	2	—	2	2	8
8. Railways	—	1	—	1	—	—	2
9. Shipping	3	3	2	4	1	—	13
10. Motor Car, Aircraft ..	—	—	—	3	1	—	4
11. Cotton, Woollen, etc. ..	2	6	2	—	1	—	11
12. Tobacco..	1	—	1	1	—	1	4
13. Drink ..	1	3	3	—	1	—	8
14. Food ..	—	—	1	1	1	1	4
15. Chemicals, Rubber	—	1	2	2	—	2	7
16. Oil ..	—	—	3	1	—	1	5
17. Transport (other than above) ..	—	—	—	1	—	—	1
18. Retailing, Catering ..	—	—	2	1	2	1	6
19. Diverse Econ. Interests (Company Directors)	1	5	1	3	8	4	22
20. Newspaper and Publishing ..	3	5	3	4	—	2	17
TOTAL ..	24	35	32	33	24	14	162
All New Peers ..	70	109	93	100	127	57	556

In view of the economic difficulties which the landed estate had to face during the past eighty years, the persistence of the 'landed interest' is in itself remarkable. It is clearly a tribute to the esteem in which the 'imponderables' of landownership are still being held. But the decline in the number of private landowners, the reduction in the size of holdings and of the public position of the landowners, are even more significant facets in the decline of aristocracy, as a comparatively distinct social group, than the absorption of new elements into the Peerage. It must be investigated in turn.

THE SLOW DECLINE OF LANDOWNERSHIP

'And you see,' Trollope makes Archdeacon Grantley say, 'land gives so much more than rent. It gives position and influence and political power, to say nothing about the game.' Considered as an investment, the landed estate was throughout the nineteenth century probably inferior to industrial or commercial property; the economic and technological progress in agricultural production has always lagged behind that of manufacture. Between 1867 and 1937, agricultural income (in monetary terms) grew only by 16 per cent while the national income increased fivefold. During the same period the income from rent (*i.e.* net rent) actually declined from 3 per cent to 0·5 per cent of the National Income.[1] And while the number of people dependent on agriculture fell steeply over this period, the decline in the income from rent, although spread over a decreasing number of proprietors, did nevertheless represent a considerable fall in the real income which landed families drew from their estates.

Between 1851 and 1877 average rents rose by about 1 per cent per annum; in the following eighteen years they fell by 32 per cent. From then, until the beginning of the Second World War, rents fluctuated, rising somewhat during and after the First War, but falling again in the late twenties and, of course, during the depression. By 1939 they were hardly higher than in 1914. But with the rising cost of maintenance, landowners' net income fell sharply. With the system of agricultural price-support during and after the war, the economic position of the agricultural community improved greatly. Rents rose too (by 83 per cent between 1939 and 1957), but even allowing for the fact that during and immediately after the war little or no maintenance or re-equipment was carried out by landowners, their income barely kept up with rising prices, and they did not share in the growing prosperity of agriculture and the rising standards of living in general. Land values rose with

[1] J. R. Bellerby and others: *Agriculture and Industry, relative Income*, 1956.

rents but they failed to match the appreciation of industrial property in the post-war boom. Between 1951 and 1954, equity prices rose by 22 per cent while land values fell by 14 per cent; return on capital was estimated at 1 per cent.[1] A further exodus from landownership was thus inevitable, the actual date of sale being generally determined by the exigencies of death and the need to pay death duties. Today the proportion of land farmed under tenure is just over half, compared with two-thirds in 1939 and a little under 90 per cent in 1914.[2]

The 1860's and 1870's were the last golden decades of land-ownership. The returns of 1873 showed that just over 4,200 individual proprietors owned between them 60 per cent of all privately-owned land in England and Wales, averaging 4,400 acres per owner. The 1,688 owners of more than 3,000 acres (with rentals of £3,000 or more) shared 45 per cent of the land and their estates averaged 8,400 acres per head.[3] This concentration of ownership emerges clearly from Table IV.

But with the agricultural depression a decline set in. Estates were sold or reduced in size, slowly at first, but more rapidly since the beginning of the twentieth century. By 1925 the number of larger properties in Bedfordshire had declined from 45 (in 1873) to 27.[4] At about that time the Country Landowners' Association estimated that approximately 700,000 acres were being disposed annually.[5]

Bedfordshire is not an isolated example. In neighbouring Oxfordshire the number of estates of more than 1,000 acres in private hands declined similarly from 68 in 1873 to 35 in 1941[6] and

---

[1] 'The Country Landowner', 1955 (vol. VI, part 5), p. 298. Since decontrol of land rents in 1957 rents have risen considerably. On rent movements in general see D. R. Denman and V. F. Stewart: *Farm Rents*, 1959 and G. Hallett: *The Economics of Agricultural Land Tenure*, 1960.

[2] Today's figures are estimates. See Hallett, *op. cit.*, p. 15.

[3] Bateman, *op. cit.* I have disregarded 'waste' and land owned by Public Bodies. These two categories account for 2,968,000 out of a total of 34,524,000 acres.

[4] H. Durant: The Development of Landownership with special reference to Bedfordshire, 1773–1925. *Sociological Review*, 1936, pp. 85–98.

[5] Country Landowners' Association Quarterly Circular, February 1922, p. 6.

[6] T. W. Gardner: *Farms and Estates of Oxfordshire* (Department of Agriculture, University of Reading), 1951.

TABLE IV

Landownership in England and Wales, 1873:*

Class	Number of Owners	Extent of Acres
Peers, etc.†	400	5,728,979
Great Landowners‡	1,288	8,497,699
Squires§	2,529	4,319,271
Others‖	—	14,453,401
Waste	—	1,524,624
TOTAL	—	34,523,974

* Based on Bateman: *The Great Landowners of Great Britain and Ireland*, 4th edition, 1883, p. 515.

† Including Peeresses and sons of Peers.

‡ Holding 3,000 acres or more, provided that their annual rental reaches £3,000.

§ Estates of 1,000–3,000 acres as well as larger estates if the rental is below the £3,000 limit.

‖ Larger and smaller farmers, cottagers as well as the holdings of public bodies. The number of these, although given by Bateman constitutes a rather meaningless aggregate as no allowance is made for the great number of lease-holders who were also freeholders both in respect of the number of farms or with regard to their size.

the proportion of the total area held by large estates (private and public) fell from over half in 1873 to just under 40 per cent in 1941. The most suggestive comparison comes, however, from the Eastern Counties. Here the number and total acreage of large estates which in 1941 were in private hands was less than half that of 1873.

All accounts suggest that these figures are fairly representative and that the process of splitting and liquidating estates has gone on apace since the wartime survey on which they were based. The Country Landowners' Association which represents letting owners and owner-occupiers has today over 30,000 members; nearly 80 per cent of these own and mostly farm 250 acres or less. While they represent only a fraction of all owner-occupiers in England and Wales, the larger landowners are almost completely organized. Thus the number of C.L.A. members, owning more than 1,000 acres, is suggestive. In the late 1950's the Association

E

TABLE V

Large Landownership in six Eastern Counties, 1873 and 1941*
(Number and area of estates of 3,000 acres and more):

	1873		1941	
	Number	Area	Number	Area
Bedfordshire	17	104,000	8	61,000
Essex	44	270,000	16	91,000
Hertfordshire	25	157,000	12	59,000
Huntingdonshire	17	100,000	11	64,000
Norfolk	70	516,000	43	286,000
Suffolk	46	265,000	28	171,000
TOTAL	219	1,422,000	118	732,000

* The 1941 figures, derived from University of Cambridge, Department of Agriculture, Farm Economics Branch: *Landownership in the Eastern Counties*, 1941 (December 1947), include private estate and estates in public hands. The overall figures given for the latter suggest that, for a true comparison the numbers and area of estates in 1941 must be reduced by about 25 per cent.

contained 1,540 members in this class. In 1873 this same group comprised, as we saw, over 4,000 persons and of those nearly 1,700 held more than 3,000 acres. The corresponding number of C.L.A. members today is 507.[1]

The mere survival of estates as economic units does not tell us enough about the survival of the gentry as a strata of interconnected landed families, passing on their property from generation to generation.[2] Nor do the entities, which we term estates, necessarily remain the same. Old ones are split up, new ones are formed. Others are held as farming syndicates or by public bodies, thus passing from individual to corporate ownership and control. The dividing line between farming, land-ownership and land-management is also becoming somewhat blurred. Landowners turn themselves into their own estate managers, or even take over a part or

[1] Information given by the C.L.A. (1959).
[2] Oxfordshire had in 1941 65 principal landowners (with estates of more than 500 acres.) All but four of these were residents, but only 27 of the estates had already been in the possession of the same family in 1873. Gardner, *op. cit.*, p. 39.

the whole of their estate and run it as one farm or, through bailiffs, as separate units. Successful farmers, on the other hand, purchase additional holdings and may thus amass what are, in effect, small estates.

The changing rôle of the owner of landed estate can be observed in the development and activities of the Country Landowners' Association. Founded as Central Land Association in 1907, when the shades of the agricultural depression were still in the memory of the landed community and when the Liberal landslide of 1906 had brought with it threats of heavier taxation and even of the possible nationalization of land, it was, at first, largely an organization of the larger landowners. Its aim was to safeguard the interests of agriculture and of the owners of landed estates. Although officially not party-political, its membership, like the class from which it was drawn, was largely Tory.[1]

In support of the claim of the landowner to more favourable treatment, the Association cited the social significance of the land-owning class and the injustice (and impolicy) of allowing this section of the population to disappear. 'We do not ask for any special favour for landowners', the C.L.A. wrote in a memorandum to the Chancellor of the Exchequer on the burden of taxation after the war. 'We recognize that we must share, equally with others, the burden of the country's expenditure. But we are charged with the duty of presenting the case of the landowning class *which has done great service to the country and has never failed in an emergency.*'[2]

After 1939, when, mostly as a result of government measures, the real income of the farming community had risen considerably, many people doubted the continued usefulness of a class of landed

---

[1] Of the original committee of 21 members eight were Conservative Peers or M.P.s and eight Liberals. But of the large landowner-Peers who graced the Association as Vice-Presidents 13 out of 14 were Conservatives. The Association did to some extent succeed in maintaining its non-party character. The first Annual General Meeting decided on an Executive Committee of 30 members of whom 20 were to be drawn from the membership of the two Houses of Parliament but with the proviso that not more than 12 should belong to one party. The extreme right-wing members did actually secede to form the Land Union.

[2] C.L.A. Quarterly Journal, February 1922, p. 7. (My italics.)

proprietors. This forced the Association to make out an economic case for landownership and for the increase of rent and the more favourable financial treatment on which, in turn, its survival depended. The Association put growing emphasis on the need for the efficient management of the estate, the combination of farming and letting in landownership, the necessity of educating land-owners and inculcating a new spirit into the activity. Without this, the owners of broad acres would slowly decay among a pros-perous tenantry. The traditional squires who looked upon their estates 'as family heritage rather than an individual possession (and) from that point of view as well as for such reasons as love of country life with its sports and amenities (were) content to accept an agricultural rent representing interest at considerably less than market value'[1] were doomed. Now they were asked to turn them-selves into agricultural businessmen, maximizing their returns through the prudent application of economic principles to the task of estate-management.

The changes in the character of landownership and the changing fortunes of 'landed' families are perhaps most clearly reflected in the successive editions of *Burke's Landed Gentry*. Published for the first time in 1833, this work sought to record the 'genealogical history of the Commoners of England enjoying territorial posses-sions' but not claiming 'hereditary honours'. It contained, at first, the records of about 400 families deriving their income predomin-antly from landed estates. Gradually its scope widened and the editors began to include men who had made their fortune in indus-try or trade but who had, at the same time, acquired a 'stake in the country'. However, until 1914 substantial ownership of land remained a necessary condition of entry. In 1921 the editors recognized the fact that changing economic conditions had forced a number of families to sell their properties and these were described as 'formerly of' their estate. By 1937 one-third of the families listed were land-less. In the 1952 edition this number had grown and the editor admitted a number of families who had never owned land but who either had an interesting pedigree or possessed a coat of arms. Thus of the approximately 5,500 families listed, only half

---

[1] From a letter of the Secretary of the C.L.A. published in the *Yorkshire Post*. Quarterly Circular, 1932, p. 131.

were actual landowners and of these 600 were newcomers to landownership.[1]

The landed gentry has always renewed itself from the group of the newly rich, and although the possession of an estate is no longer a prerequisite of acceptance into the ranks of society, or a condition for the bestowal of hereditary honours, old patterns die hard. If the very rich continue to grow richer, landownership on a large scale may one day become again an expression of conspicuous consumption.[2] But while the pleasures of country life can be obtained from the possession of a converted farmhouse and a few acres, few will as yet forgo the profitability of industrial investment and of capital appreciation for the illusions of feudal grandeur. Those whose traditions are firmly rooted in a county and its society will understandably be unwilling to change their way of life, but there is little evidence that landed dynasties are about to be founded today.

ARISTOCRACY AND UPPER CLASS

The long and progressively growing influx of new elements into the British Peerage, matched by similar changes in the character of the aristocracy, and the gradual decline of landownership, both in numbers and in the size of estates, makes it doubtful whether it is still meaningful to speak of a British aristocracy and a landed gentry. It would accord more with social reality if we spoke of a titled or landed section of the British upper (middle) class. Nowadays there is little to distinguish the recipients of honours—let alone their families—from those who occupy the same economic position or follow similar occupations without titles or honours. The members of the Peerage are today covering probably as wide a range of positions as can be found in the upper ranges of our society. Few, I imagine, believe in the magic of the accolade or agree with Nancy Mitford that ennoblement changes a man,

---

[1] cf. A. R. Wagner: 'The Land and the Gentry', *The Times*, October 1, 1952. 'These innovations', Sir Anthony Wagner wrote, 'are not editorial whim but the response of British Commonsense to major changes.'

[2] It is interesting to observe that shooting lodges of lairds and Lords have been taken over by syndicates, not by individual proprietors. They provide a day's shooting at an all-inclusive charge of something like £50 a day.

and that 'he becomes an aristocrat as soon as he receives his title. The Queen turns him from socialist leader, or middle-class businessman into a nobleman: his outlook from now on will be the outlook of an aristocrat.'[1]

We have seen how in the past one hundred years, the British aristocracy has changed from a traditionalist to a capitalist aristocracy. From a strongly endogamous group, whose individual 'houses' drew their support largely from immovable property of which the head of the family was only the temporary custodian, it has grown into a section of the population much less closely interlinked by ties of marriage and based very frequently on widely dispersed and more transient industrial and commercial property and varied economic interests. In 1922, when the House of Lords comprised 680 (hereditary) Peers, it still contained 242 landowners, but 272 Peers were Company Directors, sharing 761 directorships in a wide range of industries.[2]

Since then the process has continued; apart from the comparatively small group of Labour Peers, additions to the Peerage as we saw, have been predominantly of men with roots in industrial or commercial activity or of leaders of the professions, of the administration or the services. And subsequent generations in the 'new' Peerage have largely perpetuated this trend.[3]

In their marriages, too, the families of newly created Peers have followed the pattern of the wider upper class. Unless they were members of the aristocracy, or the landed gentry, Peers of the first generation rarely married into the aristocracy. As their ennoblement almost invariably occurred long after their marriage, this is hardly surprising. But the heirs to titles in the 'new' Peerage have not allied themselves with aristocratic families through marriage to any greater degree than their fathers and grandfathers. Sometimes, of course, new wealth does link itself with old lineage to a remarkable extent. Charles Wilson, later Lord Nunburnholme,

---

[1] Nancy Mitford: 'The English Aristocracy' in Mitford (ed.): *Noblesse Oblige*, p. 45.

[2] Labour Research Department: *Labour and Capital in Parliament*, 1923, pp. 10–11.

[3] Among 378 Directors (comprising the boards of 25 leading Merchant Banks, the 8 big Commercial Banks and the directors of a number of other banks, leading Insurance Companies, etc.) there were 69 Peers. (M. Barratt-Brown: 'The Controllers,' *Universities and New Left Review*, No. 5, Autumn 1958.)

Hull shipowner of a comparatively humble background, married a niece of the Duke of Wellington. His heirs did even better, allying themselves to the daughters of Marquises. Altogether, among the parents-in-law of his children and grandchildren, we can count one Duke, two Marquises, two Earls and one Viscount. If any trend can be observed, it is that recent creations tend to marry among themselves, while those who belong to families of long lineage still show some preference for partners from old aristocratic families. There is probably today a gradually declining section of the nobility and the landed gentry which preserves some of the features of aristocratic life as we have known it.

TABLE VI

Inter-Marriage in the Peerage, 1957*:

Father-in-Law

Peer	1st	2nd	3rd	4th	5th	6th–Other	Unmarried	Total	Percentage of marriages within the peerage
1st	5	3	—	1	3	5 144	10	171	10
2nd	5	4	2	2	—	3 118	21	155	12
3rd	6	1	1	5	2	4 62	25	106	23
4th	1	—	—	2	2	5 39	26	75	20
5th	—	2	—	—	—	4 35	6	47	15
6th	9	7	6	4	3	23 187	49	288	22
All Peers	26	17	9	14	10	44 585	137	842	17

* The above *formal* analysis does inevitably *overestimate* the marriages of real newcomers and their descendants into Peerage families, especially old-established ones: among the peers of recent creations married to descendants of ancient families, a number are really *cadets* of aristocratic families of long lineage. At the same time the table also *underestimates* the number of Peers of ancient lineage who married into their class. If the ancestry of the spouse had been traced further back, and if the families of baronets had been included, we would have found more endogamous marriages among noble families of long lineage.

The political rôle of the Peerage has also undergone considerable changes during the course of this century, and the changes cannot be ascribed merely to the decisive curtailment of aristocratic power through the Parliament Acts of 1911 and 1949. Hereditary titles, with the exception of baronetcies, have always served a dual function: the dignified and the representative. Some men, although upholding the former, have always neglected the latter.

Even in the nineteenth century, when the House of Lords was the final arbiter on many political issues,[1] many Peers were absentees. Since 1911 the House of Lords has attracted to its debates a declining number of a growing total of peers, and those who are active and attend regularly are today predominantly the 'professional' politicians, ex-members of the House of Commons and Labour Peers who were ennobled to represent their party in the Upper House.[2] In the nineteenth century a large section of the aristocracy had traditional ties with Westminster. Such ties still exist, but they are getting fewer and more tenuous as old lineages decline or die out, and the families of newly created Peers do not continue the older pattern. In the first generation, the number of M.P.s and of men holding posts in the government is, of course, very large and succeeding generations could hardly show the same degree of political activity. Given the past tradition of political families in the aristocracy we should, however, expect to find a greater amount of political activity than actually occurs.

TABLE VII

Political Activity in the New Peerage
(Number of M.P.s in successive generations):

Creations	First Generation M.P.s	Second Generation M.P.s	Third Generation M.P.s
1880–1890	37 out of 58	13 out of 36	2 out of 32
1891–1900	34 out of 61	7 out of 28	0 out of 17
1901–1910	50 out of 70	5 out of 36	0 out of 22
1911–1920	62 out of 109	6 out of 59	1 out of 20
1921–1930	50 out of 93	3 out of 47	incomplete
1931–1940	60 out of 100	5 out of 51	incomplete

The members of the administration who sit in the House of Lords also offer a good example of the prevalence of either ennobled M.P.s, 'Political Peers' or descendants of old aristocratic

---

[1] In 1911 Balfour could still refer to the need 'to ensure that whatever Party is in office the Conservative Party shall always be in power'. No doubt the Peers had the good sense to acquiesce ultimately in a number of measures which the majority of them detested (e.g. the Irish Church Bill) but their assertion of independent judgment was between 1868 and 1910 a constant check to Liberal policy. The protracted final struggle shows with what tenacity a majority held on to its power.

[2] Bromhead, *op. cit.*, ch. III.

families. Peers of the second or third generation are comparatively rare in this group.

Nor do Peers of the first generation always make a contribution to public life via the House of Lords. Of 190 such Peers, alive at the end of 1953, 69 did not speak at all in the Lords between 1951 and 1954. Many were old but 'some of these silent Peers held exceedingly powerful positions in industrial and commercial life, others were men of the highest renown in various other spheres of the nation's activities. It can only be assumed that many regarded their titles as marks of honour and distinction . . . rather than as valuable for the opportunity to contribute to debate in the House of Lords.'[1]

Thus a hereditary aristocracy fulfils few functions in our society. Divorced from its traditional roots it lacks the continuity which comes from the ownership of entailed property. Deprived of its traditional rôle in rural society, it has few natural public tasks and membership of the House of Commons is no longer a natural avenue for its members. Composed to a lesser extent than previously of rentiers, or landed proprietors, its members have fewer opportunities to participate in the discussions of the Upper House even if they have the inclination to do so. The introduction of Life Peerages in 1958 is an implicit recognition that social and economic circumstances have greatly lessened the usefulness of the traditional, hereditary aristocracy.

Politically the scheme has, perhaps, not been as successful as its advocates hoped. The eminent men and women thus ennobled are often fully occupied in a variety of useful pursuits and they have perhaps not brought much new vigour to the debates of the House of Lords. The government, by continuing to bestow hereditary honours, has re-affirmed the social value of an aristocratic order, yet one may well doubt whether transmissible titles accord with the general tenor of life in a democratic society. And while in the nineteenth century the aristocracy contributed to the political life of the community, by manning the second chamber and in general by giving service to the state, its members do this today to a much more limited extent. It would thus seem that the aristocracy, having lost its social function, has also largely lost its political *raison d'être*.

[1] Bromhead, *op. cit.*, p. 49.

CHAPTER VI

Formative Influences and Attitude to Politics: The Case of the Aristocracy

'How can those who spend their time in hunting shooting and drinking know what were the motives of those who are responsible for the Public Security.'—SIR ROBERT PEEL to his wife, December 1845.

'Politics would become an utter blank to me were I to make the discovery that we were mistaken in maintaining their association with religion.'—GLADSTONE to Manning, April 1850.

'You can rely on my carrying on father's tradition so long as I can carry on anything even in this slippery world of government. . . . And I think that Oliver will carry on: he has certainly abjured so far the paths of ease and comfort.'—BALDWIN to his Mother, June 1920.

THE analysis in terms of social class and political groupings which has been presented in the last chapters needs re-defining in terms of individual careers and of the more subjective factors determining political careers. This chapter and the next explore some aspects of the questions which arise invariably in the study of élite groups: Why do people enter, how are they chosen, how do those who are successful as full-time politicians, act in the political setting? This discussion will be continued in Chapter VIII, which asks what it is that makes some men rise to positions of leadership and great power while others remain among the rank and file.

It is easier to pose these questions than to answer them fully and in detail. Political life, especially in Britain, is more exhaustively documented than any similar field of activity; we know vastly more even about deliberations inside the Cabinet than about the discussions and decisions of the boards of the great industrial and commercial enterprises. The proceedings of no other opinion-forming and decision-making assembly are as fully recorded as those of the two Houses of Parliament. The Press has always sought to report what goes on behind the scenes of parliament and in the corridors of power. Memoirs and biographies abound. Yet it would be idle to pretend that the analysis of the written record can ever give a complete and wholly convincing account of the springs of action and the bases of attitudes of leading politicians.[1]

The study of the attitude to politics which is presented here is based primarily on the rich fount of biographical and autobiographical literature which is available for the study of British politicians, especially those of the Victorian era.[2] I have in my investigations concentrated on the innermost circle of the political élite, the membership of the Cabinet, whose published life histories are particularly numerous.[3] Moreover, as this literature is richest for the period before 1914 this chapter puts emphasis on that period. The themes touched upon here are, however, taken up in the chapters devoted to the leadership in the Conservative Party and in the Labour Party.

The analysis of the social structure of cabinet membership shows a number of distinct groups, viz. the aristocracy, and the politicians who belong to upper class families and were often closely allied to it; the 'new' men from the entrepreneurial and professional middle class, and the men and women of working-class origin who, with few exceptions, achieved Cabinet status after a career in Labour politics. In the context of this chapter the term aristocracy is not used in a strictly definitional sense, but rather as a convenient shorthand expression for the politicians who sprang from the ranks of the 'gentlemanly' class. In the same way the next chapter, which asks similar questions for the group of middle-class politicians, deals in effect largely with the 'newcomers' to the profession of politics.

This distinction between the traditional ruling class and the *hommes nouveaux* was followed in the analysis and interpretation

---

[1] I felt, on the other hand, that it is not practicable to conduct the rigorous and methodical kind of interview study of politicians which alone could have given a full and unbiased account of their attitudes.

[2] These literary tombstones, which dutiful Victorian widows and sons erected for departed 'public men', have no rival elsewhere or for any other period. They are in themselves a phenomenon of some social significance for the study of the society which they help to illuminate.

[3] Almost half of the total of 292 Cabinet Ministers have so far been the subjects of memoirs or reminiscences of varying length and quality.

of the biographical material, because the social origin of the men
here studied is an indication of the influences which shape the
political character of the individual. The presence or absence of
such factors as public school education, university experience,
the membership of dissenting churches, political family tradition,
economic independence, the connection with popular political
movements or intellectual interests are unique features in the lives
of these groups and clearly influence their entry into politics and
their attitude to it. Inevitably, not all careers can be fitted into the
institutional framework which emerged from the social analysis,
but it is sufficiently typical to serve as a guiding beacon for the
selection of the vast amount of biographical data which are available.[1]

ROOTS AND ROUTES: LANDOWNERSHIP INTO POLITICS

A study of the routes by which men enter politics, the causes with
which they identify, and the preparations which they make for a
political career is relevant for our understanding of the political
élite. Ease of entry into the parliamentary sphere and the relative
security of tenure which a 'pocket borough' gives, is, for example,
as important for our understanding of the political activity of the
landed aristocracy, as is the economic independence guaranteed by
a sizeable rent-roll and the prestige which a landowner enjoys in
his county. And to both we must add the concept of his rôle and
his duties which imbued the squire-politician. It is the territorial
character of the aristocracy which more than anything else accounted
for the close connection between titled families. Family ties and a
family's political tradition, as well as the position of prestige which
parliamentary service conferred on landowners in the society of
their county, in general contribute to that drive towards political
activity which is such a marked feature of the nineteenth century
acreocracy.

---

[1] To use biographical material for the analysis of the attitude to politics which
we can observe within the political élite it was necessary to make a fairly rigid
selection. I have tried to find certain patterns of political behaviour which appear
characteristic for certain groups within the political élite rather than present a
catalogue of all individual traits which could be observed.

The large territorial magnate felt that to sell land was a step which should be avoided. Status and prestige were linked with landed property. The urban luxuries, which industrial assets or a parcel of shares could give, were not on a par with it. When the sixth Duke of Devonshire found himself so much in debt that the sale of a part of his estates seemed the only solution, the third Earl Fitzwilliam wrote to him, counselling caution.

'In the first place,' he said, 'the gain from a sale (as against a continuing mortage) would not be very great. But in any case what do you lose in order to gain this small proportionate addition to your income? Why, you lose greatly in station.—You are now, taking all circumstances into consideration, the first gentleman in the East Riding of Yorkshire . . . the alienation of one of the great masses of your landed property is a very different affair, and cannot fail to make a sensible inroad upon your influence, and upon the position which you hold in the great national community.'[1]

The Earl's advice was not heeded and given the circumstances, not very practicable, but a generation later, the 7th Duke avoided another sale to get rid of an indebtedness amounting to close on £1 million. He would not mind selling some of his Irish properties: 'I have so many houses that to get rid of one would be a relief rather than a sacrifice.' But he realized that a sale of any of the Cavendish land 'might lower the position of my family'.[2]

The prestige of landownership was regarded as essential to give Disraeli the formal status of Conservative leader in the House of Commons to which his able and ardent defence of the protectionist cause clearly entitled him. To set Disraeli up as a country gentleman, and thus make him generally acceptable to the party, was the idea of Lord Henry and Lord George Bentinck, and although the latter did not live to see the project brought to fruition, it was eventually carried out by Lord Henry and his elder brother, the Marquess of Titchfield. They secured a loan of £25,000 from the Duke of Portland which made the purchase of Hughenden Manor

---

[1] Quoted in David Spring: The English Landed Estate in the Age of Coal and Iron: 1830–80. *Journal of Economic History*, vol. IX, 1951, p. 17.
[2] *loc. cit.*, p. 19.

possible. And so Disraeli was enabled, in his own words, 'to play the high game in public life'.[1]

Hughenden was a small estate of only 750 acres and its owner, although patron of a living and a member of the bench, had little in the way of public functions to undertake. Nor could it provide Disraeli with a material basis for his political activity; throughout his life this had to come from his wife's income. The larger landed estate on the other hand, was to its owners a source of income as well as the focal point for a series of activities and public positions.[2] They were not only patrons of livings and Justices of the Peace but on them rested generally the major share of responsibility for the running of village schools, infirmaries and other local welfare institutions. They were expected to subscribe generously to local charities, and to assume some responsibility for the welfare of their tenants and the agricultural and estate labour force. In the running of their own farms and the improvement of waste and other infertile parts of the estate, they even turned into agriculturalists, and this they often did with great benefit both to themselves and to the wider agricultural community.[3]

No doubt comparatively few squires and magnates qualify for the heroic picture of the Victorian landowner which Tennyson drew in *The Princess*:

> And there we saw Sir Walter where he stood,
> Before a tower of crimson holly-hocks,
> Among six boys, head under head, and look'd
> No little lily-handed Baronet he,
> A great broad-shouldered genial English man,
> A lord of fat prize-oxen and of sheep,
> A raiser of huge melons and of pine,

[1] *cf.* Moneypenny and Buckle, vol. I, p. 966–7. Financially the plan was hardly sensible. Disraeli settled himself with the cost of the upkeep of a large house. In 1857 the Marquess of Titchfield, by then 5th Duke of Portland, called in the loan and caused Disraeli further financial embarrassment.

[2] Of the 2,500 large landowners listed by Bateman 66 had incomes of over £50,000, 259 received rentals of £20–50,000; 541 had £10–20,000 and 702 £6,000–10,000 and 932 between £3,000 and £6,000. (*op. cit.*, p. 495).

[3] For the 'feudal' character of English landownership see Taine's *Notes on England* (pp. 137–46 of 1957 edition). Taine's account refers to the 1860's. See also E. Wingfield Stratford: *The Squire and his Relations*, 1936.

A patron of some thirty charities,
A pamphleteer on guano and on grain,
A quarter-sessions chairman, abler none.[1]

The sporting and gaming squire remained to show the ignorance, arrogance and lack of culture so frequently associated with his class. Nor did the 'improving squire' necessarily make a contribution to the solution of the wider issues of his time. The young Disraeli's attack on the 'Venetian Oligarchy' of the Whigs—but really not only of the Whigs—was part of that romantic radicalism which attacks institutions, not because of inherent faults, but because of the human shortcomings of those who were its standard bearers. The landed classes had only to put themselves at the 'head of the people', and to defend the labouring classes against suppression by the manufacturing or business classes, to solve all social ills. Yet a large part of the landowners, of whom Disraeli had made himself spokesman, deserted Peel in 1845 when, under the impact of the Irish famine, he decided on the immediate and total repeal of the Corn Laws.

Actually the landowners as a group were divided over the protectionist issue, and in the decisive votes over repeal the squires can be found in both camps in almost equal proportion.[2] When it came to the rights of the landowner over his property, and the freedom of contract to dispose of it at what rent or to whom he chose, the magnates tended to be strong adherents of *laissez faire*. This shows itself in the resistance which they tended to offer to a series of measures which sought, however ineffectually, to protect Irish tenants and to improve the state of Irish agriculture through measures which would affect freedom of contract.[3]

The exploitation of the Irish 'farming' population is clearly not unconnected with the fact that the squire was usually an alien, non-resident proprietor without any social or cultural ties with his tenants. In the setting of the English village, the desire for maximum returns from the land was frequently overlaid by those

---

[1] Sir Walter Vivian the benevolent landlord is a portrait of Tennyson's brother-in-law, Edmund Lushington. *cf.* John Killhon: *Tennyson and 'The Princess'*, 1958, pp. 61–62.

[2] *cf.* W. H. Aydelotte: *loc. cit.*

[3] *cf.* R. D. C. Black: *Economic Theory and the Irish Question*, 1960.

traditions of responsibility generally accepted by the nineteenth-century successor of the Lord of the Manor. There was also the general disdain of ostentatiousness and the emphasis on individual charity, which was such a strong element in the Victorian set of conduct and which tended to make the landowner aware of his social obligations.[1]

We must not underrate the force of the tradition of 'Public Service' demanded of the local landowner, and often willingly given. Parliamentary activity is in line with the duties of the squire in his more immediate surroundings as magistrate, guardian of the poor, Deputy Lieutenant of the County or Sheriff and later often as member of the County Council. 'Your position is fixed—that of an English Country Gentleman', Sir Francis Baring had written to his son then at Christ Church, Oxford, in 1846. 'Have English Country Gentlemen, then, any business? To my mind no one more. All men are not fitted for the performance of all these duties, but it is in the discharge of some that men of property in this country do their duty to their God, benefit their country and contribute to their own happiness. . . . You may look to public life, if your feelings turn that way, or you may lead a quieter life and still be a very useful and good man. . . . I shall be as satisfied if you are a *worthy* Squire, as if you were a leading Whig speaker.'[2]

In the eighteenth century, the particular desire of the class of country gentlemen—the smaller squires rather than the landed magnates—was the representation of their *county*, and once in Parliament they kept aloof from the grossest abuses. In the nineteenth century, territorial influence continued to be important in helping a man to enter into the House of Commons but it was seldom sufficient, especially in the counties. Personal popularity and reputation which was gained through the exercise of public duties had to be added to it. Hicks Beach's entry into the House of Commons may be cited as an example. He had inherited family property of two estates of comparatively modest size in Gloucestershire and Wiltshire even before he came of age, and later he entered on the duties connected with his Gloucestershire estate where he lived. He sat

[1] *cf.* E. Wingfield-Stratford: *The Squire and his Relations*, 1956, pp. 311–19 and *passim*.

[2] B. Mallet: *Thomas George Earl of Northbrook, A Memoir*, 1908, p. 26.

on the bench, acted as a guardian of the poor, and effected agricultural improvements. Before he entered Parliament at the age of twenty-seven he had been asked to contest two neighbouring constituencies. In 1864 the member for East Gloucestershire, his father's constituency, died. Hicks Beach was invited to stand, he accepted, a rival Conservative candidate was persuaded to withdraw and he was elected unopposed.

When Northcote, while still hoping to be returned for Exeter, considered giving up his position in the Civil Service, to devote himself entirely to the care of his father's estate, which he expected to inherit shortly, he thought of the step in the following terms: 'If in a few years, I have made myself master of my duties there and established my position in the county and learnt practically something of the wants of my own class and of my neighbours, I think I should come into Parliament naturally and with much more strength than if I were a mere official adventurer.'

The desire for personal prestige as well as the obligations of public service were factors which turned the landowner towards political activity. The extent of landownership among the members of the House of Commons is remarkable, but so is the extent of political activity in the landowning class, especially among those holding large estates. In 1868 almost 10 per cent of the squires and landed magnates sat in the House of Commons. Fifty-nine M.P.s, returned in 1868 held over 50,000 acres,[1] yet the total number of estates of that size was only 115 in the 1870's.[2]

By the middle of the nineteenth century an improved political morality, as well as parliamentary reforms, had greatly reduced the possibilities for self-seeking and self-advancement which eighteenth-century politics used to offer to all those whose moral conscience had not been too tender. What remained was the 'inevitability of a parliamentary career' for the members of the nation's leading families.

INEVITABLE PARLIAMENT MEN

The traditional character of a political career among members of the British aristocracy emerges clearly from the salient features of

---

[1] *cf.* Hanham: *Elections and Party Management,* p. xv.
[2] Bateman, *op. cit.,* p. 495.

their entry into politics. They are the early age at which aristocratic members entered the House of Commons, their representation of small boroughs or county constituencies, and the existence
of close ties between members and their constituencies based
mostly on their position as landowners in the county or
borough.

In the mid-eighteenth century a parliamentary career constituted
part and parcel of the aspirations, if not the actual career of the
landowning class. In 1761, 21 out of 23 M.P.s who were the eldest
sons of *English* peers had entered the House on the first possible
opportunity after their coming of age. 'The sons of politically
active Peers . . . owed it to their families and to their future position
to do this', Sir Lewis Namier has written. The letters 'M.P.'
after their name were 'a kind of Parliamentary courtesy title,
preparatory to the Peerage.'[1] A century later 49 M.P.s who were
the eldest sons of Peers sat in the House of Commons. They too
had generally entered Parliament when still very young.[2]

These young men were enabled to enter the House of Commons
at an early age because they were economically independent and
also because family property and influence could generally secure
them nomination and often for a safe seat at that. J. W. Lowther,
one of a long line of landowners in Westmoreland and of M.P.s for
that county and elsewhere, relates how, in 1803, Gerard Noel,
M.P. for Rutland and his uncle by marriage, applied for the Chil-
tern Hundreds. 'My family had a close connection with the county,
having lived for some generations at Cottesmore and Barleythorpe
. . . and my great grandfather, Sir W. Lowther, had been M.P. for
the county from 1790 to 1802. I was selected as the Conservative
candidate' (and elected).[3] Between 1832 and 1867 the nomination
in a great number of constituencies could still be exercised through
the ownership of burgesses votes, or through the pressure which a
landowner could exercise over his tenants: Charles Dod, surveying
the electoral scene in 1853, mentions the preponderant influence
of one family in the return of members in the case of 72 out of the

---

[1] Namier: *The Structure of Politics at the Accession of George III*, 2nd ed.,
1957, p. 2.
[2] Thirty of the forty-nine had entered the House of Commons by the age of
25 and a further eleven had done so by the age of thirty.
[3] J. W. Lowther: *A Speaker's Commentary*, 2 vols., 1925, vol. I, p. 153.

156 English constituencies.[1] This patronage was exercised in most cases by the local aristocracy and landed gentry. While the rising middle class, unless aided by the aristocracy, entered Parliament for the large boroughs with their newly enfranchised population, the young aristocrat was almost invariably sent by the rural boroughs or by one of the agricultural counties. Of the twenty-two aristocratic Cabinet Ministers who sat for borough constituencies before 1885 only three sat for towns with more than 2,000 voters and of these only one, the future Lord Derby, was returned for an industrial borough—Preston, where the Stanley family had strong influence.

In the group of men here studied—as among aristocratic M.P.s in general—it is thus the eldest son or other heir to a title who is most conspicuous. Only a career in the army offered a serious alternative, lending both additional status and honour to its bearer without being a 'job' in the material sense. In the case of sons who could not readily expect to succeed to their father's estate, the choice of a political career is a much less obvious one. We find that prudence dictates the choice of the Law, the Church or the Civil Service as a career. Throughout the period when the future third Marquis of Salisbury was not yet the heir to his father's estate and lived rather precariously on a small income from an inheritance, supplemented by earnings from his pen, the question of exchanging his place in the House of Commons for a safe place in the Civil Service arose frequently. 'I cannot but see,' he wrote, 'that if my means through life are likely to be confined to what I at present possess, a political career, though not now beyond my means, may not be consistent with due prudence in respect of after years.'[2]

The group of 'inevitable Parliament men' whose choice of a political career is dictated by family considerations, upbringing, and by their place in society, is in the middle of the nineteenth century— just as much as one hundred years earlier—to be found in the heirs to the great territorial magnates, and the old established political families, whether they belong to the aristocracy or the gentry. The borough of Woodstock was, until its disenfranchisement,

---

[1] C. Dod: *Electoral Facts from 1832 to 1852*, 1853.
[2] Lady G. Cecil: *The Life of Robert, Marquis of Salisbury*, 4 vols., 1921–32, vol. I, p. 65.

a Churchill Pocket Borough. In the 1850's the seat was held by Lord Alfred Churchill, the Duke of Marlborough's brother. Unfortunately, he showed a sympathy for the policies of Lord Palmerston and was forced to retire from the constituency. His place was taken by Henry Barnett, a neighbouring landowner who had the Duke's confidence. In 1874, at the first General Election after he had come of age, Lord Randolph Churchill was elected in place of the squire, who had conveniently retired.[1] The attitude to politics of such men has something of the cool detachment of a professional man entering on a safe career. 'I am too young, even legally speaking,' wrote Lord John Manners when asked to contest a seat in Cambridgeshire, 'but Parliament is the place in which they (i.e. his principles) must be developed and acted out.'[2] They were offered and accepted governmental office early and without misgivings about the low position which they were to hold. What counted was not the nature of the appointment but the appointment as such, provided it was compatible with the style of living to which their class had been used.

The aristocratic politicians who reached the Cabinet were largely a rentier group, deriving their income either from landed property or from investments. It is this 'annuity-based' economic independence, which distinguishes them from the politicians of the entrepreneurial middle class who, in the main, began their political career while still engaged in manufacturing or commercial activities. Political activity entails for the politician from the traditional ruling strata little or no sacrifice. To embark on a parliamentary career did not change his style of life perceptibly. He is rarely motivated by those strong moral passions which spur politicians from sections of the middle and working class, especially those who were labouring under a sense of injustice, because of disadvantages and discriminations experienced. Nor has political activity for him much of the character of the 'vocation' which completely absorbs his life to the exclusion of most other activities.[3]

Those who looked at their political activity in terms of office-holding might have to make some adjustment in their style of life

---

[1] (Sir) W. S. Churchill: *Life of Randolph Churchill*, p. 50.

[2] C. Whibley: *Lord John Manners and his friends*, 2 vols., 1925, vol. I, p. 81.

[3] On the notion of 'politics as a vocation' with special relevance to the Middle Class, see below pp. 178–180.

and material provisions; younger sons, especially, may have needed additional financial assistance from their families. Lord George Hamilton, a younger son of the Duke of Abercorn, entered Parliament in 1868. His successful maiden speech on the Irish Church Bill brought him and the Duke many congratulations. 'It was decided [therefore] that I should give up the army as a profession and devote myself entirely to politics.'[1] Yet his financial affairs were at first far from straight and by marrying a comparatively poor wife he was thought to have embarrassed his political future.[2] Occasionally a ministerial salary was itself important to augment the declining fortune of an aristocratic politician, but for the bulk of this group political activity and office holding never became essential in a material sense.

Politics was only one strand in the life of a leisured class. Interests vital for the individual lay outside it. For the traditional ruling class of the Victorian era, politics were not expected to interfere with social or literary activities, or with sport and travel. Posts as junior ministers were not, as a rule, taken very seriously. Granville had to be reprimanded for neglecting his duties as Under-Secretary for Foreign Affairs, Lansdowne's appointment to a minor post did not lead to any reduction in his social activities. A record of Balfour's daily activities when Irish Secretary at a time of great political crisis reads like this: 'Golf or real tennis, 12–2, Castle, 2–7, the work that does not get done in five hours remains undone.' When the future Duke of Devonshire was offered the same post in 1870 his first reaction was to refuse the offer. 'Most of all,' he wrote to Gladstone, 'I cannot reconcile myself to giving up almost the whole year to official duties. I imagine that the Irish Secretary ought to be in Dublin during the greater part of the year when Parliament is not sitting. This to me, with all my friends and pursuits in England, would be almost banishment for the time . . .'[3]

The period with which we are concerned saw a growing volume of platform speeches by Cabinet Ministers and party leaders, yet it is interesting to observe that aristocratic politicians, Hartington, Balfour and Harcourt apart, took little part in these campaigns.

---

[1] Lord George Hamilton: *Recollections*, vol. I, p. 15.
[2] *ibid.*, p. 40.
[3] B. Holland: *The Duke of Devonshire*, vol. I, p. 81.

No doubt the selection of aristocratic politicians which, at least before 1885 did not put a premium on good oratory and therefore did not necessarily produce men who could make a mark as demagogues, would inevitably weigh against their employment in such capacity; yet by tradition and upbringing the aristocratic politician was little suited to an age of mass democracy. Through his education and his whole way of life, he stood apart from the bulk of his fellow citizens. His attitude to the broad masses tended to be one of condescension and charity. At a time when the middle classes were agitated by the issues of corn law repeal and franchise reform, Lord John Manners advocated measures of social amelioration to be granted by a well-meaning ruling class to alleviate the sufferings of the poor. 'Let us show the people, *i.e.* the lower orders, by adding to their comforts in the only legitimate way a legislature can do, *viz.* by voting money to build public baths . . . that we are their real friends.'[1] Again, because of the traditional nature of their political career they tended to lack that decisive attitude which is the result of a strong moral passion or of great enthusiasm.

Regard for the opponent, to whom the aristocratic politician was bound by ties of a common upbringing and often of personal friendship, worked against his effectiveness as a platform speaker. Balfour, after he had attacked Gladstone rather sharply in the House of Commons recalled how he regretted what he had said almost immediately afterwards. Northcote's lack of effectiveness as leader of the House of Commons was ascribed to his deferential attitude towards Gladstone, whose secretary he had been. When Bonar Law took over the Leadership of the Conservative Party from Balfour we find that a new tone enters political controversy. Speaking at a mass meeting in the Albert Hall he abused his opponents in the most violent terms.

We shall understand the aristocratic politician better if we study some of the institutions and mores which, through their influence on his life and through the general mental climate which they created, helped to shape the attitude of the aristocratic politician to politics, *viz.* the public school and the ancient universities, London Society, family tradition and Christian religion.

---

[1] Whibley, *op. cit.*, vol. I, p. 137.

FORMATIVE FACTORS: PUBLIC SCHOOLS AND THE
ANCIENT UNIVERSITIES

The making of the future politician from the ranks of the aristocracy can be traced back to the education which they received in the public schools. The old public schools, especially Eton and Harrow, were in the middle of the nineteenth century in a process of transition.[1] Old licentiousness, archaic discipline and the untrammelled exercise of the right of the strongest were slowly giving way to greater emphasis on character training, the inculcation of a corporate spirit, and finally a more scholastic type of education.[2] But even the reformed public schools and the bulk of the new institutions, which arose in the second half of the nineteenth century to cater for a growing middle-class demand, based their education on three major assumptions: the natural sinfulness of the boys; the existence of a well-defined and naturally superior 'gentlemanly' class whose sons ought to be educated *apart* from the majority of the nation's youth and to be brought up as its natural leaders, and, last but not least, the usefulness of a so-called 'liberal' non-vocational, if not anti-vocational academic training.

The first of these led to the insistence on a rigid but formal discipline and the necessity and value of corporal punishment. It even helped to give to organized games their high place in the public school system. For Arnold, the cane lay close to the Bible. He despaired of making the conduct of his schoolboys amenable to moral principles. He would 'try to educate Christian gentlemen for Christian boys I cannot make'.[3] Following his reform at Rugby the fagging system became recognized as an institution and invested with positive educative functions. The subjection of the fag 'is not degrading for it is rendered not to an arbitrary but to a

[1] We are justified in concentrating largely on Eton and Harrow, as their rôle in educating the future aristocratic politician exceeds in importance that of all other Public Schools. This was especially so in the period before 1914. Eton was strongly aristocratic and Tory in character while Harrow had Whig leanings and was favoured by the children of the *nouveaux riches*.

[2] On this, and on the history of the public schools in general see E. C. Mack: *Public Schools and British Opinion, 1780–1860*, 1938, and *Public Schools and British Opinion since 1860*, 1941.

[3] On Arnold's educational ideals see T. W. Bamford: *Thomas Arnold*, 1960, and Chapter II of Lionel Trilling's *Life of Matthew Arnold*, 1939.

real superiority; it is shown to be a power exercised in the main
not for its own good, but for that of society as a whole . . . the discipline to which boys are thus subjected and the quickness, handi-
ness, thoughtfulness and punctuality which they learn from some
of the services required of them are no despicable part of education.'[1]

Beating was not only a prophylactic or a cure, it was regarded as
a concomitant of healthy moral development for it instilled the
acceptance of pain and punishment as an essential part of physical
courage and manhood. 'The great Victorian headmasters were
conscientious floggers, conscientiously whipping virtue in and
vice out. They took their work seriously, believing that they could
achieve by it moral improvement.'[2] Sport was an ally in the battle
against sin. To fill the spare time of the boy with tiring exercises
would counter the temptations of idleness and sex. And the
superior performance of games became too easily in itself a yard-
stick of moral rectitude. But the influence of games goes even
deeper. Cricket, in the famous words of Tom Brown, 'is more
than a game, it's an institution'; 'and it ought to be such an
unselfish game', the master replies, 'it merges the individual in
the eleven, he doesn't play that he may win, but that his side
may.'

The submergence of the individual in this group has also other
consequences. The authority exercised by the masters and by the
older boys over the younger, the emphasis put on good performance in athletics, and later also in scholarship, aims at instilling
discipline and obedience to those in command. It cannot fail to
lead to the admiration of all those who reached the highest rungs
of the ladder, be it in the political or the social field. An educational
system, which puts such a high value on the exercise of individual
superiority—often callous and brutal in its forms—and on the
leadership of the daring and imaginative, and which recognizes
existing social distinctions, is a good training ground for a political
élite in a status society. It has in itself a recognized scale of social
values, depending largely on age, strength and ability. In daily life

---

[1] Thomas Arnold: 'On the discipline of Public Schools', *Journal of Education*,
1835.

[2] T. C. Worsley: *Barbarians and Philistines* (1940), p. 156.

this was reinforced by real social distinctions within the public school community.

By the middle of the nineteenth century the public schools had long ceased to be foundations for poor scholars, yet, together with an increasing number of fee-paying pupils, they still contained a number of scholars who received a free education. These were no longer the children of the poor but the gifted sons of professional men or sometimes of local tradespeople who generally owed their 'election' to the influence of the masters. Whatever their background, they constituted a distinct class and were considered inferior to the fee-paying pupils. These distinctions were the more marked the more aristocratic the character of the school. It was alleviated where, as at Winchester, scholarship was held in high esteem and the scholar, whether Colleger or not, was accorded prestige. Mid-nineteenth-century Eton, on the other hand, showed a decisive rift between oppidans and the boys on the foundation.[1] In the lower school the separation was complete. Menial duties, such as serving at table and holding open doors, had to be performed by them, and their position with regard to sports was a distinctly inferior one.[2]

We must not forget the exclusiveness of the public school as such. While internal reforms had greatly improved the conditions under which scholars at Eton worked and lived they had also raised the social background of the applicants and a place in College became practically the reserve of sons of 'gentlemen'. Internal cohesiveness could only accentuate the feeling of social superiority of Eton as such. 'To be an Etonian was . . . in itself the real social distinction and it was much more firmly believed than it had been earlier that gentle birth both required and produced a higher moral code.'[3] The public schools effectively cut off their pupils from the bulk of the nation's youth. Neither through their

---

[1] 'The "Up Town" collegers, presumably not born in the purple, were heavily handicapped from the first. The sons of Eton masters were received on equal terms but the same privileges were not conceded to the sons of Eton and Windsor doctors or solicitors, royal servants or successful tradesmen. The poor lad was pointed at, he began his career as a pariah . . .' A. D. Coleridge: *Eton in the Forties*, 1898, p. 20. See also the Autobiography of Charles Merivale, privately printed, 1898, p. 36.

[2] cf. James Brinsley-Richards: *Seven Years at Eton (1857–64)*, 1883.

[3] C. Hollis: *Eton: a History*, p. 290.

curricula, nor through any action on the part of the masters, did the public schools attempt to break down the barrier of class prejudice which home surroundings and family tradition had erected. The boys were not taught to despise those who served on them, or the masses of those who perform the productive processes in our society—'they simply ignore them'.[1]

It might be thought that public school training would implant an unduly dominating attitude in its successful members. But we must recognize that the attitude which this education fostered was an essentially ambivalent one. It strengthened both dominance and submission. The boy advanced by the mere process of growing up from fag to fagmaster, and even in the very successful ones there was instilled that constant feeling of loyalty to the school, the tradition and finally his class. The type of boy which the upper class desired to see grow up in the public school was one 'who obeyed implicitly those who were his superiors and who, on the other hand, could command an army or head a government'.[2] 'It was assumed or so it seemed to me', someone who had passed through the public school system has written, 'that every boy would at one time or another be in such position as Viceroy of India and must be brought up with this end in view. . . . The government of the country was somewhat made almost a personal matter.'[3] We can recognize in this sentiment one of the factors which strengthened the feeling of superiority of the ruling class. As a group they believed themselves destined to rule, whatever their exact position in the status system of the public school may have been. They felt that it was only natural that those who ruled the country and administered its empire should be selected from their midst.[4] Seen in the life-cycle of the individual, the school, as a body, took the place of a harsh father who was the product of a similar upbringing, and it educated to loyalty towards the Church, the Monarchy, the Empire or whatever symbols the educational and political system might choose to express the accepted order of things. In the eyes of its members the public school thus assumes

---

[1] A. Ponsonby: *The Decline of Aristocracy*, p. 201.

[2] E. C. Mack: *Public Schools and British Opinion, 1780–1860*, p. 73.

[3] Graham Greene (ed.) *The Old School. Essays by various hands.*

[4] *cf.* G. Greene (ed.) *op. cit.*, and other works quoted. A study of the aspirations of Public School boys is badly needed.

a place much above an ordinary place of education. It embodies the traditions accepted by the class which sends its children there and hands down the social values which they cherish. 'When the call came to me to form a government,' Lord Baldwin declared, 'one of my first thoughts was that it should be a government of which Harrow should not be ashamed. I remembered how in previous governments there had been four or perhaps five Harrovians—and I determined to have six.'[1]

Another thing which the public school implanted in the mind of its pupils was the development of recreational activities. It thus emphasized and further strengthened pursuits which formed an integral part of the life of the country gentleman. During the eighteenth century, the chief pastimes of boys in public schools had been coursing, hunting and gambling. During the nineteenth century, these tended to give way to organized sports, while towards the end of the century attention begins to be paid to purely cultural and aesthetic pursuits. Teaching in nineteenth-century Eton and Harrow was almost exclusively restricted to the classics, its aim was to train intellect rather than prepare the boys for a professional career.[2] And despite the close connection which existed between the public schools and the church—both through their history and through their masters who were mostly ordained clergymen of the established church—little attention was paid to formal religion.

It is this stress on an education for social ease with its emphasis on a purely classical academic training, as well as the great importance of sport, which distinguishes the public school upbringing from the education which the sons of the professional and commercial middle class received elsewhere. The new secondary schools, the Scottish Academies, the new boarding establishments of the nonconformist denominations, like Woodhouse Grove and Wesley College, aimed at an education which was to fit boys for a career in commerce, industry or the professions. They did not seek to prepare them for the older universities, the army or the squirearchy. Consequently, their syllabuses included,

---

[1] Quoted, S. Haxey: *Tory M.P.*, 1939, p. 180.

[2] See Alfred Lyttelton's account of Eton where he excelled both at games and intellectually as portrayed in Edith Lyttelton: *Alfred Lyttelton*, 1917, and Ponsonby, *op. cit.*, pp. 217–24.

from the beginning, modern languages, natural science, history and geography as well as such eminently practical subjects as commercial arithmetic. If they did expect their pupils to proceed to a university, they prepared them more often for London University, and later for one of the newer civic universities, than for Oxford or Cambridge. The old grammar schools adapted themselves in many cases to the changing needs of the times by opening 'modern' departments.

The public school tradition was in some ways carried further in the universities. The connection between an aristocratic background and membership of the ancient universities is too striking to be overlooked. Not a single Cabinet Minister from that class who visited a university failed to go to either Oxford or Cambridge. Indeed of all those who went from the seven old-established public schools to an academic institution, only one failed to pass through an 'Oxbridge' College.

TABLE I

Class and University Education of Cabinet Ministers, 1868–1955:

CLASS

University	Aristo-cracy	Middle Class	Working Class	Tradi-tional Ruling Class	'New Men'	All
Oxford	49	60	1	86	24	110
Cambridge	26	29	1	38	18	56
English Redbrick	—	11	3	1	13	14
Scottish*	—	12	2	—	14	14
Irish and Foreign	—	4	—	—	4	4
All Universities	75	116	7	125	73	198
Not at University	18	43	35	24	72	96
TOTAL	93	159	42	149	145	294

* Those who went to Oxford or Cambridge after they had been to a Scottish University are not enumerated here.

As at a public school it was the social rather than the intellectual side of university life which counted most for the majority of the young aristocrats.

In this social life, it must be borne in mind, political activity and interests played their part. There were the debating societies and the political clubs which propelled their members towards politics. As the nineteenth century advanced, the two Union Societies became increasingly important.[1] In their procedure and in their choice of subjects they reflected the forms and standards set by the House of Commons. Curzon's career in Oxford is a brilliant example of the importance of all this, coupled as it was with low academic attainment in spite of great ability. He was Secretary of the Canning Club and became President of the Union. The connection of the latter office with future political eminence is indeed strong. Of 25 Peers who had been Presidents of the Oxford Union between 1827 and 1894, 13 reached the Cabinet.[2]

Not that Union activity brought immediate political fame or a call to political battle; only occasionally did a reputation made in the Union result in political activity.[3] If political careers started at the university we have to look to social rather than political influences to trace their origin. Ties of friendship and membership of a peer group united the Cambridge men of the 1820's who formed a group of Philosophical Radicals in the Reformed Parliament and the group of Young England on the Tory benches in the House of Commons of the 1840's has a similar origin in the Cambridge of the 1830's. It was a political *friendship* which brought Gladstone into Parliament for Newark, a seat in the gift of the Duke of Newcastle, the father of his friend, Lord Lincoln.

If, as a rule, the older universities failed to make scholars of the young aristocrats who went there, they helped to develop further the tradition of gentlemanly living which had in some way already been incipient in the public school. The keeping of horses, hunting, riding and gaming led the young man to the style of living of the landed squirearchy. The men with whom the future Eighth Duke of Devonshire associated in Cambridge were 'an idle set . . . I scarcely recall any who would be called a reading man

---

[1] *cf.* P. Craddock and others: *Recollections of the Cambridge Union, 1815–1939,* 1953, pp. 74–75.

[2] *cf. The Complete Peerage,* 2nd ed., vol. II, p. 583, for table of Peers who were Presidents during that period.

[3] W. V. Harcourt obtained a post as Leader Writer to the *Daily Chronicle* partly as the result of his Union speeches.

among them. Practically all went out as passmen . . . they were
gentlemen, manly in pursuits and ideas, insouciants, taking life
easily as it came, without ambition and with but little culture . . .'[1]
In their scholastic pursuits the majority of those who studied
seriously for a degree read classics, some chose jurisprudence and
very few mathematics or the natural sciences. Their education
laid thus little foundation for an understanding of the contemporary world. In the very field of political activity—as witnessed
in the Union debates—argument proceeded on a level of gener-
alities and was expressed in ornate phrases and allusive witticisms.
Facts and figures, the dry bones of governmental activity, counted
for little.

The effects of a stay in Oxford or Cambridge must be found in
its character-forming qualities and in the moral influence which
Christian teaching, then an integral part of university life, with
compulsory church attendance and the subscription to the thirty-
nine articles, had on the student. John Manners, writing to his
father from Cambridge, hopes 'that whether I distinguish myself
as a scholar or not I may never, for a single moment, forfeit my
character as a Christian and a man of honour'.[2]

THE INFLUENCE OF LONDON SOCIETY AND OF FAMILY TRADITION

The influence of London 'Society' in facilitating the entry of the
future politician into Parliament must not be underestimated. It
was in the middle of the nineteenth century an essentially political
'Society'—although not in the party-political sense; on the contrary, the two parties mixed freely and its members often inter-
married. We can term this Society 'political' because of the close
connections which existed between the government and the heads
of the socially influential old aristocratic houses. Trevelyan
described London Society as composed of those who were invited
by two or three great political ladies in their 'salons'. The circle
was not exclusively aristocratic, a certain number of 'men of
wealth' were accepted and artists and writers could be 'personae

---

[1] Lord Welby quoted in B. Holland: *The Duke of Devonshire*, vol. I, p. 15.
[2] Whibley, *op. cit.*, vol. I, p. 53.

gratae'. An exception was also generally made in the case of the successful politician, yet when Russell asked Bright to dine in 1866, 'London Society' was outraged.[1] The *aspiring* politician, whether Conservative or Liberal, who was not a member of the right class, was generally excluded from its sphere. Goschen and Asquith and Chamberlain, later such prominent members of London Society, had at first no access to it, neither had James Stansfield or W. H. Smith 'that successful newsvendor'. Yet for the young aristocrat there was no difficulty about gaining entry, and it offered to those whose families might lack the political or territorial influence so necessary for entering the House of Commons, a chance to make themselves known to those who had.[2]

For the aristocratic politician the political tradition of the family is of first-rate importance in determining his entry into politics and the party which he is to support.[3] Following family tradition with respect to party alignments was undoubtedly easier at a time when the differences between the parties were not so marked. In any case, we find among the aristocratic group of Cabinet Ministers only few who, as far as can be ascertained, did not follow in the political tradition of their fathers and their families. Parental ambition and control worked towards the achievement of this end in case it was not forthcoming on its own accord.[4] The young politician was usually dependent on his father's support for his

---

[1] *cf.* G. M. Trevelyan: *Life of John Bright*, p. 354.

[2] Only a minority of non-aristocratic Cabinet Ministers of this period 1868–1916 had entry into London Society before they became members of Parliament. Of the 33 whose pre-parliamentary activities are well documented only 13 moved in the circles of London Society and of these 4 belonged to landowning families and 2 were sons of Cabinet Ministers.

[3] Haldane, though not an aristocrat, comments in the following words on the move of his relative, Lord Camperdown putting his name down for Brooks and for the 'New Club' in Edinburgh. 'I am committed to Whig politics, somewhat prematurely, but this would have been the case sooner or later'. Sir F. Maurice: *Life of Haldane*, vol. I, p. 26.

[4] See the following quotation from a letter of Sir Charles Trevelyan, father of G. O. Trevelyan. 'An opening will, I hope, soon occur for his getting into Parliament. You know how much I have it at heart. It will be much the best for him, and I do not think it will be bad for the public—to give up his whole life to public affairs.' G. M. Trevelyan: *G. O. Trevelyan, a Memoir*, p. 64.

political activity, and opposition by the son to the political aspirations of the father could endanger this support.[1]

The membership of political families is so significant a feature of the political careers of members of the aristocracy that it must be discussed here more fully. It is naturally and logically connected with the territorial predominance of so many landed families in their county or in parts of it. Indeed in many cases we find that the combination of long lineage and long-standing ancestral political activity is a greater claim to distinction than old titles and coronets. The Longs in the 1870's held nearly 14,000 acres in Wiltshire (and small estates in Somerset and Merionethshire) worth over £23,000 per annum. Three successive generations of Longs represented Wiltshire throughout the nineteenth century and altogether 73 members of the Long family had sat in the House of Commons.

Parliamentary activity did frequently descend like a title—if not actually with it. Sons succeeded their fathers as 'Knights of the Shire' or borough representatives at the latter's death or retirement. This was especially so in the unreformed House of Commons. Of 5,034 M.P.s who sat in Parliament between 1734 and 1832, 3,045 belonged to 922 families and, of these, 247 families could claim 1,527 M.P.s. Indeed there were 31 families who had sent a total of 382 men into the House of Commons.[2]

Among Cabinet Members the concentration is not quite so marked although between 1832 and 1955 we can find four Greys, five Cecils and five Stanleys as members of successive Cabinets. Families furnishing two or three cabinet members also belonged almost invariably to the aristocracy. In the group of middle-class politicians, only the Chamberlains constitute something like a dynasty with three Cabinet Ministers, but even here political leadership is confined to two generations. If we define political activity more widely and include, apart from office holding, all parliamentary service in the House of Commons, as well as regular

---

[1] Salisbury's father threatened to stop paying his son's election expenditure if he did persist in his attacks on the administration. Lady G. Cecil, *op. cit.*, vol. I, pp. 85–95.

[2] *cf.* G. P. Judd, *Members of Parliament, 1734–1832*, p. 33. Judd defined a family group as two or more M.P.s who were descended from a common great-grandfather.

activity in the House of Lords, we also find the close connection between the membership of titled families and the political activity of members of successive generations.

TABLE II

Social Class and Membership of Political Families:

(a) CABINET, 1868–1955

	All	Aristocracy	Middle Class	Working Class
Father *or* Grandfather politically active	50	27	22	1
Father *and* Grandfather politically active		41	2	—
None		25	135	41
TOTAL		93	159	42

(b) UNDER-SECRETARIES, 1868–1945

	All	Aristocracy	Middle Class	Working Class
Father *or* Grandfather politically active	23	20	3	—
Father *and* Grandfather politically active	24	24	—	—
None	60	14	36	10
TOTAL	107	58	39	10

Yet political families are not just synonymous with titled families; there are among the Peerage, and even more among landed families as such, many whose members rarely, if ever, enter Parliament or otherwise occupy a prominent position in politics. This emerges clearly from the analysis of a sample of 100 families in the British Peerage in which the title descended uninterruptedly between 1800 and 1900.[1] Counting only those who

---

[1] Based on *The Complete Peerage*, 2nd Edition.

became Peers, we find the following distribution of political activity.

TABLE III

Political Activity in the British Peerage, 1800–1900*

Number of families where no Peers are known to have been politically active	31
Number of families where only one peer in three or more was politically active	18
Number of families where between one-third and two-thirds of the Peers were politically active	17
Number of families where two thirds or more (but fewer than all) of the Peers were politically active	19
Number of families where all Peers were politically active	15
	100

* The total number of Peers involved was 354.

The tradition of political activity in a man's family affects his career in two ways. It facilitates his advancement in the political arena, because an illustrious name enhances his reputation and influential members of his family can assist him in climbing the rungs of the political ladder.[1] But it also helps to determine a man's career on the subjective plane. The political activity and prominent position of an ancestor influences the entry into politics of the young descendant by raising the level of his aspiration, or by turning it to politics. Two political careers throw some light on this.

Edward Grey was very much influenced by his grandfather, Sir George Grey, a member of Russell's and Palmerston's cabinets who supervised his education as Grey's father had died when his son was twelve years old. Temperamentally Edward Grey was unsuited to the political sphere and, on his own admission, felt much more at home and at ease on his estates looking after his birds, than in the House of Commons. At election time he secretly wished for defeat.[2] What kept him in politics was a strong sense of duty, which seems, however, born rather out of an inability to

---

[1] This phenomenon is discussed further in Chapter VIII below.
[2] G. M. Trevelyan: *Life of Grey*, p. 66.

break away from a course once adopted than from any concept of a positive aim.[1]

The relationship between Balfour and his uncle, the Marquess of Salisbury, seems similarly to have transcended the traditional family relationship transferred to the political scene. Balfour had entered the House of Commons with the help of the Cecil family. He not only acted as the confidential agent of Salisbury and as his go-between with some sections of the party, but he was also for-ever deferential to his wishes. In 1885 his uncle put him at the head of the Local Government Board, where he was not a great success. Very sensitive to any criticism and afraid of being again a failure he was rather reluctant to accept office in 1886. 'Unless I can be of use,' he wrote to his cousin, 'I do not wish to be mixed up in the formation of the new government. . . . I feel no natural vocation for being a great man's great man, still less for being thought so. . . .' yet he would be prepared to come up to London if he thought he 'could be of the slightest use to uncle Robert.'[2] The political activities of Balfour and Grey, both members of political families, seem more determined by emotional attach-ment and tradition than by the 'inevitableness' of a political career which we find in the aristocratic politician of an older generation. Both often expressed a desire to leave politics for a vocation more congenial to them. Both had hobbies and interests outside the political field which absorbed much of their energy. If defeated, Balfour said on the occasion of an election, he would give up politics for philosophy.[3]

Rooted in family tradition and in the identification with a ruling élite which their public school upbringing had instilled in them, the aristocratic politicians entered into the political sphere as into their natural milieu. If they thus took their parliamentary career too much for granted we must not forget that they approached it often with great seriousness. And that sense of responsibility and feeling of service derives in no small part from their religious beliefs.

---

[1] He was unwilling to enter Campbell-Bannerman's cabinet because he adhered to the terms of the 'Relugas compact' after his two co-conspirators, Asquith and Haldane, had already expressed their willingness to serve.

[2] B. E. C. Dugdale: *Life of A. J. Balfour*, vol. I, p. 107–8.

[3] For Balfour's intellectual make-up and lack of clear-cut convictions see Beatrice Webb's sketches of him in *Our Partnership*.

THE INFLUENCE OF RELIGION

In the language of the aristocratic politician the phrase 'public duty' recurs frequently. The institutional basis of this has been discussed earlier, but its basis in individual morality cannot be ignored. Among the forces that influenced the formation of this concept in the nineteenth century the religious tradition of both Evangelicalism and of the High Church ranks high. Evangelicalism had a hold on a section of the traditional élite, comparable in strength to the influence which dissent had on a part of the classes below them. It roused the individual conscience and made man aware of his responsibility to work out his own salvation by manifestations of religious faith and by moral action. G. W. E. Russell, a nephew of the Prime Minister, who had experienced its influence, recalled 'an abiding sense of religious responsibility, an evangelizing zeal, an aloofness from the world and a level of saintliness in daily life'.[1] Such an attitude is very different from that 'latitudinarianism' if not 'laxity' in religious matters which prevailed in the circles of the aristocracy during the eighteenth century.[2]

If Evangelicals desired reform it was not because of charitable feelings, such as we find in the High Church men like John Manners. It was rather because they thought that existing abuses prevented men from reaching the state of grace, which could only be the outcome of individual piety and moral conduct. It was one of the tenets of Evangelicalism to frown on wealthy pleasures and all manifestations of luxury and ostentatiousness. Among the politicians who were influenced by the teachings of Evangelicalism, we find men like Trevelyan (whose father belonged to the Clapham sect), Grey, and in certain respects, Northcote, whose public and political life is characterized by a moral seriousness and devotion to duty which is possibly surpassed only by some of the nonconformist politicians whose careers will be examined later. And their private lives, although still in line with that of their class, are distinguished by a comparative simplicity and an absence of that ostentatious style of living which was so pronounced among

---

[1] G. W. E. Russell: *A Household of Faith*, p. 23. Quoted in Charles Smythe: 'The Evangelical Movement in Perspective', *Cambridge Historical Journal*, vol. VII, pp. 160–74 at p. 165.

[2] cf. E. Wingfield-Stratford: *The Squire and his Relations*, 1956, pp. 303–5.

another section of the same class. In this, I believe, we can see the result of that evangelical faith which as Halévy put it 'invested the British aristocracy with almost stoic dignity [and] restrained the plutocrats from vulgar ostentation and debauchery'.[1]

Evangelicalism was not alone in instilling a sense of public duty in the aristocratic politician; High-Churchmanship, especially as manifested in the romantic revival of the Oxford Movement and Tractarianism, induced it from another angle. The Oxford reformers built on Evangelical foundations. 'I believe all that you believe,' Pusey had told the Evangelicals, 'we only part where you deny.' The Tractarians were not content with their predecessors' belief in the power of individual faith; feeling alone was not sufficient. The Oxford Movement and its successors had renewed interest in questions of dogma and Christian morality. And this, linked with a romantic sensibility, caused the founders to stress the significance of ritual and form of worship.

Their theology found application in the field of politics. John Manners and George Smythe hoped for a rejuvenation of the body politic under the benevolent despotism of a Christian king. 'Complete the vision of old days when I beg that we may sit by each other in the new Parliament. . . . I believe that the government of the one is for the good of the many . . . from Monarchy results the Commonwealth, from oligarchy, oligarchy, from democracy a tyranny.'[2] Gladstone, although not a member of an aristocratic family, must be mentioned here because of his close connections with aristocratic High Church circles. Originally brought up in the evangelical movement, he was later engrossed in the idea of the Church as an institution through which salvation is achieved.[3] The particular forms in which he held his belief on the relationship between religion and politics and of a state with its membership restricted to the members of the Church and with a conscience borrowed from it, do give way, in the course of time, to a broader concept, but one where the political principles are based on Christian morality. 'I venture to say,' he declared in the House of Commons much to its surprise and to the annoyance of Palmerston, 'that every man who is not presumably incapacitated by some

---

[1] E. Halévy: *History of the English People, 1830–41*, p. 166.
[2] Smythe to Manners, quoted in Whibley, *op. cit.*, vol. I, p. 136.
[3] *cf.* E. Eyck: *Life of Gladstone*, p. 28–29.

consideration of personal unfitness is morally entitled to come within the pale of the constitution.'[1]

During the Reform crisis and the period of agricultural unrest in the early 1830's these Oxford dons and rural clergymen had ranked themselves solidly behind the defenders of the existing order.[2] A generation later the Conservatism of their successors was strengthened by the threat of disestablishment.[3] Salisbury had come under the influence of the 'movement' while at Oxford. The foundation of his belief was the acceptance of the mystery of creation and existence; the moral doctrines of Christianity appealed to him not on *a priori* grounds but on account of their spiritual authority. Such a concept must lead to a quietist attitude to life and to fatalistic acceptance of the status quo.[4] This belief helped to strengthen his opposition to the extension of the franchise. The existing social order of society was to him pre-ordained, only voluntary acts by individuals, not state action, could change and improve things. Conflict should thus be avoided. His opposition to the electoral claims of the working class entailing for him, as we saw, the threat of a conflict between Capital and Labour, did not arise in the pursuit of personal or general material considerations. He opposed the bill because he felt it was his 'duty to [oppose] every bill which in my opinion involves great danger to the state'.[5]

---

[1] *ibid.*, p. 155.

[2] *cf.* G. Faber: *Oxford Apostles* (Penguin edition, 1954) pp. 240–5.

[3] For a career which started with official activity in the Scottish Church see Lady Frances Balfour: *Lord Balfour of Burleigh, a Memoir*, 1925.

[4] 'What folly,' Salisbury wrote, 'to shape our conduct to a rule of which it is quite clear that it is precisely an even chance whether it takes us with God or exactly against Him.'—G. Cecil, *op. cit.*

[5] G. Cecil, *op. cit.*, p. 26.

Formative Influences and Attitude to Politics: The Case of the Middle Class

Give us concessions,' say the Radicals, 'and you may keep your places as long as you like.' 'Give us our place,' say Mr Disraeli and Lord John Russell with a single breath, 'and we will squeeze for you what concessions we can out of our reluctant followers.'—LORD SALISBURY in *Bentley's Quarterly*.

'British Revolutions are made by British Churchwardens. That's why they have been successful.'—ELLEN WILKINSON: *Clash*.

'The dialectic of internal politics is the conversion of a ruled class into collaborators in the art of ruling.'—R. G. COLLINGWOOD: *The New Leviathan*.

THE convictions and careers of middle-class politicians are presented here in a manner analogous to that employed for the aristocratic politicians. Our understanding of the 'new men' in the political élite will be heightened by the study of their careers in the context of some of the institutions which shaped their lives and influenced their entry into politics. Their attitude to the task of governing, and their involvement in the game of politics were very different in character from those which we found among the politicians from the traditional ruling class. They must be seen against the background of the social and cultural milieu from which they sprang.

It is as important to set the rise of the middle-class politician against the background of urban politics, as it is to see it as a stage in the upward social drive of a new class, which contains men who are anxious to add the cachet of political service to the cash which their enterprise had brought them. We would also neglect an important facet of the character of the British political élite, if we failed to investigate the connection between the intellectuals and the ideological aspect of politics, especially their identification with new ideas and with political and social reforms. These tended to lead them to identify with the parties of the Left, but it showed itself also in the Conservative Party.

BACKGROUND OF RISING MEN

Compared with the group of aristocratic Cabinet Ministers, middle-class politicians show a much greater heterogeneity of origin, occupation and wealth. They range from the country solicitor to the large non-titled landowner, from the *nouveau riche* to the member of old-established families. The division of the middle ranges of the political élite into those who belong to the 'traditional ruling strata' and the 'new men' meets this problem to some extent, and it is with the latter group that we are predominantly concerned in this section. But formal dividing lines can occasionally mislead, education in one of the exclusive public schools does sometimes follow closely on the rapid rise of a father from obscurity to affluence, and marks the *nouveau riche* character of a family. I have deliberately drawn on the life histories and political careers of men from all sections of the middle class who exhibited the characteristics prevalent among the *new* men in the political leadership.

These 'new men' are almost by definition a rising social group, but the upward social mobility within our group can be described rather than defined. We can trace it for many of these families through a few generations, but it is impossible to show it with the degree of exactness which would make it amenable to statistical treatment. We can, however, tabulate the greater variety of occupations among the parental generation of this group and thus show the extent of inter-generational mobility.

The connection between the rise of the new middle class, and the rise of its individual members, to positions of political eminence and leadership has had considerable influence on the attitude of the middle-class politician to politics. Men who came from hitherto submerged groups and whose own career was bound up with individual exertion or general social and economic changes

TABLE I

'New Men' in the Political Elite as a rising social group, 1868–1955:

Occupation	Fathers	Sons
Rentier	3	11
Services, Diplomacy, Civil Service	8	11
Clergymen, C. of E.	6	—
Barristers	7	34
Solicitors	7	7
Physicians, Surgeons	4	2
Teachers (Public School, Grammar School)	1	2
University Teachers	1	10
Journalists, Authors	5	9
Engineers, Chemists, Physicists	4	1
Accountant, Surveyor	1	1
Non-conformist Ministers	9	—
Elementary School Teacher	1	1
Works Chemist	1	—
Banking and Commerce	15	\
Industry (Entrepreneur)	12	} 23
Industry (Manager)	1	2
Estate Agent	1	—
Shopkeepers	2	—
Clerks	2	—
Tradesmen, Artisans	7	—
Skilled and Unskilled Workers	31	2
Farmers	2	—
Ranks in Army or Police	2	—
Officials of Trade Unions, etc.	—	29
Not known	12	2
TOTAL	145	145

were, as a rule, emotionally and intellectually less involved in the maintenance of the social and political *status quo* than those from the ranks above them. Their membership of religious and ethnic minority groups is another significant phenomenon. The politicians who belong to what I have termed the 'traditional ruling

class' are almost invariably adherents of the Church of England;
the 'new men' on the other hand, have strong affiliations with
non-conformity or other minority denominations. Nearly one-
half of those middle-class politicians who were neither landowners
nor the products of the seven most high-ranking public schools,
belonged to families who professed dissent, Roman Catholicism
or Judaism. Their religious beliefs were often important factors in
the shaping of their political career.

TABLE II

Religious Affiliations in the Group of Middle-Class Cabinet
Ministers, 1868–1955:

Religious Denomination	Traditional Ruling Class	'New Men'	Total
Not known	8	19	27
Church of England	50	41	91
Church of Scotland ⎫ Scottish Free Churches ⎭	—	13	13
Roman Catholic	—	2	2
Methodist	—	5	5
Congregationalist	—	5	5
Baptist	—	3	3
Unitarian	3	1	4
Quaker	—	5	5
Other dissenters	—	4	4
Jewish	—	5	5
TOTAL	61	103	164

A third factor influenced the attitude of middle-class politicians.
For want of a better term,[4] I intend to call it intellectualism. It
influenced particularly the attitude of *professional men* to politics.
We can obviously not just equate the latter with the intelligentsia,
conceived as a spiritually creative section of the community, composed of individuals who tend to discuss problems rationally and
critically, and who seek new insights and ideas and their expression
and dissemination. When considering the social structure of the
country in the period under discussion, we expect to find the

intellectuals mainly among the university-educated and in the ranks of professional men, especially among those whose professional career is least regulated: the lawyer, the person following an academic career and the 'free-lance', some of whom, may be thought to have a vested interest in intellectual pursuits.[1]

One-third of the Cabinet Membership between 1868 and 1955 had followed a professional career, mostly in the legal field; professionals account for nearly a half of the 'new men' in the political élite. The fathers of some of these men belonged to the lower ranks of the professions, others had been businessmen in a small way. The educational career of their sons progressed frequently via the grammar school to the university and their advance was often marked by scholarships, which they needed, and by prizes which they gained. Their comparative poverty was probably a spur to hard work. Yet perseverance alone did not make them what they were; many did clearly owe their successful professional career to outstanding mental equipment.[2]

Not all of them were 'mere' professionals. Many made their mark as authors and scholars, an even greater number engaged in that serious and well-paid pastime of the nineteenth century politician: writing for the periodicals. Indeed, in a few cases their contribution to the thought of their period is clearly of greater significance than the mark which they made as politicians.

Political activity as a stage in the process of upward social mobility, membership of minority groups (especially of those suffering under strongly felt disabilities or identifying *with* such groups) and intellectualism as an attitude of mind are the three most obvious characteristics which emerge from the social analysis of the middle class in politics. At the same time they distinguish these men from the aristocracy or the members of the traditional ruling class as a whole. Admittedly, we are not concerned with

[1] *i.e.* Karl Mannheim's *Freischwebende Intelligenz.*

[2] Academic Distinctions in the groups of Cabinet Ministers: 1886–1916. Middle Class Professional Men and Aristocratic Landowners compared.

	Middle Class Professionals	Aristocratic Landowners
At University.. ..	20	34
Distinctions	10	3
All Cabinet Ministers in category	24	40

completely independent mutually exclusive forces. The three institutional factors which influence the careers of middle-class politicians and their attitude to politics are obviously not isolated social phenomena. They are, on the contrary, often intimately connected. Socially and emotionally non-conformity was the religion of the less well to do. It was from the middle class and later from the working class that portions of the élite groups in a developing economy and an expanding empire were to be drawn. And in this general process of upward social mobility, the professions were important avenues—and incidentally have remained so ever since. The three factors also interpenetrate on the level of the individual personality. Attitudes to politics and factors motivating a man's career do not fall into neat pigeonholes, but the social climbers, the disinherited and the intellectuals, are sufficiently marked types to justify further analysis.

Here, too, personal testimony will be used as the basis of documentation, but the character of an individual's pre-parliamentary political activity and the means by which he gained entry into the House of Commons, afford corroborating evidence. The politician from a disinherited group is often to be found in the leadership of local and national reform movements long before he enters Parliament, while the climber will seek and find honorific status enhancing public activities to pave his way into Parliament. Both he and the intellectual tend to be parliamentary 'carpet-baggers', but while the one uses personal influence, the other succeeds often because of the reputation he had established for himself at the centre. A seat in Parliament becomes a reward for services given to his party as speaker and propagandist.[1]

[1] Businessmen, Rentiers and Professional Men in Cabinets, 1886–1916, Association with Constituency:

Mode of securing entry into the House of Commons	Business-men	Rentiers	Professionals	Total
Personal influence	6	1	5	12
Influence of friends	1	1	7	9
Offered self as candidate	2	—	1	3
Through Central Party Organization or invited	2	3	9	14
Not known	1	—	3	4
TOTAL..	12	5	25*	42

POLITICS AND STATUS-SEEKING

For some men political activity is a means of securing a higher status in society than that which they could expect to reach through their occupation. The mid-nineteenth-century House of Commons, largely aristocratic in character, offered its non-aristocratic members the opportunity for assimilation into a higher social class and opened the way to honours, titles and offices. While the type of the 'social climber' is not unknown among lawyers and professionals, it is most common among entrepreneurs and businessmen. In the middle of the nineteenth century, merchants and industrialists were not yet automatically accepted into 'Society'. The mere money-making activity of manufacture or trade was still regarded as taboo. Landownership, the Army and above all politics, were, of course, a way of ridding oneself of these stigmas and were the means of gaining entry into polite 'Society'. This prejudice against mercenary activities extended to the very process of entry into politics. W. H. Smith, the newsagent, found it difficult to recruit a committee when he contested Westminster for the first time in 1865, in spite of the fact that he was prepared to finance the election entirely himself.[1]

The attitude which regards political activity as a means of achieving status expresses itself in a variety of forms. For one we can observe a flexibility—if not laxity—in all matters of political principles, coupled with a rational approach to one's own performance in politics and a lack of squeamishness in the choice of political weapons. For status-seekers, political purism is a definite encumbrance on the path to success in politics, especially if they have no chance to obtain recognition as popular leaders, because they either lack the talents of an orator or have no connection with one of the large urban constituencies with a democratic electorate.

[1] *cf.* Sir H. Maxwell: *The Life and Times of the Rt Hon. W. H. Smith*, vol. I, p. 124.

---

* Includes one Cabinet Minister of working class origins.

These figures refer to the individual's first attempt at entering Parliament. Because of this the 'carpet-bagging' nature of the political career of professional men is not sufficiently brought out. Others than those listed had to seek the support of the party machine to secure election.

Next we can notice a craving for recognition, through office, honour or in a social setting, and finally a certain insistence on one's own dignity in political activity.[1]

Where the biographic data allow us to draw any conclusions about the intensity with which office is expected by the individual, we find that the non-aristocratic member generally shows a greater emotional concern on the occasion of Cabinet formation. Yet even here the concern for dignity is often only too apparent. An episode from the life of H. H. Fowler, 1st Baron Wolverhampton is illuminating. Disclosing to Fowler his place in the 1892 Liberal Government, Morley told him: ' "You will be disappointed but I have done all I could." My father asked but one question: "Is it the Cabinet?" "Of course, but . . ." He had fairly expected a post in the first rank,' his daughter has told us, 'and the Presidency of the Local Government Board was offered to him.'[2]

To illustrate the rise in social position which entry into Parliament entailed, we may quote from a letter of Goschen Senior to his son. 'I wish you joy from all my heart' [he wrote on the occasion of Goschen's election for the City of London] 'really in some respect this election is the very end of all my endeavours and aspirations; for up to this mark I may say that part of your success has had its origin in those things which I have been able to perform, for instance your position in society and in the commercial world. Henceforth you will owe every future success to yourself alone as far as public life is concerned . . .'[3] In the letter just quoted Goschen Senior doubts the wisdom of his son's proclaiming his political principles with such explicitness. This, he thought, could be a burden later. The son certainly shows a rational attitude to his own parliamentary performance as the following extract from his diary, referring to his resolution to intervene in a debate

---

[1] Hermann Kantorowicz, in his analysis of the spirit of British politics, has made an illuminating comparison of the influence of the two ideals, chivalry and dignity, on (national) character and political conduct. He contrasts the gentleman ideal, based on the former, with that of the Prussian Officer, whose code reflects the latter, but he recognizes that the two ideals may be found within the same person. See his *The Spirit of British Foreign Policy*, 1931. Chapter I, especially pp. 72–77.

[2] Edith Fowler: *Life of H. H. Fowler*, p. 254.

[3] A. R. D. Elliott: *Life of Goschen*, vol. I, p. 50.

in 1878, shows, ' . . . arrived mad with anger at Cross's speech and declared that I would insult him . . . I . . . had one of my greatest oratorical successes. I was never more congratulated. It is a speech which will help me very much in the House . . .'[1]

The circumstances of a man's entry into the House of Commons are an indication of his attitude to politics. W. H. Smith clearly sought recognition and status when he attempted to get elected. At the beginning of his career he followed the political tradition of his father, who was an ardent Wesleyan and a Liberal. But after he had twice failed to obtain nomination as a Liberal candidate he changed his politics and in 1865 stood as Liberal/Conservative in Westminster where he was to be successful in 1868. This change in his political conviction followed closely on the refusal of the Reform Club to elect him a member. Campbell-Bannerman's entry into Parliament was not preceded by previous experience or interest in politics, and he had not given any indication of his political convictions. He stood as a self-styled 'advanced Liberal' at a sudden by-election for Dunfermline, where the family had business connections and he took a Glasgow lawyer with him as his election agent.

While isolated incidents serve only as indications of the attitude which I intend to describe, Campbell-Bannerman's whole career offers an example of status-seeking and insistence on dignity in the group of politicians from the middle classes. His entry into politics seemed dictated by reasons other than interest in particular policies or a desire to effect reforms. During his political career he did not usually put forward any new ideas. He desired secure enjoyment of his position rather than political strife, an attitude which can be observed in his behaviour in Parliament and in office. After his election he did not speak for a year and then for a long time he spoke on Scottish and administrative matters only. In 1880 he accepted, without demur, his old post as Financial Secretary to the War Office which he had relinquished in 1874. This in spite of the fact that other ex-junior Ministers were promoted and comparative newcomers stepped straight into higher office. When in office, he was a loyal subordinate, without a personal axe to grind, consolidating the policy of his predecessor rather than carrying out

[1] Elliott, *op. cit.*, vol. I, pp. 183-5.

any new measures. When asked to contest a less safe constituency in Glasgow he retorted: 'Still I am not going to run my head against a stone wall. I have said I should require very full information before even attempting it.'[1] Whether in office or in opposition, the enjoyment of his holidays, of activities outside Parliament, were of the greatest importance to him. He laid great stress on the spending of a long holiday abroad each year, went frequently on short trips to Paris and, in the autumn, a stay of three months in Scotland was regarded as essential for the nursing of his constituency.

He felt deeply and genuinely hurt by any interference with his holiday plans even on occasions, when, as Leader of the Party, his presence in London was regarded as vital. At the time of the Transvaal crisis, he was finally persuaded to return to London from the Continent. Having consulted with his colleagues he went off again, to Paris, where he was staying on the day of President Kruger's ultimatum. On the other hand, we find that he valued highly any token of Royal favour in which he saw a sign of confidence in himself—an attitude which we find well expressed on the occasion of his receiving a knighthood. His concern with position rather than principle comes out very strongly in his conduct of political business. He loathed writing and speaking and, in preparation of his speeches made one speech carry over into another. Likewise he was not a ready debater. On the other hand, he spent much time in cultivating the relation with his constituency and engaged frequently in behind-the-scenes manoeuvres. It is in crisis situations, like the split over the Boer War, that we find examples of his conciliatory attitude, his insistence on party unity and attempts at finding unifying formulas rather than making clear-cut political decisions. Yet while insisting on unity, and paying lip-service to the need for realignment with Rosebery, he avoided any public indication that he might be prepared to serve under him. He was altogether a good hater, despite his delight in personal friendship, and men whom he disliked he labelled with bitter epithets. Thus Haldane was for him always 'Master' Haldane. Never a fluent speaker he became ruffled by encountering animosity. 'He felt deeply certain forms of attack which he believed were intended

---

[1] J. A. Spender: *Life of Sir H. Campbell-Bannerman*, vol. I, p. 174.

to damage him and to attack his dignity.'[1] According to all observers a change came over him once he became Prime Minister. He acquired security in parliamentary debates and his bearing showed both dignity and decisiveness.

Among the group of professional men in the political élite, we find a counterpart of the status-seeking businessmen in the legal careerist who held legal office and sat in the Cabinet either by virtue of office, or for personal rather than political reasons. These men came almost entirely from the new middle class and entered the House of Commons mostly at a fairly advanced age.[2] Before their election to Parliament they rarely show a deep interest in political issues, nor do they have many hobbies or interests outside their work at the Bar. Their entry into Society seems to take place only after becoming members of Parliament. For them politics is a career which would complement their professional activity and perhaps help them to enter on the lucrative career of a Law Officer, with the prospect of a pension for life if the Woolsack was reached. Failing that, a judgeship as the reward for faithful services to the party was not out of the question. When suggested to succeed the retiring speaker, Farrer Herschell (later Lord Chancellor Herschell) consulted Lord Selbourne whether the acceptance of the Speakership '. . . would prove an absolute bar to eventual promotion to the Woolsack'.[3]

A legal career in the Government, with the Woolsack, a high judicial appointment or other position at the end of it was thought to be within the reach of the loyal 'Party Advocate', the lawyer who represented the party in election petitions. That, indeed, was the career of some of them before they entered the House of Commons. Their period as backbenchers tended to be very brief. Six out of eight men whose career in the governments between 1886 and 1916 was entirely or mostly legal were appointed Solicitor General or Attorney General within four years from the day their party

[1] Spender, *op cit.*, vol. II, p. 52.
[2] Of the 33 men who held the office of Solicitor General between 1868 and 1955 only thirteen had entered Parliament before the age of forty. Of the group, twelve ended their career on the bench and nine as Lord Chancellors. Only nine can be described as leading party politicians, who had a general career in ministerial office.
[3] D.N.B. article on Lord Herschell.

came into power. Lord Halsbury was given his first legal appointment before he had found a place in the House of Commons. Before entering on his duties as Lord Chancellor—an appointment freely criticized at the time—he had already made preparations for a successor in his constituency, by sending his friend Webster to take his place.

In other cases politics may be conceived as a way out of the impasse created by a comparatively unsuccessful professional career. Gathorne Hardy, the future Lord Cranbrook, had practised with mixed success at the Parliamentary Bar. At the age of thirty he took stock of his prospect. He wrote in his diary that 'Cardwell was urging me yesterday to attempt Parliament but for what place and with what interest am I to do it? Bradford [his home town] closed for the next election and no other place open . . . and after all, am I to give up Parliamentary business if it should come my way? Again, what would my father say? That I should like it I am sure but as to duty . . .?'[1] Yet after contesting Bradford unsuccessfully in 1847 he did not stand again until 1856 when the death of his father had left him provided for and he had been refused silk for the second time in his legal career. At the beginning of that year he still hopes for preferment at the Bar. 'If Watson should succeed Park there may be a move on Circuit that might open the Q.C. ranks to me.'[2] Six weeks later he is in Parliament. He had read of a vacancy for Leominster and 'noting that a week had elapsed since so there would have been time for other candidates to come forward I hastened to town and put my irons in the fire . . .'[3]

Politics is here conceived clearly as a way of life, a profession with few material perquisites attached to it. This aspect of the political career is, of course, of particular importance in the ranks of 'Society'. A comparative newcomer to Society, who is accepted but lacks economic position and material independence, might well seek to add the profession of one to the pleasures of the other. Yet in just such a case the House of Commons was not always easily reached. Although Duff Cooper was ex-Eton and ex-Oxford

---

[1] A. E. Gathorne-Hardy: *Gathorne Hardy, A Memoir*, vol. I, p. 58.
[2] *ibid.*, vol. I, p. 98.
[3] *ibid.*, vol. I, p. 99.

his economic and social status was well below that of the daughter
of the Duke of Rutland whom he married. As a Foreign Office
Clerk, with a salary of about £300 and a somewhat larger private
income he was hardly equipped to embark on a political career.
Yet, although he advanced slowly in the Foreign Office hierarchy
he 'had never ceased to cherish the hope of sometime becoming a
member of Parliament'. As the years passed, the hope grew.[1] It
soon became a central idea in his life. 'All these days' he wrote in
his diary at the end of 1922 'our minds, Diana's and mine, have
been occupied with one subject which we call "the plan". Briefly
it is that we should go to America in order that she may, in a few
years, make a large fortune at the films. It involves me giving up
the Foreign Office. The idea is that when we come back I should
stand for Parliament . . .'[2]

Whether Duff Cooper was looking at Parliament also as a place
through which office could be obtained—and with office a much
larger income than in the Civil Service—we do not know. But
even in the twentieth century, when the opportunities opened up
by a political career were so much less than earlier, the purely
economic motive for a parliamentary career should not be overlooked. Moore-Brabazon was a Conservative 'for the thoroughly
unsatisfactory reason that my father was Conservative before me
and his father before him so it never entered my head to stand
under any other colour'.[3] He entered Parliament to regain the old
high position which he had held in the aircraft industry and which
had become overshadowed through the development of flying
during the war.[4] His political activity was clearly subordinate to his
economic one. When in 1937 he was offered the Under-Secretaryship for Air he had to refuse because 'I couldn't afford to accept
with the surtax ruining you at any moment. . . . If I were to take
the post I should be bankrupt in a year and lose my seat and my
company positions.'[5]

We are here straddling the borderline between the approach to
politics which conceives political leadership and parliamentary

---

[1] A. Duff Cooper: *Old Men Forget*, 1953, p. 110.
[2] *ibid.*, p. 110.
[3] Lord Brabazon: *The Brabazon Story*, 1956, p. 105, and 97.
[4] *ibid.*, p. 105.
[5] Brabazon, *op. cit.*, p. 181.

activity as a calling and one which looks upon it as a job.[1] The
career of the middle-class politician demonstrates this dichotomy
to a more marked extent than that of the politician from the traditional ruling strata. With few exceptions he followed an occupation
before he entered politics, and he often continued in it while in
Parliament. His political activity, unlike that of the aristocrat,
often entailed material sacrifice and was an alternative to other and
possibly very lucrative pursuits. To undertake it, a strong moral
motivation or a feeling of injustice may be needed. At the same
time politics may be regarded as a career, in the strictly material
sense, but more significantly perhaps, it will be conceived as a
profession with a corresponding sense of purpose and concept of
duty. Some facets of the ethos of the middle-class politician are
studied below.[2]

DISQUALIFICATIONS AND DRIVE

Among the group of the 'disinherited', who enter political life
largely because they had experienced disqualifications and injuries,
and had laboured under disadvantages, dissenters occupy a place
of special importance. Their attitude to politics was characterized
not only by their attempts to remove the injustices under which
they were suffering, but also by the singleness of purpose with
which they pursued political goals, and by their devotion to
political activity, even where the latter is subordinated to personal
ends, such as the search for status.

The disqualifications which affected dissenters until well into
the second half of the nineteenth century can be subsumed under
a number of specific headings and one general phenomenon. Discrimination extended mainly to the religious and the educational
field. Their agitation was directed against the religious Establishment, the discrimination in public schools and universities and
against the support of Church schools out of State funds as the
result of the 1870 Education Act. These were acute grievances of

[1] The most penetrating analysis of this distinction has been made in Max
Weber's celebrated essay 'Politik als Beruf' (1919). It has been translated as
'Politics as a Vocation' in H. Gerth and C. W. Mills (eds.) *From Max Weber,
Essays,* 1947.

[2] This general discussion is continued on pp. 373–377 below.

a clearly definable character. In addition, the whole body of dissent shared the memory of a socially ostracized minority. John Morley, the son of a man who had once followed dissent, quotes approvingly Birrell's statement: ' "that it has always been hard in England to be a Non-conformist" ', and he goes on to say that 'it demanded an effort and was to be cutting yourself off, not from the fountains of holiness, but from the main current of secular national life.'[1]

The second half of the nineteenth century is the age of non-conformist parliamentary activity and eminence. To bring dissent into the political arena needed not only the repeal of the Test Acts, accomplished in 1828, but a change of attitude on the part of the organized non-conformist communities. Officially Methodism advocated right into the Victorian age a quietist, if not outright conservative attitude in political matters.[2] It needed the pressure of minority opinion inside the Methodist Connexion to make a new departure possible. Edward Miall, editor of the influential weekly *The Non-conformist* founded the 'Dissenters Parliamentary Committee' in 1847, to oppose Russell's Education Bill. Under the Chairmanship of Samuel Morley it sought strenuously to get non-conformists selected as candidates for Parliament. The body was relatively successful and the House of Commons elected in that year contained 26 members opposed to the link between Church and State, the majority of whom were dissenters. After that date the numbers increased steadily. By 1852 the 'anti-State Church' M.P.s numbered 38, in 1868 there were 95 (of whom 63 were Protestant Dissenters). Then and for a long time to come their political affiliations were almost exclusively with the Liberal Party. In 1880 we find that of 374 Liberal M.P.s, at least 100 were dissenters.[3]

It was through dissent that Joseph Chamberlain entered the political arena. He took up the fight for educational reform before

[1] John Morley: *Recollections*, vol. I, p. 150.
[2] *cf.* E. R. Taylor: *Methodism and Politics, 1791–1851*. We must, of course, remember that it was through bodies like the Protestant Dissenting Deputies that non-conformity sought to fight against its political disabilities in the eighteenth and early nineteenth century.
[3] *cf.* W. G. Addison: *Religious Equality in Modern England, 1714–1914*, London, 1944, p. 93, and also pp. 124–51.

the 1870 Act and advocated a vast enterprise of secular education, compulsory, non-sectarian, free if necessary, and state-controlled. This movement, embodied in the National Education League, was practically a non-conformist enterprise. 'I come to you tonight,' he said in one of his political speeches, 'as one of that little knot of fanatics and of those much abused beings, a political dissenter, and I glory in it.'[1]

The characteristic of the Radical Party in politics was the preference for measures rather than men. They sought to achieve certain goals without being directly concerned with the carrying out of policies from day to day. Political power as such was suspect; it was thought to be derogatory to the strict moral conduct and the concern with one's salvation with which the religious nonconformist and the evangelical were deeply concerned, 'Give us the measures and you may have the places' was their battle cry. Those, who nevertheless accepted political office were suspect, and it was feared that they might be prepared to compromise in the policies which they had undertaken to carry out.[2] The Radical group did not regard itself bound to the Liberal Party under all circumstances. It felt free to support any group which happened to be temporarily allied with them in the prosecution of a certain policy. Thus Mundella, one of the post-1868 Radicals, who later reached ministerial office, saw his principal task in the improvement of working conditions and the introduction of a system of arbitration in industrial disputes. To that end he collaborated with a Liberal as well as with a Tory government.

Three aspects of non-conformist religion seem to influence a person's political activity and shape his attitude to politics, namely its general humanitarianism, its insistence on continuous and concentrated work, and its striving after moral purity. If, for example, we wish to understand John Bright's attitude to politics we must see it against this background. Throughout his life he insisted on the paramountcy of certain moral principles, notably that of pacifism. This led him frequently into situations where he was antagonistic to most of his colleagues and it brought about his

---

[1] J. Garvin: *Life of John Chamberlain*, vol. I, p. 152. (This particular speech did not deal with the Education Question.)

[2] *e.g.* the conflict between Forster and his supporters over his compromise in the solution of the education question through the 1870 Act.

resignation from the Government in 1882 over the bombardment of Alexandria. To many this appeared a minor issue, but to Bright it was a matter of principle.[1] He was forever in doubt whether his political activity might not be detrimental to moral integrity. Once in Parliament he would not compromise with the customs of polite society with regard to dress or behaviour at Court, nor would he make the customary contributions to charities, at that time expected of a Member of Parliament. This is in contrast to the ideal of a definite class society, held by the aristocracy, with its acceptance of electoral bribery and success in Society as the necessary corollary of a political career. The one group was clearly concerned more with the exercise of power and the other with the realization of political principles.

Puritanism, as Max Weber has shown, lays great stress on the absorption of man in his work. Success in one's work was regarded as the best sign of man's election. Not all were 'elect', but every man was to act as if he was and with this in mind he was expected to work hard and to seek success in life. Through this he would gain inner strength and would feel secure in the belief that he had been chosen to be saved and not damned.[2]

A voracity for work, often to the exclusion of recreation or reflection, lies at the bottom of much of the activities of members of the Victorian entrepreneurial class. It frequently spilled over into politics, and, while its basis was not purely altruism its aim was wider than the amassing of wealth or fame. Mundella had started his career as an apprentice in a Nottingham hosiery firm and had slowly risen to be a partner in a business. 'My success,' he wrote later, 'is really due to *hard work* and a certain shrewdness a commonsense . . . which keeps me out of blunders. My versatility is inherited, so is my elasticity: but while I know I am not a genius

---

[1] *cf.* G. M. Trevelyan: *Life of John Bright* and J. T. Mills: *John Bright and the Quakers*, 2 vols. 1935.

[2] As an example of this attitude Weber quotes from the moral exhortations given by Richard Baxter in his 'The Saints' Everlasting Rest': 'Keep up a high esteem of time and be every day more careful that you lose none of your time than you are that you lose none of your gold and silver. And if vain recreation, dressing, feasting, idle talk, unprofitable company or sleep be of any temptation to rob you of your time, accordingly heighten your watchfulness' (Max Weber: *The Protestant Ethic and the Spirit of Capitalism*, 1930, p. 261.)

I am conscious of a power and love of hard work and, though I say it, I am sincere and honest.'[1]

This immersion in one's work does not apply solely to the sphere of professional work or economic activity. The maxim that the successful conduct of this-worldly activities is a symptom of man's election led to a general methodical conduct of life in all its spheres. Spare-time activities related to political or public work, absence of recreational pursuits and participation in the life of Society, seem fair criteria of the strength of this need for 'tireless vocational activity'.[2] We find signs of such a subordination of spare-time activities to political life in the manner in which W. H. Smith, brought up in the strictest tradition of Wesleyanism, approached politics—although the whole of his activities were again subordinated to a desire to gain status in Society. He studied diligently foreign methods of administration, he sought election to the London School Board in order to show his earnest interest in education. He constantly tried to obtain information and to gain knowledge which might be applicable to problems of current politics and administration. When, as First Lord of the Admiralty, he spent his holidays cruising abroad, sightseeing ashore was undertaken as a duty with the gathering of information as its aim.

As a young man Chamberlain utilized most of his spare time for public activities and he turned to the support of these even pursuits, normally considered mainly recreational. He had received little formal education and his early work, as a Sunday and night-school teacher and as propagator of educational reforms, meant for him, therefore, constant and painstaking effort. When reading he collected quotations with an eye to their future use. 'All his reading . . . is . . . so to say pertinent' and his careful and methodical practice, by which technical ingenuity attempted to give the impression of quick wit and easy flow of speech is summed up by his biographer in the statement that 'no man of equal fame ever owed more to the capacity of taking pains'.[3] He was extremely hard-working in his business activities and later on in political

---

[1] W. H. G. Armytage: *A. J. Mundella, the Liberal background to the Labour Movement*, 1951, p. 322.

[2] Weber's 'Rastlose Berufsarbeit'.

[3] Garvin, *op. cit.*, vol. I, p. 68–69.

life. Constant activity was the very breath of life for him. 'I have been as busy as ever myself and have hardly had a moment unoccupied. So I keep my health all right which I should not if I slackened for a week.'[1]

In Chamberlain's life, as in that of some of the other radical reformers, Bright's strong moral passion or Gladstone's broad religious humanitarianism are absent. It is rather an initial disgust and a strong desire to see results, to get things done which underlies their political activity. The restless energy of Chamberlain's municipal activities is symptomatic of this attitude. 'In twelve months, by God's help, the City shall not know itself,' he exclaimed at the beginning of his Birmingham mayoralty,[2] and on the occasion of his entry into the House of Commons he writes: 'I can't say I look forward to my new life with pleasure for all change is painful to me and for some time past my only pleasure has been in work. But it is another step towards the fulfilment of my destiny and while I do not greatly care how soon the last comes I like the story to keep moving.'[3]

This particular story ended on the Treasury Bench and in a reluctant alliance with the Tories. But the adherence of a section of religious dissent with Conservatism which had resulted from the Home Rule issue was an unnatural phenomenon and with the exception of such isolated cases as Chamberlain's it was not destined to last.[4] The social and cultural background of dissenters and the anti-authoritarian character of their religious beliefs made them uneasy bedfellows for the Conservative politicians from the gentlemen-class. And the social composition of organized nonconformity caused the majority of its members to identify most naturally with Liberal and radical politics. For Matthew Arnold, the middle class was 'moving between [the] two cardinal points of ... our commercial member of Parliament and ... our fanatical Protestant dissenters'.[5] In 1869, when this was written, nonconformists and businessmen, often in one and the same person,

---

[1] ibid., I, p. 201.

[2] ibid., I, p. 188.

[3] Garvin, op. cit., vol. I, p. 230.

[4] In 1887 all but two of the Methodist M.P.s were Liberals. cf. M. L. Edwards: Methodism in England, 1850–1932, 1943, p. 170.

[5] cf. Culture and Anarchy, p. 100, of C. Dover Wilson's edition, 1932.

were the dominant group among the 'new men' in politics. But from then onwards a new type of politician begins to emerge.

THE INTELLECTUALS' ATTITUDE TO POLITICS

An examination of the attitude to politics shown by that section of the professional middle class referred to earlier as intellectuals, shows none of the deep-felt resentment of injustices and deprivations which we can observe among the group of non-conformist politicians. Even men who were brought up as dissenters or who had to struggle to complete their education with the help of scholarships and bursaries did not labour under the same sense of injustice. It seems that professional success, and the social recognition in which it resulted, compensated them for earlier deprivations.

These men did not enter on a political career because of professional failure or in order to improve their professional status. On the contrary, entry into politics took place after professional success seemed well assured. Nor was there the same urgency about embarking on a political career as we found in the cases of the 'traditional politician' from the ranks of the aristocracy. A note of circumspection and calculation on the advisability of entering politics is sounded by Bryce. 'I have some idea of fighting Bouverie in the Kilmarnock Burghs but still doubt whether it is compatible with practice at the Bar and my Oxford Chair and am excessively exercised to know which is the best course to take, whether to abjure politics meantime and stick to law alone, which hitherto has not been encouraging, or to make Parliament one's first object. As respects money, which is of course a serious difficulty, my chair and my savings together would give me enough to live on.'[1]

For Bryce, politics were clearly complementing professional activity; his scholarly work was continued right through his political career. An attitude which regarded parliamentary activities as one among a number of pursuits is frequently found among the professional group in politics. The economic need for persistent legal or other professional activity seems to explain this only partly; the lawyers, for instance, frequently had very large incomes which

[1] H. A. L. Fisher: *Life of Lord Bryce*, vol. I, p. 147.

usually exceeded a Cabinet Minister's salary. They could have dispensed with part of it had they desired to devote more time to politics.[1] But their professional life was to them not just an arduous undertaking. Bryce, Haldane and Morley, to name only three, had many and varied interests outside the professional as well as outside the political sphere, whether we think of sport or travel, literary activities, scholarly pursuits or non-political public duties.

Asquith shows in his political career a combination of intellectual flexibility and lack of deep feeling. We are told that in his family life he fought shy of emotion.[2] The rareness of his speeches in the early period of his political career suggests a reasoned plan to impress Parliament by few and carefully prepared, well-timed contributions rather than the expression of strong impulses. Snowden describes him as 'seeming to lack human sympathy, which alone could touch the responsive chords in those who listened'.[3] In the period of the split in the Liberal Party he managed to maintain contact with Campbell-Bannerman and the bulk of the party, despite the strong ties which bound him to the Liberal Imperialists. Likewise, in the negotiations which preceded the formation of the 1906 government, Asquith was the first to go back on the terms of the agreement concluded between him, Haldane and Grey, which would have made their acceptance of office dependent on Campbell-Bannerman moving to the House of Lords.

In policy decisions Asquith was cautious, giving perhaps undue weight to legalistic considerations. In the debate on the Trades Dispute Bill in 1906, Campbell-Bannerman had accepted a Labour amendment which sought to protect Trade Unions from action in tort through a specific clause in the Bill. Asquith and other Liberal lawyers on the other hand proposed to protect the Unions through changes in the Law of Agency. The effect would have been the same, but Asquith was only reconciled with difficulty to the new proposals.[4] I am quoting this incident as it seems

---

[1] Haldane's income at the time of his entry into the Government was over £20,000.

[2] J. A. Spender and C. Asquith: *Life of Lord Oxford and Asquith*, vol. I, p. 208 *et seq.*

[3] P. Snowden: *Autobiography*, vol. I, p. 127. See also B. Webb: *Our Partnership*, p. 227.

[4] Spender and Asquith, *op. cit.*, vol. I, p. 182–3.

to indicate a preoccupation with certain issues in the abstract and a lack of understanding for the forces which motivated them. Yet the same power of penetration of the gifted lawyer which made him so sensitive to the legal aspects of a particular measure was by all accounts also responsible for his *success* in politics. The intellectual approach entails both the ability to see all sides of a question and to be able to foresee the practical consequences of a certain course of action.[1] Asquith's success as Prime Minister might be ascribed to his ability to hold a team of strong-willed individuals together, not only as an efficient chairman but also as the counsellor of individual members and arbitrator of plans. Lloyd George said of him in 1913: 'He is a big man. He never initiates anything but he is a great judge. He brushes aside all small points and goes to the heart of the subject.'[2] Beaverbrook described the contrast between Asquith's approach to his government colleagues and that of Lloyd George. Asquith was interested in the mental attainments of his friends, their ideas rather than their personality, Lloyd George sought to understand them by studying their habits, their preferences, private virtues and vices.[3]

The difference in the attitude to parliamentary activity of the intellectual and the businessman could be observed when the leadership of the House of Commons passed from W. H. Smith into the hands of A. J. Balfour. Balfour, with his speculative turn of mind and his wide interests can in some respect be classified as an 'intellectual' in our sense of the word although he was not a professional man. Smith was constantly at his post, although frequently in ill-health, and he was considerate and attentive to claims and complaints of members. Balfour, on the other hand, was often nonchalant in his manners, lukewarm in the advocacy of Bills which did not interest him and frequently absent from the House.[4]

What motivated the political activity of the intellectuals? Two

---

[1] See also his refusal to commit himself unequivocally on the Chinese Labour question, which was an important issue in the General Election of 1906. *Op. cit.*, vol. I, pp. 177-8.

[2] Quoted by Lord Riddell in his diary. See R. B. McCallum: *Asquith*, 1936, p. 63.

[3] Lord Beaverbrook: *Politicians and the War*, 1928, p. 80.

[4] Maxwell, *op. cit.*, especially vol. II, p. 187 *et seq.*, and Blanche Dugdale: *A. J. Balfour* vol. I, p. 201 *et seq.*

interests seemed to induce the successful barrister, writer or journalists to enter politics. Firstly, a liking for the type of company
which membership of the House of Commons entailed: social
intercourse with the aristocracy, country house life, dinners. This
type of life is found at its purest in the group of vivacious and
spirited men and women who called themselves 'The Souls', a
group which included both the rich and aristocratic as well as
brilliant professional men. Both Haldane and Asquith had access
to this circle.[1] Secondly a genuine interest in certain measures of
reform and in issues of public policy which accounts, I think, for
the tenacity with which some of the intellectuals held on to
political activity.

Their very success in the political field was also frequently due
to the sometimes comparatively narrow expertise which they
possessed. George Cave had entered Parliament in 1905 as Conservative Member for Kingston, after a relatively uneventful
career at the Bar and in local politics. Not being as successful a
lawyer as some other M.P.s, he could not devote much time to
his parliamentary activities. 'In any case,' he wrote, 'I do not feel
much at home in the parliamentary skirmishes and debates "at
large". I like something definite to bite on like a Bill, and hope I may
get some chance soon.' His chance did come when he was asked by
his front-bench to move an amendment to the Licensing Bill. His
competent speech attracted attention, he was taken into the coun-
sels of the party leadership. He gave advice on the drafting of
amendments and on legal matters in general and became a Conservative representative on a number of committees and judicial
commissions of inquiry. He advanced from membership of the
opposition shadow-cabinet to the Solicitor-Generalship under
Lloyd George, then to the Home Office (1916) and finally the
Woolsack.[2]

The typical politicians from the ranks of the 'intellectuals' will,
however, be found in the Liberal rather than the Conservative
Party.[3] While the measures which they sought to advance were
often similar to those advocated by the non-conformist business

---

[1] 'We were not "souls",' Haldane wrote in his *Autobiography*, 'but they liked
our company and we liked theirs because of its brilliance'.

[2] For Cave's career see the *Life* by Charles Mallet.

[3] But see pp. 193–194 below and also Chapter X.

class, which entered Parliament in the wake of Cobden and Bright, their approach to them was different. The roots of their concern for political issues and the forms in which it showed itself was intellectual in character, the result of reflection rather than experience. It is illuminating to compare these 'new Radicals' if such we may term them, with the older group in one other aspect of their respective careers. The original Radicals were largely the representatives of popular movements with a loyal local following which carried them into Parliament. Many of the new Radicals had at the beginning of their political career no such following. They began their political activity as members of political coteries, debating societies or dining clubs. The Alfred Grey Committee and, following on it the 'Eighty Club' are examples of this. Their political popularity came later and depended on the Party Organization, unless parliamentary or administrative success had already created a national reputation for them.[1]

The methods by which they propagated their ideas were often conspiratorial. A new movement, such as that of the Liberal Imperialists, was born as a clique and it attempted, in the first instance, to widen its hold over Members of Parliament. Referring to these young Liberals, Haldane wrote: 'We are to look to John Morley and Fowler on the Front Bench as those with whom we are informally but in substance in touch and we are to distribute amongst ourselves the work of thinking and working out an effective programme.'[2]

Members of this group, especially Haldane, seem to have derived great satisfaction from the intrigue-cum-diplomacy which is the essence of behind-the-scenes politics. Complicated negotiations, taking decisions on new problems, battling against odds are stimulating to the intellectually curious and venturesome. Bryce was apparently extremely stimulated by an early election contest and not much upset by the fact that he did not gain the seat.[3] Masterman enjoyed an administrative tussle and opportunity for intellectual subtlety. Referring to the excitement of the railway strike in 1912 his wife noted: 'oddly enough the whole excitement seemed

[1] Only in the case of John Morley did a national reputation precede rather than follow on a 'party' political career and entry into Parliament.

[2] Sir F. Maurice: *Life of Haldane*, vol. I, p. 50.

[3] *ibid.*, p. 147.

to have done [him] more good than harm. He had gone to London in a very low state of health but returned very much better.'[1]

Haldane's life is a striking example of the identification of a political career with a number of reform measures. Even before his entrance into Parliament in 1885, he was engaged in work connected with Adult Education and began to be interested in social problems. He was not at all desirous of accepting office in the Liberal administration of 1892–95, as it would interfere with his progress at the Bar as well as with his campaign for social and educational reforms. Haldane relates how during those years higher education was 'the absorbing political subject'.[2] He intrigued on behalf of his scheme, approached the Government and induced them to introduce a Bill. In the debate he relates '. . . the prospect of the Bill seemed hopeless, I sprang to my feet when an opportunity at last offered and I spoke for once like inspired'.[3]

His interest in administrative reforms comes out clearly in his first period of office. His appointment as Secretary of State for War was not just due to Campbell-Bannerman's refusal to make him Lord Chancellor. Haldane could have become Home Secretary but chose the War Office which, according to the Prime Minister, 'nobody will touch with a pole' because a study of the defence issue had convinced him of its paramount importance. 'Here,' he wrote later in his autobiography, 'was an almost virgin field to be operated on by applying first principles'; his army, as he told a baffled Army Council, was to be a 'Hegelian Army'.[4] Although this sphere was completely outside his previous experience, he rapidly acquired expert knowledge and seems to have devoted all his energies to the achievement of far-reaching reforms. Beatrice Webb describes Haldane during those days as 'completely absorbed in his office, thinking out problems of Army administration'.[5] It would be wrong to forget in this connection Haldane's

---

[1] Lucy Masterman: *C. F. G. Masterman,* 1939, p. 208. See also the account of Masterman's activity in connection with the early administration of the National Health Insurance Scheme, *ibid.,* p. 239–40.

[2] Haldane: *Autobiography,* p. 124.

[3] *ibid.,* p. 126. Haldane supported the Conservative Education Act of 1902 much to the chagrin of his party.

[4] Haldane: *op. cit.,* pp. 183 and 185.

[5] B. Webb: *op. cit.,* p. 363.

failure as a speaker, his inability to enthuse, except when he was personally attracted, as well as a certain intellectual arrogance, all of which undoubtedly combined to make him less effective in the Cabinet and the House of Commons than in his department. Yet if anything reflects the genuineness of his identification with certain measures of reform as a positive force, it is the persistence with which he sought to take over the Admiralty after having completed his scheme of Army reform, in order to ensure the success of his plans for an Expeditionary Force. He even went so far as to threaten resignation if his wish should not be complied with. The strong hold which novel measures of policy had on his mind, his delight in the showing of wit, ingenuity and subterfuge and a general lack of emotion, all combined to shape his rôle in the Liberal government. His post, he said, 'was much more at close quarters with individuals than with the Cabinet as a whole. I was not really good in that Cabinet partly from temperament partly because I found it difficult to get really interested in its detailed work.'[1]

McKenna displayed a similar interest in administration and a liking for tackling problems of administrative reform together with a lack of sociability, and awkwardness and pedantry as a public speaker. His whole career is a proof of this. As a young barrister he had already thought of an administrative career in the City. While a Junior Minister, he was offered the post of Permanent Secretary to the Treasury which was about to fall vacant and he seriously considered accepting it. 'Work for its own sake attracted him when honours left him cold,' says his biographer.[2] In his administration at the Admiralty he showed the same inflexibility to the views of the War Office as Haldane showed to those of the Navy, and like Haldane he thought of resigning. His exit from politics to become Chairman of the Midlands Bank may also be regarded as an indication of his preoccupation with administrative skills. Although he was prepared to return to politics should the solution of a specific question require it, he characteristically left the decision about there being a need for such a step in the hands of the directors of the Bank.[3]

---

[1] Maurice, *op. cit.*, vol. I, p. 162.
[2] S. McKenna: *Reginald McKenna, A Memoir*, 1948, p. 120.
[3] *ibid.* p. 287.

The rôle of the intellectuals as stimulators of thought and leaders in action in continental progressive movements has been widely commented upon.[1] Though less conspicuous, similar influences can be seen at work in Britain. Even when they were formally outside the political sphere the Webbs are the best examples of intellectuals supporting and partly shaping progressive forces, after they had arrived at new political concepts by reasoning and speculation. Haldane's propagation of university reform and Masterman's devotion to schemes of social reform may be seen as characteristic of a similar process. When in office as Under-Secretary of the Local Government Board, and frustrated by Burns in his wish to carry out reforms, the latter pondered whether he should not act on his own, 'try and come out into the open, agitate and lead in the hope of doing something *soon*, independent of this rather baffling and impotent and ineffectual life'.[2]

In general, new ideas were taken up by the intellectuals more eagerly than by other groups. Beatrice Webb relates how during the Poor Law campaign, when they were at the height of their fame as reformers and investigators, and were consequently frequently entertained, there was a 'scramble for new ideas. We happen just now to have a good many to give away, hence the eagerness for our company. Every politician one meets wants to be coached.'[3]

It must again be borne in mind here that the intellectual cannot simply be equated with the professional man and we should therefore be wrong if we regarded the receptiveness to new ideas simply as characteristic of the professional middle class alone. Among aristocratic politicians we can also find men of high academic distinctions and wide intellectual interests, *viz.* Rosebery and Balfour. Lord Curzon had produced scholarly books on Persia and the Far East and Salisbury undertook chemical experiments of some originality. His early political writings, too, have profundity and trenchancy. Yet the receptiveness of such men to new ideas is often restricted by their inability to understand ideas which seem incompatible with their tradition and the firmly rooted belief,

[1] See among others R. Michels: *The Sociology of Political Parties,* K. Mannheim: *Ideology and Utopia.* Also, from a critical point of view, J. Benda: *The Great Betrayal* (Le Trahison des Clercs), 1928.

[2] Masterman, *op. cit.,* p. 116—written in 1909.

[3] *Our Partnership,* p. 402.

G

based on this tradition, that theirs was a pre-eminence in governmental function. The most enlightened of them were certainly not
concerned just with the material advantages of a privileged position but, like Balfour, who once told Beatrice Webb that he wished
'to maintain existing institutions', they felt that the foundations
of the existing order should not be tampered with.

Conservative intellectuals of the same mould as those in the
progressive movements were, on the whole, less likely to enter
politics, and if they did so, they tended to achieve positions of eminence and leadership to a much smaller extent than their colleagues
in the opposite camp. Of the men who were closely associated with
the Round Table, and among the 'ideologues' of Protection and
Empire Preference, only Amery reached a comparatively elevated position in the Conservative hierarchy; and at times he was
left out of the inner group of Conservative politicians.[1] Some
members of this circle did hold office as junior ministers but the
influence of men like W. A. S. Hewins and Lord Lothian was
exercised on the propagandist plane and on the political back-
stage rather than in the parliamentary arena. Others, like Dawson
and Brand, reached positions of great power and influence but they
were formally, at least, outside the sphere of politics proper.[2]

It seems to me to be of considerable social significance that this
group of imperialist reformers contained many 'new men' as well
as others who were only very marginally connected with the traditional ruling class.[3] The Conservative Leadership, which was so
full of members of that class, may well have been antagonistic to
these intellectuals with their insistence on a new policy based,
above all, on the imperial idea. Their very partisanship did not
always endear them to the pragmatic Conservative politicians.
Success and failure in the field of politics is a compound of personal
influence and partisanship, of individual drive and the exigencies
of the hour. The working of these factors remains to be unravelled.

[1] Lord Milner's membership of the War Cabinet hardly counts in this respect.
He owed his place to eminence and experience rather than political partisanship.

[2] The history of the 'Round Table' group remains to be written. Useful in-
sight can be gained from biographies such as J. R. M. Butler's *Life of Lord
Lothian* and L. S. Amery's *My Political Life*, 3 vols., 1953–55. See also A. P.
Thornton: *The Imperial Idea and its Enemies*, 1959.

[3] L. S. Amery and Edward Grigg (Lord Altrincham) went to Harrow and
Winchester respectively as scholars.

The Career of Politics

'The interest of the party can never require an improper appointment: an improper appointment is a job and nothing injures party more than a job. But at the same time there is nothing more injurious to political connection than the fear of justly rewarding your friends ... it is not becoming in any minister to decry party who has risen by party. We should always remember that if we were not partisan we should not be ministers.'—BENJAMIN DISRAELI.

> It happened to Lord Lundy then
> As happened to so many men:
> Towards the age of twenty-six,
> They shoved him into politics;
> In which profession he commanded
> The income which his rank demanded
> In turn as Secretary for
> India, the Colonies and War.
>
> —HILAIRE BELLOC.

BRITISH politics has long depended on the existence of an independent leisured class, willing and able to devote the greater part of their days, or at least of their ample spare time, to the business of government. It has benefited by the high esteem in which the political career has been held and the eagerness with which men have always sought to enter it. And through the years this has changed only slowly, even at the national level, where men have for some time been paid for the political functions which they perform. The prestige of politics has, no doubt, prevented it from becoming 'a gainful profession, like advocacy, stockbroking, the dry goods trade or the getting up of companies'.[1] Such a type of politician had arisen in the U.S., so Bryce thought, primarily because of the low esteem in which politics were held, the location

[1] James Bryce: *The American Commonwealth*, 2 vols., 1889, vol. II, p. 28.

of much of state government activity in comparatively small places, the greater frequency and complexity of the electoral system, and, last but not least, the vastly greater number of 'political' offices, whether elected or otherwise.[1]

In contrast, the 'Inner Circle' of politicians in Britain was, in the 1880's, infinitesimal in size. It still is. Bryce concluded that the total number of those who engaged full-time in political activity, *i.e.* M.P.s, active members of the House of Lords, candidates seriously nursing a constituency, political journalists and editors and 'the persons who in each constituency devote most of their time to politics' numbered 3,500.[2] Today's figures, based on slightly different categories, are given below.

TABLE I

Active Politicians and Political Functionaries, 1962:

Category	Numbers
M.P.s	630
Peers who regularly attend the sittings of the House of Lords*	50–100
Officers of National Party Organizations†	60
Officers of quasi-party organizations and political pressure groups at the National Level‡	50
Party Agents, local and regional§	772
Parliamentary candidates, *seriously* nursing a constituency‖	600
TOTAL	2,162–2,212

* cf. Lord Chorley and others: *Reform of the House of Lords*; A. P. Bromhead: *The House of Lords in British Politics*.

† Only full-time professional staff with political responsibilities are counted, not the clerical or technical employees.

‡ Based on own calculations.

§ According to the Party Organizations.

‖ According to estimates by Professor Austen Ranney.

[1] 'Probably over 200,000 persons whose chief occupation and livelihood is politics.' *ibid.*, p. 31 and pp. 24–36 *passim*.

[2] cf. Bryce, *op. cit.*, vol. I, p. 31, for detailed figures.

The above is the more remarkable if we reflect that since Bryce wrote, the population of Britain has increased by 50 per cent, and that during the same time there has taken place a considerable growth of what is alternately described as 'bureaucracy', 'organization' or the 'aparat' in all spheres of social and economic life.

The circle of 'professional' politicians is also comparatively stable in its composition. An electoral system based on single or double-member constituencies tends, as we know, to react violently to the changing electoral fortunes of parties. Considering that since the eighteenth century, party warfare has greatly increased in scope and volume and that elections have taken place at shorter intervals, the continued stability of the personnel of Parliament is rather astounding. Between 1734 and 1832 a total of 5,034 men sat in the House of Commons. During the period between the two Reform Acts, including the House elected in 1868, there were a total of about 3,800 candidates, of whom about 2,650 were elected. Between 1885 and 1918 the House of Commons knew approximately 2,350 M.P.s. In the inter-war years there was a total of 1,823, but of these, several hundred M.P.s had already sat in Parliament during the war of 1914–18 or earlier, and the majority of members elected in 1935 continued in Parliament until the end of the Second World War or even afterwards.[1] If we compare the length of parliamentary service at the two extreme periods we find that the M.P.s who sat in Parliament during the 100 years after 1734 served on average 13·4 years. For the period between the two World Wars, Ross calculated that the average length of membership of the House of Commons was 15 years.[2]

The stability of the ministerial group is only a little less marked. During the inter-war period, 113 men and one woman reached the Cabinet. Yet the chance to sit and deliberate around the long table in No. 10 and to belong to the body that, formally at least, makes the vital decisions, is today probably greater than at any previous period in British history. The 'Labour Turnover' in the Cabinet has steadily increased during the past 150 years. Lassitude and

---

[1] Figures for the number of M.P.s at given period are derived as follows: 1734–1832—G. P. Judd: *Members of Parliament, 1734–1832*, 1955. 1832–68—James Acland: *Imperial Poll Book 1832–69*, 1869. 1885–1918—*Constitutional Yearbook*, 1919, pp. 341–78. 1918–39—F. J. S. Ross: *Parliamentary Representation*, 1943.

[2] cf. Judd, *op. cit.*, p. 27, and Ross, *op. cit.*, p. 40.

political longevity were probably responsible for the long tenure of office by Ministers at the beginning of the nineteenth century. In the 15 years of Lord Liverpool's administration, 21 men held the 15 offices which ranked as Cabinet; their tenure of office in that administration alone averaged nearly 12 years. Peel's ministry (1841–46) saw on the average one change of personnel per annum in a Cabinet of 14 or 15.

We can evaluate the extent of changes in the membership of Cabinets by relating changes involving the entry of new men to the size and duration of each Cabinet.

TABLE II

Personnel Changes in individual Cabinets, 1868–1955:

Administration	Duration	Coefficient of change*
Gladstone	1868–74	5·4
Disraeli	1874–80	6·9
Salisbury–Balfour	1895–1905	9·5
Campbell-Bannerman–Asquith	1905–14	9·5
Bonar Law–Baldwin	1922–23 ⎱ 1924–29 ⎰	12·5
MacDonald	1924 ⎱ 1929–31 ⎰	19·5
Baldwin–Chamberlain	1935–40	15·5
Attlee	1945–51	12·5
Churchill	1951–55	15·6

* This coefficient expresses the number of entrants into a Cabinet after its formation, per annum as a percentage of the Cabinet size.

The opportunity to reach the Cabinet, albeit for shorter periods, has thus increased during the past century. But it is still small, so small as to offer comparatively little hope to the average M.P. that he will manage to scale these heights.[1] The opportunities for governmental office as such have possibly increased a little more over the years, as the widening of the administrative sphere has led to a proliferation of junior posts and of departmental headships out-

[1] The above figures suggest that the odds against getting into the Cabinet are at present of the order 1 : 15 or more.

side the Cabinet. The ministerial body is today half as strong again as before the First World War and, depending on the size of the parliamentary representation which a party enjoys, between 15 per cent and 20 per cent of all M.P.s belonging to the majority party in the House will be in office at any time.[1]

WHAT PRICE OFFICE?

How important is office as the goal and rationale of political activity? Given the comparatively small chances of the average private member to reach even the bottom rungs of the ladder, let alone to hold a major ministerial post for any length of time, it could hardly be great and it might not be worth while to investigate careers inside Parliament further. Much evidence, however, points in the other direction and suggests that office is a powerful driving force both inside Parliament and on the way to it. Those who seek it are hardly attracted by its financial rewards. '£1,200 per annum paid quarterly' was never a realistic assessment of people's ideas 'of political science and human nature', not even at the time when Disraeli wrote these words and when the salary of even a junior Minister represented a considerably larger real income than that of his Cabinet colleague today.[2]

The desire for office must rather be seen as a product of the twin desires: Power and Prestige. It is strengthened by the competitive emulation which is at work throughout society. When George Wyndham was offered the Under-Secretaryship for War, after much deferred hope, he wrote to his mother: 'I gather it has been a very tight fit, anyway all's well that ends well. My two principal reasons for being delighted are: 1. Because it will please you and Papa, and 2. Because I have set my heart on being a Minister of Victoria.'[3] Our knowledge of the political pressures that shape governmental policy may make us doubt whether office,

---

[1] If years of government alternate regularly with years of opposition the long-term chances of office are, of course, correspondingly reduced.

[2] Ministerial salaries have remained fairly stable in monetary terms. Allowing for changes in the price level, the salary of a Secretary of State which was £5,000 in 1832 would today be in the region of £25,000.

[3] G. Wyndham and J. W. Mackail (eds.): *Life and Letters of George Wyndham*, p. 67.

especially junior office, does indeed confer on its holders real power, but it seems that success inside parliamentary politics is becoming increasingly equated with front-bench status and thus inevitably with office-holding. The valuation of office by individual M.P.s will vary with personality structure, individual beliefs and party affiliation. How many M.P.s are there like 'Arthur Brookfield [who] rated his own capacity very high and when, in 1885 he was not offered the Under-Secretaryship for War on which he had set his heart he boycotted the House of Commons and did not put in an appearance there for many years'.[1]

There is no measuring of frustrated ambition, nor can we know how many M.P.s have lacked the desire to leave the status of a private backbencher. Percy Wyndham took up 'parliamentary work as a duty like other duties but rather an irksome one. During the 25 years in which he had sat for West Cumberland he won great esteem as a private member and did valuable work on many committees. But he held his own principles unswervingly: and they were not always those of his party. He represented the country interest . . .'[2]

The House of Commons has had its quota of independent-spirited individuals, rebels, cross-benchers, iconoclasts who preferred to exercise political influence as private members. Indeed, their political power may have been greater this way. Nor must we forget the leaders of political cabals although, like individual rebels, they may well have a price-tag on their independence and may be willing to shift their power from attempts at coercion from the outside to the exercise of power from the inside.

MILESTONES ON THE ROAD TO OFFICE

In the analysis of parliamentary and governmental career patterns we can, in the first instance, proceed along the lines of quantitative analysis. Age, experience, the steps that lead from office to office; quick ascendancy and sudden dismissal, each tell their tale and are at the same time symptom and causative factor in a career. '*Le*

---

[1] *cf.* J. W. Lowther: *A Speaker's Commentary*, 2 vols., 1925, vol. I, p. 179.
[2] Wyndham and Mackail, *op. cit.*, p. 32.

pouvoir des positions déjà prises' (Proudhon) is probably nowhere as important as in the inner circle of politics. Some men are selected for office, others select themselves. But in this sphere, the formal shades rapidly into the informal and the undefinable. How important are the ties of friendship and kinship in the selection of men for office; what is the influence of expertise and experience on an individual's career? Is the race to the good House of Commons man, or rather to the adroit wire-puller behind the scenes? How many political animals who started as fiery colts end their days fattening themselves on some rich pasture of their own choice? We can sometimes see how hidden forces work, but a quantitative analysis of such factors is rarely possible. It is easier to show the governmental career and to trace the stepping stones on the road to office. We can describe the 'how' but not necessarily the 'why' of a political career.

Seniority rather than age counts towards success in Parliament, and those who enter politics young have a greater chance of obtaining office than those who become M.P.s only when they are well advanced in middle age. One of the factors influencing the careeer of the aristocratic politician is his opportunity to enter Parliament at a comparatively early age. 'You will be in Parliament by the time you are twenty-one,' Lord Chesterfield wrote to his son, 'and you must make your mark there if you wish to make a mark in your country.' Five generations later, Lord Winterton, the son of an Irish Earl and possessor of estates in Surrey, found himself, 'thanks mainly to the support and influence of Lord Leconsfield . . . chosen at the age of twenty-one years and six months to be the Conservative candidate in an important by-election'.[1] Of the 93 aristocratic Cabinet Ministers, 58 had entered Parliament before the age of thirty, yet of the 159 middle class politicians who reached the Cabinet, only 31 had reached the House of Commons by that age.[2] An early start is thus an obvious advantage; a late start is a certain handicap. Less than 10 per cent of all Cabinet Ministers who held office between 1868 and 1955 had entered Parliament after they had attained the age of fifty; before 1916 such a career was practically unheard of, only three future Cabinet

---

[1] *i.e.* Horsham, Surrey. Earl Winterton: *Pre-War*, 1932, p. 1.

[2] In the case of peers who were never M.P.s the relevant age is that at which the subject became a peer, or twenty-five years, whichever is the later.

Ministers had entered Parliament so late in life. But even among those who entered Cabinets for the first time after that date, the late start accounts for only 14 per cent, exactly half the proportion which it formed among the M.P.s of the period.[1]

The ten years which, on the average, separate the aristocratic entrant into Parliament from his middle-class or working-class colleague reveal themselves in their subsequent careers. The higher your position in the social scale, the earlier tends to be your entry into the Cabinet. Politicians with a working-class background have, on the other hand, a particularly steep ascent to the top: only one of their number entered Parliament before the age of thirty.

But time also affects the age-structure of Cabinets. We find that in each period its membership is older than in the preceding one.

TABLE III

Age at Entry into Cabinet:

(*a*) According to Class—

	Aristocracy	Middle Class	Working Class	All Cabinet Ministers
Under 30	2	—	—	2
31–40	22	15	—	37
41–50	37	54	8	99
51–60	27	61	25	113
61 and over	5	29	9	43
TOTAL	93	159	42	294

(*b*) According to Period—

	1868–86	1886–1916	1916–35	1935–55
Under 30	1	1	1	—
31–40	16	23	11	10
41–50	16	43	34	28
51–60	13	25	44	46
61 and over	3	9	18	15
TOTAL	49	101	108	99

[1] Ross, *op. cit.*, p. 22.

This reflects both changes in the class composition of the Cabinet as well as the increasing age at which each group enters Parliament.

What happens to politicians during the interval between their entry into Parliament and their joining the Cabinet? The average politician needs between 15 and 20 years before he reaches what must be for all practical purposes the final stage of his political career.[1] The process of selection and promotion occurs in and through his activity in Parliament. At least parliamentary conduct and activity within one's party strongly influence the *cursus honorum*, if only in a negative sense, by preventing the selection of those who, for one reason or another, will not pass muster as parliamentarians or as colleagues.

Selection and success in terms of office-holding can take a number of routes. A man can step straight into a Cabinet post— he may even, like MacDonald, move to 10 Downing Street without any previous apprenticeship in junior or departmental office. On the other hand, he may move upwards by stages, holding posts at different levels of importance and power and finally reach the Cabinet. The length and stages of the route seem to depend above all on party affiliation. Where power is held regularly and over long periods, as in the case of the Conservative Party, comparatively few Cabinet Ministers will be without previous experience in administrative office. When a party achieves office irregularly and for rather short periods, a number of the newly appointed Ministers will enter the Cabinet without previous governmental experience. In the Labour Ministries of the 1920's only a third of the Cabinet Ministers had held office before; and the Liberal administration of 1906, which was separated from the previous Liberal government by more than ten years, contained also a large number of untried men.[2]

---

[1] The chances of becoming Prime Minister are so absolutely remote as not to come seriously within the purview of calculable chance for the aspiring politician. Among the 294 Cabinet Ministers whom I studied only 16 eventually became Premiers. They had, on the average, spent 26 years in Parliament before forming an administration for the first time.

[2] Mr Attlee's administration, on the other hand, could make use of the experience which Labour politicians had gained in the wartime coalition and in consequence only Aneurin Bevan and George Isaacs among Cabinet Ministers were without previous governmental experience.

As in all organizations with a hierarchy of offices the world of government knows its own formal ladder of advancement, although not all Prime Ministers pay the same attention to the claims established by previous service. 'Gladstone is very strange and old-fashioned,' Hartington told Lady Rosebery, '. . . he takes Sir Robert Peel as his model and talks of seniority and previous claims.' Yet such 'old-fashioned' ideas have possibly become more important since. In Labour administrations, previous experience in a department has very frequently led to the promotion to more senior appointments in the same field. Some career lines within a department do actually start at the Parliamentary Private Secretary level. Sir Kingsley Wood had started his official career as P.P.S. to the Minister of Health. He then advanced to the Parliamentary Secretaryship of the Ministry, an office which he held for five years. After a further five years in other offices, he returned to the Ministry of Health as its departmental head. Among the men who had started their career in governmental office as Parliamentary Secretaries, a significantly large proportion stayed at least for some time in the sphere in which their career began originally; the number of those who actually became Heads of the department in which they were junior Ministers is greater than it would be if promotion were random in respect of previous experience.

Internal cohesion of a party, and the acceptance of a hierarchical system of leadership, as we find it inside the Conservative Party, generally favours a step by step advance towards high political office. Parties of the Left are, however, more like permanent coalitions and in the formation of his Cabinet, the Prime Minister is often forced to accommodate faction and to protect himself from eventual stings from the party's tail by giving office to actual or potential rebels.

THE HIGH ROAD TO POWER

Political careers which lead straight into Cabinet Office are worth investigating in greater detail. The 75 men who achieved Cabinet Office in one step, straight from the parliamentary ranks, can be divided into two main groups; one containing men with little or no previous connection with political parties, the other composed of those who enjoy great power and influence in the ranks of the par-

TABLE IV

Cursus honorum and Party:*

Career before entering Cabinet	Conservative	Liberal	Labour	All
Advanced straight into Cabinet	28	21	26	75
Held only Departmental Headship or equivalent†	16	6	5	27
Held only Junior Office	81	52	23	156
Held both Junior Office and Departmental Headship†	18	9	9	36
TOTAL	143	88	63	294

* In the case of a politician who shifted his political allegiance this refers to the party to which he belonged when he entered the Cabinet for the first time.

† These categories contain two or three men who would undoubtedly have reached Cabinet status more directly if Mr Churchill's wartime Cabinet had not been limited to very few members.

ties. We can with justifiable exaggeration speak of the 'outsiders' and the 'insiders', the 'experts' and the 'partisans' the '*dei ex machina*' and the 'machine-politicians'. And the directness of the route to high office has lately been enhanced by the rapidity of the advancement. The hierarchical structure of the British executive, its close connection with the life of Parliament, especially the House of Commons, and service for the party on the floor of the House, meant that for a long time it was uncommon to enter the Cabinet soon after entering Parliament. Recent developments have changed this. Of the 124 men who sat in British Cabinets between 1868 and 1916, only eight had reached that body within five years of entering Parliament. Of the 170 who achieved Cabinet rank between 1916 and 1955, 34 did so after such a comparatively short apprenticeship. It is not really surprising that the majority of this group should advance straight into the Cabinet. These are the outsiders *par excellence*.

This development is largely the result of those extra-parliamentary and often even non-political factors which are increasingly

determining the selection of men for governmental office. Membership of either of the Houses of Parliament is generally considered
to be a necessary condition of holding governmental office, but
sometimes men enter Parliament only because they have been
selected for office. Others enter it in the usual way with the knowledge that they will not have to kick their heels in subordinate
office if their party comes to power. Sir Walter (later Lord) Monck-
ton entered Parliament in 1951 and he became a member of the
new Cabinet on the morrow of the election which brought the
Conservatives back to power. The inability to get a man who was
chosen for office into Parliament had, at times, constituted a
barrier to this kind of appointment, but nowadays governments
normally find a way to effect this via the House of Lords, if not via
a seat in the House of Commons.

The rest of those who enter the Cabinet without previous ministerial experience tend to be rather on the opposite side of the
governmental spectrum. They are generally men the very strength
of whose parliamentary and political position makes their elevation to the Cabinet almost a foregone conclusion. In contrast to
these two groups, the run of the mill of our political leaders proceed more slowly and less directly to the apex of political power,
but if their rise is less meteoric the staying power of their course
is perhaps a little greater.

Social status also plays an important rôle in the process of reaching office and it cannot be neglected when considering the rank of
office held. High social position has often tended to support a
claim to an appointment commensurate in importance with the
appointee's status outside the Government. And at a time when the
lustre attached to high rank was vastly greater than it is today, the
illustrious name of a great nobleman could bestow prestige especially on a weak government. When Palmerston wished to give office
to the young Marquess of Hartington, he addressed himself to the
Duke of Devonshire, the Marquess' father: 'Young men in high
aristocratic positions should take part in the administration of
public affairs and should not leave the working of our political
machine to classes whose pursuits and interests are of a different
kind.'[1] The Duke of Argyll refused the first offer to enter Russell's

---

[1] cf. Holland, op. cit., p. 55. The future Duke of Devonshire was promoted
to the Cabinet three years later.

government in 1851. The offer was conveyed through Lord
Carlisle, his wife's uncle, who intimated to him that while not
a Cabinet place, the appointment would be 'at the door of the
Cabinet'. A year later, aged twenty-nine, the Duke entered the
Cabinet as Lord Privy Seal, a post which, Lord Aberdeen rightly
observed 'would not impose any serious amount of official labour
upon you'.[1]

A classification of the background of the men who were called
straight into the Cabinet is given below. It shows that specialists
entered the Government soon after entering parliamentary politics.
The representatives of factions, on the other hand, generally have
a considerable parliamentary apprenticeship behind them.

Before 1868 the 'factions' were composed predominantly of the
followers of leading politicians. They were held together by personal loyalty rather than political principles. In the more democratic polity which followed, the basis of faction became more
ideological.

In 1868 Gladstone regarded it as a great triumph that he had
persuaded Bright to enter the Cabinet; he had wrestled with him
for hours to obtain his consent. He was, of course, not concerned
with Bright's administrative ability; indeed there is little doubt
that at that time Bright was no longer capable of sustained work,
but Gladstone needed Bright as the elder statesman of the radical
camp and his appointment was a token of goodwill towards that
group.[2] The other two leading spokesmen of the Radicals, Forster
and Stansfield, were given junior office and their elevation to the
Cabinet came only later, and in Stansfield's case grudgingly at that.

---

[1] A generation earlier another great nobleman was offered the same appointment on even less onerous terms. Writing on behalf of her husband, Mrs Canning asked her brother-in-law, the Duke of Portland, to 'lend [his] name, as a
sleeping partner in the firm. . . . The office proposed for your acceptance is . . . in
point of rank second in the Government but has absolutely nothing to do in the
way of business and you need not remain an hour longer in Town for holding it
nor need you . . . even attend Cabinet Councils while you are in Town . . .'
Quoted in A. S. Turberville: *A History of Welbeck Abbey*, 2 vols., 1938–39, vol.
II, p. 333.

[2] *cf.* the letter of Clarendon to Delane written after the formation of the
Government. 'He [Bright] rightly declined India as being too laborious and takes
the Board of Trade where he will not have much to do.' A. I. Desant: *J. T.
Delane*, 2 vols., 1908, vol. II, p. 229.

TABLE V

Causes of direct elevation to the Cabinet:

Causes	Attained Cabinet Rank within five years of entering Parliament	Others	Total
1. High-ranking aristocratic position	1	—	1
2. Representatives of factions	3	13	16
3. Leaders of Party Organizations	—	2	2
4. Members of First Labour Cabinet*	2	12	14
5. Nepotism?	2	5	7
6. Brought into Cabinet as 'Specialists'	15	—	15
7. Representatives of T.U. Movement	1	1	2
8. No specific reason found	6	12	18
TOTAL	30	45	75

* It was natural that the first Labour Government should be composed largely of men without previous experience in government. The appointment of some (*i.e.* Wheatley and Thomson) seems, however, to have been due to the special position which the one held as spokesman of the Left wing and to the fact that the other was a personal friend of MacDonald. Others were brought in as non-party 'specialists'.

Glyn, the Chief Whip, suggested to Gladstone in 1870 that Stansfield should be offered the Post Office which was then vacant 'but in a deterring manner', and this, in spite of the fact that with Forster out of favour with a considerable part of Radical opinion, there was a need to placate this group.[1]

In 1880 the representation of the advanced Liberals in the Cabinet again formed an intricate problem which demanded much adroitness on the part of the Premier, who was unwilling to concede much, and considerable pressure on the part of the Radical leaders, Chamberlain and Dilke, who jointly hoped to force Gladstone to give them Cabinet posts. Dilke was the older and more experienced of the two, but he had antagonized the Queen by a series of strong attacks on the monarchy. Chamberlain had been in Parliament for a shorter period, but he had recently been elected Chair-

[1] *cf.* Gladstone–Granville Correspondence, (*loc. cit.*) letters 418–21.

man of the National Liberal League and this gave strength to his claim. In the end, it was Chamberlain who entered the Cabinet as President of the Board of Trade, while Dilke had to be content with the Under-Secretaryship at the Foreign Office.

Men in strong political positions are naturally apt to set their sights high. When two years later, after the Phoenix Park murders, Dilke was offered the Irish Secretaryship without a seat in the Cabinet, he resolutely refused, and even Chamberlain's entreaties were without avail.[1] He was promoted when the next vacancy occurred, but it needed the shifting of Dodson, from the Presidency of the Local Government Board to the Chancellorship of the Duchy of Lancaster, to enable him to take a post which would not meet with the disapproval of the Queen.[2]

When Morley entered Parliament at a by-election in 1883, he had already gained a national reputation as an outstanding radical journalist and publicist. On Courtney's resignation from the office of Financial Secretary of the Treasury, his name was mentioned as that of a possible successor. But this was hardly a big enough bait. He wrote to his sister: 'I was not asked but I don't think I would have taken it. My time will come and will come before I want it.'[3] It came only two years later, when he was appointed Irish Secretary with a seat in the Cabinet.

It was equally certain that Lord Randolph Churchill, who had constituted himself almost a one man party within the Conservative ranks, should be offered a Cabinet post at the first possible occasion (1885) after his meteoric rise inside his party.[4] Indeed, his position was so strong that he could press for the removal of Sir Stafford Northcote from the leadership of the House of Commons. He refused to join the Government unless this condition was met.

---

[1] Dilke's opposition to the acceptance of this post (traditionally associated with Cabinet rank) was strengthened by the fact, contrary to custom, that the Lord Lieutenant (Lord Spencer) was to be a member of the Cabinet. Gladstone wanted to offer him the Duchy but the Queen regarded this as a 'peculiar personal post'.

[2] cf. R. H. Jenkins: *Sir Charles Dilke*, 1958, p. 151–62.

[3] Francis Hirst: *The Early Life and Letters of John Morley*, 2 vols., 1927, vol. I, p. 207.

[4] During the first six years of his membership of the House of Commons he failed to make much of an impression on the House. He also spent a good deal of his time in Dublin where his father was Viceroy.

Salisbury had to acquiesce and had to send Northcote to the House of Lords after Hicks Beach had equally declined to serve because he regarded 'Lord Randolph Churchill's active assistance as a member of the Government vital to any hope of Conservative success at the General Election, for his popularity with the new electorate was greater than that of any other member of the party'.[1]

The closest parallel to Randolph Churchill's rise inside the Conservative Party is perhaps the inclusion of Aneurin Bevan in Mr Attlee's government in 1945. Bevan was appointed to a position inside the Cabinet although (or because) he had been the most vocal of the opponents of the wartime Coalition Government and also directly, or by implication, of the Labour Party Leadership. Unlike Randolph Churchill, Bevan was for the next fourteen years a serious challenger to the Labour Party leadership from the Left. Earlier Labour governments, too, had their 'representatives' of the Left; Wheatley in 1924, and Lansbury in 1929, were appointed to pacify the Left wing, but neither had previously been an outspoken opponent of the Party Leadership.

In giving office to men like Asquith in 1892, and to Burns and Lloyd George in 1905, the Liberal leaders were equally concerned with strong parliamentarians and representatives of important sections inside the Liberal Party. Others, less important as leaders of parliamentary factions, came in as representatives of the Liberal organization in the country. When Acland was appointed to the humble office of Vice-President of the Council in 1892, with a seat in the Cabinet, Gladstone gave office not only to the son of an old friend but also to a leading member of the directorate which governed the Liberal Federation. In 1905 the same office (by then styled 'Presidency of the Board of Education') was given to Augustine Birrell, who had been President of the National Liberal Federation during the preceding three years.

At the same time, Campbell-Bannerman gave the post of Secretary of State for Scotland to a man who lacked personal or parliamentary distinction, but who had been one of his most trusted lieutenants and a mainstay of the Liberal organization in Scotland. John Sinclair, later Lord Pentland, was a man with a large private income. He went to Sandhurst and then spent some years in the

---

[1] (Sir) W. S. Churchill: *Life of Lord Randolph Churchill*, vol. I, p. 403.

Army. He married a daughter of Lord Aberdeen and his acquain-
tances included Arnold Morley, the Chief Whip, and Edward
Marjoribanks, the Scottish Whip. The latter introduced him to the
Inverness Liberals who were in search of a candidate. Inverness
was the first of a series of Scottish constituencies which Sinclair
nearly contested, contested and lost and, in two cases, contested
and actually won. He sat in Parliament from 1889 and 1895, and
was Assistant Private Secretary to Campbell-Bannerman during
part of that time. He re-entered the Commons in 1897 and continued his activities in Scotland and was a general factotum to the
Liberal leader; he arranged the General Election in 1900 for him
and acted as a channel of communication between his leader and
the Scottish Liberals. He eventually became Scottish Liberal
Whip. In 1905 he helped Campbell-Bannerman in the task of
Cabinet formation and was himself rewarded with office.[1]

Midway between the leaders of powerful minorities and the
representatives of the party organization are the two men who
owed their elevation to the Cabinet to their leading positions in the
Trade Union movement. Ernest Bevin was appointed Minister of
Labour and a member of the small War Cabinet even before he
had found a seat in Parliament.[2] He had, of course, been a leading
figure inside the Labour Party and, earlier in life, had sought to
enter Parliament, but it is doubtful whether he would again have
tried to become a politician had it not been for the war and the
offer of a Cabinet post. George Isaacs, General Secretary of
NATSOPA, was less well known inside the Labour movement and
comparatively obscure inside the House of Commons, where he
had sat, with interruptions, since 1923. Yet there is little doubt that
when Attlee offered him Bevin's Ministry in 1945 he sought
thereby to strengthen the Trade Union representation in his
Cabinet.[3]

The appointment of these two Trade Union leaders to positions
which directly affected the working conditions and well-being of
the industrial wage earners was, of course, no accident. These

---

[1] For the life and career of Sinclair see: *The Rt Hon. John Sinclair, Lord
Pentland, A Memoir* (by Lady Pentland), 1928.

[2] Bevin was returned unopposed for Wandsworth Central six weeks later.

[3] Isaacs had been General Secretary of NATSOPA since 1909. He had previously
only held the post of Parliamentary Private Secretary.

were posts which the heads of industrial organizations were well
qualified to fill. In wartime an appointment such as Bevin's was
undoubtedly also designed to secure the whole-hearted co-operation of the industrial workers to the war-effort. In this Churchill
followed the pattern set by Lloyd George. During the First World
War, Labour politicians—who were in all cases Trade Union
leaders—were generally given appointments on the industrial side
of the Government administration and not in the general economic
field, or in foreign affairs.

EXPERTS AT THE HELM

Neither Bevin nor Isaacs were invited as 'experts'. Since the
beginning of the First World War, however, the specialist has
entered the uppermost echelons of governmental power. A sizeable group of Cabinet Ministers were given office because of their
expertise, their experience as administrators or merely because of
the prestige which they had gained in fields of activity quite outside
politics—mainly in Industry and in the Army. Those who were
members of the House of Commons entered Parliament practically simultaneously with their appointment to Cabinet Office;
those who were members of the other house had generally received
their peerage as a reward for non-political services.

It is, of course, significant that this movement started during the
First World War, when a vast increase of governmental activity
almost doubled the number of posts in the Government. It led to
the establishment of many new offices which demanded knowledge
and experience not readily available in the House of Commons or
the House of Lords.[1] The first man thus to come into the Cabinet
was Lord Kitchener. In appointing that eminent soldier as War
Minister, Asquith selected not only a specialist but also a popular
hero. The choice was made 'in deference both to the overwhelming
pressure of Public Opinion . . . and to the views of the opposition',
and both were largely the result of the hero's personality. Yet his
reputation, Lord Beaverbrook has reminded us, 'was partly sub-

---

[1] Apart from new Ministries in such fields as Blockade, Shipping, Food,
Pensions, Labour, Munitions and Reconstruction, a host of Boards and Committees were set up, often with considerable executive functions.

stance and partly that longer shadow which concrete objects cast in the rays of a setting sun'.[1] It is in the nature of such reputations that they are made late in life. The eminent soldiers and men of affairs who, in the evening of their careers, were invited to sit around the Cabinet table, were often men whose experience was no longer matched by performance.

One of the men who came into politics in this way during the First World War was H. A. L. Fisher. He entered the Government —and with it Parliament—when he was already over fifty. Until the outbreak of war, Fisher had not figured prominently in politics or in public life. After an uneventful career as an Oxford Don, he became Vice-Chancellor of Sheffield University in 1912. Two years later he was asked to serve on a committee appointed to investigate the alleged German atrocities in Belgium. This led to an interest in the impact of the war in the sphere of education. Appalled by the loss of life among so many of the ablest university students, he urged the Government to reserve some of the 'intellectual leaders of the future' for non-combatant service. Through this plan Fisher became known to members of the Government. He was sent to France to study the French system of propaganda and began to attend Lloyd George's 'breakfast parties'. When Lloyd George formed his coalition government he made Fisher President of the Board of Education, and although Fisher continued to act as special confidant of the Prime Minister, his time was mostly spent in the preparation of the reforms which were embodied in the Education Act of 1918, known as the Fisher Act.[2]

Lloyd George brought another seven outsiders into the inner governmental circle. Beatrice Webb noted with some scorn in her diary that 'Under Lloyd George each department has been handed over to the "interest" with which it is concerned. In that way, our little Welsh Attorney thinks, you combine the least political opposition with the maximum of technical knowledge. The Insurance Commission is controlled by the great industrial companies; the Board of Trade is controlled by the Shipowners, the Food Controller is a wholesale grocer (Lord Devonport), the Ministry of Munitions is largely manned by the representatives of

---

[1] Beaverbrook: *Politicians and the War*, 1914–16, 1928, p. 190.
[2] *cf.* David Ogg: *Herbert Fisher*, 1947.

the manufacturers of munitions while a duke's land-agent (Pro-
thero) has been placed at the head of the Board of Agriculture.
Finally a T.U. official is Minister of Labour (Hodge) and has been
given, as the permanent head of his department, an ex-Trade
Union Official (Shackleton). The one shining example of this
"vested interest cum expert" government is the distinguished
University Professor—H. A. L. Fisher—now President of the
Board of Education.'[1]

MacDonald felt equally in need of special talents for his two
governments. He asked Lord Chelmsford—whose career had been
at the Bar and in Colonial administration—to take charge of the
Admiralty; he selected G. H. Oliver, a retired Colonial Civil
Servant (albeit an old Fabian) as Colonial Secretary with a seat in
the House of Lords and appointed a non-political lawyer as Lord
Chancellor. Two later Lord Chancellors, who had not been
previously politically prominent, were selected from members
of the Bar. But the appointment of experts and outsiders recurred
on a significant scale only under the threat or impact of the Second
World War.

It was thus that two Civil Servants became Ministers of the
Crown. Sir John Anderson exchanged the post of Permanent
Secretary of the Home Office, formally for the post of Lord Privy
Seal, but in reality for the planning of the Civil Defence side of the
War; Sir James Grigg became the political head of the Department
of which he had been the Civil Service head. Grigg's appointment
to the War Office, extraordinary as it appears on the face of things,
is less surprising. As a Civil Servant his career had been rather
unconventional. From a Private Secretaryship to Warren Fisher,
the head of the Treasury, he advanced to become Principal Private
Secretary to a succession of Chancellors, including a five years'
stint with Winston Churchill. In 1934 he went as Finance Member
(*i.e.* Minister) to India and expected to have the reversion of the
Permanent Secretaryship of the Treasury on his return to England.
In the event the post went to Sir Horace Wilson, and Grigg became
Secretary of the War Office. He remained in that capacity for three
years when Churchill selected him as political head in succession
to Margesson. No doubt he was selected equally as an old friend, a

---

[1] Beatrice Webb: *Diaries, 1912–24* (edited by Margaret I. Cole), 1952, p. 83.

politically loyal subordinate and an experienced administrator.[1] The Prime Minister had proposed to him that he should take office as a Peer but Grigg expressed preference for the House of Commons and he was in consequence returned for East Cardiff. The appointment created some consternation, surprise and, on the part of seasoned politicians with expectation of office, a little envy. Grigg himself admits to a feeling of discomfort because, despite his administrative experience and his background as Minister in India, he was very much 'a new man as a politician'.[2]

With administrative and military exigencies largely determining the actions of the Prime Minister, the appointment of such 'outsiders' to government posts does not assume quite the same significance as in peacetime. There is inevitably less political and parliamentary control of the executive and there is less need for the administrator to be a politician. On the other hand, the expert turned minister may use the prestige gained as administrator in furthering a political career. Lord Woolton was appointed Minister of Food on the strength of his experience as the head of a department store empire, without strong party ties. After the war he became the most successful head of the Conservative Party Organization.

When Mr Churchill returned to the Premiership, he brought two distinguished non-politicians into the Cabinet. He appointed Lord Alexander as Minister of Defence and Lord Ismay as Secretary of Commonwealth Affairs. He also appointed Lord Leathers, who had been War Minister of Transport, but who could hardly be called a politician, Secretary of State for the Co-ordination of Transport, Fuel and Power. Lord Cherwell was given the sinecure office of Paymaster General and was put in charge of scientific development and research. In these appointments the technical and the extremely personal often combine. Lord Ismay has told us how anxious he was not to accept office and how he could not resist the pressure of the man whom he so greatly admired.[3] Cherwell

---

[1] One cannot read Sir James Grigg's autobiography (*Prejudice and Judgment*, 1948) without becoming aware of the 'political' character of the office of Private Secretary to an important Minister. In this particular case a powerful politician and an intellectually outstanding Civil Servant reinforced each other on a political plane which they both shared.

[2] *cf.* Sir P. J. Grigg, *op. cit.*, p. 352.

[3] *cf.* Lord Ismay: *The Memoirs*, 1960, p. 37.

had been Churchill's adviser on scientific matters since the 1930's. During the war he held a government post to carry out similar functions, and when Churchill returned to power he again brought in Cherwell, who occupied his position as the Prime Minister's friend and adviser, his research assistant, sounding board and listening post.

In these cases the appointment of a man on account of his expert knowledge merges with his eligibility as a personal friend. There can be little doubt that, in the selection of men for office, personal considerations play an important part. Parliamentary performance, general ability, expertise and experience all affect the selection. But in a world where advancement so often depends not on men's knowledge as on the knowledge of men, it would be surprising to find the stratosphere of politics composed entirely of those particles which had risen there by the sheer thrust of ability and perseverance.[1]

Among those, who advanced right away to Cabinet positions, five or six appear to have owed their appointments to the strong ties which bound them to the source of power inside the administration: *i.e.* to the Prime Minister. These men tend to be relatives or close friends. But sometimes the placing of men in the Cabinet is due to their connection with another leading member of the administration. Henry Matthews, a Catholic lawyer from Birmingham, clearly owed his surprising advance from backbencher to Home Secretary to his friendship with Randolph Churchill. It is, however, in the first steps inside the political élite that we can best observe the work of a guiding hand. The whole gamut of social forces inside a political party, and on the parliamentary scene as a whole, are operative here, and members of the Government, especially the departmental head of a junior minister about to be appointed, exercise considerable influence. Such forces must be investigated if we are to understand the formation of the political élite.

THE INFLUENCE OF KINSHIP AND FRIENDSHIP

Clearly, we must start here with the phenomenon discussed in the previous chapter: the membership of political families. The inci-

---

[1] Leathers and Cherwell had previous government experience outside the Cabinet during the war. Neither could, however, be termed a 'politician' and they were originally appointed as 'experts'.

dence of this is too great to be without significance. Parliamentary activity and political service in one generation is, as we saw, frequently linked with similar activity on the part of members of an earlier generation of the same family. One-tenth of the Cabinet members studied were the sons of ministers, many of whom had sat in Cabinets. But the tradition of political service acts not only as a spur towards success, it is also a lever in the process. In the attempt to reach the first rung on the political ladder, the tyro is often helped by the elder members of his family, who are active in politics and perhaps, even more subtly, by the veneration in which an ancestor may have been held. In his later political life, his own qualities and achievements are important. Referring to the appointment of the future Lord Salisbury as Secretary for India in 1866, Disraeli's biographer refers not only to the former's parliamentary reputation but also to the fact that he was the son—and now the heir—of an old friend and colleague.[1]

The effect of political careers in the direct line of descent is strengthened and enhanced by the political activity in the wider kinship group. Throughout the nineteenth century, the British aristocracy was a highly endogamous group. The heir to a peerage or any member of a titled family who entered the House of Commons would very likely find there not only members of his father's family but also men who were related to him on his mother's side. Moreover, endogamy was not only a social phenomenon inside a fairly large class; it was also significant within the various layers which we can observe inside it.[2] The intermarriage of members of the families of the *larger* landowners is bound to strengthen the cousinhood inside Parliament because these are the families which, more than any others, tended to provide recruits for the House of Commons. It is instructive to follow the ramifications of kinship as they manifest themselves among Cabinet Ministers of different periods and various parties.

The daughter of the Duke of Argyll married the brother of A. J.

---

[1] Moneypenny and Buckle, *op. cit.*, vol. II, p. 178.

[2] The endogamy of the British Aristocracy was, of course, customary rather than legal. The term *mésalliance*, so frequently found in the continental discussion of aristocratic status is neither used nor is it meaningful in any sense. We can simply observe that in the Victorian era at least members of the 'landed classes' tended to marry within that class.

Balfour. Balfour was a nephew of the 3rd Marquess of Salisbury. When Balfour became Prime Minister, he appointed Alfred Lyttelton as Colonial Secretary. Lyttelton was Gladstone's nephew[1]; his mother and Gladstone's wife[2] were sisters. Lyttelton's sister had married Lord Frederick Cavendish, M.P. and Minister and brother of the Duke of Devonshire, who had sat in Gladstone's Cabinet and was now a colleague of Balfour. The Duke was succeeded in his title by his nephew, who sat in the House of Commons from 1891 to 1908 and who was, in turn, Financial Secretary to the Treasury (1903–05), Governor-General of Canada (1916–21) and Secretary of State for the Colonies (1922–23). His son, the future 10th Duke, married a daughter of the 4th Marquess of Salisbury. One of his daughters married James Stuart, son of the 5th Earl of Moray, at one time Secretary of State for Scotland. Another daughter married Harold Macmillan. By tracing Lady Dorothy Macmillan's ancestry along another line, more kinship ramifications of the great Whig and Tory landed families emerge. Her maternal grandfather was the 5th Marquess of Lansdowne, Salisbury's Foreign Secretary, Governor of Canada and Viceroy of India. Lansdowne's brother-in-law was Lord George Hamilton, with whom he sat in the same Cabinet. Lord Winterton, a Cabinet Minister of a later generation, was his nephew. Lansdowne's son married the daughter of another Viceroy and, through him, we can follow a direct link with Lord Grey of the Reform Bill and, through his wife, to Lord John Russell. Indeed if we cast the net of cousinhood wide enough, it would contain most of the Prime Ministers who held office during the period here studied, as well as a large number of Cabinet Ministers and Members of Parliament.

By constructing kinship charts centred around a few leading aristocratic politicians and indicating on them those who were in Parliament and especially those who held office, incidence of family ties can be shown in a more systematic form.[3] Given the

---

[1] Lyttelton was also brother-in-law of Asquith through the latter's second wife, but as the marriage took place some years after the death of Mrs Lyttelton, this connection is somewhat tenuous.

[2] Her mother was a cousin of the younger Pitt and a niece of Lord Granville, head of the Government of All Talents, 1806–7.

[3] These kinship charts will be found at the end of the chapter.

general kinship pattern, the operation of kinship and friendship in individual cases of political appointments becomes of interest.

In the general cousinhood of the great Whig families, to which Lord John Russell attributed the prevalence of the Woburn Bench in the 1850's, the Barings were comparative newcomers. But they rose rapidly and connected themselves well. Sir Francis Baring, the third Baronet, was Chancellor of the Exchequer in 1839. He had married a niece of Lord Grey (of the Reform Bill) and, through this marriage, he became brother-in-law of Sir George Grey and Henry Labouchère, and was more distantly related to (Sir) Charles Wood, later Lord Halifax, all of whom held ministerial office. These connections proved to be very useful in the political career of his son. On leaving Oxford in 1848, G. T. Baring became Private Secretary to his uncle Labouchère when the latter was Irish Secretary; he followed him to the Board of Trade and then turned to serve his other uncle, Grey, in a similar capacity and from him went to work under Wood at the Admiralty. When nearly ten years later he entered the House of Commons, he continued his attachment to the latter two men and served as junior minister at the Admiralty, the India Office and the Home Office. It was Sir Charles Wood who some years later suggested Baring as a suitable candidate for the post of Governor General of India. His qualifications for the post are obscure although he had two necessary prerequisites: wealth and a peerage, both of which he had acquired in 1866 on the death of his father. He returned from India in 1877 after a stay of five years and, as an 'Elder Statesman', he was given Cabinet office by Gladstone in 1880.

Private Secretaryship, the unpaid service to a public personage, is a frequent opening to a political career and even when the first step, membership of the House of Commons, has been made, a Parliamentary Private Secretaryship is a suitable stepping stone for further advancement.[1] Sir Edward Grey, Lord Northbrook's nephew, began his public activity as Private Secretary to the British Resident in Egypt, Sir Evelyn Baring who was a relative of

---

[1] Others have deliberately eschewed such a ladder of possible advance. A friend who was Parliamentary Private Secretary to Baldwin suggested to Duff Cooper that he might possibly attach himself to Winston Churchill in a similar capacity. Cooper, however, rejected the advice and decided to make his way up by his own effort.

Northbrook and had been his private secretary in India. Gladstone advised him to make politics his career. Balfour began his political career as Private Secretary to his uncle to whom he also owed his first appointment. We have seen how agitating he found the ensuing conflict between feelings of loyalty and feelings of dependence. Balfour's own Parliamentary Private Secretary in 1877 was George Wyndham, whom he later helped to obtain his first governmental post. Asquith appointed his brother-in-law as his Parliamentary Private Secretary and thus 'gave him his first political chance'.[1] During the war he made him first Under-Secretary for War and later Secretary of State for Scotland.

To be the son of a leading politician is, of course, of inestimable benefit to those who seek a political career. In 1880 just before setting off on his 'Midlothian Campaign' Gladstone conceived the idea of getting a seat for his son, Herbert. The latter noted in his diary that he 'was summoned to London' (from Oxford). He met Adam—the Liberal Whip—who told him of these plans but indicated that 'all the boroughs were snapped up'. 'On Wednesday morning,' the diary continues, 'I was summoned to Parliament Street (the Liberal Central Office) and Adam told me a deputation was waiting to ask me to contest Middlesex . . . I could not refuse, though I felt annihilated.'[2] The fight for Middlesex was, of course, a rather hopeless proposition but another opening was soon found. Mr Gladstone's election for Midlothian left the Leeds seat, for which he had also been elected, vacant. The son was suggested as a substitute for the father, was accepted and elected unopposed at the age of twenty-six. A year later he was appointed a Junior Lord of the Treasury. The post was unpaid but his father gave him £45 a month, partly no doubt in recompense for the work which he did for him as a Secretary and go-between. In 1886 he became Financial Secretary at the War Office and then advanced slowly via the Under-Secretaryship of the Home Office, the Office of Works, the post of Liberal Chief Whip until he reached the Home Office and the Cabinet in 1905.

Even in the 1960's the personal element cannot be taken out of politics. Personal favourites will continue to be appointed and the

---

[1] cf. Margot Asquith: *Autobiography* (Penguin Ed.), 2 vols, 1936, vol. I, p. 13.
[2] C. Mallet: *Herbert Gladstone, a Memoir*, 1932, p. 73

antagonism between leading politicians do today affect the smooth working of a government probably as much as they did a century ago.[1] A Cabinet is a team of individuals thrown by necessity much into each other's company; it would be absurd to expect that its composition would not show the influence of personal ties. In 1958, seven Cabinet Ministers out of nineteen were related by marriage to the Prime Minister, and for the whole of the Government, the proportion of Mr Macmillan's relatives was even higher.[2] 'Nepotism is one of the strongest human emotions,' Christopher Hollis has written, 'and everybody would at all times give jobs to as many cousins as he is let.'[3] To do this is comparatively easy where the group from which men are selected for office is one that is already closely interrelated. The choice of 'cousins' is then inevitable, and must, in many cases, be entirely fortuitous.

At the same time we must not neglect the influence of party. Today parliamentary leadership, governmental office and public eminence is closely linked to party leadership. Party loyalties, buttressed by the marked although decreasing antagonism and conflict between the two major parties, help towards cohesion of the leading groups of politicians. It is as partisans that political leaders keep their status when electoral defeat has swept them from office. Others gain prominence through the parties with which they identify. Service to party brings loyal followership and in the end often rewards of office. To study the British political élite in the twentieth century means also to study the leadership of the two major political parties.

---

[1] cf. the recent autobiographies of leading Labour politicians, e.g. Attlee, Dalton, Morrison and Shinwell. See also L. Hunter: *The Road to Brighton Pier*, 1959.

[2] *John Bull*, January 4, 1958.

[3] C. Hollis: 'The Conservative Party in History' in *Political Quarterly*, vol. 32, No. 3. July–September 1961, p. 220, commenting on the article cited in the preceding note.

DIAGRAM B: THE DERBYS

Derby[12]

Derby[13]

Wilton[2]

Wilton[3]
M.P.

Wilton[4]

Derby[14]
P.M.

Skelmersdale[1]
M.P.

Alvanley[1]
M.P., M.

Crawford[26]
M.P.

Clarendon[4] C.M.

Widow of Salisbury[2]

Derby[15]
M.P., C.M.

Derby[16]
C.M., M.P.

Manchester[7]

Devonshire[8]

Derby[17]
M.P., C.M.

Lord Stanley
M.P., C.M.

Oliver Stanley
M.P., C.M.

Derby[18]

Members of the aristocracy

Non-aristocrats

Unmarried

No descendants

Descendants did not contain M.P.s or Ministers in first generation and were consequently not traced

M.P. Member of Parliament
M.   Minister
C.M. Cabinet Minister
P.M. Prime Minister

DIAGRAM C: THE SALISBURYS

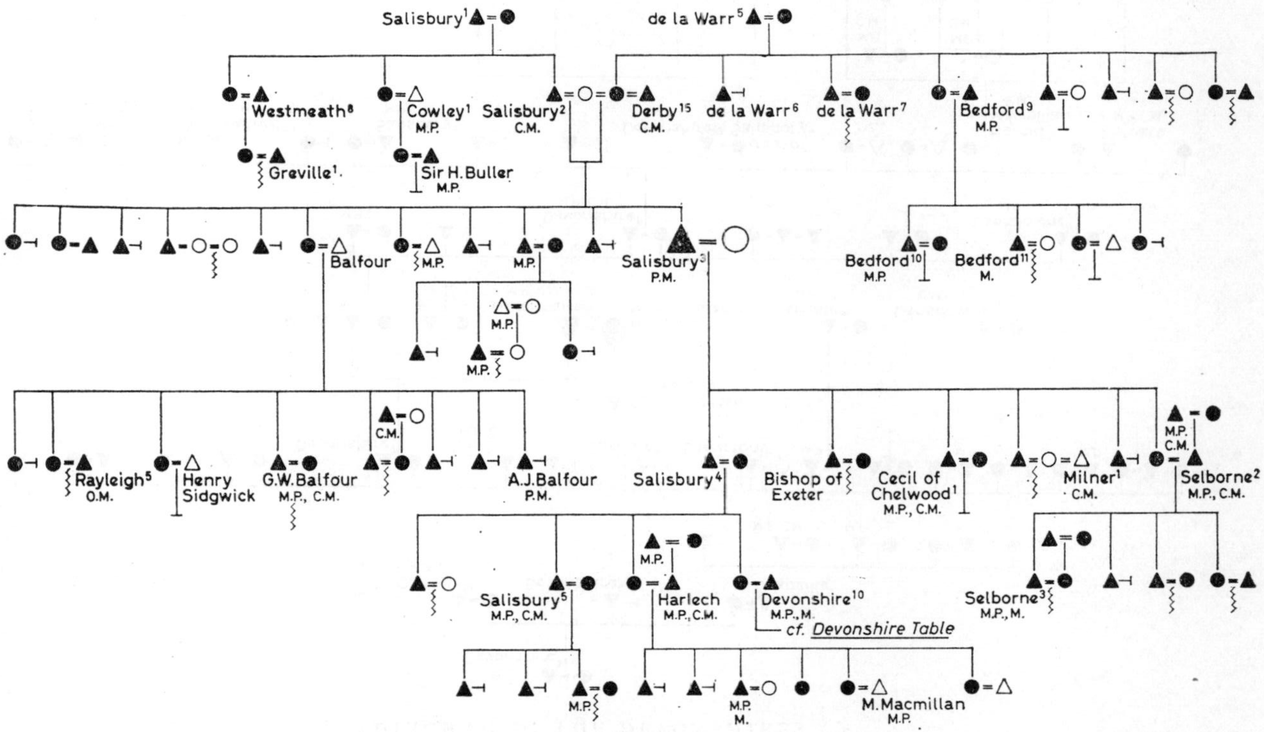

DIAGRAM D: THE DEVONSHIRES

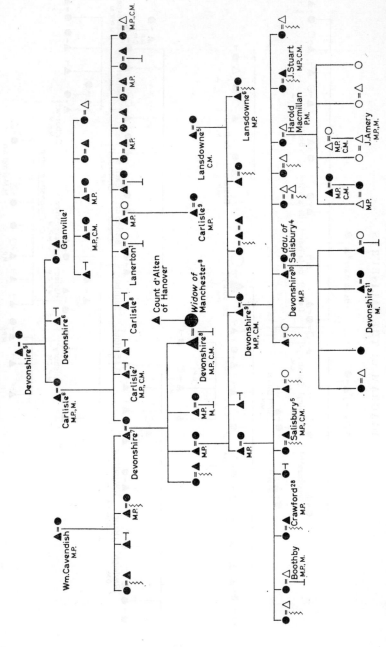

224

CHAPTER IX

Labour Leaders and Labour Led

'The power of the movement lies in the massive obstinacy of the rank and file. Whenever this massive feeling can be directed for or against any particular measure it becomes almost irresistible. Our English Governing Class would not openly dare to defy it'.—BEATRICE WEBB.

> *O but we dreamed to mend*
> *Whatever mischief seemed*
> *To afflict mankind, but now*
> *That winds of winter blow*
> *Learn that we were crack-pated when we dreamed.*
> —W. B. YEATS: *Nineteen Hundred and Nineteen.*

A SOCIOLOGICAL analysis of the leadership of a political party such as is attempted in this chapter must seek to study definite groups over a definite period of time. With the growth of Labour's Parliamentary representation and with the decline of sectional organizations within the party, the Party's national leadership has become increasingly synonymous with the group of Labour M.P.s and Cabinet Ministers. Those who reached prominent positions in the labour movement have drifted sooner or later into Parliament and in the struggle to achieve national renown, membership of Parliament is a considerable asset.[1]

---

[1] The only men who are influential in the Labour Party and who are not included in the above groups are, of course, those trade union leaders who participate to a significant extent in the *political* activities of the labour movement without, however, occupying formal political or parliamentary positions. Their influence is based solely on their position in the industrial movement. To have included this group would, however, have presented considerable problems of definition and selection. By studying, for example, the men who occupy the trade union seats on the National Executive of the Labour Party we would have missed most of the really influential trade union leaders. Even if a representative group could have been found the paucity of biographical material would have presented serious obstacles to the evaluation of their rôle and contribution. I therefore decided to leave out this group except for those trade union leaders who were in Parliament.

The character of the Labour Party élite has so far only been drawn in broad outline and largely in respect of the Labour Cabinets.[1] Here the emphasis will be on the evolution of a representative leadership cadre within a new and non-traditional political party and on the relationship between the various levels and groups of the Labour Leadership.

Labour movements, especially those exercising governmental power or aiming to do so, are customarily rent by a conflict between a 'left' and a 'right' wing—or rather between conservative 'go-slowers' and radical 'whole-hoggers'. To throw light on this phenomenon, the social antecedents of those members of the P.L.P. who have shown determined opposition to certain aspects of Labour policy, are examined. While this 'left-wing' is not a socially homogeneous subgroup of the élite, there are indications that even *within* the Labour Movement social background and career lines are correlated with political attitudes.

A merely formal analysis of the leadership of the Labour Party would, however, be of limited interest. The British Labour movement has a strong democratic tradition and greatly developed local loyalties. From a loose federation of trade unions and socialist societies composed almost entirely of working-class men and women, it grew into a nation-wide organization, which was centrally directed and with a significant portion of its members belonging to the middle class.[2] When at the beginning its leadership faced the serried ranks of aristocratic and bourgeois politicians in the House of Commons the two groups were separated not only by great social differences but also by the prevalence in Labour's ranks of anti-traditional attitudes towards political power. Yet parallel with Labour's own *embourgeoisement*—and hardly unconnected with it—we find that its concept of leadership has largely assimilated the attitudes traditionally held by representa-

---

[1] See Chapter IV, pp. 92–96.

[2] Professional people and white collar workers are especially noticeable among the active party workers and in local Management Committees which, among other things, select the party's Parliamentary candidates. Detailed investigations of the membership of Labour Party constituency organizations and of their activities are unfortunately rare. But see J. S. Gould: Riverside: a Labour Constituency, *Fabian Journal*, November 1954; W. Fienburgh and others: Put policy on the agenda: A Study of Labour Party Organizations, *Fabian Journal*, February 1952; A. H. Birch: *Small Town Politics*, 1959, ch. 5.

tives of the older political parties. Its own representation grew on the whole into a 'responsible opposition' and 'learned how to govern'. In order to understand the evolution of the Labour Party élite we must thus also take account of the ideological factor and of the changing concepts of the rôle of political leadership held by Labour leaders.

NOVITIATE IN OPPOSITION AND GOVERNMENT

In 1906 the British Public was startled by the fact that the Labour Representation Committee, which had only been founded just over five years earlier, succeeded in returning 29 members to the House of Commons.

From the very start Labour's rôle was circumscribed by the limited objectives which the Labour Representation Committee (L.R.C.) had set itself. In putting itself forward as the spokesman of 'Labour' it thought in terms of the specific interests of an economic group. The 1906 election manifesto of the L.R.C., endorsed by each candidate, spoke of the House of Commons which 'is supposed to be the people's house and yet the people are not there. Landlords, employers, lawyers, brewers and financiers are there in force, why not labour? The trade unions ask the same liberty as capital yet they are refused. . . .' This allusion to the encroachment on trade union liberty by judicial decisions (such as the Taff Vale case) preceded reference to a small list of specific reforms and, finally, in a general way, to the need for the social amelioration of the condition of the very poor.

Without exception, the 29 men who were elected under L.R.C. auspices were men of working class background. Labour leaders of middle-class origin, who came predominantly from the ranks of the Fabian Society, the Social Democratic Federation, and to a lesser extent from the Independent Labour Party, either did not seek election, or if they did, they were unsuccessful, like J. B. Glasier. Labour M.P.s and their 'Lib-Lab' colleagues who joined them in 1909 were born mostly in the 1850's and 1860's, and although the majority had received some formal schooling this rarely extended into their 'teens. Their subsequent self-education must be seen against this background. From their own accounts of their early reading, and of the books which influenced them most, an

interesting picture emerges.[1] We find that specific socialist literature is referred to only by a minority and even the English
utopian thinkers and Philosophical Radicals are rarely mentioned,
with the exception of John Stuart Mill. Of later reformers Henry
George's name is frequently given. There is some influence of
the Fabians and two lone voices mentioned Marx. In general we
find that the most influential social thinkers are Carlyle and Ruskin,
but it is significant how often religious writings (the Bible and
sermons) are mentioned and how many of these working-class politicians referred to the influence of poetry.

It is true that some Labour leaders, *e.g.* MacDonald and Snowden, had in the course of their political careers moved upward and
had entered the lower strata of the middle class through marriage
or by their own efforts. But before the introduction of salaries for
M.P.s, political activity meant for the majority continued material
hardship. Their hardship, moreover, is the more significant as it
must be seen against the background of well-to-do, if not opulent
living, which was the rule among M.P.s and the higher social
order to which most of them belonged. Jowett was later to write
that 'Labour members who entered Parliament after state salaries
were paid had little idea of what it meant to be an I.L.P. M.P.
during the first four years of my Parliamentary life'.[2] M.P.s who
belonged to the I.L.P. were allowed two hundred pounds annually
out of the Parliamentary Fund created by the Labour Party. This
sum had to pay not only for their expenses at Westminster but
also for the needs of their families. It proved hardly sufficient, and
men like Jowett and Snowden tended to supplement their salaries

---

[1] *cf.* 'The Labour Party and the books that helped to make it', *The Review of
Reviews*, Vol. 33, 1909, pp. 568–82. This article gives the responses of 45 (out of
51) Labour and Lib-Lab M.P.s to questions on early reading and intellectual
influences.

[2] Fenner Brockway: *Socialism over 60 Years: the Life of Jowett of Bradford
(1864–1944)*, 1946, p. 70. Yet even the position of salaried Labour M.P.s was not
an easy one, certainly not in the period of high prices immediately after the
First World War. With a parliamentary salary of £400 and a grant from his
trade union, Shinwell found in 1922 that he had just over £5 a week to spend in
London. Of this he paid 15s. for a small room in an unfashionable district.
'Meals in the House were quite beyond the means of most Scottish members
and we used to walk miles to discover cheap and clean food.' Emanuel Shinwell:
Conflict Without Malice, 1955, p. 82.

by outside activities—mainly journalism. Those M.P.s whose candidature had been sponsored by trade unions were generally better off. If they were officials of the unions they continued to draw their salaries—or at least a part of them. In many cases they received a special allowance to permit them to carry out their parliamentary work.

As a group, the Parliamentary Labour Party (P.L.P.) lacked discipline. The men who formed it were united only in their class background. Their political views, the extent of their parliamentary activity and attitude towards other parties, varied with character, intellectual activity and integrity. Professed socialists like Keir Hardie, MacDonald and Snowden mixed with independent-minded trade union leaders (Clynes, Crooks, and Hodge) as well as with those who were really Liberals at heart (Shackleton, Bowerman, or Roberts). The majority of them owed their successes at the polls to electoral agreements with the Liberals, or, at best, they were returned on minority votes in three-cornered contests.[1] The leadership of the Party reflected this uneasy alliance between the socialist and the trade union element. In the first five years the office was held by four men—Keir Hardie, Shackleton (during Hardie's illness), Henderson and Barnes. In 1911 MacDonald took over.

The changes in the leadership were also partly due to the currently held view of the rôle of the chairman. He was regarded more as a spokesman and representative than as an initiator of policies and a leader of men. Keir Hardie found the burden of his office irksome and the effects stifling. 'The strongest reason to get out of the Chair,' he wrote to Snowden, 'is that I may be able to speak out occasionally. In the last session the party has practically dropped out of public notice. The comic papers and the cartoonists are ignoring us, a fatal sign. . . . By another session those of us who believe in fighting will have to get together occasionally on our own account and if we cannot drag the party with us we will "gang oor

---

[1] Of the 29 M.P.s elected under the auspices of the L.R.C. in 1906, 24 were elected without Liberal opposition or with implied Liberal tolerance. They had either a straight fight in a one-member constituency or they were running tacitly in harness with a Liberal against Conservative opposition in double-member constituencies. cf. F. Bealing and H. Pelling: *The Labour Party in British Politics, 1900–1906,* 1958, pp. 298–9.

ain gait".'[1] On the other hand, Shackleton, who would have been
Hardie's natural successor (having already exercised the chairmanship during the latter's illness) refused nomination in 1908 because
he thought that he could not be sure of the support of the socialist
Labour M.P.s. Henderson was elected instead, but did not succeed any better than Keir Hardie in impressing the stamp of his
personality on the P.L.P. The party continued to be an uneasy
alliance between trade union representatives and socialist politicians. The bulk of the work in the House of Commons was carried out by a small number of active and devoted members and it
is hardly surprising that this group was almost synonymous with
the convinced socialists on the Labour benches. The I.L.P. members were in any case the only ones who were quite free to devote
the whole of their time to affairs at Westminster. For the trade
union leaders and officials who were in Parliament, politics had
mostly to be combined with union activity and few of them had
undergone the kind of apprenticeship to parliamentary activity
which is to be found on the speaker's platform or in political
journalism. Snowden tells us, that even when at Westminster they
tended to 'spend their time in the smoking-room or on the
terrace'.[2] The more humdrum the work, the less the attendance.
On the Standing Committee on the Housing Bill in 1908, Labour
M.P.s had recorded only half the possible attendances.

In 1911 Barnes, as Chairman of the P.L.P., put his finger on a
tender spot when he complained about 'the irregularities of
attendance on the part of some of the members. The main cause
(of which) is no doubt the fact that the unions have not sufficiently
released their members from trade union work', and, he went
on to say, 'it was a matter for serious consideration . . . whether
(the party) should prolong indefinitely a system of dual service
which operates so as to prevent efficient work being done in
Parliament'.[3]

The loyalties and sense of cohesion among Labour M.P.s were
put to a further test by the events following the 1910 elections. The
decline in the Liberal Government's majority meant that the

---

[1] P. Snowden: *An Autobiography*, 2 vols., 1934, vol. I, p. 174.

[2] *ibid.*, p. 216.

[3] *Report of the Labour Party Conference of 1911*, p. 31 (from the report on the
work of the P.L.P.).

Labour Party occupied a strategically important position at Westminster. A move against the Government could result in its defeat in a general election, should the Conservatives decide to support it. If that were to occur, the position of the Labour Party would be precarious. With depleted funds it would have to meet at the polls with Liberal opposition where there had been none so far. In the following years the Parliamentary Labour Party certainly tended to refrain from too violent criticism and opposition of Liberal policy and measures.[1]

MacDonald, who had just succeeded to the leadership of the P.L.P. and who clearly meant to keep it, was the chief advocate of a policy of limited objectives and tactical advances and he defended this policy with great force at the 1911 Labour Party Conference. 'The foundations of the new Jerusalem,' he averred, 'could not be laid by simply quoting meaningless sentences.'[2] The trouble with his policy was probably not that he was mistaken, but as Snowden put it later, that he failed to combine a policy of co-operation with reasonable aggressiveness and thus conveyed the impression that he was willing to sacrifice the independence of the party to political expediency. This led in the following years to a growing estrangement between the parliamentary leadership of the party and sections of its rank-and-file supporters in the country. The conflict over policy and parliamentary tactics showed itself also within the P.L.P. but here the most decisive break occurred over the attitude towards the war. While the majority supported the Government, five of the seven I.L.P. members opposed it and desired an early peace.[3] The proposals for military conscription, however, aroused considerable bitterness in Labour's ranks and opposition to it lasted a long time. Yet in the end, after the Bill had been so

---

[1] Only 31 (of 42) Labour M.P.s voted in favour of a 'Right to Work' resolution in 1908 and only 17 supported Hardie's motion denouncing the use of police and soldiers to break up a strike in a colliery. On the other hand, a minority on the Left, mainly I.L.P. members, decided to vote on issues according to their merit and in this frequently defied the decisions of the group. Thus Jowett, Lansbury, Snowden, O'Grady and Thorne voted against the National Insurance Bill, as they objected to the contributory element in its financial structure. cf. P. Snowden, op. cit., p. 228.

[2] loc. cit., p. 218.

[3] i.e. Hardie, MacDonald, Snowden, Jowett, Richardson and, on the other hand, Clynes and James Parker.

amended as to meet some Labour objections, only ten Labour M.P.s voted against it.[1]

Having thus overcome its scruples and followed the general trend of public opinion, Labour received recognition in a concrete form. With the advent of the coalition in May 1915, the Party entered the Government. Of the thirty-odd Labour M.P.s who supported the war, nine found their way on to the Treasury Bench. Three served under Asquith; later, under Lloyd George, Labour had six places in the Government. Three men reached Cabinet rank and the rest served mainly as junior ministers or as whips. The Labour Ministers were mostly in their fifties and sixties; they had been in Parliament for about ten years. With a few exceptions they had neither opportunity nor outstanding ability to make their mark as administrators, or to contribute to the war policy in general except as defenders of governmental policy in the trade union movement. It seems significant for the character of this first group of Labour leaders that only a minority continued to play a leading part in Labour Party politics after the war. Only Clynes, Henderson and Walsh held office in the first Labour Government.[2]

In this Administration, as in later ones, the Party had to rely largely on men with little or no experience in government office. Over 40 per cent of all Labour Cabinet Ministers (26 out of 63) advanced straight from a position of a private Member of Parliament into Cabinet office, in most cases without even the indirect experience of government which the Conservative or Liberal back-bencher tended to receive by contact with colleagues when his party was in office. The experience of departmental administration enjoyed by many others was likewise limited, owing to the short duration of the earlier Labour administration. Only during the life of the third and fourth Labour Governments do we find anything resembling the usual *cursus honorum* inside the administration.[3] Labour politicians, who had sprung from the working class were especially liable to be pitchforked straight into Cabinet

---

[1] *cf.* J. H. S. Reid: *The Rise of the British Labour Party*, 1935, p. 217.

[2] Indeed, four Labour Ministers actually defied the decision of their party to withdraw from the coalition after the end of the war. However, after the General Election of 1922 even the last of these disappeared from the political scene.

[3] Labour's share in the wartime coalition helped in this.

office. They reached the governmental front bench without the preparation for political office which family background and education tended to give to members of the other two parties. Their training ground for politics had not been the debating society of one of the older Universities, or the Officers' Mess, the Board Room or the landed estate, but the platform, the office desk or the negotiating table. Their entrance into politics was that of men who represented their union or their movement and not of men who sought to embark on a public career or seek office. MacDonald and Snowden, David Kirkwood thought, were 'aloof from sectional interest', and in consequence 'always seemed to have a wider outlook on political affairs than the men who came into politics through industrial channels'.[1] Smillie, who was offered the post of Food Controller during the first war, declined because 'he felt that [his] life's work was with the miners [and that he] had no special qualifications for such a post'.[2]

The Webbs poured scorn on the narrow-minded and slow-thinking trade union officials who formed the bulk of the P.L.P. between 1918 and 1922. Yet after the formation of the Government, Beatrice Webb was forced to report that the Civil Service was pleased with their new masters, that they eagerly devoted themselves to business, were anxious to learn and lacked any 'side' in the exercise of their duties. 'Whether its policy is right or wrong, Labour will prove itself emphatically fit for *administration* and that is what the Service likes.'[3]

To be a learner in the exercise of government can lead to a neglect of wider issues. Absorption in administrative action by which positive results can be achieved comparatively quickly may make men more ready to accept existing conditions. Sir Almeric Fitzroy, then Clerk of the Privy Council, reports a conversation with Clynes, then Deputy Food Controller:

'Whose period of office has clearly been of great educational value . . . Clynes has profited greatly by contact with the larger outlook of Lord Rhondda of whom he spoke with sincere praise. It was significant to hear from him that Labour at large had ceased to take any strong

---

[1] David Kirkwood: *My Life of Revolt*, 1935, p. 217.
[2] Robert Smillie: *My Life for Labour*, 1924, p. 176.
[3] *op. cit.*, p. 4.

interest in the reform of the House of Lords and gave as his principal reason the sturdy defence of individual rights for which members of that assembly had made themselves conspicuous.'[1]

Seven years later, when he held office again, Clynes apparently still felt himself very much a beginner in the art of government. His civil servants were always at his side 'advising, coaching, checking and, in short time, I gained a measure of knowledge necessary in matters where perhaps national safety and the spending of millions was concerned'.[2]

There is, of course, nothing peculiar in this situation. Every Cabinet Minister is invariably dependent on his permanent officials for advice and guidance. In the context of our discussion it is only interesting to observe how Labour leaders conceived their own rôle in the exercise of power. MacDonald expressed probably not only his own views when on the advent of the first Labour Government he said to a vast gathering in the Albert Hall in London:

'We shall take office . . . in order to try and settle the manifold and pressing difficulties that beset our nation, Europe and the whole world at the present moment. My task and my colleagues' task is going to be to mobilize all men and women of goodwill and sane judgment. . . . I want a Labour government so that the life of the nation can be carried on. 1924 is not the last year in God's programme of creation. We shall be dead and gone and still the journey will be going on, still the search for the Holy Grail will be made by knights like Keir Hardie.'[3]

Even allowing for the fact that the scope of action of the first two Labour governments was severely limited, there is little evidence that newer lines of policy, aiming at far-reaching changes, even of a non-controversial character, were attempted by any of the departments. Beatrice Webb refers to her husband's work in the 1924 Government in the following terms:

'Sidney does his level best for his country and his party; he works up to the limits of his strength during the working months. But in his

---

[1] Sir Almeric Fitzroy: *Memoirs*, 2 vols. (1925), vol. II, p. 45.
[2] John Robert Clynes: *Memoirs*, 2 vols., 1937, vol. II, p. 45.
[3] Quoted in M. A. Hamilton: *J. R. MacDonald, 1923–1925*, 1925, p. 29.

heart of hearts he remains essentially a detached observer without any keenness for one way or another or as to his own continued participation in the exercise of power.'[1]

This absence of personal involvement in the general issues of political power which Mrs Webb noted in her husband's activities as a Cabinet Minister is confirmed by a study of his correspondence. We can observe it during 1924 and to an even greater extent during the period of the second Labour government when Sidney, then Lord Passfield and aged seventy, was continually longing for the day when he would be released from office. His frequent letters to his wife show great absorption in his administrative tasks and little mention of the general issues with which the Government was confronted. 'I am snowed under with papers and problems which leaves me little time for anything else', he wrote to her in 1930 when he was Secretary of State for the Colonies and the Dominions.[2] It is ironical to find how little the authors of the 1909 report on the 'Prevention of Destitution' apparently thought about the vast misery in their midst.[3]

Mr Attlee could command more trained talent when he formed his government in 1945. This, and the freedom of manoeuvre which his large majority gave him, led to a record of number of new legislative measures and policies implemented. At the same time the purely administrative tasks which the Government faced had grown in size and complexity since before the war. Those who form the Cabinet are still primarily heads of departments and this sets limits to the amount of planning that can be done collectively.

'Ministers conceive a deep distaste for embarking upon projects that will entail more and larger meetings with their colleagues. This means that even Socialist Ministers are selective about the sector of the national life that they can attempt to plan.'[4]

---

[1] *Diaries, 1924–32* (Ed. by Margaret I. Cole), 1952, p. 42. (Entry for 30.8.1924.)

[2] Letter of 13.3.1930 in Passfield Papers.

[3] Beatrice Webb's Diaries for 1929–31 are equally silent about the unemployment problem.

[4] Patrick C. Gordon-Walker: On Being a Cabinet-Minister, *Encounter*, April 1956. Morrison has given a similar picture of the burden of a Cabinet Minister in charge of a major department. *Government and Parliament*, 1954, pp. 62-63.

The problems that arise at the intersection of administrative exigencies with those of personal relationship go to the very heart of governmental planning. The representatives of a new class in the political leadership, aiming to establish a new social order, could have been expected to create new political institutions to carry out its policies. It is surely significant that the Labour Party has not sought to introduce any (constitutional) measures which might have facilitated the task of planning its reforms or eased the burden of collective decision-making at the national level. The development and widespread use of the system of Cabinet Committees hardly merits such a description.[1]

LABOUR BETWEEN WORKING CLASS AND RULING CLASS

The composition of Labour's parliamentary representation which emerged from the General Election of 1918 did not differ materially from that of the old Parliamentary Labour Party. Indeed, the defeat of most of the I.L.P. candidates (including MacDonald, Snowden and Jowett) increased even further the narrow sectional character of Labour Representation. Of the 57 M.P.s who were elected 49 had been sponsored by the trade unions and only 8 were elected under the auspices of the newly founded Constituency Labour Parties. Four M.P.s, although elected as Independents, joined the Labour forces shortly afterwards. One of these, Brigadier-General Sir Owen Thomas, whose career in the Labour Party was short-lived, was the only Labour M.P. who did not belong either by origin, up-bringing or occupation to the working class.

From then onwards, however, the character of Labour representation changes and widens. It becomes a national party and contests a growing number of seats. No longer exclusively active in constituencies predominantly working-class in character, it works through local party organizations open to individual members of all classes of the community. Accordingly, it begins to draw its parliamentary candidates from outside the working class. While 'safe seats' still tend to be held by trade union candidates, and while their chances of success are thus great, the expansion in the

---

[1] There has been little thinking by Labour politicians about the problems of Cabinet government. The division between departmental ministers and those in charge with specific functions was discussed very briefly by Attlee in *The Labour Party in Perspective*, pp. 128–30 of 1949 ed.

numbers of Labour M.P.s is largely accounted for by candidates with other backgrounds. The total number of seats fought by trade union sponsored candidates fluctuated within comparatively narrow limits throughout the period from 1918 to 1955 and the trade union bloc found its strength within the P.L.P. almost inversely related to the magnitude of the Labour Party's victory. Not all T.U. sponsored candidates were Union officials. Some were rank-and-file members while others had been active members, but had left manual work altogether while keeping their Union Membership card. But on the whole, the trade union spon-sored M.P.s tended to be men of working-class origin, even if some had moved away from the working-class occupationally and possibly socially, even before they entered the House of Commons.

The middle-class element in the Parliamentary Labour Party originated largely among those who did not even formally enter politics via the trade union route. It was a political army which waxed and waned with the strength of Labour's parliamentary representation. A breakdown into its social components shows clearly how the Labour Party absorbed into its leading strata the representatives of older radical groups (mostly of upper middle-class origin, rentiers or professional men) who had lost their political footing with the decline of the Liberal Party. The analysis presented in Table I also shows how the Labour Party attracted into its leader cadre men from the intelligentsia and the new middle class, including some who had themselves risen from the working class. It shows that only about one-third of this group still belonged to the traditional class of Labour M.P.s; that is, only a third had spent their pre-parliamentary careers in factories or mines, followed possibly by a spell of office in a trade union or other working-class organization. If we consider the over-all per-centage of Labour M.P.s who had followed originally working-class occupations, whether or not they were trade union sponsored M.P.s, we see that the proportion was as high as 92 per cent in the 1918 period. It dropped to 70 per cent for the years 1922–1923–1924; it fell further to 60 per cent in 1929, rose to 75 per cent two years later, and fell again to 64 per cent after 1935.[1]

---

[1] For the social character of the P.L.P. after the last war see tables V and VI of this chapter.

TABLE I

Occupations followed by Non-Trade Union Sponsored Labour M.P.s:

(Refers to last occupation followed before entering House of Commons.)

Percentage Distribution	1918	1922	1923	1924	1929	1931	1935
Working Class Occupations	64	28	38	34	33	20	33
Professions..	18	46	42	47	44	67	49
Other Middle Class Occupations	18	26	20	19	23	13	18
TOTAL	100	100	100	100	100	100	100

Numerical Distribution (in detail)							
Working Class:							
Manual and Clerical Workers	1	8	20	12	25	2	11
Officials of Trade Unions etc.	6	8	14	9	31	1	12
Middle and Upper Class:							
(a) Professions:							
Journalists	2	6	9	5	20	1	3
School Teachers	—	8	10	7	19	2	6
University Teachers	—	4	3	5	7	2	5
Doctors	—	2	3	3	9	2	2
Lawyers	—	4	8	5	13	3	11
Ministers of Religion and others	—	2	4	4	6	—	8
(b) Other:							
Managerial, Administrative, Military	—	3	4	3	9	1	2
Estate Agents, Builders, Farmers etc.	2	4	4	2	9	—	2
Entrepreneurs	—	5	6	5	11	1	9
Rentiers	—	3	4	2	9	—	—
Total Ascertained	11	57	89	62	168	15	71
Not Ascertained	1	—	1	1	5	—	4

We are helped to an even better understanding of the social character of the Parliamentary Labour Party by looking at the educational background of the same group of M.P.s. As we advance into the 1920's and 1930's and as Labour representation grows, we can observe an increasing proportion of M.P.s who had received more than just an Elementary school education. At the other end of the spectrum we find that in the inter-war years only one in six of this group could be said to have received a conventional ruling class education—Public School with possibly Oxford or Cambridge thereafter.[1]

TABLE II

Education of Non-Trade Union Sponsored Labour M.P.s:

	1918	1922	1923	1924	1929	1931	1935	All
Elementary School only	10	26	42	29	69	5	36	98
Grammar School only	—	6	10	6	24	3	6	32
Boarding School only	—	—	2	1	1	—	1	3
Elementary School & University	—	1	3	2	5	1	3	5
Grammar School & University	1	10	12	10	26	2	10	33
University, schooling unknown	—	3	5	4	13	1	1	14
Public School only	—	2	4	3	6	1	3	10
Public School & University	—	7	8	7	14	1	8	20
Not known	1	2	4	1	15	1	7	22
TOTALS	12	57	90	63	173	15	75	237

It is against this background that the first two Labour administrations must be viewed. Looking back on their personnel and their policies after a quarter of a century, it is difficult if not impossible to understand the fear and apprehension caused in 1924 by the prospect of a Labour government. Asquith told Parliament

[1] In the post-1945 P.L.P. the proportion of public-school educated M.P.s has increased to between 10–15 per cent of the total (20–25 per cent of the group of non-T.U. sponsored M.P.s).

that his postbag had been heavy with letters from people of all political persuasions, imploring him to save the country from the impending catastrophe by agreeing to a coalition. He himself regarded these fears as exaggerated, but, in any case, he thought that 'if a Labour government was to be tried in [Britain] it could hardly be under safer conditions'.

In preparing the distribution of portfolios for his first government, MacDonald is said to have expressed to some of his colleagues his disgust at the poor material at his disposal. Even allowing for the disdain felt by the leader of the Labour Party for his intellectually and socially less well endowed colleagues—a disdain which seems to have bordered at times on the pathological —there is substance in his plaint. A British Cabinet tends to be based on the personnel and tradition of its predecessor Cabinets. MacDonald could not utilize much experience of office among his colleagues. Moreover, he was not bent on making an impression of daring innovations. Contrary to those who thought that Labour's task in office should be the formulation of a bold socialist programme, he desired to show to the public that his government was composed of competent and level-headed administrators. He felt that he had to satisfy the desire for office among his senior colleagues and give representation to the trade union movement, yet he desired at all costs to secure for his Cabinet some of the *cachet* connected with persons of accepted social position and political renown.[1] Only five days after the election, in December 1923, MacDonald met Haldane by arrangement and 'offered me anything I should choose; the leadership of the House of Lords, the Chancellorship, Defence, Education and the carrying out of my plans' (probably concerning defence and reorganization of the administration of justice).[2] Parmoor, too, was approached and persuaded to accept the office of Lord President of the Council. Noel Buxton, J. C. Wedgwood, C. P. Trevelyan and Lord Chelmsford

---

[1] Beatrice Webb wrote in January 1924 that 'Sidney came away feeling that the Cabinet would err on the side of respectability—too many outsiders, too many peers. J(ames) R(amsay) M(acDonald) oddly enough does not like the plebeian element and chooses as his intimate associates not the workman but the lawyer or big administrator with the manner and attitude of the ruling and thoroughly comfortable class.' *Diaries, 1912–1924*, 1952, p. 263.

[2] Sir Frederick Maurice, *Haldane*, 2 vols., 1937–39, vol. II, p. 137.

completed this group of former Liberal or Conservative politicians who had come to support the Labour Party.[1]

This group of Cabinet Ministers, which belonged to the traditional ruling class of Great Britain, of aristocratic, upper or middle-class origin, is nearly as large as that of the men who had entered politics via a professional career in trade unions or political organizations. Only a mere handful of Labour Cabinet members reached leadership and office by different routes. Table III presents a breakdown of the 1924 and 1929 Labour governments on the one hand and the two post-Second World War governments on the other. Using a combination of class background and occupational career lines to establish the types discussed above, it demonstrates clearly the bare majority given to working-class representatives in the Labour governments of both the earlier and the later period. On the other hand it shows that the representation from the aristocratic and upper middle class, declined slightly between the two periods, and gave way to professional men from the middle and lower middle class.[2]

From this evidence, it would seem that the social composition and character of Labour Cabinets remained substantially unchanged from the time of the first Labour government. The balance struck by MacDonald in 1924 between working class and traditional ruling class did not only affect the kind of Cabinet which he formed in 1929, it equally expressed itself in Mr Attlee's choice. Yet the third Labour government, in 1945, was separated from the first two by more than just a gulf of fifteen years which in turn meant that only a minority of its members had seen office in 1929.

---

[1] We can include in this category also Lord Thomson, a friend of MacDonald's who had joined the Labour Party after a distinguished military career. He was made Secretary of State for Air.

[2] Beatrice Webb analysed the 1929 Labour Government along similar lines and came to the following division of the Government, including the Under-Secretaries:

Manual Workers	17
Lower Middle Class ..	9
Old Governing Class ..	10
Aristocrats	4
	—
	40

Diaries, 1924–1932, p. 210. See also *Political Quarterly*, 1930, pp. 104–9.

TABLE III

Career Patterns of Members of Labour Cabinets, 1924–50:
(*In terms of class background and occupational routes*)

	1924	1929	1945	1950
1. Aristocratic or upper middle-class background, with a professional, entrepreneurial or rentier career	7	5	4	3
2. Middle or lower middle-class background with a professional career	2	2	4	5
3. Working-class background, with a professional career leading to middle-class status	—	2	1	1
4. Working-class background, with a business career leading to middle-class status*	1	1	—	—
5. Working-class background, with a career as an official of a trade union or other working-class organization	9	9	10	9
6. Working-class background, with a career occupationally confined to the working class	1	—	1	—
TOTAL	20	19	20	18

It is rather interesting to note that there was no Labour Minister with a middle-class background and a business career in any of the Cabinets examined in this table.

By 1945 the party had become a genuinely national party. Its record poll of nearly 12 million contained about 3 million middle-class votes and the Parliamentary Labour Party showed a larger proportion of middle-class members than before the war.[1] Nothing

---

[1] Bonham: *The Middle Class Vote*, 1954, estimated that one-third of the middle-class vote went to Labour in 1945 and less than one-fifth in 1951. The middle-class vote accounted for 18·5 per cent of total Labour votes in 1945. See also J.F.S. Ross: *Parliamentary Representation*, 2nd ed., 1948, and R. B. McCallum and A. Readman: *The British General Election of 1945* (London, 1947) *passim*. This trend has continued in all post-war elections. The breakdown for the 1951 P.L.P. is given in Table V.

illustrates this more pointedly than the fact that the teachers had ousted the miners as the strongest occupational group on the Labour benches.

For a comparison of Attlee's post-war team with the group of Labour ministers in the inter-war years, we must study the occupational and political career data of Labour ministers more closely. All but two of the members of MacDonald's Cabinet who did not belong to the working class had started their political careers in the older parties. Some could say with C. P. Trevelyan:

> 'I was born a Liberal for I had behind me two generations of eminent service given through that Party to their country by Lord Macaulay and Sir George Trevelyan. I was, however, much more than a Liberal by inheritance. I remained a Liberal by deliberate choice, though many influences compelled me to seek a more advanced party. ... The war has brought a wholesale transference of the working-class vote from Liberalism to Labour and with that has come, in my view, the end of the supremely valuable part played in our history by the Liberal Party.'[1]

Others felt moved to join the Labour Party because that party embodied among its aims particular reforms dear to their hearts. Haldane was propelled towards the party by his interest in education, Parmoor and Ponsonby became pacifists during the war and were fervent advocates of the League of Nations.

The Trade Union leaders and party officials, who formed the bulk of the working-class party leadership in MacDonald's day, differed in career patterns from their successors who achieved office twenty years later. Not only was their own early experience often formed under Liberalism and not only was their first step in local politics often taken under the Liberal banner, but the formative influence on most of them was that of the industrial struggle and the work needed to put the union organization on its feet. From experience as back-benchers in a small isolated party, they moved almost at once straight into Cabinet office. Only four of them entered the House of Commons before reaching the age of thirty and their Cabinet experience covered their fifties and sixties.

Mr Attlee's middle-class colleagues in the Cabinet received their

---

[1] C. P. Trevelyan: *From Liberalism to Labour*, 1921, p. 29.

TABLE IV

Labour Cabinet Ministers Contrasted: 1916–35 and 1935–55:

	Period when in Office	
	1916–35	*1935–55*
(a) Age of Entry into Politics—		
Under 30	3	1
From 31 to 35	3	6
From 36 to 40	8	11
From 41 to 45	5	10
From 46 to 50	7	3
From 51 to 60	3	3
Sixty-one and over	4	—
(b) Class Background—		
Aristocracy	3	1
Middle Class	12	14
Working Class	19	19
(c) Occupation—		
Landowning	2	—
Rentier	2	1
Profession	10	15
Commerce and Industry	2	2
Trade Union Officials, etc.	14	15
Other	4	1
(d) Education: School—		
Elementary	17	18
Grammar	8	5
Public	6	11
Other	3	—
(e) Education: University—		
None	20	17
Oxford	5	6
Cambridge	2	5
Other Universities	7	6

	Period when in Office	
	1916–35	*1935–55*
(f) Ministerial Career—		
Stepped straight into Cabinet office	24	3
Held only office as departmental head or		
equivalent before entering the Cabinet	1	4
Held only junior office before entering the		
Cabinet	9	18
Held both junior office and departmental		
headship before entering the Cabinet	—	9
ALL LABOUR CABINET MINISTERS	34	34

political training mainly inside the Labour Party. Their occupational careers followed more clearly a definite pattern, for many of them it had included public-school education, university training and a professional career—predominantly in law or in teaching. Those who stepped into politics from officialdom in trade unions or in other working-class organizations did so earlier in life than their predecessors a generation earlier. Their experience in office before they entered the Cabinet had been varied. Moreover, through their activities as Members of Parliament, they had slowly acquired middle-class standards and the outlook of professional politicians.

In Table IV a number of comparisons are made between the groups of Cabinet Ministers for the two periods under discussion. They bring out the contrast in background and training which has been discussed. The development of Labour leadership as shown in this profile, highlights the changing character of a cadre of politicians in a highly complex democratic society. It illustrates quite clearly the trend away from politicians who live *for* politics to those who live *by* politics. The number of politicians for whom politics is not only a way of life but a livelihood has been steadily increasing in our society. As the Labour Party advanced towards political maturity during the time when this process was going on, it shared in this development to a greater extent than its opponents. Relatively speaking, Labour politicians have also tended to benefit more from those rewards and opportunities which come to them by virtue of the position which they hold than their colleagues on the opposite benches. There are nowadays probably increasing opportunities for outside earnings even for those who do not pursue part-time commercial or professional activities. M.P.s are in demand as journalists, lecturers, broadcasters and as Public Relations men. In addition, a vastly greater number of perquisites and privileges are falling to the lot of even the unknown back-bencher than ever before. Governments and business dispense a much greater degree of hospitality than before the war, let alone before 1914. Places on foreign missions and delegations are within the reach of M.P.s who will bestir themselves; these in turn widen the opportunities for extra parliamentary activity and earnings. Being an M.P. has become a marketable commodity—even without such dubious forms of activity as guinea-pig directorships.

Finally, the Government has today an increasingly large number of offices at its disposal with which to reward its followers. This is not only through jobs in the administration itself, but also through posts in the nationalized industries, other government agencies or foreign missions. With such avenues of advancement at its disposal, a major party can promise its followers a fair degree of security in their political pursuits.

By thus making politics more like a profession it is also making it more middle class. As the only Party whose political representation was not already entirely middle or upper class in character, the Labour Party leadership is clearly influenced by this process. Yet the adjustment of the rising group of Labour politicians to the traditional middle and upper-class environment in which the game of politics had customarily been played was neither easy nor unquestioned. Labour was 'handicapped' not only by its own social background but also by those elements in its ideology which implied a rejection of the rules of the game itself.

In this connection it is important to distinguish between the occasional Member of Parliament of working-class origin who had entered Parliament during the last quarter of the nineteenth century and the representative of a working-class organization seeking to represent the aspirations of his class in the House of Commons and doing this within the framework of a distinctive Labour Party. The earlier working class M.P.s regarded themselves as closely bound to the Liberal Party. More often than not their Parliamentary careers were the steps in a general process of upward social mobility. Keir Hardie observed that 'the working man's representative (in Parliament) thinks more of his own reputation in the eyes of the House than of the interests of his suffering brethren in mill and mine. He desires to be reckoned a gentleman, fit to take his place as a member of the "finest club in the world".[1] On the other hand, the early Labour Party M.P.s were quite clearly condemned both by their politics and by their poverty to stay outside the circle. Hardie's cloth cap and grey woollen suit (although meant as an act of defiance) were a symbol of distinctiveness which even top hat and frock-coat could not have surmounted.

The European War caused some breaking down of social barriers between Labour M.P.s on the one hand and the members of the ruling class and of the two major parties on the other. The coalition brought Labour leaders into social as well as political contact with the bourgeois parties, a process which was helped by the innumerable governmental and departmental committees and missions which flourished as a result of increased governmental activity. The situation was eased further by the fact that from 1916 onwards the Prime Minister was a man of lower-class background.

The post-1918 House of Commons with its aggressive reassertion of Conservatism and of the entrepreneurial spirit might have isolated the Labour Party socially as well as politically. Instead we find a growing integration of the Labour Benches into the community of the House of Commons and eventually in the wider 'Society'. With few exceptions, Labour M.P.s submit like others to the traditions of the place, and succumb to the *genus loci*. Parliamentary life itself becomes an educative and moderating influence. The mores of the House lessen antagonism. The great formal egalitarianism of the rules of the House, the privileges which the Member of Parliament enjoys, the deference shown to him by officials and servants of the House strengthen the individual's self-esteem, and do, no doubt, combat feelings of separateness. New loyalties are created. It needs a very strongly developed feeling of loyalty to one's own group, together with a set of clear cut differentiating factors, for a section of M.P.s to keep entirely apart from the main stream. The Irish Nationalists, who had both these characteristics, achieved such distinctiveness. The Labour Party was not so favoured by external circumstances.

---

[1] In *The Miner*, 1887.

Observers used to the rigid social and ideological divisions of continental Parliaments were astonished by the degree of intermixture in the British House of Commons. 'A division of tables in the dining-room of the House of Commons in the same manner as in the restaurant of the Reichstag would be unthinkable in England', wrote a German journalist in 1929.[1]

The only attempt at complete parliamentary and social isolation by Labour M.P.s came from the group who were elected for Glasgow and neighbouring constituencies in 1922, the so-called 'Clydesiders'. Representing constituencies with traditions of militant unionism and elated by the unexpected size of their electoral victory (all but two of the eleven Glasgow constituencies returned Labour candidates) they came nearest to expressing sentiments of class war on the Labour benches. During the period of the first Labour Government they sought resolutely to stay away from all social functions which might be regarded as corrupting or compromising. Yet with that quixotic combination of extreme radical views and strong national pride which we do find in the British Labour movement, David Kirkwood, one of their leaders, could not disguise some admiration for his opponents. He relates that he was rebuked for abusing some of them and was told that such behaviour was pointless, that 'these people have a code! They will listen to argument but abuse does not interest them.' This he found true. 'The "conventions" of the House of Commons are strong to bind. At first I thought they were nothing more than surface politics. They are not, they are the foundations of the parliamentary system.'[2] Kirkwood himself was to embrace parliamentary conventionality to the full; he accepted a peerage from Mr Attlee and without explicitly accepting the contemporary social system, he thought that those who directed it were sincere people and within their lights, disinterested men.[3] Robert Smillie, who as a politician was admittedly never in the front ranks, expressed similar sentiments:

'In my young and callow days I was probably a little prejudiced in favour of my class and hot with resentment against those whom I

---

[1] Egon F. Wertheimer: *Portrait of the Labour Party*, 1929.
[2] D. Kirkwood, *op. cit.*, p. 202–5.
[3] See especially the last two chapters of his Autobiography.

regarded as their oppressors. But experience teaches and I now know that a gentleman is a gentleman whatever his rank in life may be and always will be trusted as such.'[1]

The violation of accepted rules of parliamentary conduct and offences against the decorum of the House which occurred occasionally, and which emanated mostly from members from the Clyde, was abhorred by many. Snowden regarded the speeches of the Clydesiders as soapbox stuff delivered for consumption at home. MacDonald was very apologetic to the King about the singing of 'The Red Flag' when the latter remonstrated with him about this. He begged the King to remember 'the very difficult position he was in *vis-à-vis* his own extremists... his followers had got into the way of singing this song and it will be by degrees that he hopes to break down this habit.'[2]

The singing of the 'Red Flag' was repeated after the victory in 1945[3] but despite Labour's great parliamentary majority and the much more radical character of its policy there was comparatively little class and party antagonism between 1945 and 1951. The wartime coalition and the large middle-class contingent on the Labour benches weakened the feeling of antagonism and helped the party to add social to political recognition. During the 1920's a Labour M.P. with a solid middle-class background and upbringing might experience a cooling off of social relationships with friends and relatives;[4] this was less likely to happen after 1945.

The integration of Labour politicians in the middle class, while the population as a whole was still rather deeply divided socially, put the Party and its leadership into a dilemma. The socialist beliefs to which the Party subscribed rejected the existing social system and the style of life of its ruling groups. Since its inception, the Labour movement in Great Britain had criticized the British

[1] *My Life for Labour*, 1924, p. 133. See also G. N. Barnes: *From Workshop to War Cabinet*, 1924, pp. 70–75.

[2] Harold Nicolson: *King George the Fifth*, London, 1952, p. 386. (From Lord Stamfordham's Memorandum to the King on the formation of the first Labour Government.)

[3] Herbert (now Lord) Morrison found this slightly disturbing and contrary to the rules of the House. He diagnosed it as 'first day high spirits'. Lord Morrison: *Herbert Morrison, an Autobiography*, London, 1960, p. 251.

[4] *cf.* Sir P. Hastings: *Autobiography*, 1948, p. 226–9.

upper class and had poured scorn and invective on the extrava-
gances and economic wastefulness of the lives of the rich. Its
spokesmen had agitated against the snobbishness of Britain's
antiquated class structure, and the 'accoutrements' of upper-class
life which helped to perpetuate the pattern. Court ceremonials
formed an important part of this. On taking power, Labour leaders
were faced with this aspect of the problem as one calling for personal decision. How much of the decorative part of the British
Constitution were they to observe? The first and most obvious
case arose in connection with the wearing of court dress. George V,
as we now know, was a stickler for etiquette and deeply concerned
to preserve the traditions of the Court, of which dress seemed to
him of paramount importance. Already before Labour came to
power, the King had expressed his concern about the Party's position with regard to dress when, before inviting MacDonald to the
Palace in 1922, he inquired through Lord Stamfordham, whether
the Leader of the Opposition would come in Court Dress when
invited to Buckingham Palace.[1] MacDonald replied in the affirma-
tive, which we can now readily understand: 'He liked pomp and
ceremony; he had an intense and abiding sense of the picturesque
and a deep love of the ordered and ancient and the hierarchical.'[2]

The problem arose again on a wider scale when it came to the
presentation of the Cabinet. With the exception of Jowett and
Wheatley, the whole Cabinet appeared in knee-breeches when
kissing hands. This was no doubt partly due to MacDonald's
influence, but it also showed the rather unquestioning acceptance
of tradition on the part of the majority of the Labour Cabinet.[3]
Many Labour leaders and their wives regarded social recognition
by the Court as an achievement which was desirable in itself rather
than as an irksome duty, and Mrs Clynes wrote to the papers
suggesting that the daughters of Labour leaders should be presented at Buckingham Palace.

On the other hand a minority made a great effort to prevent this
involvement with 'Society'. Beatrice Webb tried to create for the

---

[1] Hugh Dalton: *Call Back Yesterday*, 1953, vol. I, p. 145.
[2] M. A. Hamilton: *Remembering My Good Friends*, 1934, p. 128.
[3] In the case of the second Labour Government, MacDonald sent out a
circular requesting the wearing of Court Dress for the swearing-in ceremony.
Attlee did away with this custom in 1945 (in agreement with the Palace).

Labour leadership something equivalent to a 'social' life without being 'Society' in the traditional sense. Her vehicle for doing so was the 'Parliamentary Labour Club', which she helped to found and which, she hoped, would bring the various strata of the Party leadership, especially their wives, together for friendly social intercourse. She did not want 'the P.L.P. to become the plaything of London Society and the despised of the more serious elements in the Labour movement . . . the personal conduct of the Labour members and their wives will be just as important as the political policy of the Labour Cabinet, perhaps even more so, as [the latter] must be qualified by the fact that the Party is in a minority and personal conduct can be settled with a single eye as to what is desirable from the standpoint of the future society.'[1] It is significant, however, that the club, set up with much thought and care, proved to be a comparative failure. The various social sets among Labour Ministers kept apart. Those who could, sought entry into real society. And 'Society', always eager to absorb the *arriviste*, extended a helping hand. The Snowdens, Beatrice Webb noted in her diary, in September 1929, 'had spent yesterday with the Connaughts and the day before with the Balfours at Fisher's Hill'.[2] Barnes, Snowden, Thomas and Henderson could be found at Cliveden on occasional week-ends.[3] MacDonald's own liking for 'Society' is well known. 'He went out of his way to tell me,' Beatrice Webb relates, 'that he was going to stay with Mrs Biddulph—the Honourable Mrs Biddulph, he added—and then described her as a patron of good English craftsmanship in furniture. Then I am going to stay at —— with the Princess Hartsfelt. She was a Cunningham, you know, do you know her? A remarkable woman.'[4] Such conduct was to embitter sections of the Labour movement and to contribute to the antagonism which was felt increasingly by the Left Wing for the leadership of the Party: it was bound to weaken the opposition to the economic system which formed one of the bases of Labour's political appeal.

In addition to 'High Society' there was, of course, the political society formed by Labour itself—or rather by the progressively

---

[1] *Diaries, 1924–32*, p. 5.
[2] *Diaries, 1924–32*, p. 220.
[3] Thomas Jones: *A Diary with Letters*, 1954 p. xxxv.
[4] Beatrice Webb, *op. cit.*, p. 117.

minded counter-élite of which the intellectual wing of the Labour
movement formed a significant part. With the increase in 'respectability' of the Labour Party, this group increased in size and significance. Its scope is difficult to define. Its economic basis was a
middle-class salary (possibly a small private income), a week-end
cottage and a motor-car, not much spare cash but a fair amount of
spare time. The ties which connected these circles were intellectual
interests rather than social pursuits, common concern with social
and cultural endeavour rather than family connection. The men
and women who belonged to them were writers and journalists,
lawyers, university teachers and artists, left-wing professional
politicians and younger administrators. They met in central
London flats or in smaller houses in the inner suburbs, on week-
ends and at holiday parties. The Webbs attempted throughout
their lives to be a centre of such a society, although Beatrice's
unselfconscious self-importance and her 'sense of mission' probably did not encourage genuinely spontaneous social intercourse.
She writes of one such week-end in her diary:

> 'A really useful week-end with Lion Philimore who left me to select
> the party. The Alexanders, Greenwoods, Colonel Williams and our-
> selves went down to Kendal on Saturday. Patrick Hastings and his
> wife motored down for lunch and tea on Sunday, the Bernard Shaws
> came over in the afternoon, and the Oswald Mosleys motored down
> to lunch. The conversation was exclusively political—I doubt
> whether during these forty hours there was a single allusion to
> women, wine, horses, sports, scandal or money-making . . . undiluted
> public affairs and the philosophy upon which these are based was the
> order of the day.'[1]

The effectiveness of such gatherings is difficult to assess; their
impact on politics in the short run may have been small. In the
long run the mental climate which they created is important. In
such circles—as on a more institutionalized level in Fabian Summer Schools—newcomers are introduced into the political scene,
they see the ropes which support the props, they get a feel for the
political stage and possibly they meet some of the chief actors.

'Left Wing' Society served, and probably still does serve in its
own way, as much as a centre for political advancement of those

[1] Beatrice Webb, *op. cit.*, 24.3.1924, pp. 16–17.

who aspire to a 'political' (not necessarily Parliamentary) career in the Labour Party as real 'Society' has done for the 'bright young thing' on the Right. Lord Pakenham, who held ministerial office between 1948 and 1957, relates how, after his defeat at Oxford in 1945, his friends, especially Evan Durbin, insisted that he 'must nevertheless be got into Parliament and at once'. The whole episode, as related in his diary, is instructive:

> 'He swept aside my dubieties. Action had to be taken and was taken forthwith. By Sunday, Hugh Dalton was Chancellor of the Exchequer; he was staying with Bill and Mary Piercy at Burford and [we] were motoring over to tea, hoping for something though I knew not what. [Dalton] visualized my position with alacrity, insisted that I must at all costs be associated with the great social experiment that was about to be conducted, and that evening found time to write letters to half a dozen leading members of the Government, commending me to their attention.'[1]

Like all 'Societies', the British Left Wing Society is exclusive. It is true, breeding or wealth are not prerequisites for entrance; but intellectual ability, middle-class cultural tastes, and a university background probably are. The trade union leaders of the middle ranks, energetic and able local councillors of working-class origin, are unlikely to find their way into it. Labour 'Society' is also strongly centred on London and favours men with connections in the Metropolis. Embryonic groups are found in the universities, especially in Oxford, where the circle around G. D. H. Cole was by all accounts a breeding ground for future Labour politicians.[2]

Beatrice Webb described in her diary a visit of a woman organizer of the Labour Party for north-east England and her husband; she was a graduate, he a scientific worker, probably also university-trained. The diary provides a candid picture:

> '[They were] distinguished people, intellectually and morally, but possessing no social status . . . we took them to see the Snowdens and

---

[1] Francis A. Pakenham: *Born to Believe*, 1953, p. 132. *cf*. Hugh Gaitskell: 'At Oxford in the Twenties' (on G. D. H. Cole) in A. Briggs and J. Saville (eds.) *Essays in Labour History in Memory of G. D. H. Cole*, 1960.

[2] There were, of course, also non-bourgeois social nuclei which became influential in the Labour Movement. They are, by the nature of things, even more difficult to trace. For an account of one such see T. Brennan: 'The White House', *Cambridge Journal*, January 1954.

also the Ponsonbys, both being among Mrs Fenn's forty M.P.s for whose women's section she is responsible. But by the Snowdens she was treated just as a salaried subordinate to whom they were distantly civil. Arthur Ponsonby was more forthcoming but in neither case was there the remotest recognition that this man and woman were among the élite.'[1]

THEORIES OF LEADERSHIP

The Labour Party did not originate in the tradition of the two patrician parties, which had gradually broadened their bases and had grudgingly given way to pressure from their 'popular' organizations below. Its constituent bodies, Trade Unions, Socialist Societies and the I.L.P., were imbued with a spirit of democratic organization and sentiment. Members and leaders were social equals acting in a fairly close cameraderie which facilitated the discussion of policy issues at all levels and permitted a vigorous criticism of aims and policies. As we have seen, the organization of the P.L.P. after 1906 was loose. The office of Chairman was conceived more as that of the formal head and organizer than that of 'leader'. MacDonald who became *de facto* leader of the party in 1911, when he was elected to the Chairmanship, stressed the need for a unified and disciplined party. Leadership for him was clearly much more than an administrative task. When his name was mentioned as a possible successor to Hardie in 1908 he wrote to Bruce Glasier that 'to take the job for a period of two years at the maximum is a bit discouraging'.[2] He saw the Labour leader as a pacemaker and a disciplinarian at the same time. It might be left to the movement to set its sights on the far horizon, but the leader was to determine the road and the tempo of advance:

> 'The responsibility of leaders to the mass must be secured but democracy which gives leaders no power will soon discover that it can do nothing. The problem of democracy is how to retain leadership with authority and yet to limit the authority so that it is not dictatorship.'[3]

The political (*i.e.* legislative and administrative) function he

[1] *op. cit.*, p. 83.
[2] Godfrey Elton: *The Life of James Ramsay MacDonald*, 1939, p. 161.
[3] MacDonald: *Socialism*, p. 230.

regarded as an essentially specialized one, which only a minority could undertake. This minority ought to be small, certainly smaller than the House of Commons.[1] He recognized that governmental office and political leadership in general demand a man's full-time attention and that the job of politics is a professional activity like any other. 'The art and science of government is one of the most difficult of all arts and care should be taken to enable it to command the most skilled intelligence.'[2] According to him, the Labour Party had so far not adopted its method of selecting candidates to the need of the House of Commons; it still chose men because of their 'status in local bodies or in organizations whose method of work and training are not those of the House of Commons.'[3]

In opposition to the view that a political leader should be an expert and professional, deciding alone and unfettered on the line of policy to be pursued, other leaders of the I.L.P., especially Fred Jowett, advocated a different theory of leadership. For them the politician remained in close contact with his followers and carried out, in Parliament, the policies on which the party had agreed. MacDonald saw political tactics as determined by the parliamentary situation, he regarded a group of Labour M.P.s as good in itself, and in consequence, was loath to weaken the power of the Liberal Party and possibly cause a general election which might weaken Labour's position. Jowett, on the other hand, believed that Labour M.P.s should pursue a vigorous socialist policy. To vote on issues according to their merit, to carry one's convictions into the division lobby was not only a matter of intellectual honesty but also essential to gain mass support. Jowett further believed that such a policy would have beneficial effects on the whole system of parliamentary government.

'I believe that the Party which sets itself to establish the authority of the elected representatives of the people against the successive juntas of which governments are composed will do a great service to the country and increase the respect of the public for parliamentary government.'

[1] *Socialism and Government*, 2 vols., 1909, vol. I, p. 107–26.

This he declared in a speech as Chairman of the 1910 Conference of the I.L.P. He went on to join the issue:

'The ordinary wayfaring man cannot understand why Members of Parliament should not vote for the things he had advocated merely because such a vote would be considered as a vote of censure on the government of the day. All this jiggery pokery of party government, played like a game for ascendancy and power, is not for us.'[1]

Jowett's point was taken up in a publication emanating from some of his Bradford friends. Known as a 'Green Manifesto', it reverberated throughout the Labour movement. The authors condemned the opportunist tactics of the majority of the Labour Party leaders, claiming that individual M.P.s were more concerned to keep their seats than to pursue definite policies. If the Labour-Socialist alliance, which formed the basis of the Labour Party, was so ineffective, it might not be worth while to continue with parliamentary activity. Alternatively the authors thought it might become necessary for 'our movement [to] assert its democratic claims by definite mandate.'[2]

This was one of the few concrete proposals made for a reform of the relationship between leadership and mass movement. Another was that of the committee system which Jowett sought to apply to governmental policy-making. He thought that each department of the administration should be assisted in its work by a committee of M.P.s, which would discuss all proposed measures and have access to all relevant information before the matter was brought to the whole House of Commons.[3] This was clearly more than a procedural device. It aimed at making Parliament more directly democratic and the Cabinet less omnipotent.

MacDonald, on the other hand, regarded the concentration of power in the Cabinet as the logical outcome of social development. Parallels to it could be found in all large organizations. He maintained that in order to combine such a committee system with responsible government, the committees would have to be party committees, but that this would only enlarge further the power of

---

[1] Quoted in Brockway, op. cit., p. 104.
[2] L. Hall and others: Let us reform the Labour Party, 1909, p. 14.
[3] cf. Jowett's article in Clarion on 24.7.1908.

the government *vis-à-vis* the House of Commons. MacDonald clearly envisaged that a socialist party would be like other parties and would work the parliamentary system in the same way as they had done in the past. All other views were regarded by him as retrograde and utopian at the same time. Socialism could be achieved only through a 'socialistic' party *i.e.* one which will be victorious when, as one of the major parties, its principles and policies have been naturally accepted by a majority of the population; a 'party which accepts the socialist point of view and approaches the industrial problems of society with socialist assumptions in mind'. Men who instead seek to establish a 'socialist' party with new methods, hitherto not used in the British parliamentary system, will fail 'because its methods would be contrary to those by which society evolves'.[1] He regarded as beneficial the fact that the British electoral system compels a party to attain a majority representation because it forced a socialistic party to be active in local politics and serve an apprenticeship in municipal affairs so that the party 'is entrusted with legislative responsibility only after it has proved itself in administrative work'.[2] Thus for MacDonald the Labour Party was set firmly on the path already trod by the other two parties.

The way in which the first Labour Government was formed is a proof both of MacDonald's ascendancy and of the status of the leader. After the General Election of December 1923, when the question of a Labour Government was first mooted, discussions took place at various levels of Labour Party leadership. The N.E.C. of the party, the T.U.C. and a group of leading Labour M.P.s met to discuss the problem. All declared themselves in favour of taking office and at each of these meetings Sidney Webb was at pains to emphasize the enormous difficulties at all times, and in all parties, of constructing a Cabinet. . . . It was realized that the only conceivable way of doing the job was to leave it entirely to the one person who might be charged to do it, namely MacDonald; and I got the meeting to acquiesce in a self-denying ordinance that no one of us would seek to interfere for himself or otherwise. I had very vividly in mind the possibility of an attempt to get all appointments

---

[1] *Socialism and Government*, vol. II, p. 12.
[2] *ibid.*, vol. I, p. 137.

I

made by vote of the party meetings and I was delighted to find that this was not proposed or even mentioned by anyone. Nor was it ever suggested when the party meeting came to be held on the assembly of Parliament. The responsibility of so sudden and unexpected an assumption of office gave the party a shock which sobered even the wildest shouters.'[1]

It was MacDonald's view, not Jowett's, which determined the structure of the Labour Party and of Labour leadership. The defeated view erupted from time to time, however, and the controversy was renewed, but whatever the intellectual strength of the argument of those who have sought to widen the extent of direct democracy inside the Labour Party, it has received little support from men in key positions. The Webbs were firmly convinced of the importance of strong Cabinet rule and of the assertion of strong leadership. Their criticism was merely directed at the type of men who tended to emerge in this process hitherto. MacDonald's veneration for the established institutions of leadership was not shared by them. Instead of the existing governing class, they desired 'an élite of unassuming experts who would appear to be no different in status from common men'.[2]

The 1918 Constitution of the Labour Party which laid the basis for a mass party did, at the same time, strengthen the hands of the big battalions, *i.e.* the power of the large unions which in effect meant the power of their leadership. Until then the Labour Party had been a federation of trade unions and Socialist Societies and power rested in a National Executive Committee (N.E.C.) elected separately by each of the constituent sections. The new constitution laid down that all members of the N.E.C. were to be elected by the whole conference from three lists representing respectively the affiliated societies (*i.e.* trade unions and bodies like the I.L.P.), Constituency Labour Parties and the women on a card basis.[3] As cards were roughly proportionate to membership this

---

[1] Passfield Papers, IV/18, f. 4. This memorandum has been published in *The Political Quarterly*, Jan–March, 1961.

[2] Beatrice Webb: *Diaries, 1924–1932*, 1956, p. 171 (21.8.1928) in reference to Haldane's death and their difference of opinion on the subject of the ruling class.

[3] In 1937 the party reverted, however, to its old practice. The representatives of the various sections are now elected by the sections (Trade Unions, Constituency Parties, Socialist Societies). Only the five women members of the Executive are elected by the Conference as a whole.

meant that the unions, who in any case paid for the party, could also call the tune if they wished. If bodies like the I.L.P. had lost considerably in power they gained ideologically through the fact that the basic tenets of socialism were written into the Constitution.

The exercise of power and the adherence to principles (as some conceived it) were soon to come into conflict but in the first few years after the war this was not yet acute. Informal power in the Parliamentary Labour Party was concentrated in the Leadership, and this was widely accepted. By 1922—when it occupied one-quarter of the seats in the House of Commons—Labour was recognized as the official opposition. The parliamentary leaders of the Party felt that they had arrived politically. They were revered and deferred to by new entrants into the House of Commons. They were the men who had raised the banner of the Party in the dark days, who had struggled against great odds, had been hounded for their convictions (like MacDonald and Snowden). On them rested the patina of tradition, theirs was the glory of the head which had turned grey in the service of the movement. Frequently uncritical followership was matched by demands for unquestioned trust. In 1924 large groups in the Labour Party and many of the 'experts' on foreign affairs tried to bring pressure to bear on MacDonald to persuade him to weaken the ties of alliance with France. These attempts at forcing his hand angered the Prime Minister. 'What we want,' he told Norman Angell, who had sought to intervene, 'is for the *New Leader* to carry on socialist propaganda and I want the I.L.P. to carry on socialist propaganda, instead of which everybody wants to be a Cabinet Minister, or, if they do not want to be a Cabinet Minister, they want to make a Cabinet of their own.'[1]

A Labour movement which, in its lower echelons, was still essentially democratic and egalitarian in the form of its organization, was bound to react to this attitude. It came with force when the events of 1931 had turned the party's attitude towards Mac-Donald from admiration to bitter hatred. His character was re-assessed; his conduct of Labour policy was questioned. Moreover the party sought to guard itself against a repetition of 'the great

---

[1] Norman Angell: *After All*, 1951, p. 243. Some sections of the I.L.P. took a very similar view to that of MacDonald of their task. See Clifford Allen's speech as Chairman of the I.L.P. Conference in 1924.

betrayal' by restricting the power of the leader of the party, especially in his rôle as actual or potential Prime Minister. In 1932 C. P. Trevelyan, an early critic of MacDonald (he had resigned from the Government in 1931 because of its failure to advocate a Socialist policy), expressed the view that 'we are a more democratic party now than ever, and new times require new systems—not necessarily by great breaking changes, but by great evolutionary developments in the direction of giving the mass of the movement a chance of saying how it shall be ruled'. Eventually, the N.E.C., which had consulted other sections of the Labour Movement, produced a report which it submitted at the 1933 Annual Conference. It advocated therein that in the event of Labour forming another government, the Prime Minister should consult with a committee of three members of the P.L.P. and the Secretary of the Labour Party about the formation of his Cabinet. It also proposed that the Prime Minister should be subject to majority decisions of the Cabinet, and that he should ask for the approval of the Cabinet and of the P.L.P. before deciding on a dissolution. The hedge around the powers of a Labour Prime Minister which these proposals erected was hardly made of thorns, and it was only natural that a more rigorous policy should have been advocated. However, a resolution to vest the selection of the Government in the hands of a committee composed of members of the National Joint Council of the Labour Party and of the Co-operative Party was defeated by a majority of three to one. In any case, even the mild proposals advocated and adopted in 1933 were forgotten in 1945. 'The passage of time and further experience had led to these proposals being tacitly dropped', Attlee has told us in his autobiography.[1]

What he did not say then, but what he and others have revealed since, is that a proposal was made to convene a meeting of the Parliamentary Labour Party and to elect or re-elect the Leader of the Party and thus submit the selection of the future Prime Minister to the body of Labour M.P.s[2] The pressure behind this move was based on personal as well as on party-constitutional

---

[1] Attlee: *As It Happened*, 1954, p. 156, quoted in R. T. McKenzie: *British Political Parties*, 1955, p. 332. I have drawn frequently on McKenzie in describing the post-1931 development.

[2] *cf.* Lord Attlee: *A Prime Minister Remembers*, 1961, pp. 2–4, and Lord Morrison: *Herbert Morrison, An Autobiography*, London, 1960, pp. 245–6.

grounds. Attlee, on the other hand, thought that on general constitutional grounds alone he was bound to accept the King's commission without delay. The formal authority of the elected leader of the Parliamentary Labour Party has since been firmly established although the position, which is still subject to annual confirmation, has been twice contested. Moreover, in allocating office in the Shadow Cabinet freely to men who were not members of the Committee of the Parliamentary Party, Gaitskell had possibly strengthened further the authority of his office.

It is rather on the question of the relationship between Parliamentary leadership and the authority of the Annual Conference that the issue has been joined. The formal relationship between the two bodies was defined in the 1918 Conference in the famous but already slightly ambiguous formula which laid down that the Labour Party Conference gave the general direction in which the Party was to travel, but the Party in Parliament was to determine the order of advance.[1] Throughout the inter-war years the pressure of sections of the Labour Movement to bind the Parliamentary Party was as persistent as the success of the latter to avoid such mandating. If the political leadership was upheld this was clearly due to the distribution of power at the Labour Party Conference and in the N.E.C. and not, I think, due to 'implicit but well observed assumptions [underlying the constitution] that policy was made ultimately by the political leadership [because it] personifies the party to the broader public' and because 'it is to [the political leadership] that the elector is asked to give its confidence'.[2]

The leadership following the principle that it determines priorities has frequently disregarded Conference decisions but as late as 1954 it was still felt that to do so with regard to major issues was fraught with dangers and difficulties for the Parliamentary Party. Speaking at the Scarborough Conference of that year in defence of German rearmament, both Attlee and Morrison stressed

---

[1] The actual reference occurs in section 3 of clause IV stating the Party objects. It declares that the Political Labour Party would 'give effect as far as may be practicable to the principles from time to time approved by the Party Conference'. On the other hand it lays down (clause IX) that an endorsed parliamentary candidate (must) 'accept and conform to the Constitutional Programme, Principles and Policy of the Party'.

[2] 'Union and Party', Editorial, *Socialist Commentary*, October 1960, p. 3.

the fact that a rejection of this policy would put the leadership in an anomalous and invidious position. To take an unequivocal decision on this problem in a constantly changing international situation would only 'tie and fetter' a future Labour Government.[1] The leadership was eventually spared this particular embarrassment as their policy was approved by a narrow majority. When six years later the Executive was faced with defeat on the issue of nuclear disarmament there was some clamour for a re-definition of the rôle and function of the Parliamentary Labour Party vis-à-vis the Party Conference, in order to prevent the recurrence of a similar situation in the future. Some suggested a direct representation of the Parliamentary body on the N.E.C. while others proposed to divorce the industrial from the political movement, or at least a re-definition of the terms of the alliance. The Editors of 'Socialist Commentary' thought that the Unions should concentrate their attention on industrial policy and the party was bound to recognize the weight of their claims in that field, but 'any attempt [on the unions' part] to dominate the Party in its parliamentary and political work would be fatal'.[2]

At the same time the supporters of nuclear disarmament and those on the Left in general sought to reassert the supremacy of the National Party over the parliamentary representation. John Stonehouse, M.P., moved at the Scarborough Conference that: 'This Conference reaffirms that the policy of the Labour Party to be pursued nationally and in Parliament on questions of principle shall be determined by Annual Conference. While acknowledging that the day-to-day actions in Parliament must be the job of the Parliamentary Party, the Conference declares that Labour policy is decided by the Party Conference which is the final authority.' Here was an attempt to lock the stable door before the horse had bolted. The Executive was prepared to accept the motion, Mr Len Williams, the National Agent of the Party declared, provided it was recognized that the resolution did not change anything and 'as

---

[1] Report of 1954 Labour Party Annual Conference, p. 108. Attlee had spoken earlier of the fact that in negotiations with Russia a future Labour Foreign Secretary would be 'tied and bound because the Russians would know that under no circumstances will there be any rearmament of Western Germany' (ibid., p. 1).

[2] Socialist Commentary, October 1960, p. 3.

long as it is clearly understood that nobody at all has the power to instruct, control or dictate to the Parliamentary Labour Party on the way it carries out its responsibilities'. In many ways this proviso went further than previous statements on this subject and the bulk of the Parliamentary Labour Party did indeed pursue its policy in the field of defence unperturbed by the Conference's endorsement of nuclear disarmament.

Although the Parliamentary leadership was strengthened by the reversal of the Scarborough decision in the following year, this triumph did not herald the end of Labour's dissensions. Their roots go deep.

COHESION AND CONFLICT

'From the very first the ties which bound the Party together were of the loosest possible kind. It has steadily, and, in my opinion, wisely, always declined to be bound by any programme, to subscribe to any dogma or to lay down any creed . . . on the contrary, its strength has been its catholicity, its tolerance, its welcoming of all shades of political and even revolutionary thought, providing its chief object—the unifying of the workers' political power, was not damaged.'[1] The words in which Mr. G. J. Wardle, the Chairman, characterized the Labour Party at its annual conference in 1917, could hardly describe the true relationship inside the party at its lowest, and even less at its highest, levels today.

The crystallization of a clearly defined party leadership and the development of traditional leader-follower relationships have been described. The emphasis on internal party discipline and the insistence on a party programme, however lax one might be in its execution, followed the evolution of the party from minority to majority status. Nevertheless, the insistence on formal unity could not abolish conflict at all levels. No amount of disciplinary action against local party members or parliamentarians could prevent the expression of conflicting opinions and the occasional revolt of minority groups.

In the early days of the Labour Party, the conflict of opinion

---

[1] *Report* of the Labour Party Annual Conference, 1917, p. 82, quoted in McKenzie, *op. cit.*, p. 473.

was most obvious in the movement at large. With the emergence of a large leadership group, both inside the House of Commons and in the country as a whole, controversies centre increasingly on these groups; indeed, they may well be regarded as the initiators of controversies. The movement as a whole and local party organizations often reverberated with the issues this posed.

A fairly formal analysis and description of some phases of the opposition inside the Parliamentary Party, given here, cannot account fully for the emergence of conflict or the strength of rival factions, but it may give some indication of the bases of certain lines of division within the party. The divergencies of opinion and the extent of factions are best observed during periods when the party is in office. Then political opinion is put to the test of departmental policies and day-to-day administrative decisions. At the same time, loyalty and unfailing support in the division lobbies is expected of every Labour member. To oppose your own government by your vote, even on comparatively minor issues, incurs the opprobrium of fellow M.P.s and even more of the party leadership; we must take its expression generally as a sign of fundamental conflict.

During the 1924 Government the Labour back-benchers, although restive, never failed to support the Government. What criticism there was, was centred naturally around the I.L.P. which could count more than two-thirds of the Parliamentary Party among its members and which had endorsed the candidature of 45 M.P.s. The latter probably formed the bulk of the 'regular I.L.P. meeting [where] the business of the week is discussed, not with a view to developing points of difference but mutually helping one another in giving more efficient service. On some matters there are differences of opinion but they are never allowed to impair the splendid unity which is characteristic both of the I.L.P. group and the wider parliamentary party to which it is proud to belong.'[1] There was criticism of the Government's foreign policy and still more of its ability to tackle the unemployment problem by other means than those of orthodox public finance, but none of this led to any tangible repercussions inside the P.L.P. Only the 'Clyde-

---

[1] *Report* of the N.A.C. of the I.L.P. to the 1924 Party Conference (*Conference Report*, p. 45).

siders' engaged in a silent opposition to the Government by boy-
cotting its social functions.[1]

Scottish I.L.P. members were to be prominent among the small
knot of M.P.s whose opposition to the policies of the second
Labour Government carried them into the division lobbies, but
only a minority of the I.L.P. group followed this line. Nearly half
the M.P.s elected in 1929 were members of the I.L.P. and 37 of
them had been I.L.P. sponsored candidates, but those who were
prepared to turn against their front bench were considerably
fewer. This group, which acted definitely as 'a party within the
party', deciding regularly on its parliamentary tactics, had only 14
to 16 members. It originated in a resolution of the 1930 Conference
of the I.L.P., which declared that the I.L.P. was an independent
socialist organization with 'a distinctive position within the party',
and that it was 'unreasonable to ask members of the party to
accept without question all the proposals of the Government when
these proposals are not themselves subject to the decisions of the
Parliamentary Party . . . and often do not agree with the Party
Programme as defined by the Party Conference.'[2]

The I.L.P. M.P.s who followed conference decisions believed
that they were carrying out the wishes of the movement in the
country. J. Kinley, M.P., said at the I.L.P. Conference in 1931, that
comrades who criticized their action should reflect that those who
were Labour M.P.s were not the Labour Party. The Labour Party
was in the country. The movement sent the members to the House.
Their main task should therefore be to put the programme of the
party into legislative form. 'If the government would do so, there
would be no need for a "left-wing" group.'[3]

The opposition to one aspect or another of government policy
was, of course, not restricted to the I.L.P. faithfuls; others took
part now and then. Indeed, a total of 119 Labour M.P.s voted
against the Government in 17 different divisions between August
1929 and January 1931.[4] The I.L.P. cadre, however, formed the

---

[1] cf. Letter of Sidney Webb to his wife of 12.2.1924. (Passfield Papers.)

[2] Quoted in G. D. H. Cole: *A History of the Labour Party from 1914*, 1948, p.
246.

[3] *Report* of the 1931 Conference of the I.L.P., p. 34. See also Jowett's defence
of his part in the opposition, in the *Bradford Pioneer* (Brockway, *op. cit.*, p. 289).

[4] cf. F. Brockway in the *New Leader*, January 23, 1931.

nucleus of most of the opposition moves. The bulk of this opposition arose over the treatment of the unemployed or other financial measures to restrict the numbers of those entitled to certain kinds of financial assistance, such as educational grants. When the 'Left Wing' attempted to express more general disquiet at the policy of the Government, as in the amendment to the vote on the King's speech at the beginning of the session in 1930–31, they failed to attract support. Only 13 M.P.s expressed their regret that the speech contained no proposals for 'a socialist reorganization of industry, agriculture and banking . . . and for a fairer distribution of the National Income'.

Even at the end of the Labour Government's term of office, therefore, its support had not decreased perceptibly. Opposition concentrated on the Government's policy towards the unemployed. During the reading of the (1931) Bill for the regulation of Unemployment Benefits, I.L.P. members challenged the Government on seven different occasions. But neither specific amendments to the Bill, nor general opposition, ever resulted in more than 25 Labour M.P.s voting against the Government. Only four of these were trade union M.P.s; only eight had originally followed working class occupations, and the same number had finished their education in elementary school. Those who subjectively identified themselves most strongly with working-class demands were occupationally much less working-class than the P.L.P. as a whole. The bulk of the working-class M.P.s remained loyal to the party leadership and so, of course, did the majority of middle-class M.P.s. How, then, did the faithful and the rebels look at each other?

The prophets of 'socialism in our time' saw the faithful whipped to dance around the golden calf of the leadership. Jennie Lee told us that 'she was totally unprepared for the solid rows of decent well-intentioned, unpretentious Labour back-benchers [who] in the long run . . . did the most deadly damage. Again and again an effort was made to rouse them from their inertia. On every occasion they reacted like a load of damp cement. They would see nothing, do nothing, listen to nothing that had not first been given the seal of MacDonald's approval.'[1]

_____

[1] Jennie Lee: *Tomorrow is a New Day*, London, 1939, p. 145.

For the middle-of-the-road Labour M.P.—earnest, hard-working, unambitious and unimaginative—the opposition was just a group of cranks. For one of them:

'The sincerity of these difficult members . . . was never questioned . . . but they were in essence . . . political individualists and insofar as they considered their own convenience before the needs of the party, they were bad colleagues. They believed themselves to be moved by principles, whereas they were really the victims of pride . . . what for the sake of the Labour Party others had to endure they would not have. The immaculate purity of their socialist conscience was not to be fouled by such base contacts and compromises as others had to make . . . as players in the party they would do everything except pass the ball.'[1]

The opposition inside Labour's ranks in Parliament during the period of the post-war Labour Governments and the years which followed them provides a more detailed knowledge of what, by and large, constitutes Labour's 'Left Wing'. Opposition has been more widespread in more recent years, involving both larger numbers of individuals and a wider range of issues. In addition, the size of Labour's majority in the first post-war Parliament and the suspension of the standing orders of the P.L.P. during most of these years, have combined to facilitate the expression of opposition to the Government. Pressure from the whips and the strong feelings of loyalty did no doubt dissuade some critics of the Government from expressing their views in the division lobbies, but by and large, deed seems to have followed thought. This view is borne out by the fact that the distribution of voting in opposition to the party whip or the party line does not follow a purely random spread. During the period 1945–54 the Government (or after 1951 the party leadership) found itself opposed by its own tail on twelve important occasions.[2] These involved a total of 540 individual acts

---

[1] Henry Snell (Lord Snell): *Men, Moments, and Myself*, 1936, p. 231 (Snell was at that time Chairman of the P.L.P.)

[2] The following 'acts of opposition' were analysed: (Numbers in opposition in parentheses).

1. Amendment opposing the appointment of part-time directors moved in the Committee stage of the Civil Aviation Bill, August 1946 (21).
2. Amendment on foreign policy tabled during the debate on the Address but not voted on when called, November 1946 (43).

of opposition and 213 M.P.s—just under half of the total number of those who sat on the Labour benches during these years.

Among those who opposed, four groups can be distinguished:

(a) Pacifists (i.e. all those who rejected outright the Government's conscription bill)—39 members.

(b) Those of the non-Pacifists who voted only once or on one issue against the Government—97 members.

(c) Those who opposed the Government twice or more often—77 members.

(d) 24 members included in (c) whose opposition was persistent, extending to four, five or even seven different occasions.

Pure pacifism inside the P.L.P. was very much an issue which moved older and more seasoned politicians. A large number of them had passed through the I.L.P., over one-third had sat in the House of Commons before 1945, mostly already in the 1920's. The character of this group is similar to that of the opposition during the second Labour Government; indeed, we can find many direct links between the two groups. Originating largely in working-class or lower middle-class homes, many had risen through the educational ladder and had become members of the professions; only 15 were still following working-class occupations or

3. Amendment on conscription during the same debate (46).

4. Second Reading of National Service Bill opposed, March 1947 (73).

5. Third reading of the same bill opposed, May 1947 (39).

6. Signatories to the 'Nenni' telegram, congratulating Nenni on his electoral victory, despite the fact that Nenni's party opposed the Saragat Socialists with whom the L.P. had ties as fellow members of the Socialist International, March 1948 (31).

7. Motion opposing Government policy on the employment of Civil Servants who were Communists or Fascists. Supported by only five signatories when forced to a division, March 1948 (41).

8. Second reading of Palestine Bill opposed, March 1948 (30).

9. Critical amendments to Government of Ireland Bill, April–May 1949 (58).

10. Conservative Government's Statement on Defence opposed in division, contrary to Party policy of abstention, March 1957 (57).

11. Motion to approve Order in Council to extend National Service Act from 1954 to 1959 opposed, November 1953 (40).

12. Amendment to Atomic Energy Bill, aiming at the banning of the Hydrogen Bomb, April 1954 (61).

worked for working-class organizations by the time they entered Parliament.

When we look at the general, not specifically pacifist opposition, and compare this group with the P.L.P. as a whole, an interesting picture emerges. The more frequent the opposition the less representative of the Labour benches as a whole is its character. Thus one third of all Labour M.P.s in the 1945 House of Commons had been in Parliament before that election; among those who opposed the Government on only one issue the corresponding percentage is below 25; of the 24 'persistent offenders' all but two had entered the House in 1945 or later. Nor did the opposition tend to come from trade union sponsored candidates. The percentage of trade union M.P.s during the three post-1945 Parliaments was 33 per cent. For the group of M.P.s who opposed the party leadership on only one issue the percentage was 25 per cent; for the 'persistent offenders', 12 per cent. By comparing the social character of all those who opposed the leadership two or three times and of those who did so four times or more, further light is shed on the character of this intra-party opposition.

It is significant that the opposition to the actions of Mr Attlee's Government and to his subsequent leadership of the Party in opposition concerned largely the field of foreign affairs and defence. We find that on the economic plane and with regard to the implementation of the Welfare State, the Labour Government proceeded to carry out its declared aims and in consequence aroused less antagonism. But in foreign affairs and in defence the policies of the Government came into conflict with traditional socialist sentiment and, according to some people, with the declared aims of the party. Yet these issues never did rouse much interest in the masses of the working class and when raised by the opposition within the Parliamentary Labour Party, they did not at first evoke much opposition from the mass of Labour's followers. It is probably for that reason rather than for any other that the opposition had, at least in its beginning, little *organized* support outside Parliament. Unlike the opposition during the period of the second Labour Government, it had lacked an organizational and to a certain extent an ideological basis. The Bevanite 'rebels' received the bulk of their support from the Constituency parties who gradually increased their hold over the Constituency Party

TABLE V

The 'Rebels' Contrasted with the whole of the Parliamentary Labour Party:

| | Rebels | | Parliamentary Labour Party[1] | |
	Occasional Defectors	Persistent Offenders	Totals in 1945	Totals in 1951
Education:				
Elementary School only	13	5	—	74
University	29	13	c.101–136	122
Oxford or Cambridge	(11)	(6)	(c.46–59)	(57)
Occupation:				
Professional	28	16	c.130–165	133
Lawyers	(5)	(4)		
Teachers, Lecturers	(4)	(3)		
Journalists, Authors	(13)	(4)		
Other professions	(6)	(5)		
Entrepreneurs, Managers	5	2	c.23–31	17
Manual, clerical, T.U. officials, etc.	16	5	c.125–155	108
Others	4	1	c.20–38	37
Unknown	—	—	c.23–78	—
Numbers involved	53	24	394	295

N.B. – 'Occasional defectors' opposed the leadership twice or three times while 'persistent offenders' did so at least four times.

representatives on the N.E.C. of the Party. Their hour of triumph, however, came only in 1952 when this group captured six of the

---

[1] The figures for the composition of the P.L.P. in 1945 are taken from Ross, *op. cit.*, and from R. B. McCallum and A. Readman: *The British General Election of 1945*. Neither figures are complete nor entirely reliable. The 1951 figures are derived from D. Butler: *The British General Election of 1951*.

seven seats in that section. When Parliament reassembled after the recess a meeting of the Parliamentary Labour Party decided to ban all organized groups within the Parliamentary Party and together with the re-imposition of Standing Orders this did much to muzzle the opposition.

Not that the original opposition on the Labour benches was really a monolithic group. A comparison of individual divisions shows clearly that each attracts a slightly differently constituted opposition. Bearing in mind the fact that in any case we are concerned with small numbers, the divisions show the degree of representativeness of different opposition views. Thus the revolt against '18 months conscription' attracted a most widely scattered support; the attack on Mr Bevin's Palestine policy, on the other hand, seems the most narrowly based of oppositions.

TABLE VI

Composition of the 'Revolt Inside Labour's Ranks' in Post-war Years:

	Broke with the Leadership on the Issue of:				
	Con-scription (in 1947) per cent	Pales-tine (in 1948) per cent	Defence (in 1952) per cent	Hydro-gen Bomb (in 1954) per cent	P.L.P. [total] (in 1951) per cent
Trade-union sponsored M.P.s..	19	3	18	18	46
Elementary School only ..	48	4	27	25	25
University education	32	75	56	46	41
Manual workers, party or trade union officials..	36	—	26	26	37
Professionals	36	76	62	56	45
(Numbers involved) ..	(73)	(30)	(57)	(61)	(295)

Yet it would be completely wrong to regard each issue as unique and independent. The series of votes which we have considered show a much greater degree of inter-relation than would have resulted from complete randomness. Through its different configurations there persists a 'general opposition'; it has links with acts of defiance towards the party line in the period before 1945 and we can pursue its continuance after 1954.[1]

---

[1] After 1959 it became more crystallized as a Left-wing opposition which has challenged the leadership on a number of occasions and in 1960 and 1961 contested the leadership and deputy leadership of the P.L.P.

In its latest phase the opposition inside the Labour Party has, however, taken on a new character. 'Bevanism', both in Parliament and in the Movement at large, had comparatively little support in the trade union element of the Party. On the other hand the strength which it displayed among the active Party workers owed much to its intellectual appeal, an appeal which was particularly strong in a section of the middle-class adherents to the Labour Movement.

During the last few years, however, the leadership has been challenged on two apparently unrelated issues; unilateralism and nationalization. The official line in favour of collective security (with reliance on the deterring power of the arsenal of atomic weapons) and a pragmatic policy in the economic field have both been challenged by a strong section of trade union opinion. The support for unilateral nuclear disarmament by such an obviously working-class element of the Labour rank and file is a surprising phenomenon and the permanence of this allegiance is not certain. It is more obvious that a considerable section of the trade union movement should support a more vigorous nationalization programme. It lays bare an ideological split at the roots of the tree of Labour, but it also reveals a conflict of interest inside the Labour Movement which is of considerable social significance.

A GROWING ÉLITE IN A CHANGING SOCIETY

The advance of the Labour Party, from a small organization led by a group of parliamentarians of varying views and sometimes conflicting loyalties, to a mass party which eventually became the sole bearer of governmental power, is a unique social and political phenomenon. This chapter has analysed the development of its leadership cadre and the attitudes and problems of its élite.

In the course of this development the character of the Labour leadership underwent considerable change. In its *status nascendi* the Party was devotedly served by three groups of functionaries, each of whom fulfilled an essential task at that particular juncture. It had a group of local leaders who set out to organize the supporters of socialist policies mainly in the industrial areas of Scotland and northern England, Lancashire and the Midlands. Secondly, there were the officials of sympathizing trade unions, regional or national, who were active in municipal politics and in the House of Commons. Finally, there was a small group of socialist propagandists, publicists, and intellectuals, who gave a considerable part of their time to further the cause of Labour. The qualities required of the early generation of Labour leaders were those of character, coupled with the ability to put oneself across, facility in writing and speaking, oratorical gifts and physical endurance rather than intellect or expertise.[1]

Since then, political leadership in the Labour Party has become institutionalized. Parliamentary activity or trade union leadership have become more frequently *the* road to political eminence. The N.E.C. of the Labour Party is today composed either of second-ranking trade union leaders,[2] of representatives of the Women's section or of leading parliamentarians, especially ministers or ex-ministers. This has meant also that the leadership is increasingly centred in London where, apart from the Labour Party, the T.U.C. itself as well as all the major trade unions and other semi-political working-class organizations have their headquarters.

The Constitution of the I.L.P. provided for the representation of all the regions on the Party's governing body. At the beginning the Labour Party Executive still contained men whose political reputation was largely made in the provinces. Whatever regional, as distinct from *local* activity, exists today inside the Labour Party it is entirely directed towards organization and education. The regional conference of the I.L.P., where policy was discussed, has no present-day equivalent. Today political reputation is increasingly made in Parliament itself or in junior office, and the selection occurs largely through the existing leadership. It is only when a vociferous and able opposition group in the P.L.P. succeeds in gaining first the ear and then the votes of an active minority in

---

[1] *cf.* some of the biographies and autobiographies of early Labour Leaders, *e.g.* Stewart's *Life of Keir Hardie*, Brockway's *Life of Jowett*, Snowden's *Autobiography*. See also John Paton's *Left Turn* and, for a slightly later period, Shinwell's Autobiography.

[2] The General Secretaries of Unions will prefer to sit on the General Council of the T.U.C., and no one may sit on both bodies. Sometimes a trade union Leader achieves eminence through service on the N.E.C. Thus, Mr Sam Watson, the Miners' representative, has frequently spoken for the Executive and Labour Party Conferences and has been a firm supporter of the Party leadership. On the relationship between the Unions and the N.E.C. see M. Harrison: *Trade Unions and the Labour Party since 1945*, 1960, ch. 7.

local party organizations, as was the case with the Bevanite 'rebels', that a change in the composition of the Party leadership can take place. It is perhaps in consequence of this that the influence and importance of the charismatic leader has declined in the Labour Party. To gain leadership a strong personality and the ability to achieve transference are probably essential, and an attractive voice and mien are no doubt helpful, but we must not forget that modern means of mass communication can achieve much even with mediocre talents. It is also clear, as Max Weber pointed out forty-odd years ago, that the very act of a democratic election invests leaders with a charismatic authority.[1] Professor Laski's suggestion to Attlee, apparently made in a conversation between the two men, that Attlee should hand over the leadership to someone who had 'more of the essential gifts' seems based on a misconception of what is required. Attlee's reply that, as Laski had pointed out, he had 'neither the personality nor the distinctiveness to tempt [him] to think that [he] should have any value apart from the party which he served', is, on the other hand, a typical Attleean understatement.[2] It is the very identification of leader and party which makes for the strength of his position.

The leadership is also helped in the maintenance of its position of power by the party bureaucracy. The growth of the Labour Party headquarters and especially of its research and publicity departments, has put at the disposal of the leadership a Civil Service which is invaluable during the period when the Party is in opposition, and which gives the leaders a great advantage over Party members in the lower ranks, including probably the majority of Members of Parliament.

This largely self-recruiting leadership becomes increasingly distant from the rank and file of the Party membership. Indeed, it might be accurate to speak of a series of concentric and increasingly narrower circles into which the Labour Party is divided, each fairly self-contained, and with recruitment proceeding generally only from one parallel to the next. The ideal type of *cursus honorum* inside the Labour Party is still that which starts from local party membership and proceeds via officership in local organizations, or

---

[1] See M. Weber on the inversion ('Umdeutung') of the charisma in *Wirtschaft und Gesellschaft*, ch. II, para. 14.

[2] *cf*. K. Martin: *Harold Laski*, 1953, p. 162.

trade unions, to elected municipal office, and then via the House of Commons to the Treasury Bench. In this the British Labour Party is distinct from the Conservative Party, but of late years other and extraordinary ladders of advancement have increasingly been used. Sir Stafford Cripps, to give but one example, was recruited for the Labour Party largely through the endeavours of Herbert Morrison. He was not expected to start his activities in the local party organization. The question of finding a seat for him was apparently discussed at the highest level, as his father could write to him after a visit to the Webbs, that 'the question of a proper London constituency for you arose . . . they [the Party leaders] have a very sympathetic attitude *to your claim.*'[1]

In an increasingly mobile society it seems only natural that a growing proportion of Labour M.P.s should belong occupationally to the middle class. Although many of them will have risen from the working class, their attitudes must be coloured by their own social position. In addition, the very atmosphere of the House of Commons, of which the Labour Party now forms an integral part, conditions its members. All this need not necessarily mollify them or weaken their socialism—we have seen that the Left Wing opposition counted a large number of middle class M.P.s among its supporters—but it hampers communication between leaders and followers. Thus in the political field the Labour Party seems to be creating or maintaining a static system of stratification which it is seeking to destroy in the economic and social field.

Up till now the influx of men and women from the ranks of wage earners, or their representatives, into the House of Commons has been maintained largely through the 'proprietary boroughs' which are in the hands of the trade unions.[2] This pre-emption of a third or a quarter of all Labour seats by trade union nominees is, however, only a custom, although one hallowed by tradition and also apparently supported by Party headquarters. It need not necessarily continue on that scale, and recent displays of unrest in local Labour parties suggest that it may not do so. We have even less reason to assume that the composition of future Labour

---

[1] E. Estorick: *Stafford Cripps*, p. 79 (my italics). Pethick-Lawrence's entry into Labour politics proceeded in a similar fashion.

[2] Recent happenings in connection with nominations to traditional trade union seats suggest the use of this ancient term.

Cabinets will follow the tradition of shared representation between the middle-class and the working-class element in the P.L.P. Beatrice Webb thought in 1930 that 'every succeeding Labour Prime Minister in the construction of his Cabinet will be confronted with the necessity of including . . . the representatives of the great organized industries' (*i.e.* the principal trade union leaders).

'. . . just as the P.M. 200 years ago had to have the Duke of Newcastle or some equivalent nobleman in his Cabinet, so the Labour P.M. in the twentieth century will find it necessary to include in his administration the General Secretary or other official of the miners, cotton operatives (etc.), together with the representatives of the Consumers' Co-operative Movement. This firm anchorage of the Labour Party in the working class organization may be deemed a guarantee that Labour administrations will continue to represent adequately four-fifths of the population.'[1]

Attlee's government still followed partly in this tradition. But with the exception of Bevin, the ministers who had entered politics via the trade union movement did not really belong to the top ranks of trade union leaders, nor perhaps even to the second drawer. Since then there has been even less evidence that leading trade union officials are eager to exchange the real power which they hold in the industrial field for the vague and possibly wholly illusory power which might be theirs as members of the House of Commons or even as junior ministers. When Attlee formed his government in 1945 there were still six Cabinet Ministers as well as six departmental heads outside the Cabinet in addition to thirteen Parliamentary Secretaries who held Trade Union-sponsored seats. By 1951 this number had fallen significantly: four Cabinet Ministers, three Ministers outside the Cabinet and eleven Parliamentary Secretaries come into this category. In the contemporary Shadow Cabinet they are even less strongly represented.[2]

---

[1] Beatrice Webb: 'The Disappearance of the Governing Class', *Political Quarterly*, 1930, pp. 104–9.

[2] In 1955 only four minor trade unions were represented in Parliament by their General Secretaries: *cf.* B. C. Roberts: *Trade Union Government and Administration*, 1957, p. 387. For lists of T.U.-sponsored M.P.s in the four Labour Governments see V. L. Allen: *Trade Unions and the Government*, London, 1960.

Beginning with MacDonald, it has been held increasingly inside the British Left, that the professionalization of political activity and the existence of a comparatively small nucleus of leaders who make the vital decisions (subject to referendum-like approval through general elections or party congresses) are necessary developments in the modern state exercising wide economic and social controls. It is clear that this development increases the social stratification inside the field of politics, either directly through power as a dimension of social differentiation, or indirectly through the importation of socio-economic standards from the world outside into Labour politics. There is little evidence that 'successive Labour administrations [have] maintained by precept and example, the modest personal expenditure and unpretentious ways of social intercourse implied by the idea of equality between man and man'.[1]

This is not the place to consider whether they should have done so, nor to ask whether the above-mentioned trend has been inevitable. One thing seems clear: the rise of a Labour leadership claiming great power and using the full panoply of the State when in office, has led to tensions inside the wider Labour Movement. The practice of central control has come into conflict with the ideological precepts of a primitive (*i.e.* original) egalitarianism and the tradition of direct democracy which have been inherent in the British Labour tradition.

---

[1] Beatrice Webb, *loc. cit.*, p. 109.

CHAPTER X

Leadership in the Conservative Party

' "If not with me, at any rate be against me", he would have said to every representative of the people in the name of the great leader whom he followed. He thought that debates were good—because they served to create that public opinion which was hereafter to be used in creating some future House of Commons; but he did not think it possible that any vote should be given on a great question either this way or that as the result of a debate; and he was certainly assured in his own opinion that any such changing of votes would be dangerous, revolutionary and almost unparliamentary.'—ANTHONY TROLLOPE.

'The Conservatives do represent big business and I think that makes them the more efficient Party. Running the country, after all, is just the biggest business of them all.'—A SKILLED ENGINEER, 1959.

IN discussing the character of authority in the Conservative Party and the rôle of the leader *vis-à-vis* his followers, it has lately been fashionable to stress the similarities between the two great parties of the right and the left. In the Conservative Party, we are told, party 'democracy' is as much a reality or a shibboleth as in the Labour Party. R. T. McKenzie, who first put forward this thesis and documented it with a wealth of material, saw the present position between the two parties as analogous to that which existed in the last quarter of the nineteenth century in respect of the Liberal and the Conservative Party. He quoted with approval Professor Lowell's dictum about the rôle of party organization in the British political system. 'Both are shams,' Lowell wrote, 'but with this difference that the Conservative organization is a transparent and the Liberal an opaque sham.'[1] If one substitutes Labour for Liberal, this sentence, it is held, sums up the present situation.

The workings of a party machine whose main purpose must

---

[1] A. L. Lowell: *The Government of England*, 2 vols., 1908, vol. I, p. 570.

inevitably be the conquest and maintenance of political power rarely corresponds to the image which the propagandists seek to create. Rank-and-file followers, who are ideologically committed and attracted by broad principles, will project their own conviction on the party leadership and see the relationship of leaders and led in the light of their general views about the position of authority in our society.

In the last chapter the realities of leadership in the Labour Party were set against a background of a popular protest movement, whose followers believe in a more radical and direct form of democracy, and are critical of many of the accepted social values and traditional expressions of authority. Such an 'image', however unrealistic it may have been, could not fail to affect the actual exercise of authority in a party and the internal struggles of the Labour Party have clearly born this out.

The formal relationship between leaders and followers in the Conservative Party cannot be discussed without reference to the views about the rôle of leaders and the function of leadership held by those at the top and those at the bottom of the political hierarchy. The 'mythos of leadership' affects the attitudes and expectations of those who exercise authority as well as of those who merely serve and vote.

After discussing the factors which make for conformity, we must examine those which engender conflict. If the analysis of cohesion and dissension inside the P.L.P. is followed here by a study of the group of Conservative Parliamentarians this is not done for mere symmetry. The body of Conservative Parliamentarians has during the past forty years experienced rifts of considerable dimensions. It is well known that the causes around which such conflicts have centred were predominantly in the field of foreign and imperial policy. Their core was not the internal structure of British society, but the place of Britain in the world and the character of the Empire and Commonwealth.

At first glance such trends inside the upper level of Conservative politicians would appear to be rooted in purely ideological factors unconnected with social and economic reality. Such a view is, however, superficial. In some ways the leadership ranks of the Conservative Party are probably socially as monolithic as that of any political party in the world. Seen through its leadership cadre, it is the Conservative Party rather than the Labour Party which has the character of a class party. A more subtle analysis of the social background of the Conservative leadership shows, however, some lines of social division within that admittedly very narrowly confined group.

LEADERS AND FOLLOWERS

In the General Election of 1929, the first to be fought on the basis of *complete* adult suffrage, the Conservatives suffered defeat. Their representation in Parliament fell from 396 to 260. The Labour Party, which with 289 M.P.s, was the strongest single group in the new House of Commons, did not have an absolute majority either.[1] Under these circumstances there was some division of opinion whether the Government should resign forthwith or await its defeat on the floor of the House. Baldwin favoured the former course, so did Lord Stamfordham who, as Private Secretary to the King, was involved in the question of the succession to the Premiership. 'Democracy is no longer a meaningless set of shibboleth,' he wrote to Sir George Murray, 'and with the enormous increase of votes by the women's franchise it is the actual voice and, for better or worse, the *political* voice of the state.[2]

The final act in this advance towards adult suffrage—as the first —had been carried out by a Conservative Government against a mere handful of opponents from its own ranks. During the sixty years that lay between the enfranchisement of the male urban householder and the granting of the 'flapper vote'[3] Conservatives had, perhaps reluctantly, come to terms with political democracy on the national plane. The Conservative concept of leadership was, however, formed in the early years of this advance, at a time when the two parties became more clearly crystallized and when their followers in the country at large confronted each other in the broadly based phalanxes of their respective Party organizations.

---

[1] In popular votes the Conservatives polled actually slightly more votes than the Labour Party.

[2] H. Nicolson: *George V*, p. 435. Baldwin's course of action was eventually adopted.

[3] The term given to the new electorate of women between the ages of twenty-one and thirty.

Its leader and spiritual architect was Benjamin Disraeli. 'The Party today is recognizably the party of Disraeli, of two generations of Chamberlain, of Stanley Baldwin and of Sir Winston Churchill. If a guiding principle must be looked for it is simply the assumption that the Conservative Party ought to govern and will govern even though there be no other principle to guide it when in power, or dictate its pattern of revival when it goes through the rare, unnatural but at the same time calcining process of electoral defeat.'[1]

When the edifice of the 'new' Toryism was erected conditions were conducive to the rise of a charismatic and authoritarian leader-personality, and Disraeli filled the part to perfection. He reunited a party which had been broken and dispirited by Peel's acceptance of a free-trade policy and which in consequence had been out of office for twenty years. Disraeli led his party in fact—if not formally—for longer than any of his predecessors. He had engaged in a long combat with Gladstone which had stirred popular imagination. LOYALTY, DISCIPLINE, DEFERENCE and TRADITION, these formed the bases for the Conservative Leader's large powers over his followers.

Loyalty inside the Conservative Party leadership has deeper roots than the degree of mutual trust which is necessary for successful co-operation inside a group. Conservative politicians were, as we noted, even more closely connected by ties of friendship and kinship than their Liberal opponents and these ties were stronger the greater the social homogeneity of the group from which they were recruited. Their contacts, as we saw, exceeded those provided and necessitated by the political life. Reading the biographies and autobiographies of Conservative politicians, one is struck again and again by the extent and intimacy of these personal contacts. They are inevitably related to the greater freedom and ease of intercourse which stems from a considerable degree of material independence. And such personal ties extend, of course, over a wider area than the group of ruling politicians and include the world of the (very) rich, the leadership of the Armed Forces and the circles around the Court. It is inconceivable

---

[1] 'The adaptable Party' in a special number of *The Political Quarterly* devoted to the Conservative Party (July–September 1961, p. 210).

that George V, who addressed Sir Austen Chamberlain as 'My dear Austen', would have written to a Labour Secretary of State using his Christian name. Loyalty to colleagues and respect for the wishes of others are closely bound up with the code of honour which governs 'gentlemanly' conduct. One stands by one's friends, keeps one's word, is absolutely truthful and seeks to avoid hurting other people's feeling.

This clearly enhances a Prime Minister's position enormously and it equally affects his conduct. In response to Randolph Churchill's complaint about the lack of drive and punch on the part of the Conservative Leader in the House of Commons, Salisbury stressed the fact that he was 'bound to Sir Stafford Northcote as a colleague by a tie not of expediency but of honour and that he could not take part in anything which would be at variance with entire loyalty to him'.[1]

Neville Chamberlain, who was not slow in noting down in private criticism of his colleagues, wrote in his diary fifty years later that 'the question of leadership is again acute. . . . I am getting letters and communications from all over the country. . . . I cannot see my way out. . . . I am the one person who might bring about S(tanley) B(aldwin)'s retirement, but I cannot act where my action might put me in his place'.[2]

In emergencies such ties can, of course, be disregarded. Salisbury removed Northcote from the leadership of the House of Commons when Sir Michael Hicks Beach added his voice to that of Randolph Churchill in 1885. Strongly felt convictions, too, are sometimes readily and inexplicably changed. Lord Birkenhead (F. E. Smith), one of the most outspoken Unionist opponents of Home Rule, became later, as a Minister in Lloyd George's coalition, one of the leaders in the negotiation with the Irish 'rebels'. His *volte face* and general arrogance were mainly responsible for Lord Robert Cecil's remark in a parliamentary debate of that period that 'England prefers to be ruled by second-rate intellects rather than by second-rate characters'.

Yet the support of the majority of Conservative Leaders for the Coalition Government was based on some feeling of loyalty for that

---

[1] W. S. Churchill: *Life of Randolph Churchill*, vol. I. p. 386.

[2] Entry of 23.2.1931 quoted in Feiling: *The Life of Neville Chamberlain*, p. 185. See also entry of 1.3.1936 (*ibid.*, p. 278).

extraordinary conjurer of human emotions, David Lloyd George. Austen Chamberlain, a man of greater depth of feeling than his half-brother, describes how his attitude towards the Prime Minister had changed from mistrust to admiration. It was unthinkable to overthrow him.[1] The motives of others may have been more complex, but the issue of personal loyalty was clearly involved in the support of the coalition. They would have succeeded with this appeal had there not been another leader around whom rank and file opposition could concentrate. Bonar Law was out of the Government, when the question of the coalition came to a head in 1922; a serious breakdown in health had forced him to resign office a year before. On the eve of the famous meeting at the Carlton Club, at which the question of Conservative support for the coalition was to be debated, Salvidge, the Liverpool Tory Boss, visited Law. He heard from him that he would attend next day's meeting, would oppose his ministerial colleagues, and that Lord Curzon, the Foreign Secretary, had sided with him. This spelt the death of the Government. From Kensington, Salvidge went to see Lloyd George in Downing Street and found him in conclave with a part of the Cabinet. Salvidge related what he had heard. When he had finished, Salvidge tells us, 'Balfour . . . banged the table with his fist and shouted, "I say fight them, fight them, this is wrong. The Conservative Party has always acted on the advice of its leaders. Is the lead of Law and Curzon to count as everything and the advice of the rest of us as nothing? This is revolt and should be crushed." '[2]

The military metaphor has always been close to the Conservative mind and this language does express one aspect of Conservative 'Realpolitik'. The actual organization of the Conservative forces in the country at large was originally conceived by the leadership as that of the infantry of the political battle, the

---

[1] Sir C. Petrie: *Life of Austen Chamberlain*, 2 vols., 1940, vol. II, pp. 158, 159, 163.

[2] S. Salvidge: *Salvidge of Liverpool*, 1934, p. 239. Salvidge is a unique phenomenon in British Politics: the local boss who exercised a considerable influence on national politics. He controlled the Conservative Party Machine of Liverpool, was a powerful figure in the National Union and, probably as a result of it, the confidant of Prime Ministers and Party Leaders. His diary is a valuable source for the internal history of the Conservative Party.

'handmaid to the Party'. In one of the few speeches, which he made to the Conservative Organization in the country, Disraeli stressed the need for discipline on the part of the Conservative Army. 'All men have agreed that in the conduct of public affairs there is nothing more precious than discipline and it is a great mistake that discipline is *incompatible with the deepest convictions*. . . . Nature herself is organized, (without it) there would be nothing but volcanoes and deluges. In public life without discipline—organization—similar effects would be produced. It is for you now, the assembled officers of the great constitutional army that you have formed, to feel convinced of these views. . . . Act upon these views of organization . . . it is only by encouraging discipline that you will be able to maintain yourself in that power which you have obtained.'[1]

Disraeli clearly conceived the Conservative organization in the country as primarily of local importance. Its principal purpose was to gain the support of the lukewarm and the waverers and to keep them to the right course. His immediate successors sought to confine it in that rôle. Neither Salisbury nor Balfour 'showed more than a faint interest in the functions of the National Union (of Conservative Associations) in reporting on the state of opinion among their supporters'.[2] The local organizations did largely agree with the subordinate positions which had been assigned to them. 'Our organization,' an officer of an important Conservative Association told Ostrogorski, 'is a military organization. It is led by a Commander in Chief who is called "President", by so many Brigadier Generals who are styled Chairmen, by so many Colonels', etc.[3]

The success of the system is clearly connected with the extent and depth of the feeling of deference which affected the distribution of power inside the National Union. Although it originated in local

---

[1] *The Times*, 7.8.1878, quoted in Ostrogorski: *Democracy and the Organization of Political Parties*, vol. I, p. 259. In 1872 the Earl of Shrewsbury in a speech to the Sixth Annual Conference of the National Union said: 'The duty of a soldier is obedience, and discipline is the great characteristic of the army and the navy, and I may also say in a like manner it is characteristic of the Conservative Union', McKenzie, *op. cit.*, p. 156.

[2] *ibid.*, p. 178.

[3] Ostrogorski, *op. cit.*, p. 604, note 2.

Associations of Conservative Workingmen the latter enjoyed little or no power in the wider local or national leadership. Nor is there evidence that they sought it. The Patrons, Vice-Patrons, Presidents and Vice-Presidents, were, as their titles suggest, to be recruited from men of the highest social eminence. At the foundation of the National Union a number of workingmen were proposed for election to the Council alongside with 'noblemen and gentlemen'. Some of the former objected to this honour. The union, one of them said, ought not 'to have second-rate names on the committee. His own name was there and he objected to it very strongly. The committee was not the place for a workingman but should be composed of the best men they could possibly obtain.'[1]

While the National Union rose, so to speak, from below, the Primrose League, that other popular Conservative body in the country, was organized from above, and its whole structure was permeated by the spirit of hierarchy.[2] With its knights and dames, its gamut of 'office holders' of varying rank, dependent on the size of their contribution, its subtle admixture of the great and the noble, of garden fêtes and soirées, it appealed to middle-class and lower middle-class snobbishness. At the same time it brought in the 'lower orders', paying only nominal contributions. By this 'union' of social classes and by the adroit mixture of refreshment, entertainment and a little politics the League gave the conservative workingman, his wife, his sons and daughters, the experience of civility and apparent care by the members of the middle class. And the local leaders, in turn, received their portion of civility and condescension on the part of a 'real' Lady or perhaps a Cabinet Minister or ex-Cabinet Minister who might receive them in London or in their country houses.[3] Its programme, in as far as it can be said to exist, featured the maintenance of the 'hallowed' institutions of the Realm, the defence of established religion and

[1] Quoted McKenzie, op. cit., p. 153.

[2] Founded in 1883 and named after Disraeli's favourite flower, its membership reached the million mark by 1890 and topped 2,000,000. On the early history of the Primrose League see J. H. Robb: The Primrose League, 1883–1906, 1942.

[3] On this see the very lively account in Ostrogorski, op. cit., pp. 538–47. (Ostrogorski incidentally thought that the activities of the Primrose League did actually bring about a lowering of class barriers.)

the belief in the imperial ascendancy. It chimed in well with the fundamental obedience and deference to the demands of the Party leadership.

In the day-to-day political struggle the troops of the beribboned and bemedalled attendants of Primrose League habitations were anything but a stage army. Keeping up registers, disseminating propaganda through lectures and tracts, converting and canvassing were among their tasks. 'The territorial area of each habitation is parcelled out among its districts and blocks which wardens and subwardens work systematically for the good of "the cause", that is to say for the triumph of the Tory Party at the next election.'[1]

Neither the 'combination of bric-à-brac with well contrived modern machinery' nor the limited powers of the local Conservative Association and of the National Union in which they were organized, satisfied fully all local politicians and would-be politicians. Ostrogorski thought that rank-and-file dissatisfaction with the aristocratic and exclusive character of the Conservative administration of 1874–80 prepared the way for Randolph Churchill's attempt to turn the National Union into a policy-making body. However small this movement may have been, there was from that time onwards, a tendency for the rank-and-file to seek greater influence over the inner councils and policies of the Party, and at times, in the decades that followed, they became vocal. Occasionally, when allied with sections of the Conservative politicians, they even came near to rejecting the policy of the leadership in voice and vote.

In 1921 the Annual Conference of the National Union almost repudiated the Irish policy of the Government. Salvidge countered with an appeal to the loyalty of the delegates to the political leaders and to himself as their own leader, who had been a champion of Ulster and an arch-enemy of Home Rule in the struggle before the war, and who now supported the Government in their new policy.[2]

To trust the Leader, not to stab the Government in the back, not to wreck its power in the country, and through this let loose revolution and misgovernment, these were the arguments used for warding off opposition and effective criticism.

---

[1] Ostrogorski, *op. cit.*, p. 539.
[2] Salvidge, *op. cit.*, pp. 209–11.

Such criticism is, of course, loudest when the inexplicable has happened and the Party has been defeated at the polls. In 1923 there was much evidence that Baldwin's decision to appeal to the country over Protection was unwise. It had certainly been taken without adequate discussion with local Conservative Leaders or M.P.s. Smarting under defeat, some M.P.s and defeated candidates tried to enforce closer consultation before important decisions were taken. Austen Chamberlain opposed any such attempts. Speaking in support of Baldwin at a meeting of Conservative M.P.s, Peers and defeated candidates, he said: 'Do not weaken the hand of the man you choose for your Leader and do not ask of him, or of any of us, that we should remit executive decisions to be debated in public meetings. That way confusion and disaster lie. That has been the practice of the Labour Party and unless their arrival in power leads to a direct breach with their past traditions, leads to their giving to their leaders a confidence, a responsibility and a power that they have never been entrusted with so far, they will come to an early and speedy disaster.'[1]

The power of the Conservative rank-and-file to use the National Union at least as a pressure group would be greater if the character and process of Conservative policy did give them something to fasten on. But as we know the Party, and especially its leadership, has always eschewed detailed programmes of any sort; instead it has rested its appeal on the broad set of Conservative principles and on the record of the Government when in power. At election times this has traditionally been supplemented by the 'appeal of the Leader to the Nation', issued on his own responsibility and without formal consultation with anybody. 'Mr Snowden', Baldwin said, 'suggests that the Conservative Party has never committed the folly of issuing a list of a few dozen items of reform which it proposes to carry out. Nor will it ever do so as long as I am leader.'[2]

---

[1] Conservative Party: *Gleanings and Memoranda*, 1924, p. 237, quoted in McKenzie, p. 117.

[2] Speech at Yarmouth in 1928, quoted by G. M. Young in his *Life of Baldwin*, 1952, p. 136. In 1949 Churchill, addressing the Party Conference, accepted the programme 'The Right Road for Britain', but added: 'I have advised you consistently during these years not to commit yourselves to rigid detailed programmes'. (*Report* of Annual Conference pp. 118–19.)

The annual conference of the National Union has frequently passed resolutions in an attempt to influence policy-making, although the delegates knew full well that this did not bind the leadership in any way. Only once since the war did such a vote influence party policy. In 1950 the Conference passed, against the advice of the platform, a resolution committing a future Conservative Government to the building of 300,000 houses annually. This was accepted with a great gesture by Lord Woolton, the Chairman of the Party, but it certainly inconvenienced the Party Leadership.

Unrepresentative as the Conference is—those sent as delegates of individual parties do not necessarily attend and even if they do, they come without anything even faintly resembling a mandate from their constituencies—it may yet influence party or government policy on specific issues where there is a strong feeling among the staunch stalwarts in the constituencies.

The real power of Conservative constituency organizations lies, however, in their power over their M.P., and this has been enhanced by their newly found financial independence. The Maxwell Fyfe reform of the Conservative Party organization put an end to the large financial contribution which M.P.s and candidates were wont to make to their constituency parties and which were indeed often essential for their solvency. This made it undoubtedly easier for some local Conservative organizations to oust M.P.s who had opposed the Government's Suez policy.[1] But, as Maxwell Fyfe himself saw, their powers were bound to go further. Party organization, he thought, must 'satisfy the constituencies which were raising large sums of money for their own work and for the Party as a whole. There must be a method by which they were satisfied that the money was well spent and that their representatives had a voice in its expenditure. The National Union, through its Executive Committee, should have a voice in the formulation of policy without fettering the leader of the Party, who was the ultimate arbiter.'[2]

In the selection of men for Parliament the basic character of Conservative Party leadership is generally perpetuated. Local

[1] cf. Leon Epstein: British M.P.s, and their local Parties: the Suez Case. *American Political Science Review*, June 1960, pp. 374–90.

[2] *The Times*, 16.7.1949, quoted in S. Beer: The Conservative Party, *Journal of Politics*, 1952, pp. 41–47 and p. 68.

selection committees, composed of the leaders of the local organization, men and women of worth and status and generally of advanced years, are inevitably and perhaps almost unconsciously prejudiced in favour of men who in their social background are like themselves or above them. For 'the English nation is a class-conscious nation. The reaction from Socialist egalitarianism has made the conservative English probably more class-conscious than they would otherwise have been and by and large they prefer to be represented in Parliament by Public Schoolboys.'[1]

If we wish to probe further the dissensions inside the Conservative Party we must begin by investigating the apparent homogeneity of its parliamentary phalanx.

MEN OF SUBSTANCE

In 1919 Lloyd George related to A. J. Balfour his impression of the new House of Commons. 'I addressed myself,' the Prime Minister is reported to have said, 'first to the Opposition benches in front of me. They were very cold and hostile; I could not get a cheer. This, said I to myself, is not the House of Commons it's the Trades Union Congress. So I turned, as one does in such circumstances, to the benches behind me but neither was that the House of Commons; it was the Associated Chamber of Commerce.'[2] This impression was widely shared and the Parliament elected after the holocaust has entered into history as that of the 'hard-faced men who looked as if they had done well out of the war'.[3]

The House of Commons which was dissolved at the end of the war had been elected nearly eight years earlier. Time, and four years of war, had changed many individual fortunes and it was hardly surprising that the new Parliament should contain many new faces. On the Conservative benches alone there were 158 new members out of a total of 333. Among them were clearly a fair number whose entry into Parliament crowned a rapid rise in fortune and social position and to whom the 'coupon' gave easy (but

---

[1] Christopher Hollis: The Conservative Party in History, *Political Quarterly*, July–September 1961, p. 222.

[2] Sir C. Petrie: *Life of Sir Austen Chamberlain*, vol. II, p. 139.

[3] Phrases very similar to those of Keynes were used by J. C. Davidson in a letter to the King's Private Secretary. *cf*. Nicolson, *op. cit.*, p. 333.

probably hardly free) access to political eminence. The list of newly elected M.P.s shows many engineers, contractors, ship-builders and shipowners, men from industries which had gained considerably by wartime activities. Yet in the whole group of new Conservative M.P.s those with a background of industry and commerce are in a minority; they formed 40 per cent of the total. In 1950, when after the débâcle of the immediate post-war election, Conservative fortunes were again on the mend and when 88 Conservative M.P.s entered the House of Commons for the first time, the percentage of entrepreneurs, businessmen and managers among the newly elected was almost exactly the same. In other respects there are differences between the groups of Conservative M.P.s who set their feet on the bottom rungs of the political ladder after two periods of comparatively great social change (as outlined in Table I) which are illuminating. If we look at their educational background we find that between one-third and one-half of the M.P.s who were newly elected after the First World War were men who were socially 'on the make'.[1] The new M.P.s of the post-1945 generation seem much more solidly linked to an upper middle-class background. Nearly two-thirds were Public School educated, compared with 35 per cent in 1918; the proportion of those recruited from the most exclusive Public Schools has actually doubled.

A few of the group of newly-elected Tory M.P.s in 1950 were men who had risen from comparatively obscure origins. Two could definitely be described as of a working-class background: Aubrey Jones, whose father was a miner and Henry Price who was the son of a builders' labourer. But both had managed to advance into the middle class before entering Parliament. Aubrey Jones was actually to rise further through politics; he became Minister of Supply in 1950. They are, however, exceptions to a general pattern.

In the post-war years the concept of the 'Opportunity State' has been widely used in Conservative thinking and propaganda. Even so the middle-aged and middle-class men and women who form the backbone of local Conservative organization and with whom

---

[1] Those who do not give their education or who declare that they were educated 'privately' can generally be assumed to have had 'inferior' schooling.

TABLE I

Background of newly-elected Conservative M.P.s, 1918 and 1950 (in percentages):

	1918	1950
(a) Education: School—		
Eton	10	23
Harrow	7	6
Winchester	3	1
Rugby	3	3
Other 'top 20' Public Schools	10	20
Other Public Schools	2	11
Grammar School	21	25
Elementary School only	4	2
Other	5	2
'Privately'	12	1
Abroad	4	4
Not known	19	2
(b) Occupation—		
Landowners	6	—
Army and Navy	12	3·5
Rentier	2	3·5
Entrepreneurs, Businessmen, Managers	40	41
Barristers	14	15
Solicitors	4·5	7
Physicians and Surgeons	3·5	2
Journalists, Authors	2·5	7
Other Professional Men	4·5	6
Civil Service	1	2
Farmers, Land Agents	1·5	5·5
Political Organizers	1·5	3·5
No occupation	—	2
Married Women	—	1
Not Known	7	1
TOTAL	154	88

the selection of Conservative candidates, and hence Conservative M.P.s rests have rarely failed to choose their future M.P.s from among their equals or their betters. The process by which those who already start high are again selected to a predominant degree for political office cannot be based on this. It must rather be sought in the social milieu which prevails in the House of Commons and in the Government and which favours men with a certain social background. In the comparison of Cabinet membership with the membership of the House of Commons, this process of selection emerged clearly. Bonar Law was aware of the difficulties which he faced in assuming the leadership of the Party. 'The fact that he had no experience of government did not trouble him when he took the leadership. What he was afraid of was his wanting of birth. He was confident that he could lead without experience but afraid that the Party might follow unwillingly because he had not blue blood in his veins.'[1]

Those who enter the House of Commons in any particular period were described earlier as a parliamentary generation. Largely irrespective of the age at which they become M.P.s their careers are determined by the part which they play inside the chamber in debates, on committees and finally in administration. The bloom of Conservative success in the Coupon Election of 1918 soon faded: the gathering of Labour strength in succeeding elections returned to the limbo many of those who had entered Parliament in 1918. Only ten of the newly elected Tories achieved office; all but three of them were Public School educated. In the more balanced parliamentary situation after the Second World War the average Conservative M.P. had a much greater chance of obtaining office. Of the 88 Conservative M.P.s newly elected in 1950, 31 did so by 1961. Some passed through office—and through the House of Commons—but the majority were still politically active and in Parliament ten years later. A tabulation of success and failure shows how the former is still closely related to social background as measured by the type of a man's education.

The Public School image was perhaps not impressive to all Conservative leaders at all levels. Those who ran the organization at the local and even at the national level are not generally drawn

---

[1] Petrie. *op. cit.*, vol. II, p. 159.

TABLE II

Political Success and Educational Background in the Group of
M.P.s first elected in 1950:

| | Political Status Achieved | | |
School	Backbencher	Parliamentary Secretary	Ministerial Status
Eton	11	2	6
Harrow	2	2	—
Other 'top 20' Public Schools	9	3	4
Other Public Schools	14	2	1
Grammar School	14	3	5
Other	7	2	1
TOTAL	57	14	17

from quite the same circles as the Party leadership. This was a
source of conflict at the beginning of the Conservative Organization and the lack of social background of early party officials appear
to have made their work difficult. J. E. Gorst, the first Secretary of
the National Union of Conservative Associations, suffered under
this disadvantage. *Blackwood's Magazine* suggested in the 1880's
that the London Agent of the Party, *i.e.* its principal officer, should
be a man of high social standing comparable to the Chief Whip so
that he could mix with the wealthy supporters of the Party.[1] Yet
such men were often unsuited or unwilling to undertake the many
humdrum tasks of party work. Salvidge encountered problems of
this kind in his Liverpool Party organization. Attacked about his
refusal to give young men a chance he denied that he was 'so keen
on demonstrating the democratic nature of Liverpool Conservatism that no one of the so-called better class, even if he served a
lifetime could hope to exercise authority under his leadership.' Yet
he 'would not have men, young or otherwise, monopolizing the
limelight merely because they had been to Public Schools. They

---

[1] Quoted by E. J. Feuchtwanger: 'J. E. Gorst and the Central Organization of
the Conservative Party', *Bulletin of the Institute of Historical Research*, 1959,
pp. 192-208 at p. 202, note 3.

must share the dust as well as the palm.' He 'had never any use for the old Tory prayer "God bless the Squire and his relations and keep us in our proper stations. . . ." '[1]

Whatever the position in local Conservative Parties, the selection of men and women for positions at the top of both the National Union and the Central Party Organization, whether elected by the Conference or appointed by the Leader, show comparatively little 'democratic' influence. Of the 15 Officers of the National Union who between 1950 and 1955 held office as Presidents, Chairmen, Vice-Chairmen and Chairmen of the Executive Committee, six were Conservative Ministers and one was a minister's widow. Among the Businessmen and the few married women who form the rest, a single Conservative Trade Unionist stands out. The 10 officers of the Central Party Organization during the same period were similarly composed of five politicians who held ministerial office, the wives of two others,[2] the brother-in-law of a third,[3] a City Businessman and a former Chief Organization Officer of the Conservative Central Office.

There are, of course, subtle gradations in the background of men who held different offices, such as we must expect in a party so hierarchically arranged as the Conservative Party. The office of President of the National Union—an office of purely honorific status—has generally been held by men of the highest social eminence. Before 1914 the Presidents were invariably members of the Peerage, sometimes Dukes or others of high rank. Since then this has changed; less than half of those who held office lately have been aristocrats but compared with the appointed Chairmen of the Party Organization and the elected Chairmen of the Executive Committee of the National Union they still present more completely the picture of the traditional Tory politician.

It is clear that the 'silent social revolution' of the past half century has largely by-passed the leadership of the Conservative Party. Its leading strata have remained firmly fixed in the upper levels of our stratified society. Admittedly wealth rather than birth has become significant and professional men are not prominent

---

[1] Salvidge, *op. cit.*, p. 301.

[2] Lady Maxwell Fyfe (Lady Kilmuir) and Mrs Henry Brooke.

[3] Mr C. J. Holland Martin, M.P., who married a sister of Lady Dorothy Macmillan.

TABLE III

Background of Officers of the Conservative Party, 1914–60:

	Presidents of National Union	Chairmen of Executive Committee of National Union	Chairmen of Party Organization
(a) Class—			
Aristocracy by descent	13	3	2
Middle Class	19	10	11
(b) Education—			
Eton and Harrow	20	3	6
Rugby and Winchester	3	2	2
Other 'top 20' Public Schools	1	1	1
Other Public Schools	3	3	2
Grammar Schools	3	2	2
Other and Not Known	2	2	—
(c) Occupation—			
Landowners	12	1	—
Rentiers	9	3	2
Commerce and Industry	8	6	7
Professions, Administration	2	3	3
Other, Married Women	1	—	1
Total	32	13	13

in the hierarchy of the Conservative Party Organization. As their educational career amply testifies, few are without a comfortable middle or upper class background. Lord Woolton is, of course, an example of the self-made man who went from the University into business and through business reached governmental office and stepped from there into Party politics. But on the whole the scholarship ladder has prepared men for a career in the Conservative Party only to a very limited extent. This is, of course, in striking contrast to the pattern of career lines in the party of the Left where a number of professional men had risen from the working class.

At the same time those changes in the character of the Conservative political leadership which we discussed, reflect changes in the economic structure of the upper and middle class section of the population. The entrepreneurial ladder, which was of such obvious significance in the case of the post-1918 generation of Conservative M.P.s, is less important today. The types of business career followed by Conservative politicians have also undergone a change.

In the inter-war years the connection between the party in the House of Commons and 'big' business was close and pronounced. The 181 M.P.s described as 'Company Directors' in 1938 held between them 775 directorships, some of them in very large and powerful concerns.[1] Connections of this kind persist, but the economic 'weight' of the average Conservative politician has probably diminished since the pre-war period. In 1958 only 79 M.P.s could be traced in the *Directory of Directors*, our principal source for tracing the holders of directorships in Public Companies and in a large number of private companies. The directorships held by them totalled 379, or just under five per head.[2] In 1961, when the House of Commons contained slightly more Conservative members, Andrew Roth counted a total of just over 490 directorships among M.P.s of all parties and noted an increase of 70 over 1959.[3] The coverage of the *Directory of Directors* is, of course, not complete. Haxey used other sources in addition to it and the total number of Conservative M.P.s with business connections, either past or present, is considerably higher.[4] On the other hand, the odd directorship, especially in small, inactive companies, may not be of great significance. What is significant is the character of the economic interests of Conservative M.P.s and the changes which these have undergone during the past thirty years. The economically powerful or the very rich are today less frequently represented in Parliament than at an earlier period. A number of owners of family firms can still be found in the House of Commons as well as some directors of large enterprises in manufacturing, transport and construction industries. They sit almost invariably on the Conservative benches. The general tendency, however, has

---

[1] S. Haxey: *Tory M.P.*, 1939, p. 37.
[2] Actually 4·8 directorships per director counted compared with 4·3 in 1938.
[3] cf. A. Roth: *The Business Background of Members of Parliament*, 1962, p. xv.
[4] *ibid.*, p. xiv.

been towards activities in the field of finance and in the service industries in general. The latter categories do not only claim *more* alignments than the manufacturing and processing industries but the number engaged in them has risen lately while the former has remained stationary. Investment Trusts, Insurance Companies, Property Development Companies, Advertising and Public Relations Firms and the Entertainment and Communications Industries claim an increasing share of M.P.s.[1]

Parallel to this change in the economic background, and possibly connected with it, there appears to have been a decline in the wealth of Conservative M.P.s. Politicians of the 1920's and 1930's had very frequently considerable fortunes. Of 43 Conservative M.P.s who died between 1931 and 1938 Haxey traced the estates of 33. Five of these left between £10,000 and £20,000; 14 between £20,000 and £100,000 and 14 more than £100,000.[2] Contemporary figures do not suggest similar riches among the post-war generation of M.P.s. Between 1951 and 1960 twelve Conservative members died. Three of these—who incidentally had entered Parliament well before the war—left estates worth more than £100,000; 2 left between £50,000 and £100,000; 3 left between £20,000 and £50,000 and 2 less than £10,000.

It is clearly not as easy today as it was a generation ago to combine service in the House of Commons with entrepreneurial activity outside it and those whose earning power or economic interests are greatest may sacrifice much.[3] Today Parliament sits for longer hours, more time is taken up by government business and the parties tend to be more evenly balanced. M.P.s are increasingly used as 'Welfare Workers' by their constituents and as 'instruments' by pressure groups of various kinds. All this makes greater demands on members' time and helps to 'professionalize' the political career. This development is already influencing the character of Conservative Party representation and it is bound to do so even more in the future.

The new types of business affiliations which we noticed among

---

[1] Roth: *op. cit.*, p. xvii.

[2] Haxey: *op. cit.*, p. 29.

[3] It is worth noting that lately a number of Conservative junior Ministers relinquished office and gave as their reason a desire to return to their business interests.

M.P.s facilitate this kind of parliamentary rôle. The provisions of services rather than goods or of speculative or financial enterprises are probably more easily combined with political activity at Westminster than activities in manufacturing industries. Some men may actually use the skills of persuasion which are a concomitant of parliamentary activity in their business pursuits. The much commented on connection between a comparatively small number of Conservative M.P.s and Public Relations and Advertising firms is only an extreme example of this tendency.[1] It is clear that the age of the patricians in politics is drawing to a close. Is that of the spokesmen about to begin?

Before we can approach this question we must look at the 'rebels' in the Conservative camp and describe the ways in which opposition did express itself in the past.

DISSENT AND DISSENSION

During the 1950's the Labour Party was deeply—and some thought irrevocably—split into two warring factions. At the same time the serried ranks of the Party opposite presented at least overtly a picture of unity and cohesion. The Conservative Party, although shaken by a *crise de conscience* caused by the Suez adventure, and attacked by a fringe within its ranks for the Suez settlement, appeared a solid block. And when, in Home affairs, the Conservative Government accepted many of the measures of social and economic reform carried out under Mr Attlee its 'acquiescence' met with little disapproval. Between 1945 and 1951 the Conservative opposition to Labour's policies had been loud and vigorous. After 1951 the critics of the Welfare State spoke only with a muffled voice.

This apparent unity within the Conservative Party today stands in marked contrast to the position before the war. During the inter-war years opposition against the leadership was not only vocal, it also expressed itself in open acts of defiance in Parliament.

---

[1] In 1961 20 Conservative M.P.s were connected with advertising and Public Relations firms compared with 4 Labour M.P.s and 1 Liberal. *cf.* Roth: *op. cit.*, pp. 153–5. On the growing political significance of this whole field see Morris Davis: 'British Public Relations; A Political Case Study', *Journal of Politics*, February 1962.

Clearly, the size of the Conservative majority during the 1920's and 1930's made it certain that limited acts of opposition in the division lobbies would not endanger the position of the Government. But given Conservative principles of leadership and policy-making, such flagrant acts of indiscipline have a greater significance than opposition inside the Parliamentary Labour Party whose standing orders provide, after all, for a right to opposition on grounds of conscience.

It is equally significant that the opposition from the Conservative back-benchers to acts of its own government were almost invariably restricted to measures in the field of imperial and foreign policy or defence. In the economic and social field Conservative Government policy met with little criticism from its supporters in the House of Commons. Occasionally a particular interest group would manage to muster some opposition and would sometimes even achieve some success. In 1921 eleven Conservative M.P.s opposed the Corn Production Acts (Repeal) Bill—together with some Liberal and most Labour M.P.s. The landowning interest was still marked in the ranks of the Conservative Party and occasionally it could score a success against the Government. Such opposition was largely organized by the Country Landowners' Association which had a sizeable following among M.P.s and Peers. Thus Sir George Courthope, M.P., the Chairman of the Executive Committee of the Association, told the 1926 Annual General Meeting that 'in both Houses of Parliament we have been able to pull our weight and exercise a good deal of pressure when proposed legislation has been inimical to rural landowning interests. Several Bills have been very successfully amended in both Houses . . . (recently) we were putting forward an amendment to the Law of Property Amendment Bill . . . the Government representatives . . . would not accept it but decided to oppose it. But such was the power of the Central Landowners' Association that we carried the amendment against the Government. I do not say, from the point of a Conservative member [which I am] that this is always a desirable thing to do,' he went on to say, 'but it is useful to feel that when we have a good case we can make an impression upon the House of Commons.'[1]

---

[1] Country Landowners' Association, *Quarterly Journal*, August 1926, p. 132.

Commerce and Industry, too, would find obvious allies in the ranks of the Conservative Party in Parliament. In 1937 Neville Chamberlain, eager to forestall profiteering on the growing volume of defence contracts and to raise an additional revenue of about £25 million, proposed a graduated tax on profits, styled National Defence Contribution. The Chancellor of the Exchequer was aware that such a measure would lead to strong opposition among his supporters. 'I reckon it to be the bravest thing I have ever done since I have been in public life, for I have risked the Premiership', he wrote in his diary.[1]

The opposition proved to be even stronger than he expected. Economists, City men and a host of economic pressure groups expressed their hostility. The latter declared that the Bill required 'drastic amendments to make it acceptable to the tax-paying community'.[2] The Finance Committee of the Conservative Party begged Chamberlain to withdraw the proposals on the day on which he accepted the Premiership. It was indeed dropped and replaced by a flat-rate tax on profits.

These, however, are rather isolated instances. On the whole the economic policy of the Conservative Governments in the inter-war years was in accord with the economic interests which the party represented in a more narrow sense.

The issues which turned dissent into dissension were those which touched vitally on Britain's position in the Empire and in the world. The strong feeling which they aroused made people forget other more immediate loyalties. Lord Lloyd, one of the most fervent protagonists of the imperial ideal, thought that 'when the future of the Empire is at stake, does Mr Baldwin really expect that we should subordinate the fate of an Empire to considerations of Party harmony?'[3]

Three issues above all caused acts of rebellion in the ranks of the Conservative Party in Parliament: the Irish settlement, the proposal eventually to grant Dominion status to India and the policy of appeasement and inadequate re-armament. In some respects

[1] Feiling, op. cit., p. 292.
[2] From Memorandum submitted by the Association of British Chambers of Commerce, the Federation of British Industries and other organizations in the economic and commercial field.
[3] C. F. Adams: Life of Lord Lloyd, 1948, p. 244.

they culminated in the vote of censure on the policy of Neville Chamberlain in May 1940 when 35 supporters of the Government voted with the opposition.[1]

The issues involved were clearly far-reaching enough for the opposition not to be restricted to the House of Commons and we find that support for the alternative policies was widespread in the lower levels of the Conservative leadership. This did not only apply to the strength of feeling which supported the diehard opposition to the establishment of an Irish Republic. The danger that this might sway the National Union of Conservative and Unionist Associations into a hostile vote was, as we saw, narrowly averted, but Austen Chamberlain did not minimize the threat which would spring from it. 'I am fighting for my political life,' he wrote in his diary. 'What Liverpool has in store I don't know. The diehards are organizing fiercely and strenuously. If we are beaten then it won't be the end but it will be very unpleasant.' Motions in favour of a protective tariff and a system of Empire-preference were repeatedly passed by Conference and Council of the National Union, which acted in this field as a pressure group trying to influence a rather reluctant and cautious Party leadership.

The fight against the India policy of the National Government was also carried into the lower ranks of the Conservative Party—and with considerable success.

At the Annual Conference in October 1933 in Birmingham, a motion opposed to the granting of full self-government received

---

[1] Below are the dates and issues on which significant numbers of Conservative M.P.s voted against the Government together with the number who did so. (a) 28.5.1919: Motion critical of the 'Sale of Honours' introduced by H. Page Croft (52); (b) 31.10.1921: Censure motion, moved by Col. Gretton, deploring the Government's entering into negotiations with delegates from Southern Ireland (40); (c) 24.9.1931: Motion re Tariff Reform, moved by H. Page Croft (46); (d) 22.2.1933: Motion in favour of adopting the report of the 'Simon' Commission—implicitly repudiating the idea of responsible Central government in India—moved by Croft (42); (e) 12.12.1934: Government motion in favour of adopting the report of the Parliamentary Joint Committee on India (80 Conservative M.P.s either voted against it or were paired); (f) 11.2.1935: Second Reading of India Bill (82); (g) 5.6.1935: Third Reading of India Bill (77); (h) 7.10.1938: Motion approving 'Munich' settlement (22 abstentions); (i) 8.5.1940: Motion of Lack of Confidence in the Government's conduct of the War (35).

344 votes against 737 in favour of the official party line. The Imperialists fought and fought again. Next year the critics gained even more support and their motion was lost by a small majority (520 to 543). The struggle was carried further at a meeting of the Central Council of the National Union in December 1934. Both sides brought their biggest guns to bear on the assembly. L. S. Amery moved that the Council should approve the general principles laid down in the report of the Parliamentary Joint Select Committee, and the Marquess of Salisbury proposed an amendment urging that Parliament should not take the irrevocable step of establishing responsible Central Government in India.[1] 'The meeting,' R. T. McKenzie has written, 'became a grand council of the party.'[2] The Council, which had a much fuller attendance than normally, debated the issue with great seriousness and in comparative calm. In the end the motion was carried by 1,102 votes to 390.

The attack on the Conservative Government's policy of appeasement and on Britain's military unpreparedness for war, which a small but vocal section of the Conservative Parliamentarians launched after the Indian issue had been settled, did not receive similar support from staunch Conservatives in the provinces. For our understanding of the nature of opposition in the Conservative party this is of considerable significance.

The life and activities of Sir Henry Page Croft throw much light on the working of this opposition.[3] Croft was one of those rare phenomena in British political life: a rebel of the Right and one who remained throughout a generation of political activity a pugnacious but consistent defender of the views which he held

---

[1] Among those who took part in the debate were Lord Eustace Percy, Lord Derby, the Marquess of Linlithgow—a former Viceroy, Viscount Bridgeman and Austen Chamberlain (for the Government) and Viscount Fitzalan, Churchill, Sir A. Knox (Chairman of the India Defence Committee), The Marquess of Hartington and Sir Henry Page Croft. cf. R. T. McKenzie: *British Political Parties*, p. 204; Lord Croft: *My Life of Strife*, 1948, pp. 227-39.

[2] McKenzie, *op. cit.*, p. 204.

[3] See his revealing autobiography: *My Life of Strife* completed just before his death in 1947. Unlike much contemporary memoir literature the book is autobiographical almost to excess. Thus even if the subject is not quite the hero to the author the actual importance and effectiveness of Croft's political activities were probably not as great as the reader is led to believe.

when entering politics.[1] A member of a family of squires and soldiers, educated at Eton and Cambridge, a maltster by occupation, a soldier during the First World War (he rose to the rank of Brigadier-General), his political conduct was anything but orthodox. He entered Parliament as a lieutenant of Joseph Chamberlain and he employed throughout his career many of the methods which the latter had used. Intelligent, although anything but an intellectual, he pursued his aims with considerable drive and stratagem both behind the scenes and on the public platform. He was a believer in the British 'race', something of a xenophobe and somewhat lukewarm in his defence of Parliamentary democracy. 'For forty-odd years,' he wrote, 'I waged war for tariff reform, Empire Unity and National Defence with hardly any respite; the only relaxation I have had in this incessant struggle was when twice I waged war against Germany, once in the field and the second time as a member of the Army Council.' His desire to *fight*, both for something and against somebody was certainly strong at all times.

At the end of the Great War, Croft was the founder, the leader and, after the election of 1918, one of the two survivors of the National Party.[2] Its aim was to end 'the old party system which for years had been nothing better than an organized mockery of the true spirit of the nation'. Its manifesto spoke of the need for military strength, unity of the Empire, concord between classes, fair return to Capital and labour and 'such opportunities in life, work and play as will ensure a contented patriotic race',[3] all tunes which have since received a far grimmer orchestration at the hands of more unscrupulous politicians elsewhere. The National Party put up 23 candidates in the Coupon Election of 1918 but it returned only two M.P.s and it soon faded away. It was resurrected— under the name of 'National Constitutional Association'—to fight the Government over Ireland. The Association 'used the old machinery of the National Party to stage most of the Die-Hard

[1] In the consistency of his beliefs and the ardour of his struggles we ought to rank Croft higher than the author of an autobiography of a similar title: David Kirkwood: *My Life of Revolt.*
[2] Croft asserts that he had originally the support of twenty M.P.s but that as the result of pressure from their constituency organizations two-thirds withdrew from the party.
[3] Croft: *My Life of Strife,* pp. 130–2.

meetings . . .' At one of these Croft declared that 'he hoped there would be no schism in the patriotic ranks of the country. People talked as if such persons as Colonel Gretton and himself were apart from the Conservative Party,' on the contrary, he added, 'we are the Conservative Party.'[1]

Whilst they failed to influence the course of events over Ireland, Croft and his friends certainly sought to make their claim come true on later occasions. The National Constitutional Association dissolved itself in October 1922 in order to foster unity among Conservatives. On the eve of the Carlton Club meeting at which the future of the coalition was to be decided, Croft addressed an appeal to the Party. The rank and file, he asserted, were determined that the coalition should end. But he thought that whatever the views of the forthcoming meeting proved to be, an assembly from which Peers were excluded could not lay down the future course of the Party. And, in any case, nothing should be done to forestall the decision of the Conservative Party Conference in November.

It is difficult to assess the importance of the organized pressure and propaganda from the right wing in bringing about the dissolution of the coalition. The same applies to the agitation for tariff reform. In 1924 Amery, with the assistance of George Lloyd (later Lord Lloyd) and Neville Chamberlain, founded the Empire Industries Association to educate the country on the issues of protection and Imperial preference. Originally non-party, it later became under the Chairmanship of Croft a growing pressure group of and among Conservative politicians. The number of Conservative M.P.s who belonged to it rose from 100 in 1927 to 280 on the eve of the General Election of 1929.[2]

This body sought to exert pressure on the Party leadership through memorials and deputations; it also tried to influence Conservative candidates for Parliament and to adopt a tariff policy for their platform. The Empire Industries Association was very active in 1931 when, as the result of the formation of the National Government, the hopes for a vigorous tariff policy seemed to fade.

---

[1] ibid., p. 160.
[2] Croft: My Life of Strife, p. 181. Amery: My Political Life, vol. II, p. 291. Amery's activities among business men had assured the Association of an income of nearly £20,000 for the first few years.

Amery, Croft, Lloyd and Patrick Hannon were instructed to wait on Baldwin and to urge an immediate dissolution. In the coming General Election it tried to ensure that in constituencies, where Conservative candidates were asked to withdraw in favour of Liberals, the local party organizations would extract from them a pledge to support a protective tariff and Empire preference.[1] By 1932 their efforts had borne fruit; for Croft 'the long long trail had ended'.[2]

At the same time the Government's India policy began to agitate the right wing. Before the publication of the report of the Round Table Conference proposals Croft wrote to forty of his friends in the House of Commons and urged them to enter the ballot at the next private members day 'to call attention to the Indian Reforms and move a resolution'. On the following Wednesday, Croft himself was successful and carried 42 M.P.s with him into the Lobby. From the debate developed a parliamentary group which styled itself the India Defence Committee; 64 M.P.s attended its first meeting. In order to propagate their ideas within the Conservative Party in the Country the 'India Defence League' was formed with Lord Somers[3] as President and Lords Fitzalan, Howe,[4] Carson, The Duke of Westminster, Field-Marshal Sir Claud Jacob, The Marquess of Hartington, Rudyard Kipling and Croft as Vice-Presidents. Not unnaturally it received the support of large numbers of retired members of the British Army in India.

There was, of course, a British India *lobby* in favour of the *status quo* as there was a manufacturer's lobby in favour of a tariff.[5] Yet if we look at the men, who expressed the strongest opposition to the leadership on some fundamental issues of Conservative policy, we find that they were hardly motivated by particular sets of economic

---

[1] *ibid.*, pp. 195–6.

[2] *ibid.*, p. 212.

[3] A former Lord of Appeal in Ordinary.

[4] Better known as Viscount Curzon, a violent opponent of the Irish Settlement.

[5] Writing to Lord Irwin (the Viceroy, later Lord Halifax) Sir Clive Wigram, George V's Private Secretary, expressed the King's regret at the attitude 'which the Conservatives, egged on by the retired die-hards from India, are adopting' . (Nicolson, *op. cit.*, p. 507.)

or other interests. The parliamentary lobbies were really lobbies of the ideologically or the emotionally committed. Many would have subscribed to the tenet that 'in Empire we have not merely the key to glory but the call to duty and the means of service to mankind'.[1] Ireland, or even India were regarded as an integral part of Britain; to agree to self-government would immediately stamp Britons in the Empire as aliens on foreign territory. 'Once we lose confidence in our mission in the East,' Churchill had declared in 1929, 'then our presence in those countries will be stripped of every moral sanction'.[2] A loss of possession entailed a loss of self-esteem and so did any decline of national strength. And a strong but narrow nationalist feeling underlay much of the opposition from the right. Occasionally such feelings showed themselves unbridled in the House of Commons. This was the case when E. S. Montague defended the Cabinet decision to dismiss General Dyer after the Amritsar shootings in 1919. 'Our party,' Austen Chamberlain wrote in his diary, 'has always disliked and distrusted him. On this occasion all their English and racial feeling was stirred to passionate display. . . . A Jew, a foreigner, a rounding on an Englishman and throwing him to the wolves—that was the feeling' . . . and Chamberlain added that 'a Jew may be a loyal Englishman and passionately patriotic but he is intellectually apart from us and will never be purely and simply English.'[3]

What in the case of a Jewish Cabinet colleague was conceived mainly as a feeling of separateness turned towards the starving and illiterate masses of Asia and Africa into a feeling of superiority. By a strange process of intellectual blockage, those who were ardent nationalists themselves failed completely to understand the nature of Asian nationalism and the strong drive behind it. They did, of course, recognize the political independence of the self-governing territories of the Commonwealth, but they hoped for an ever-

---

[1] Curzon: 'The true Imperialism', *The Nineteenth Century*, January 1908, quoted in A. P. Thornton: *The Imperial Idea and its Enemies*, 1959, p. 72.

[2] Thornton, *op. cit.*, p. 213 quoted from *Hansard*.

[3] Petrie, *op. cit.*, p. 153. General Dyer, the British Commanding Officer in the Punjab, had ordered his troops to open fire on a large unarmed crowd of demonstrators who had assembled in defiance of an order. Some 400 people were killed and over 1,000 injured. A judicial Committee of Investigation condemned his act.

growing bond between the Mother Country and the dominions. The goal of Imperialism lay in an association of states, linked economically by a system of preferential tariffs, united by a common policy, directed eventually by a central authority and strengthened demographically by emigration from Britain to the Dominions.

TABLE IV

Opposition Groups among Conservative M.P.s:

	Irish Treaty	India Bill	'Munich' *	Chamberlain, 1940
(a) Education—				
Eton	6	7	8	10
Harrow	8	5	4	4
Winchester and Rugby	3	5	2	5
Other 'top 20' Public Schools	10	12	6	4
Other Public Schools	4	11	—	4
Grammar Schools	4	9	—	4
Other	1	16	2	3
Not known	6	12	—	1
(b) Occupation—				
Landowners, Rentiers	5	10	3	3
Armed Services	11	9	3	4
Civil Service, Diplomacy	1	3	4	4
Lawyers	10	14	1	3
Authors and Journalists	—	1	3	5
Other Professions	4	7	—	—
Commerce and Industry	8	22	3	7
Not known/None?	3	11	4	7
Other	—	—	1	2
TOTALS for (a) and (b)	42	7	22	35

* Those who deliberately abstained from the vote in support of the Munich Agreement.

Ideologically committed as they were, the Conservative 'Right' was yet not quite a cross-section of the Conservative Party in the House of Commons. A social analysis of the groups which at different times—and on a variety of issues—voted against the official Conservative policy makes this clear. (See Table IV).

Compared with the whole body of Conservative M.P.s, the rebels of the right correspond in some respects more to the traditional image of the Conservative M.P. than to his modern counterpart. There were among them even more men who had been educated in public schools than we find in the Parliamentary Party as a whole, and while there are comparatively few of aristocratic descent we have also a distinctly smaller proportion of businessmen than we find in the Party in general. Their place appears to be taken by military men and by those who followed careers in law, journalism or other professions. The numerical strength of former officers serves as evidence of a professional as well as of an intellectual connection between occupational background and political action. The regular officer has obviously an occupational interest in adequate defence and the retention of Britain's overseas position. At the same time his ethos makes him receptive to the ideals of Imperialism and to the appeals to national strength and independence.

In the Conservative as in the Labour Party we can trace some connection between intellectual pursuits and independence of thought and action. Indeed, a party which puts such great store in the trusting of the leader and the discipline of the ranks requires possibly greater conviction for the open expression of rebellious thoughts. Tariff Reform and the desire to strengthen the imperial bond were first conceived and were later assiduously propagated largely by ideologues and intellectuals. A number of these found their way into Parliament and, when occasion arose, some flocked into the divisions lobbies opposite to those used by the majority of their colleagues.[1] Professors Oman and Marriott voted against the Irish Treaty; former members of the Foreign Service opposed

[1] On the whole the Opposition has a higher proportion of men who were University-educated than the Party as a whole. More than two-thirds of those who voted against Chamberlain in 1940 were educated at either Oxford or Cambridge; on the whole of the Conservative benches only 50 per cent were University Graduates.

Chamberlain in 1940. The fact that posterity has generally condemned the one act and approved of the other has no relevance to
the suggested connection between intellectual activity and right
wing opposition.

In any case we cannot look at individual acts of opposition in
isolation. On the right, as on the left, there is an overlap between
various groups of rebels although the longer period of time
covered makes this less apparent in the case of the divisions analysed. Seven of those who opposed the conclusion of a treaty with
Ireland in 1921 sought to deny responsible government to India in
1935 and of those who expressed their opposition to Munich by
withholding their vote, half voted with the Labour Party in con-
demning Chamberlain's policy in May 1940. If more divisions had
been analysed a greater consistency in acts of opposition would
have been observed. Apart from the actual voting, those who
defied the whips and embarrassed the Party leadership often
worked in small informal but effective groups, which met at regular
intervals and took counsel on tactics and policies. We noted how
Croft was the erratic centre for all sorts of eddies on the right.
Amery marshalled those in favour of far-reaching tariff reforms
and Churchill acted as a magnet for those who opposed Indian
self-government root and branch. Both were centripetal forces for
the enemies of appeasement. A group of dissident Conservatives
opposed to the Government's policy on defence and foreign affairs
centred after Munich around Amery—a dozen or so met regularly
until after the beginning of the war.[1] 'Churchill, though in general
agreement with our point of view, did not, so far as my recollection
goes, normally join in our discussion,' Amery has written. He
'formed the centre of a parallel and to some extent overlapping
group'. [2]

---

[1] Amery: *My Political Life*, 3 vols, 1953–1955, vol. III, p. 298. According to
him, those who took part were, Duff Cooper, Cranborne (Salisbury), Wolmer
(Selborne), Macmillan, Richard Law, Ronald Cartland, J. P. L. Thomas, Sidney
Herbert, Robert Bower, Hubert Duggan, Derrick Gunston and P. E. Evans.

[2] *ibid.*, p. 298.

PATRICIANS INTO PRESSURE GROUP?

In discussing the evolution of Labour Leadership the emergence of a class of professional politicians has been stressed. This is clearly linked with the general character of the Labour Party as a movement of rebellion thrusting upwards from below. Its representatives are sent to Westminster to agitate for radical changes in society. Ideally speaking, they must regard parliamentary politics and the business of legislation as an activity of the highest importance which demanded a man's complete and undivided attention. Historically and functionally it is difficult to divorce the part which Labour parliamentarians have played on the political scene from the attempts of the working class at social emancipation. Indeed, for many Labour M.P.s full-time politics actually provided an emancipation of this kind.

The overall economic interests of the Conservative Party, its predilection for the social *status quo* have been stressed earlier. Acquiescence in things as they are was underpinned by a scepticism about man's perfectibility and by a belief in fundamental, immutable inequalities between men. Politics was in the nature of a palliative. 'Everyone who thinks poetry, money-making, love and sport more important than politics . . . these are the Conservatives.'[1] While this statement refers to the Conservative voter, rather than to the man who chose politics as a career, we still find that the link between the latter and his craft, even if compelling, was often non-specific. The aspiring and ambitious Conservative M.P. was in the past generally interested in government as such and not in specific reforms or a particular office. The Conservative Minister has, as a rule, passed through a far wider range of offices than his counterpart in Labour governments. The latter was much more frequently an administrator on a comparatively narrow front.

Such an attitude to politics and to office is, of course, more attuned to older forms of government which gave more scope to the skilled dilettante and the man gifted and experienced as a parliamentarian rather than as an administrator. It also presupposes that close link between financial independence, early

---

[1] R. J. White in the Introduction to his edition of Conservative writings ('The Conservative Tradition', London, 1950, p. 1). For a more sophisticated statement see Quintin Hogg: *The Case for Conservatism*, London, 1947.

entrance into Parliament and successful leadership, to which attention has been drawn. A tradition which had grown out of an undemocratic political system, and which was rooted in an anti-quated social structure, assumed for some almost the character of a dogma. Lord Hugh Cecil in one of the few attempts at stating a philosophy of Conservatism, wrote in 1923: 'only by having a class of men born to be politicians can you ensure the very early training which has often produced that notable skill in parliamentary methods so highly valued in both Houses [of Parliament] for many generations.'[1]

The patrician-politician has a long ancestry, whether in the shape of warring factions of Republican Rome, the oligarchy of Renaissance City States or as the relatively disinterested Victorian Gentleman. And in the Conservative Party he has had his most vigorous existence, exhibiting the best and the worst features of the species. His decline, already touched upon, does bear further investigation. Looking in somewhat greater detail at the strata which have taken its place, we might profitably discuss another and more contemporary hypothesis about the nature of the Conservative Party and its leadership: namely that the party is tending to assume the character of a combination of pressure groups, or, put on a more intellectual plane, that 'the Tory Party is a coalition of interests in continual debate'.[2]

Whether true or not, this represents a new departure in the self-assessment of the Conservative Party and the image which a section seeks to project. The leadership of Mr Churchill, a man of great dynamism and charismatic qualities, did not change the character of the upper echelons of the Conservative hierarchy. In distributing office in his wartime administration, he did, indeed, reward some of the men who fought with him in the years during which he was in opposition to the Conservative Party leadership. He thus gave office to some *new* men but, with admittedly important exceptions, his appointees belonged to

---

[1] Lord H. Cecil: *Conservatism*, 1923, p. 232.

[2] W. J. Biffen: 'Party Conference and Party Policy', *Political Quarterly*, July–September 1961, p. 259. Biffen's two corollaries are: (1) The Party leadership is not immune from the strongest criticism within the Party. (2) The Tory approach to politics is such that compromise is considered, if not virtuous, at least good form.

the traditional types of Conservative politicians. Likewise, his post-war government did not divert much from the accepted pattern. Among the 65-odd who received office at his hands in 1951, only 8 were not Public School educated; 47 had passed through the 'top 20' Public Schools. Ten years later the lump had been leavened a little more: of 69 Cabinet Ministers and Junior Ministers 17 had passed through Grammar Schools or similar establishments.

Other changes in the character of Conservative leadership, which took place within the last ten years, point in a similar direction. Of the men who served under Mr Churchill only a minority were in office in 1961 (15), and the new men were often of a somewhat different background from those who held minis-terial posts in 1951. The fact that fewer of the Ministers today are patricians, points, of course, to the continued decline of this class in politics. But it also reflects the fact that the function of leader-ship and the task of governmental office require other qualities than those customarily displayed by the traditional Tory poli-ticians. For the 'patricians' have not disappeared. On the con-trary, they continue to have some power and influence in the Conservative ranks and their comparative weakness in the Govern-ment is matched by the strength of their representation on back-bench committees.

Unlike the opposition of the Left in the Labour Party, the men who direct the Conservative Back-benchers (1922) Committee or the increasing number of specialist committees do not represent a 'counter-élite' to challenge the leadership of the Party. There is, as yet, no coherent and unified representation of, for example, the Conservative Right which is either willing or able to present an alternative policy on a wide range of issues. There may be the beginnings of such a grouping in the field of foreign and imperial policy but the expression of back-bench opposition in recent years does not permit an easy division into a left or a right wing in respect of home *and* foreign policy. In the field of social policy, some Conservative back-benchers are favourable to the claims of working-class or lower middle-class groups, while others have sought to lighten the burden of the propertied and the heavily taxed. Yet even here we cannot think in terms of Left or Right. 'To attempt to do so,' we are reminded, 'is to impose a pattern borrowed from the Labour Party, which is not appropriate to the Conservatives. The

TABLE V

Background of Conservative Leadership Groups, 1951–61:

	Ministers* 1951 (per cent)	1922 Committee† 1957–59 (per cent)	Ministers* 1961 (per cent)
Educational Background—			
Eton and Harrow	36	22	35
Other 'top 20' Public Schools	34	22	32
Other Public Boarding Schools	12	15	9
Other Schools	15	34	24
Women, not classified	3	7	—
Social Background—			
Acreocracy	32	15	19
'Noblesse de Robe'‡	3	—	3
Pluto-Aristocracy§	3	—	3
Military Men	6	26	—
Businessmen	12	26	25
Professional Men	26	15	28
Middle Class Rentiers	12	—	3
Middle Class Career Politicians	3	—	16
Women	3	7	—
Rising Working Class	—	4	—
Other	—	7	—
Numbers involved	34	27	36

* Cabinet Ministers and others of ministerial status.
† The officers and the 12 Committee members (18 generally).
‡ Descendants of ennobled politicians, lawyers, etc.
§ Descendants of ennobled industrialists, etc.

picture there is rather one of a succession of specific, unrelated pressures by different Members on behalf of a number of distinct groups.'[1]

[1] cf. S. E. Finer, H. B. Berrington and D. J. Bartholomew: *Backbench Opinion in the House of Commons, 1955–59*, London, 1961, ch. 3 (Quotation at p. 102.) This is the only attempt at a systematic and quantitative analysis of factional views in the two major parties today.

Sentiments and views on this left–right continuum arise mostly on an informal *ad hoc* basis. The Early Day motions, in which they usually find expression, do not commit their signatories to any action and they may be as much an expression of opinion as any action taken in response to pressure from constituencies.[1] On a few issues only has opposition to a governmental measure been carried into the division lobby.

The formal organizations of back-benchers perform probably much more effectively the function of pressure groups, combined with that of a debating-chamber in miniature. While officially we know nothing of their deliberations, the carefully prepared leaks and inspired guesses, which emerge from time to time in print make it clear that they play a part in policy formation—if only in, the application of brakes to government proposals. Their rôle, *vis-à-vis* the Government, is further stressed by the two-way movement which takes place between leading positions on back-bench committees and posts on the Government front bench. M.P.s with special knowledge or experience frequently become officers of the specialist committees and they may then move to a government job in their sphere. Five of ten Committee Chairmen who held office in 1951 moved into government jobs in the succeeding years. Thus Mr Dodds-Parker, a former officer in the Sudan Political Service, held the Chairmanship of the Imperial (now Commonwealth) Affairs Committee. He subsequently became Under-Secretary at the Foreign Office and Parliamentary Secretary at the Commonwealth Relations Office; Mr George Ward, a former regular R.A.F. Officer, moved via the Civil Aviation Committee to junior office at the Air Ministry and eventually to the Secretaryship of State for Air. Others make the journey in the reverse direction. Mr Deedes became Chairman of the Home Affairs Committee after he had resigned from the Under-Secretaryship of the Home Office and Mr Enoch Powell was elected to

---

[1] Finer and his colleagues who base their study predominantly on these motions are fully aware of the informal nature of these expressions of concern and opposition. Their work would have gained immensely if they had tried to investigate the motives as well as the background of the signatories. 'M.P.s are notoriously susceptible to the infectious disease of writing their names in support of motions', the *Letter to Licensees* of the National Trade Defence Association wrote in 1949 (*cf.* A. Potter: *Organized Groups*, 1961, p. 290).

the Chairmanship of the very powerful Finance Committee barely a year after his resignation from the Government following a disagreement over fiscal and economic policy.

If the achievement of office is regarded as the measuring-rod for the success of a particular internal pressure group, no section of Conservative back-benchers has done as well as the small congeries of young vigorous Tory intellectuals who were first elected in 1950 and who called themselves the 'One Nation' group. Limited in numbers, connected largely by their past work in the Conservative Political Centre, it presented something of an ideological ginger group. Its original publication—*One Nation*—did much to secure acceptance for the principles of the Welfare State in Conservative ranks; since then it has moved more in the direction of a rather extreme economic liberalism. As a group its membership was limited in numbers and replacements had to secure unanimous approval. As many of the founders joined the Government, there was fairly rapid and frequent promotion. The Founding Fathers include C. J. M. Alport, Enoch Powell, Iain Macleod and Ted Heath, all of whom achieved full ministerial or even Cabinet status. By 1960 we find that of the 22 who formed its total membership over the years 13 had obtained office, including some who had subsequently resigned and rejoined the group.[1] In its origin and rôle, the One Nation group has much in common with 'The Group', an informal association of young Conservative M.P.s formed after the First War. The members of 'The Group' were also interested in social questions and their careers were even more successful. Of the seven founding members six became Cabinet Ministers.[2]

The essentials of pressure group politics inside Parliament, however, are of a different kind. They presuppose a direct connection between organized groups outside the parliamentary parties and the

---

[1] *cf.* Julian E. Critchley, M.P., 'The Intellectuals', in *Political Quarterly*, Special Issue on the Conservative Party, July–September 1961. Compared with the One Nation group the M.P. members of the Bow Group have been singularly unsuccessful politicians.

[2] *i.e.* E. F. Wood (Lord Halifax), Viscount Wolmer (Earl Selborne), W. E. Guinness (Lord Moyne), Sir Samuel Hoare (Lord Templewood), P. Lloyd-Graeme—later P. Cunliffe-Lister (Lord Swinton) and Mr Ormsby-Gore (Lord Harlech). Unlike the 'One Nation' group this was a set of *gilded youths*.

political activities of individual politicians in either of the two
Houses. There is nothing new in such a nexus. Economic and
ideological interests have for a very long time used members of
Parliament to further their interests. It is only the weight of such
pressures and the force behind them which have increased of late.
It is equally obvious that the Conservative Party, whose leader
cadres are drawn to such a significant extent from important
groups in the economic life, should provide a suitable field for such
pressuring. For where definite interests are unilaterally aligned
with the fortunes and performance of one party, we can observe
what Professor Finer has called the 'Esau phenomenon', namely
the tendency for the aims of specific pressure groups to be
absorbed into the general programme of the party. 'A lobby in
either Party is stronger than a lobby outside a Party. The Party is
often speaking for "its" lobby. The voice is Jacob's but the hands
are the hands of Esau.'[1]

This does not preclude the existence of more limited pressure
groups within a party via men who have strong ties with particular
interests. We noticed already that compared with the inter-war
years the extent and weight of specific economic interests of Conservative M.P.s has declined. But there remained in the post-
war Parliaments men who combined membership of the House
of Commons with a leading function in representative organizations
outside. We thus find or found among Conservative M.P.s the
President of the British Legion, a Vice-President of the National
Union of Manufacturers, the Chairman of the Country Landowners' Association and the Secretary of both the Yarn Spinners'
Association and the Pharmaceutical Society.[2]

Such men may act as spokesmen and on suitable occasions their
status outside the House will lend weight to their activities inside
it. Or they may form a lobby in favour of a particular policy. The
campaign to introduce commercial television was started and
actively supported by a small group of Conservative back-benchers
nearly all of whom had connections with one or the other economic group who stood to gain from such a policy—Advertising and

---

[1] S. E. Finer: 'The Political Process in Britain' in H. W. Ehrmann (ed.) *The
Political Process in Four Continents*, Pittsburgh 1958, pp. 117–48 at p. 135.
[2] *cf*. A. Potter, *op. cit.*, ch. XV.

Public Relations Agencies and Consultants, Manufacturers of Equipment, Sales Management, etc.[1] Yet dislike of the B.B.C. and opposition to Monopolies all played their part. 'The whole controversy became "a soufflé of high principles and politics" and one may add, of direct economic interest.'[2] Inside the Conservative Party opposition to commercial television came predominantly from a group of older politicians, mostly in the Lords, under the implicit leadership of Lord Halifax.[3] As many of the older members of the Government were originally not very strong in their support of Sponsored Television we can speak here perhaps of a conflict between the 'patricians' and a pressure group.

As yet the singularly committed spokesmen in the Conservative Party are in a minority, but pressure and counter-pressure on M.P.s are likely to continue and to increase. They will find expression in Party Committees and back-bench bodies in general rather than on the floor of the House. The really significant debates do today take place 'upstairs'. Whether conflicting views can be resolved successfully does not just depend on the general acceptance of the belief, cherished by Conservatives, that compromise, if not virtuous, is at least good form. It rather centres around the question: 'Have we achieved a consensus of opinion which would enable one Party to contain most conflicting interests or is our society still an expression of fundamental conflict and tension?'

An astute American observer of British politics has recently concluded that such a consensus has been achieved.[4] The decline in fundamental intra-party conflict and the recent tendency for the two parties to move towards the centre from more extreme positions on the left and on the right would point in that direction. But this consideration neglects the fact that the apparent consensus reflects the activities of the parties and of their propaganda as much as it is responsible for it. If the Conservative Party is indeed

---

[1] cf. H. H. Wilson: *Pressure Groups*, London, 1961, pp. 81–84 and *passim*.

[2] *ibid*., p. 81. (The phrase in quotation marks comes from *The Economist*.)

[3] Only comparatively few Conservative Peers voted in favour of Lord Halifax's critical motion in November 1953, but about 100 were thought to have deliberately abstained. The Government majority was 70 in a vote of 244. Wilson, *op. cit.*, p. 193.

[4] cf. S. Beer, 'Democratic One-party Government in Britain', *Political Quarterly*, April–June 1961, pp. 114–23.

'a coalition of interests in continual debate', the range of this debate will be determined by the intellectual outlook, interests and built-in prejudices of the participants. Our analysis has shown the extremely limited background from which Conservative politicians are drawn and it cannot be said, as yet, that the pressure groups which express themselves through them, widen the democratic discussion perceptibly. Before taking up this theme[1] we must look at the political élite within the setting of those institutions and groups which form the penumbra of politics.

---

[1] *cf.* Chapter XII

CHAPTER XI

Power Elite or Ruling Class?

'... Everybody here has private interests: some are directors of companies, some own property. ... Then there are those people who come to represent particular bodies, particular groups of a non-political character and there again we must recognize that as one of the conditions of our varied life. We are not supposed to be an assembly of gentlemen who have no interests of any kind and no association of any kind. That might happen in heaven but not, happily, here.'—SIR WINSTON CHURCHILL in the Committee of Privileges of the House of Commons, 1947.

'The British Empire is governed by Christian names.'—J. R. J. MACNAMARA, M.P., 1938.

THROUGHOUT the past one hundred years the political élite has remained rather firmly wedded to the upper strata of British Society. New men have entered it, but they have generally become assimilated into the groups from which the majority of their colleagues sprang. The leadership of the two parties between which governmental power has lately alternated do still represent two distinct profiles, but with the decline of ideological commitment in the Labour Party, the flames of social antagonism in the sphere of politics have tended to die down. At the same time the character of political leadership, and even more the nature and function of governmental office, has undergone a change. The faculties which helped men to pre-eminence are no longer solely those which are displayed in the debating chamber, the lobbies of the House and the corridors of politics. Skill in projecting oneself into the masses on the one hand, administrative experience on the other, help men to build up a reputation in politics. Positions of power outside the political sphere do sometimes enable men to shift to a similarly high position within the governmental hierarchy. And a reverse process is also at work.

319

Thus the contemporary élite cannot easily be seen in isolation and apart from the character and power of a wider upper class from which so many of its members are recruited. Given the rise of large-scale organization, and the agglomeration of power in the economic and the social field, the analysis of the membership of the Cabinet and of the House of Commons is artificial unless it is considered in connection with the structure and function of other élite groups.

Whether politicians of today have really lost much of their ancient prestige and whether the 'mere' parliamentarians do indeed belong to the middle ranks of power will be discussed below. One thing is certain. Side by side with a political élite of limited size, there has grown up a penumbra of quasi-political bodies with their own largely independent and powerful leadership. And right outside the public sphere growing power has become concentrated in fewer hands. Despite the vast increase in the sphere of governmental activity and the power of the executive, comparatively small groups of men hold strategic positions of control over a large tract of territory in industry and finance. Not only has the unit of management increased throughout the economic field, the enterprises themselves have grown in size through amalgamations and through measures of financial control. Such concentration is most significant when the bulk of a particular enterprise is in the hands of a few firms; that is where size and monopolistic position reinforce each other.[1]

In the cultural and social field also, large organizations and great enterprises are controlled by a constantly decreasing total of directors and governors. Such tendencies can be clearly observed in most spheres of the 'cultural' life. In publishing, concentration is most marked in the magazine field where two vast enterprises share today almost the whole market. In the theatre world, the ownership of a declining number of houses rests in few hands, and with ownership goes, ultimately, effective artistic control. Film production and distribution is likewise heavily concentrated. Outside the commercial sphere, grant-giving bodies, especially the Arts Council, have great strategic power. The B.B.C. is still the

---

[1] *cf.* P. Sargant Florence: *Ownership, Control and Success of Large Companies*, 1961, especially ch. II.

greatest of the mass-media enjoying a partial monopoly. Independent Television, with one foot in the commercial world and with the other in the world of culture and entertainment, occupies a similar position. This chapter will look at some of these other élite groups, their recruitment and their interconnection, and seek to relate this to the composition of the upper class and to the political élite proper.

THE POLITICAL ELITE AND THE ELITES

It is a *paradox* of power today that whilst it is democratically based, its actual exercise is highly concentrated. Far fewer people can be said to hold real power, than enjoy either a sizeable income, or wealth or even social prestige.

The British upper class—if defined arbitrarily as composed of people with a gross income of £5,000 or more—comprises less than 1 per cent of all households.[1] In the late 1940's the topmost 1 per cent measured in terms of wealth, owned property worth more than £10,000,[2] and the boys who are currently educated at one of the 'top 20' most exclusive Public boarding schools comprise about 0·5 per cent of their generation.[3] While these three groups are, of course, not completely identical they do overlap to a considerable extent. The membership of élite groups is largely recruited from men who belong in any case to the upper layers of society.

---

[1] In 1959 higher incomes were distributed as follows:

£3–4,999	: 156,000
£5–9,999	: 65,000
£10–19,999	: 14,000
£20,000+	: 3,000

These figures are related to a total of 20 million incomes, including those of women and adolescents. The number of households was 14·5m. in 1960. *cf.* Board of Inland Revenue: *Report for the year ended 31.3.1961*, Cmnd. 1598.

[2] This figure is based on A. M. Cartter: *The Redistribution of Income in Post-War Britain*, 1955. Cartter calculated that of persons aged twenty-five or over 1·1 per cent owned £10–25,000; 0·4 per cent £25–100,000 and 0·06 per cent over £100,000.

[3] The total number of pupils at these schools was 12,400 in 1960. On this basis the annual intake would be above 2,000. The total number of boys aged thirteen in that year was 504,000.

L

The significance of this identification will be discussed later, at the moment we are concerned with a more quantitative estimate of the wider élite.

One of the groups which flanks the political élite and which enjoys today wide and largely independent powers is the Civil Service. The British system of government has been defined as a 'Parliamentary Bureaucracy'[1] and the rôle of the minister *vis-à-vis* the administrator as that of the man 'who tells the Civil Service what the public will not stand'. Even if we cannot ascribe such an inactive rôle to the Government there can be little doubt that the men right at the top of the administrative hierarchy do exercise real power not only over the vast administrative machinery, which affects materially policy at the lower levels, but also over the general lines of national policy. The actual political leadership has recently been defined as 'an oracle managed by its priests'[2] (*i.e.* the permanent bureaucracy). By preparing policy decisions and tendering expert advice on them, top level Civil Servants exercise a strong and sometimes irresistible influence.[3]

This applies not only to the heads of the major departments and their immediate deputies but also to men of corresponding rank elsewhere. The Royal Commission on the Civil Service recognized this in its discussion on the grading of the Service. 'Specialized staff,' it said, 'will in practice shed many of their specialist labels and assume responsibility which places them definitely in the policy-making grades.'[4]

Apart from the Civil Service, the Government is also becoming increasingly dependent on its technical advisers in formulating policies. The men in question may be those at the head of the Armed Forces or leaders in the field of Commerce, Industry,

---

[1] K. C. Wheare: 'Machinery of Government,' Inaugural Lecture at Oxford, reprinted in *Public Administration*, Summer 1946, p. 76. The origin of the term, however, is older.

[2] E. Strauss: *Ruling Servants*, 1960, p. 83.

[3] The supreme example of the form of political leadership which requires the highest Executive merely to choose between alternative plans put forward by his advisers has been realized in the Eisenhower administration. See M. D. Irish: The Organization Man in the Presidency, *Journal of Politics* 1958. pp. 259–277.

[4] Report of the Royal Commission on the Civil Service (BPP. 1955–56, vol. XI), sec. 363.

Members of the General Council of the T.U.C. or those who are eminent in the world of learning. They serve as consultants to government departments and they sit on the large number of advisory committees set up by departments. They man the committees of the many semi-autonomous bodies founded by the governments during the last forty years. They congregate with ex-Civil Servants, ex-politicians, around the tables of the board rooms of the Public Corporations.

How large are the various élite groups which we are about to study? The total of the administrative class of the Home Civil Service and the equivalent class of the Foreign Civil Service in 1962 was 3,200. But it is meaningless to single out the administrative class whilst there are large numbers of men of similar ranks in the professional, scientific and technical groups. The Royal Commission adopted the term 'Higher Civil Service' and defined it as those 'whose salary maximum or whose fixed rate exceeds that of the Principal'. These groups contained in 1956 just under 3,000 men and women.[1] Many of these are nevertheless occupied with responsible routine matters. Those belonging to the policy-making élite are a much smaller body. Speaking from intimate experience of the Service in the pre-war years, H. E. Dale, a member of the Civil Service Commission, thought that 'a rough criterion of place in this élite is personal contact, sometimes infrequent, sometimes daily, almost hourly, with the Parliamentary Chiefs of the Department'. He thought that before the war only about 480 members of the Home Civil Service qualified for inclusion in this group and that only 80 of these belonged to the 'élite of an élite', *i.e.* the departmental cabinets of Ministers.[2] The inner enclave of the administration corresponds roughly to the group of the 'Highest Civil Service', defined by the Royal Commission as those above the rank of Under-Secretary or equivalent.[3] They numbered 169 in 1955.[4] The salaries of this group in 1961 were £5,000 or above.

---

[1] *loc. cit.*, sec. 357.

[2] H. E. Dale: *The Higher Civil Service*, 1943, p. 1.

[3] Report of the Royal Commission, §15. In 1961 there were '29 Permanent Secretaries and 59 Deputy Secretaries (including officers of equivalent rank who are heads of minor departments)'. (Information from Treasury, 14.6.1961.)

W. J. M. McKenzie: 'The Royal Commission on the Civil Service'. *Political Quarterly*, 1956. pp. 129–40 at p. 139.

Salaries payable in the Public Service are now to be fixed at the level of those paid outside Whitehall for posts demanding similar skills and entailing similar responsibility. However, if we attempted to use income criteria as measurements of élite group membership in commerce or industry our total would be extremely large and meaningless. It would include a great number of men from the upper managerial rank and file of industry who are essentially executants of decisions made elsewhere; their expertise may have an influence on company policy but they are not really policy-makers. It would include the owners of many small factories or even retail establishments whose income may well exceed £5,000 per annum.

Nor should mere directorships of companies qualify for inclusion in the business élite. The total number of those described as 'Company Directors' is today upwards of 30,000.[1] Many of these are the directors of small, often minute private companies. To qualify for inclusion in this sector of the élite, our industrialists, bankers or financiers must be sufficiently powerful or influential for their decision to affect the general economic development of the country. Directorship of a large industrial undertaking or of a financial organization of considerable size generally implies such power, and the holding of a number of such posts does so to a particularly large extent.[2] The organization of finance and the structure of industry in Britain are such as to justify the emphasis on the large company and the vast enterprises which exercise control over a number of subsidiaries. One-half of all economic activity (55 per cent in 1955) was due to the economic activity of Public and Private Companies but of this the lion's share belongs to the industrial giants. According to Sargant Florence 1,700 firms, each with a capital of over £200,000, forming just over 1 per cent of all registered companies, accounted nevertheless for 61 per cent of all company income, 1955–56. The share of the real giants

---

[1] This is the number of appropriate entries in the *Directory of Directors*. It does *not* include the owners, Managing Directors, etc., of the bulk of the Private Companies or of firms entirely in individual and family ownership and unincorporated.

[2] Comparatively great economic power is sometimes vested in the small enterprise if it occupies a strategic position in the industry and the industry, although small, holds a key position in the economy.

of industry is even greater in relation to the smallness of their numbers.[1] We can also observe a not inconsiderable degree of plurality of directorships, interlocking the boards of several companies. They are especially important as a link between the world of finance and the world of industry. Looking at members of the leading merchant banking houses and the boards of the 'Big Eight' commercial banks, we find that they held in addition 561 major directorships, some in other banks but the majority in the 150 leading British industrial enterprises operating at home and overseas.[2] The Boards of the leading banks and insurance companies, together with the directors of the principal industrial companies, clearly qualify for inclusion in the British business élite. Of the latter just under half have been recruited from the managerial ranks or from amongst the actual managing directors of the firm. The Boards of the largest fifty industrial companies operating at home and overseas had on the average 13 members. 'Two of these are bankers . . . two others are non-banking controllers with seats on other quite different industrial boards and insurance companies; one is a member of the family with large property rights in the firm but not himself a banker or non-banking controller; one is a scientist or engineer, one is an accountant; one is a solicitor or stockbroker or local trustee; only four are managers directing the operations of the firm and its subsidiaries.'[3]

The nationalized industries are giant undertakings by all standards yet their controlling bodies are comparatively small. Including all the area boards of the Electricity and Gas Industry, the full-time as well as the part-time members of the various boards add only a mere 345 to the industrial directorate.[4] Linked to the

---

[1] 109 Companies had a capital of more than £3m.; their income amounted approximately to 20 per cent of the total accruing to all trading concerns. Florence, op. cit., p. 13.

[2] M. Barrett-Brown: 'The Controllers', Universities and Left Review, No. 5, Autumn 1958. (The figure refers to 120 Merchant Bankers and 168 Directors of the commercial banks with an apparent overlap of 29—a total of 259.)

[3] ibid., p. 56.

[4] cf. Cmnd. 1250. This figure does not include the Court of Directors of Cable and Wireless, the Colonial Development Corporation, the Iron and Steel Holding and Realization Company or the minor boards, such as the Sugar, White Fish and Herring Industry.

latter group are the spokesmen of the major organizations representing entrepreneurs in commerce, industry and agriculture.
The 'elected' and nominated representatives of the major organized interest groups in the economic field are not always those who
as individuals hold powerful positions in commerce and industry.
Heads of comparatively small firms may obtain office or become
members of Executive Councils of employers' organizations. The
importance of these organizations does not, however, lie in the
power which they exercise throughout the economy. The central
bodies generally represent such a wide and varied membership to
make concerted action difficult, to say the least. The power of these
men lies in the fact that they tend to represent the interest of
owners and employers on a whole host of Government committees, councils and advisory bodies in general.[1] On these they
will tend to meet the representatives of organized labour. The
trade union movement is vastly more democratic than the employers organization, yet effective power rests often with a small
number of full-time officials: the General Secretaries, full-time
Presidents and with the members of the General Council of the
T.U.C.[2]

Finally we should consider the academic and scientific élite. In
this field it is even more difficult to define the limits. As a mini-
mum we are bound to include the Vice-Chancellors and Principals
of the British Universities and University Colleges, the heads of the
larger colleges of London, Oxford and Cambridge University, the
Registrars of the latter two Universities and the heads of
the principal scientific and learned Associations and Institutions.[3]

The total in this category includes admittedly only a fraction
of all those who have actually reached academic or scientific
eminence, but such eminence does not necessarily imply élite

---

[1] Employers representation was restricted to the F.B.I., the N.U.M., the
B.E.C., the Federation of British Chambers of Commerce and the N.U.F. For
a list of professional organizations and the method of selecting their officers see
note 15 to Table I, of this chapter.

[2] The process of consultation, whether formal or informal, while facilitating
the expression of pressure group interests may, at the same time, impose new
and conflicting loyalties on the men holding such positions.

[3] cf. note 12, Table I.

position. The opportunity to make important decisions and to influence the influential in other élite groups comes more readily to those who hold official positions, than to many who are merely distinguished.

The above categories,[1] and the totals which we derive from them, must inevitably be in the nature of approximation. They only attempt to put a certain numerical value to the vague term 'élite'. They also provide a first line of approach to the measurement of movement between different élite groups. In distinguishing between the gross and the net size of individual groups we see in the first place to what extent their members occupy more than one position in a particular élite group; the kind of pluralism which is most pronounced in the world of business.[2] In addition there is the overlapping of membership between élite groups. Such overlaps occur most frequently between the leadership of the private sector of the economy and the public sector, between the latter and the leaders of labour and finally between the membership of controlling and advisory bodies and all other circles of the élite. A number of men are members of two of the élite groups listed, while one admittedly small section holds positions in three and very occasionally in four groups. A figure of 300 for the pluralities of élite positions would be a conservative estimate. The membership of these bodies thus becomes a focus through which the composition and interlocking of élite groups can be studied.

THE BACKGROUNDS OF DECISION-MAKERS

In the study of the development of the British political élite it was necessary to investigate in detail the origins and careers of several hundreds of Cabinet Ministers and Junior Ministers and to compare and contrast this with the social composition of the House of Commons. Only a biographical approach along similar lines could elucidate comparable data for the membership of other élite groups. We lack complete data about many of the leaders in the economic and administrative fields and I have not attempted to parallel the

---

[1] See Table I, p. 328.

[2] The net figures are by necessity only approximations based on samples and estimates.

TABLE I

Membership of certain Élite Groups:

Élite Group	*Size* Gross	Net
1. Members of the Government	68 ⎫	
2. M.P.s	630 ⎬	730
3. Peers active in the House of Lords	100 ⎭	
4. Highest Civil Service	169	169
5. Judiciary	77	77
6. Military Leaders	319	319
7. Boards of Nationalized Industries	350	345
8. Industrial Directorate:		
(a) Top companies, Capital £1m and over	2,725	2,450
(b) Medium companies, Capital £200,000 —£1m.	6,750	6,100
9. Boards of major Banks and Insurance Companies	422	340
10. Governors of major autonomous and semi-autonomous agencies	161	150
11. Principal Government Advisory Committees	363	330
12. Leaders of Science and Learning	200	200
13. Leaders of major economic Pressure Groups	53	53
14. Trade Union Leadership	60	60
15. Spokesmen of the Professions	40	40
16. Heads of Churches	70	70
TOTAL	12,557	11,053

Notes on Sources, etc., *re*:
   1. All except Assistant Whips and Members of the Royal Household.
   3. See above, p. 196.
   4. See above, p. 323.
   5. Lords of Appeal in Ordinary, Judges of the Supreme Court and of the Scottish Court of Session.
   6. All above and including ranks of Major General, Rear Admirals and Air Vice-Marshals, Retired Field-Marshals, Admirals of the Fleet and Marshals of the R.A.F. included.
   7. Cmnd. 1250 (1960) Public Boards.
   8. *cf*. S. Florence, *op. cit.*

study of the political élite with a similar investigation of neighbouring élite groups. Instead, I have based my analysis mainly on
the available data on the leading strata of our society, and supplemented it with fresh material about certain semi-political élite
groups.

As we saw, Cabinet Ministers, lesser politicians and the mere
rank-and-file members of Parliament on the back-benches of the
House of Commons were recruited predominantly from the rentier,
and the business and professional sections of the population. Nearly

---

9. T. Lupton and C. Shirley Wilson: 'The City Men Who Decide', *Manchester
   School*, January 1959. (Figures give directors of the Big Five Banks, of
   the Bank of England and of 14 Merchant Bank Houses all with an author-
   ized capital of £2m. or more and the directors of 8 Insurance Companies
   with a capital of over £3 million.)
10. See Table IV below.
11. For list see note on p. 340. An indication of the overlap between com-
    mittees is given in P.E.P.: *Government and Industry*, 1952, p. 131.
12. Includes Vice-Chancellors and Principals of all Universities and Univer-
    sity Colleges, Heads of Oxford, Cambridge and principal London Col-
    leges, Heads of the Medical Colleges, the Principal Officers of the Royal
    Society, the British Academy and major Scientific Societies.
13. The officers and leading members of the Association of British Chambers
    of Commerce, the British Employers' Confederation, The Federation of
    British Industries and The National Union of Manufacturers, as well as
    the permanent heads of their organizations. In the case of the A.B.C.C.
    and the N.U.M. the numbers refer to Presidents, Deputy Presidents,
    Vice-Presidents, Hon. Secretaries and Hon. Treasurers. For the B.E.C.
    and the F.B.I. it seemed more appropriate to list the Chairmen of the
    principal committees in addition to Presidents and Deputy Presidents.
    The selection was not just based on formal considerations: it is from
    these groups that the greater number of the representatives of the organ-
    izations on Government committees, etc., were chosen.
14. General Council of T.U.C. and all General Secretaries of Trade Unions
    with membership of 25,000+ who are not also members of the General
    Council.
15. *i.e.* General Secretaries and Presidents or Chairmen of the principal
    organization which represent the major professional groups (Lawyers,
    Doctors, Teachers, Higher Civil Servants, Accountants, Engineers
    and Nurses).
16. Archbishops and Bishops of the Church of England, Roman Catholic
    Archbishops, the Heads of the Non-conformist Denominations, of the
    Church of Scotland, the Scottish Free Churches and of the Jewish
    Community.

half of them belonged to those aristocratic or upper class families who send their children customarily to the most exclusive public schools and from there to the universities. Only one in six of the Cabinet Ministers studied can be said to have risen socially within a generation.[1] Indeed, if we exclude the group of Labour Cabinet Ministers of whom such a large proportion has risen from the working class, the amount of significant upwards social mobility in the Cabinet membership would be very small indeed, and much of it would be found among nineteenth century politicians rather than in the present generation.

This absence of a wide field of recruitment must be seen against the background of a very imperfect social mobility, especially near the top of the social pyramid. At present almost half of the traditional middle class—members of the professions, businessmen, managers, Civil Servants and the like—are recruited from men who have grown up in middle class families. Nearly two-thirds of the men in the highest occupational groups, comprising less than 3 per cent of the population, are the sons of men who belonged to the same group[2]. Once middle class does not mean always middle class but the fall is slow and is usually spread over a number of generations. So is the rise. In the immediate post-war period, to which the above figures refer, less than one in four of the members of the traditional middle class were the sons of manual workers or those in the routine grades of non-manual workers.[3]

The one great driving force towards wider social mobility is, of course, education. During this century working-class boys and girls have been enabled to reach middle-class status, via the Grammar Schools and the universities, and the widening of the educational net will no doubt improve the prospects of such advance. The scholarship ladder has helped men to rise most where selection on the basis of intellectual ability has been the principal mode of entry for a comparatively long time. This applies to a great degree to the Civil Service where we find that the area of recruit-

---

[1] cf. Table I of Chapter VII supra.

[2] cf. D. V. Glass (ed.): Social Mobility in Great Britain, 1954, p. 183 and passim.

[3] The study of Professor Glass and his colleagues shows that there has not been any significant change in the extent of social mobility among the different age-groups whose backgrounds were studied.

ment has perceptibly widened in the course of the years. Before the First World War, only 6 per cent of the entrants to junior posts in the Home Service had received their schooling in Local Education Authority Grammar Schools. By the advent of the Second World War, the share of pupils from the public sector of the educational system amounted to nearly 20 per cent. Among those who entered in 1949–52, former public Grammar School pupils accounted for just over a quarter, and 42 out of 223 were the sons of manual workers. But the bulk of the entrants into the Administrative Class of the Home Civil Service have clearly always been from middle or upper-class families. Indeed, between 1909 and 1934, 20 per cent of all those who joined at the lowest level had been educated at the nine 'Clarendon Schools' and, after the war, 61 per cent of all those who entered by open competition were sons of men who followed administrative, professional or managerial occupations. Almost five times as many as the corresponding group of the population as a whole.[1]

Comparable figures for other professions do not exist and we do not know what influence the gradual widening of educational opportunity has had on their recruitment. It probably did not have a very marked influence on industry. Throughout the process of industrialization in Britain, entrepreneurs and managers have been recruited regularly from among men who had entered the industry as manual workers or at least were the sons of such.[2] A study of British industrialists in the hosiery and the iron and steel industry from the middle of the nineteenth century onwards does not suggest that opportunities for advancement increased significantly. In hosiery a small-scale system of manufacture had always facilitated the entry of men from below the middle class, and the high peaks of this movement were the times when the industry was expanding and innovating.[3] On the other hand, the steel industry, which requires comparatively large investments of

---

[1] R. K. Kelsall: *The Higher Civil Servants in Britain*, 1955. The comparison is with the group of males aged 20–64 given in the 1951 Census.

[2] The recent tendency to recruit managers from the technological and scientific personnel may provide new avenues for the working-class boy.

[3] *cf.* C. Erickson: *British Industrialists, Steel and Hosiery, 1850–1950*, 1959, pp. 93–106.

TABLE II

Class and Educational Background of certain Middle Class Occupational Groups: (in percentages)

	1	2	3	4	5	6	7
	All Middle Class Males	Steel Manufacturers, 1953	Hosiers, 1952	Civil Service Entrants 1949–52	Business Leaders, 1949	Managers I 1952–54	Managers II 1955
(a) Class Background—							
Social Class I*	47	62	54	63	..	20	36·5
Manual Working Class	19	18	18	19	..	33‡	}37 30
Father 'Businessman'	..	34	47	..	51	28§	..
Father Professional or Administrative	..	..	..	..	22	..	..
(b) Education received (School)—							
Elementary School only	}36·5†		..	..	{11	20	36·5
Ordinary Secondary			..	25·5		33‡	..
L.E.A. Grammar School	..	..	..	43·5	..	28§	..
Independent Secondary Day Schools	..	..	..	..	..	..	..
Public Schools (Headmasters' Conference)	..	..	..	11	58	19	26
'Top-20' Public Boarding Schools‖	..	..	..	19	..	4	8
Other Boarding Schools	..	..	..	..	..	..	..
Numbers to which figures relate	262	138	111	223	1,243	2,650	646

For notes see opposite

capital, has always been much more closely linked with upper and upper-middle-class families. Only in the group of industrialists active after the last war can we observe an increase of men of working-class origin.[1]

On the whole the managerial ladder does not seem to have widened perceptibly during the last thirty years. A considerable proportion of managers has always been recruited from men who had entered the industry on the factory floor—not all of them necessarily the sons of working-class families. On the other hand, a sizeable minority of managers were educated in the more exclusive public schools. This is less so in large enterprises where family influence is less marked and promotion follows a more bureaucratic procedure. In a sample of managers in the Manchester region, comprising largely small and medium-sized firms, it accounted for nearly a tenth.[2] R. V. Clements found also that,

---

[1] *ibid.*, Chapter II, especially pp. 11–24.

[2] R. V. Clements: *Managers*, 1955. A study of managers above the level of foremen in comparatively large firms found that recruits from the same schools amounted to only 4 per cent of the total (Acton Society: *Management Succession*, 1956).

Table II; Sources:

1. D. V. Glass (ed.): *Social Mobility in Britain*, 1954 (Based on Sample Survey).

2 and 3. Erickson: *British Industrialists, Steel and Hosiery, 1850–1950.*

4. R. K. Kelsall: *Higher Civil Servants in Britain.*

5. G. H. Copeman: *Leaders of British Industry*, 1955 (Based on a Questionnaire study).

6. Acton Society: *Management Succession*, 1956. (Managers of 27 large Companies each employing more than 10,000.)

7. R. V. Clements: *Managers*, 1955. Refers to Managers in a sample of firms in the Manchester Region of varying size.

* Erickson, Glass: Hall-Jones scale 1 + 2; Kelsall: Registrar-General's Scheme of Social Classification Social Class I.

† *i.e.* Elementary and Higher Elementary.

‡ *i.e.* Higher Grade Schools, Central Schools, Secondary Modern and Secondary Technical.

§ Including Grammar Schools *not* in the Headmasters' Conference.

‖ *i.e.* Charterhouse, Cheltenham, Clifton, Eton, Fettes, Haileybury, Harrow, Loretto, Malvern, Marlborough, Oundle, Radley, Repton, Rossall, Rugby, Shrewsbury, Sedbergh, Sherborne, Uppingham, Winchester.

while the war years had brought a comparatively large influx of men who had risen from the bench or other positions at the bottom of the factory hierarchy, the public school men reasserted themselves in the post-war years.

Other studies of the social origins of men in middle-class occupations only amplify the general tendency for self-recruitment inside the professional and industrial middle class. Table II, which summarizes some of the available data, is given here largely to allow a comparison with the social background of élite groups proper.[1]

One fact emerges clearly from the above figures: the large place occupied by those who received their schooling either in public boarding schools or in independent day schools. This may suggest that the educational and social mould into which boys are pressed during their public school education and the sound academic training which the most gifted undoubtedly receive in the best of these schools does help in their future career.

On the other hand, the importance of the public school sector may be merely a reflection of the fact that a considerable proportion of well-to-do middle-class parents send their children to fee paying schools and that public school membership, especially membership of the most exclusive boarding institutions, invariably implies the high social rank of the boys' father. The public school may thus merely reinforce the natural social and economic superiority of the boy who goes there. Arthur Ponsonby, who had looked at the system as an insider, clearly thought so. 'We segregate our upper class children in special institutions, by charging higher fees, not for superior education, but for the object of keeping certain children in a privileged position, free from the contact of the middle and lower classes because as gentlemen they are supposed to require a particular training and as far as possible socially uncontaminated surroundings.'[2] If such men are successful in their later careers, their success is the result of their superior social and economic background and the general influence which their families can bring to bear on their careers.

---

[1] In the comparisons of data from widely scattered sources allowance must be made for the inevitable differences in the classification.

[2] A. Ponsonby: *The Decline of Aristocracy*, 1912, p. 193.

Whatever the decisive aspect, public school membership and parental or family wealth are inevitably correlated. It is hardly surprising that in ascending the grades within a profession, we should increasingly come across the men who did not start the road to the top at the bottom rungs of the social ladder. If we look at the bureaucratic hierarchy we find that the higher the administrative rank, the greater its correlation with the level of parental occupation and the school attended. In 1950 nearly two-thirds of the Permanent Secretaries or Deputy Secretaries of Government Departments had been educated either in boarding schools or in independent day schools. For those of the rank of Assistant Secretary, the corresponding figure is only just over two-fifths. In the Civil Service this gap has gradually narrowed. Promotion from the ranks has brought men to the top who, although they 'lacked the polish of the typical senior servant of pre-war days, had all the necessary qualifications otherwise'.[1] Such 'polish', parental wealth and influence, and those vague 'leadership' qualities, whether genuinely fostered by the public schools or only part of their mystique, are important also to those who step up on the management ladder.[2] Thirty-three per cent of all top-managers in large Companies had been educated in public schools compared with 17·5 per cent of those in the junior and middle grades.[3]

In the business-world, 'success' can largely be equated with income. On the basis of the available data it is evident that the higher the social background, the higher the income. Among Manchester managers, the average income of men of middle-class descent was £2,253 per annum, while the sons of manual workers received only £1,280.[4]

The legal career has offered some opportunities for the talented but the bulk of the profession has been recruited from a narrow

---

[1] Kelsall, *op. cit.*, p. 156.

[2] The careers of Wykehamists, studied by Mr T. Bishop, show that while success in the professions is closely related to scholastic performance and achievement this is not so for those who entered business. See his as yet unpublished dissertation: *Origins and Achievements of Winchester Pupils, 1836–1934*, Ph.D., London University, 1962.

[3] Acton Society: *Management Succession*. The percentage of those educated at 28 most exclusive public schools was 11 and 3 per cent respectively.

[4] Clements, *op. cit.*

TABLE III

The Social Background of some Contemporary Élite Groups:

	1 Labour Govt., 1945	2 Labour Govt., 1951	3 Cons. Govt., 1951	4 Cons. Govt., 1960	5 Heads of Civil Service, 1958	6 Ambassadors and Ministers, 1953	7 Leaders of Industry and Business, 1950–55	8 Directors of large Insurance Cos., 1958	9 Directors of Bank of England and 'Big 5', 1958	10 Army, 1953	11 Judiciary, 1953	12 Bishops, 1953
Aristocrats	2	3	14	15	..	..	3	..	..	..	..	..
Working Class	38	30	1	1	..	..	1	..	..	..	..	..
Etonians	5	5	24	17	3	..	8	46	50	..	..	..
Harrow, Winchester, Rugby, Marlborough	2	5	16	10	11	..	8	34	33	..	..	..
All Public Schools	15	23	52	48	..	65	29	..	..	..	36	27
Sandhurst, Dartmouth, Woolwich	..	..	1	..	..	..	1	..	..	21	..	..
Grammar Schools	11	16	8	18	..	..	15	12	8	..	..	..
'State Secondary Schools'	30*	22*	..	..	..	..	1	..	2	4	..	..
Elementary School only	15	23	..	..	..	..	..	..	..	..	..	..
Oxford or Cambridge University	9	8	40	46	50	..	22	57	83	..	..	..
Other Universities	..	8	3	3	15	..	8	10	14	..	8	7
TOTAL IN CATEGORY	66†	66†	65	66	73*	75	65	149‡	166‡	34	58	43

base. Among those who entered Lincoln's Inn between 1886 and 1913, the sons of working-class parents were practically absent, and even for the 1920's the percentage is negligible.[1] As we ascend the legal hierarchy the area of recruitment narrows further and today's Judges, largely members of the last generation which Professor Ginsberg studied, are even more predominantly upper middle class in their background than the group from which they were selected.

It is in the light of these trends that the social composition of certain contemporary élite groups must be seen.

---

[1] *cf.* M. Ginsberg: *Studies in Sociology*, 1933, pp. 170–1. For the years 1923–27 Professor Ginsberg found that 1·8 per cent of all entrants were the sons of skilled wage-earners, 84 per cent had an upper or middle-class background, while less than 15 per cent belonged to the class intermediate between these two (*i.e.* salaried workers, small employers, etc.).

Notes on Sources, etc., columns:

1–4, 7. Original analysis. 'Leaders of Industry and Business' are leading officers (Presidents, Chairmen, Vice-Presidents, Vice-Chairmen, Hon. Gen. Secretaries, Hon. Treasurers of the British Employers' Confederation, the Federation of British Industries and the Association of British Chamber of Commerce).

5, 8, 9. T. Lupton and C. Shirley Wilson: 'The City Men Who Decide', *Manchester School*, January 1959. No data for post-school education were available for 82 of the 388 men in the three categories.

6. Sir R. Williams: *Whose Public Schools* (Bow Group Pamphlet), p. 14.

10, 11, 12. Harvey and Hood: *The British State* (Army: Rank of Lieutenant General and above; Judiciary: Members of Supreme Court and the Lord Justices of Appeal).

* Data about schooling were not available in the case of 9 members of the 1945 Government and in 4 cases in 1951. Internal evidence does suggest, however, that the majority, if not all of them, received only elementary education.

† In the case of Labour ministers the figure of those with a working class background is to some extent an estimate based on educational and occupational background. Information about Father's background was in many cases not available.

‡ No data for post-school education were available for 82 of the 388 men in the three categories. Figures for those educated at grammar schools and at other public schools are not available separately.

THE GOOD AND THE GREAT[1]

Politicians, Bureaucrats, Brass Hats, Bishops, Academics and Judges occupy *traditional* 'élite' positions. Some of these have increased slightly in numbers; others, like the Civil Service, have grown vastly both in size and in influence. The significance of the business élite lies in the vast increase in its power, not in any novel position as such.[2]

But outside these groups new and increasingly powerful sets of institutions have given rise to a new range of élite positions. Such are the host of advisory committees which form a link between government departments and powerful pressure groups or expert opinion outside it, as well as the bodies charged with the supervision and direction of semi-autonomous agencies in the public sphere. While these are subject to ultimate governmental control and are dependent on government funds they are, at the same time, largely independent of day-to-day parliamentary and political supervision. Some of the authorities which come under this heading disburse annually large sums of money and their members wield considerable power.

Formally, the majority of these bodies are unconnected with the other élite groups, but through their members they are mostly closely linked to élite positions in other fields, either contemporaneously or chronologically. The 'good and the great' are largely men of power and influence independent of the momentary positions on the advisory committee or supervisory body to which they have been appointed. It is through their position in industrial professional or other élite groups that men are drawn into the orbit of governmental activity. Officially or unofficially they tender advice, suggest lines of policy and criticize others. Under certain condi-

---

[1] The Treasury have 'a comprehensive list of likely people . . . for various . . . kinds of public service'. (Oral evidence to the Franks Committee on the Procedure of Tribunals, Fourth Day, p. 110.) Legend has it that the names are contained in a drawer marked G. & G standing for 'The Good and the Great'.

[2] Bishops, Generals and Judges today and in 1868 (in parenthesis):

Bishops	..	..	..	43	(27)
English High Court Judges	..	..	62	(20)
Major-Generals and above	..	..	137	(281)

tions they actually regulate aspects of the economic sphere with which they are intimately connected in other ways.

In one sense this is not a new development. Ministers and high-ranking administrators have always sought the counsel of experts on particular issues and 'experts' have always used officials and politicians to further their cause especially when they happened to be at the same time protagonists of particular policies.[1] The difference between the position today and that of the period before 1939 and 1914 lies in the frequency, formality and much greater effectiveness of the system.[2] Advisory bodies lack specific powers although they are often based on statutory provisions, but they help Whitehall to make up its mind, and through published reports and press publicity, they influence Parliament and Public Opinion. In 1958 there were a total of 484 effective central and national advisory councils of one sort or another; in 1939 the number was only around 200[3]; before 1914 these bodies hardly existed. A large number of them were admittedly of a highly specialized and frequently of a very technical character, such as the Committee on the Preservation of Wooden Vessels, or the bodies which advised on the Storage and Transport of Explosives or the Licensing of Bulls and Boars. Others have a much wider range. They often represent pressure groups and organizations of differing importance and include such simple bodies as the 'Standing Conference on Ironstone (Landowners)', or the more important Joint Committees set up by the Ministry of Labour and the Board of Trade, which are concerned for example with the general economic situation of particular industries or with specific problems affecting health and safety in them. Indeed a formal representative structure is specifically laid down in the case of some committees. Thus the National Joint Advisory Council of the Ministry of Labour consists of 17

---

[1] The Webbs come to mind largely because Beatrice Webb has documented their activities in this field with such engaging candour. 'You can't wire-pull old experienced wire-pullers like ourselves', she wrote when someone had sent them a personal appeal which was very obviously part of an organized campaign.

[2] cf. R. V. Vernon and N. Mansergh (eds.): *Advisory Bodies*, 1940 and C. K. Wheare: *Government by Committee*, 1955.

[3] P.E.P.: *Advisory Committees*, 1960, p. 23. This figure includes committees concerned only with Scotland and Wales but not those which have a regional basis only nor any sub-committee of major national advisory bodies. The inclusion of the latter has led to the quoting of a much larger figure.

representatives of the British Employers' Confederation, 17 members nominated by the T.U.C. and 6 from the nationalized industries.[1] But even where Councils and Committees do not have a formal representative structure, their members, although they are serving as individuals, are mostly appointed following discussions with representative bodies in the particular field. This helps to gain acceptance of the policies and measures proposed by the committee, through the prestige which members enjoy in their respective organization. Conversely participation in the work of such advisory bodies enhances the prestige and influence of organizations among its members.

While membership of advisory committees is widely based—the total number of names has been estimated at 5–6,000—only a fraction serve on the 15–30 really important committees concerned with fairly broad questions of National policy.[2] Including overlaps and official representatives, the 17 Major Committees have a total membership of 363.

It is not always easy to draw the dividing line between Advisory Bodies and Executive Committees. The Ancient Monuments Board and the Historical Buildings Council have advisory as well as administrative functions. Others are clearly almost policy-making bodies. Within the general framework of statutory control exercised by Parliament they shape events over a broad range of national affairs. The rise of such a number of important autonomous or semi-independent agencies is thus a comparatively new development of the British political system and those who govern such bodies are a new and growing section of the British Political

---

[1] The National Production Advisory Council of Industry and the Economic Planning Board are similarly constituted. cf. P.E.P., op. cit., pp. 133–44.

[2] e.g. (Membership in parenthesis.) National Production Advisory Council on Industry (31), Economic Planning Board (7), National Joint Advisory Council of Ministry of Labour (40), Consultative Committee for Industry (20), Central Transport Consultative Committee (20), Air Transport Advisory Council (6), Central Health Services Council (41), Central Advisory Council for Education (31), National Insurance Advisory Committee (9), Central Housing Advisory Council (30), Advisory Council on Scientific Policy (7), Advisory Committee on Education in the Colonies (26), Advisory Committee on Social Development in the Colonies (16), Overseas Migration Board (12), Engineering Advisory Council (22), Council for Wales and Monmouthshire (28), Agricultural Improvement Council (17).

élite. The sphere and the complement of some of these auxiliary vessels of state is charted below.

A large part of the scientific research activities carried out in Britain today are undertaken under government auspices or are financed by the Government. Their supervision is entrusted to advisory council or committees, appointed by the Lord President of the Council. These bodies decide on the overall direction of research and on the priorities which particular projects should have.[1] The B.B.C., The Arts Council and the British Council are quasi-independent bodies with their own 'Civil Service' disbursing comparatively large sums of money. Their accounts are presented to Parliament but their detailed administration is not subject to parliamentary control. The University Grants Committee is an independent body, appointed by the Government. It distributes government grants to the universities and thus acts as an intermediary between the Government and the universities.

To leave the supervision of publicly financed activities in academic institutions and in the field of culture and propaganda largely to practically autonomous, self-governing agencies has been widely praised as a necessary safeguard for the freedom of intellectual and artistic pursuits. It is conceived as a pre-condition of the genuine independence of thought and research, if not the very midwife of its birth. But those who argue thus should reflect that in appointing the supervising bodies of such agencies, the Government has the means *to shape the agency in its own image*. Hence conflict between the Government and autonomous bodies is largely excluded. The infant B.B.C. was put to the test in this respect by the tensions of the General Strike. A section of the Government, led by Churchill, wanted to commandeer it. The Director General, Sir John Reith (as he was then), protested against such measures. 'If the Government be strong and their case be right they need not adopt such measures', he wrote in a memorandum to the Prime Minister. '*Assuming the B.B.C. is for the people and that the Government is for the people, it follows that the B.B.C. must be for the Government in this crisis too.* . . . Speaking with the authority of its own reputation for sincerity and impartiality *it would emphasize and initiate statements likely to counteract*

[1] A fourth body, coming under the jurisdiction of the Lord President is the Nature Conservancy, but it is of a much lesser importance than the other three.

a spirit of selfishness and hostility.[1] Given the premise, the conclusion is convincing enough and the B.B.C.'s refusal to allow the Archbishop of Canterbury to broadcast a manifesto on behalf of the churches, is perhaps the natural outcome.[2]

Who are the hidden governors? The agencies listed below are, I think, the most important bodies in respect of money spent by them, or in view of their influence on intellectual trends, public thinking and economic, social and cultural affairs in general. Some are, in fact, the equivalent of the boards of the nationalized industries in the non-productive field. But as their business is not conducted like that of commercial organizations and as the product of their activities can not be purchased or easily measured, their success or failure is difficult to assess.

The period 1950–55 has been chosen for the analysis of the personnel of some of these agencies, which is presented below. Where the numbers would have been otherwise unduly small, a further four years were added. The analysis thus reflects appointments made by the Labour Government in the period 1945–51 as well as those of Conservative ministers since they took office. There is little evidence to suggest that the selection carried out by the two parties has shown very different features. The pattern of the National Assistance Board has hardly changed over the years. The Labour Government appointed as its chairman George Buchanan, who had entered Parliament as one of the original 'Clydesiders' in 1922 and who had held ministerial office for a few years. The Conservative Government appointed as his successor Sir Geoffrey Hutchinson, a Conservative back-bencher, a Barrister with a public school and a university background. In its composition the Board leant in 1950 towards Labour and in 1959 towards the right in politics, but its membership has otherwise been very similar: minor businessmen and former officials or professional men with experience in local rather than national affairs. Of its ten members (1950–59) only one had received a public school education.[3]

---

[1] Lord Reith: *Into the Wind*, 1949, p. 109. (My italics.)

[2] *ibid.*, p. 109-110. The Archbishop's sermon at St. Martin's-in-the-Field was however broadcast on the following Sunday. A broadcast by Ramsay MacDonald was vetoed by the Prime Minister.

[3] The Conservative Government actually appointed a former Labour M.P. and a leading Welsh Labour Party member to the Board.

TABLE IV

Governors of Autonomous and Semi-autonomous Agencies:

Agency and Directing Body	Year Founded	Size of Board	'Budget' (in £m.) 1960–61	Remarks
B.B.C. Governors	1927	9	35·0	Semi Independent Corporation
British Council	1934	6	3·25	Financed by Grant-in-Aid.
I.T.A.	1955	10	3·8	Regulatory Body; owns stations.
University Grants Committee	1919	17	58·0	Disburses Grants in Aid.
Agricultural Research Council	1931	18	6·4	Established by Royal Charter.
Medical Research Council	1920	12	4·3	Financed by Grant-in-Aid.
Advisory Council of D.S.I.R.	1916	12	15·1	Directs a Government Department.
Arts Council	1946	15	1·2	Financed by Grant-in-Aid.
Colonial Development Corporation	1948	7	160·0	Public Corporation, money borrowed.
Development Commission	1909	8	1·1	Allocates grants to rural communities.
National Research Development Corporation	1948	11	—	Public Corporation.
National Assistance Board	1935	6	143·7	
National Economic Development Council	1962	17	n.a.	To initiate economic planning and co-ordination.
National Parks Commission	1949	13	0·05	Co-ordinating body.
TOTAL		161		

Not so the membership of the 'Cultural Directorate'. During the 1950's, 52 men and 13 women were responsible for the direction of the British Council, the B.B.C. and the Arts Council.[1] Only 7 were connected to the aristocracy either by descent or marriage but the number of those who are known to be of working-class origin was even smaller. The B.B.C., the senior of the three, has, by tradition always included a representative of 'Labour'; it has also always included a woman. The Postmaster General has often managed to combine these two 'inevitables' in one person. The first Chairman of the Governors of the B.B.C. was the 6th Earl of Clarendon, who had been Government Chief Whip in the House of Lords and also, for one year, a junior minister at the Dominion Office. His deputy was Lord Gainsford, a former Liberal Minister and the Chairman of the private company which ran the radio prior to its incorporation. Their colleagues were a retired high-ranking Civil Servant, the former Headmaster of Winchester and Mrs Snowden. 'As to Mrs Snowden,' Lord Reith has written, 'the Postmaster General had to find a representative of Labour and a woman. He said he had done well to find them in the same person.'[2] When Mrs Snowden's term of office came to an end, the happy combination was repeated, and another Postmaster General found in Mrs Mary Agnes Hamilton a suitable successor. The Postmaster General's predecessor in office, however, had a more important decision to make. Lord Clarendon resigned during the tenure of the second Labour Government, before his term of office had expired. The method of selection adopted is illuminating. Lees-Smith told Reith that 'he had racked his brain for a suitable Chairman. . . . In desperation he had gone through the alphabetical list of Privy Councillors; and at the end of it—John Henry Whitley. And with him light, and understanding and excellent wisdom.'[3] Lord Attlee has left it on record that in making the appointments which inevitably, or by tradition, are the prerogative of the Prime Minister, he paid no attention to political views, merely to the fitness of the person appointed and to the require-

---

[1] Four actually held office in two of the three organizations.

[2] op. cit., p. 114. Incidentally MacDonald had not been consulted over Mrs Snowden's appointment and he refused to regard her as representing Labour.

[3] The Rt Hon. J. H. Whitley had been a Liberal M.P. and later Speaker of the House of Commons.

ments of the post. When, owing to Lord Inman's appointment as Lord Privy Seal, the Chairmanship of the B.B.C. fell vacant in 1947, the Government chose Lord Simon, a former Liberal M.P. and a man of progressive views and independent judgment, who had only recently joined the Labour Party. Of the twelve appointments to the board which the Labour Government made, only three could be called Labour Party supporters. More significant than political background is the fact that those at the head of organizations which direct cultural life in Britain, and those who are responsible for the propagation of British culture abroad, are drawn almost exclusively from members of the traditional middle class. Only one member of this group had concluded his education in an elementary school, as against 14 who passed from a public school to Oxford or Cambridge.

It is only natural that those responsible for scientific research should be drawn from a much more restricted circle than the group just discussed. Those who direct research, even if only in the most general sense which is represented by the adjudicating of conflicting claims for financial support and the approval of general guiding lines for future projects, must be able to bring scientific talent and ability to bear on it. Moreover, the members of the three great advisory boards are often chosen in consultation with the representative scientific organizations in the field. The social background of their membership will thus reflect the character and the social background of the scientific community or at least of that section of it who have reached scientific and worldly eminence. Yet even here, the public school products account for nearly one-third of the total, although the Scientific Directorate shows a somewhat more 'plebeian' character than its counterpart in the cultural field.[1]

Other facts, too, reflect on the narrow area of recruitment to bodies which are assuming constantly widening responsibilities. While three-fifths of the total are drawn from the universities and one-fifth from industry (mostly recruited from the directors of

---

[1] The social difference with the Cultural Directorate may, however, be more apparent than real if we allow for differences in the regional recruitment. A considerable percentage of the scientists came from Scotland where the Public School tradition in the middle class is not so marked. On the other hand, the English Public Schools have paid little attention until recently to a scientific training and the academic prestige has rested all too heavily on the classics.

TABLE V

The Governors of Culture and the Arts in the 1950's:

	I B.B.C.	*2* British Council	*3* Arts Council	*All*‡
EDUCATION:				
(*a*) Schools—				
Eton	5	2	4	11
Harrow	1	—	—	1
Winchester	—	—	2	2
Rugby	2	—	—	2
Other Major Public Schools	1	—	6	6
Other Public Schools	2	3	1	5
Grammar Schools	9	3	9	20
Elementary Schools	1	—	1	2
Other and Abroad	2	1	2	5
Privately and not known	2	3	7	11
All Public Schools	11	5	13	27
(*b*) University—				
Oxford	5	4	9	16
Cambridge	9	2	5	16
Scottish	2	—	1	3
'Redbrick'	1	1	4	5
None (or none known)	8	5	13	25
OCCUPATION:				
Rentier	2	1	2	
Politician	3	3	—	5
Diplomats, Foreign Service	1	2	—	6
Academic	2	2	4	3
Professions, Administration	2	—	7	7
Armed Forces	2	1	—	9
Journalists and Authors, Musicians, etc.	2	—	6	3
Commerce and Industry	6	2	4	8
Married Women	2	1	6	12
Trade Union Officials	1	—	—	7
Other	2*	—	3†	1

large and very large industrial enterprises), only two men represent the industrial working class. (See Table VI, page 348.)

The membership of Royal Commissions and *ad hoc* committees appointed by the Government to consider and report on specific issues has some of the elements of the group of expert advisers just considered, but it has others which bring it into line with the governing bodies of institutions like the B.B.C., or with the major advisory committees in the economic and social field. Royal Commissions and Departmental Committees are generally considered to represent the vocal and interested parties in particular problems as well as the independent minds of the eminent, but non-committed and the more common sense judgment of the *homme moyen intellectuel*. Lastly they are reckoned to include 'persons who are qualified not so much by knowledge or experience or by "interestedness" in the narrow sense as by the fact that they "stand for" or "speak for" sections of the community which are politically important'.[1] The composite character of the membership of such bodies alone would warrant investigation, but their importance in the British system of government makes an analysis of its personnel and internal working essential for our understanding of policy-

---

[1] R. V. Vernon and N. Mansergh (eds.): *Advisory Bodies*, 1940 (In the introduction by R. V. Vernon at pp. 27–28).

CLASS:

Aristocrats	5	2	3	10
Known to be working class	3	—	1	4
	—	—	—	—
Numbers involved	25	12	32	65†

* Lord Kenswood, Musician and Welfare Worker for the Blind, and Sir Arthur Fforde, Solicitor and Headmaster of Rugby.

† James Welsh, Sir E. Pooley, Clerk to the Drapers Company, 1908–44, Mr R. Capell, Musician and Music Critic.

‡ Excludes 4 overlaps in membership.

1 B.B.C., 1949–59.

2 BRITISH COUNCIL, 1950–59. Figures refer to President, Chairman and Vice-Chairman.

3 ARTS COUNCIL, 1950–55.

TABLE VI

Members of Research Councils, 1950–55:

Category	A.R.C.	M.R.C.	D.S.I.R.	Total*
Class—				
Aristocrats	I	2	I	3
Known to be ex-Working Class	I	—	I	2
Education—				
Eton	—	2	I	3
Harrow	2	—	—	2
Winchester	—	—	—	—
Rugby	—	I	—	I
Other Major Public Schools	I	2	5	8
Other Public Schools	3	3	3	9
Elementary Schools	—	—	I	I
Grammar Schools	13	9	13	34
Abroad	2	4	—	5
Not known and privately	5	5	I	11
All Public Schools	6	8	9	23
Oxford	2	I	2	5
Cambridge	6	5	9	20
Scottish	5	2	I	8
Other English Universities	9	10	4	22
Abroad	7	3	—	9
None	2	I	7	10
Occupation—				
Academic and Research	19	18	10	47
Industry and Commerce				
(Directors and Entrepreneurs)	I	3	11	15
Professions	—	3	—	3
Civil Service	4	—	—	4
Trade Union Officials	I	—	I	2
Other	I	2	2	5
TOTAL	26	26	24	74*

* Two overlaps.

making. As it is, this aspect of the Royal Commissions and Committee system has received scant attention.[1]

The nineteenth century is generally regarded as the golden age of the Royal Commissions, and the reports of their modern successors are held to be only a pale reflection of their ancient glory. Such a comparison rests too much on the consideration of a comparatively small number of Royal Commissions which paved the way for fundamental reforms. Between 1830 and 1900 a total of 388 Royal Commissions were appointed. In the 1850's, at the height of this mass of commission creation, the flood ran at eight Royal Commissions per annum.[2] Most of these dealt with minor topics, often of the kind which are nowadays delegated to the deliberations by small expert bodies if they are not decided wholly inside government departments. During this century the number of Royal Commissions has rapidly declined. In the fifty years between 1911 and 1960 only eighty-eight were appointed, less than two per annum, and two-thirds of these were set up in the 1910's and 1920's. Their place has, however, been taken by departmental or interdepartmental committees and the kind of subjects with which they have dealt have often been indistinguishable from those with which Royal Commissions have been concerned.[3] Many reports, often the most contentious ones, are left on the shelves where they rest with equally bulky blue books containing outdated statistics and the like. Others have changed important aspects of social policy and the conditions under which men will live to quite such an extent as their famous and statelier predecessors. Equality of pay for women, the settlement of the 'surplus' population of the large urban centres in new towns of limited size, which assumes implicitly the social and aesthetic values of the Garden

---

[1] It is perhaps not surprising that neither Bagehot nor Dicey deal with it, but even Lowell in his two volumes on *The Government of England* fails to discuss it. Since then three works have dealt at some length with *ad hoc* committees (*i.e.* Clokie and Robinson: *Royal Commissions of Inquiry*; Wheare: *Government by Committee* and Vernon and Mansergh (eds.); *Advisory Bodies*.

[2] Thirty-two of these Royal Commissions, however, dealt with questions of bribery.

[3] The difference between a Royal Commission and a departmental Committee has been held to be one of dignity. Thus 'Common Land' and 'Justices of the Peace' have been accorded the status of a Commission while Common Prostitutes and Administrative Tribunals qualified only for a committee.

City kind of environment, are examples of this. So is the principle of Civil Service remuneration, based on comparability with private employers advocated by the Priestley Commissions. Its acceptance by the Government widened further the gap in incomes between the grades, which tended to narrow in the immediate post-war years.[1]

In order to understand the policies advocated by Royal Commissions we ought to know the climate of opinion in which they work and the pressure brought to bear upon them by the interested bodies in the field. Above all we must know the intellectual presumptions and prejudices with which its members approached their tasks and the 'bias' with which they sift and interpret the facts before them. The Webbs thought that such bias 'is especially noticeable among those who have attained any position in the public eye. Hence when we are told that a particular person has been appointed on a Royal Commission or a Government Committee . . . on the grounds that he is—or claims to be—an independent person, we may rest assured that this merely means that the selector and the selected agree in their bias.'[2]

An analysis of bias is obviously impossible, although much might be done if the study of particular reports were accompanied by intensive biographical research and the interviewing of participants.[3] Instead an attempt has been made here to give an account of the *background* of 'government committee men' who form an important section of the semi-political élite. Between the end of the last war and 1960 successive governments appointed sixteen Royal Commissions. Two of these dealing respectively with 'Awards to Investors' and with 'Common Land' seemed rather specialized and were in consequence not included in the analysis. A total of 179 men and women sat on the other fourteen Royal Commissions.[4]

---

[1] The principle of comparability also affected salaries in other branches of the public services. When the history of the reassertion of the middle classes during the 1950's comes to be written, the Government's salaries policy may well be found to have been of strategic importance.

[2] S. and B. Webb: *Methods of Social Study*, p. 45.

[3] The only detailed account of the working of a modern Royal Commission is that of the Poor Law Commission described by Beatrice Webb in *Our Partnership*.

[4] Actually the aggregate total is 187, but 8 duplications of membership occurred.

Only 150 of these could be traced, and in some cases full educational data were not available, but it seemed that the analysis of the 85 per cent whose identity could be established, was justified. A similar analysis is presented for the Chairmen of 57 important committees appointed between 1955 and 1960 which dealt with problems of social and economic policy.[1]

Compared with the inter-war years, or the nineteenth century, this group has indeed shown some changes in character. Former politicians and renowned noblemen are today less in evidence, either as members or even as Chairmen of Royal Commissions or government committees. Of thirteen committees appointed by the Postmaster General between 1921 and 1938, five were chaired by Peers and of about 100 advisory bodies set up by the Ministry of Health between the wars a quarter had Peers as Chairmen.[2] If we exclude Law Lords, on whom a great deal of committee investigation has recently fallen, we find that only 14 of the 71 Royal Commissions and Departmental Committees studied here had Peers as Chairmen and five of these were new Peers of middle-class origin.

Like other 'temporary and indirect governors', Royal Commissioners and Committee Chairmen are recruited predominantly from the ranks of the (upper) middle class. Working-class occupations are not represented among those for whom data were available and although 34 of the members were women, the revolutionary departure by which the Royal Commission on Population included the wife of a West Hartlepool factory worker does not seem to have been repeated. Nor has a trade union leader ever headed a Royal Commission or chaired an important Government Committee in recent years.

The majority of these 'honorary advisers' are 'inevitably distinguished, as distinction is reckoned in the Athenaeum or in the Reform Club',[3] and, indeed, one cannot help thinking that

---

[1] A list of 67 Committees was given by the Prime Minister in a parliamentary reply (*Hansard*, 3.3.1960, written answers, col. 169–74). Ten of these seemed highly technical, *e.g.* Committees on Anthrax, Sheep Recording and Importation of Charollais cattle and were in consequence left out.

[2] *cf.* Appendices in Vernon and Mansergh (eds.), *op. cit.*

[3] O. R. McGregor: 'Social Fact and Social Conscience', *Twentieth Century* May 1960.

TABLE VII

Government 'Committee Men':

Category	Royal Commis- sioners*	Chairmen of Committees†	All‡
Class—			
Aristocrats	11	7	17
Known to be Working Class	12	—	12
Education—			
(a) School:			
Elementary School only	11	1	12
Grammar School	42	20	60
Eton	13	9	20
Harrow	1	—	1
Winchester	5	6	11
Rugby	5	2	7
Other Major Public Schools	19	5	24
Other Public Schools	22	8	28
Other and Abroad	8	3	11
Not known	24	3	26
All Public Schools	65	30	91
(b) University:			
None	34	13	45
Oxford	43	17	58
Cambridge	26	13	38
Scottish	15	5	19
'Redbrick'	8	8	15
Abroad	4	1	5
All University	116	44	155

* Figures refer to 150 of 179 members of Royal Commissions between 1944 and 1960.

† Appointed 1955—February 1960.

‡ Includes seven overlaps.

Occupation:

Landowners	1	1	1
Rentiers, 'Company Directors'	4	5	8
Politicians	5	1	6
Barristers, Judges	21	17	37
Clergy	2	—	2
Civil Servants	9	3	12
Diplomats and Colonial Admini- strators	3	—	3
Public Administrators and Local Government Officials	8	—	8
'Academic'	29	12	38
Teachers	4	—	4
Physicians and Surgeons	5	2	6
Accountants	2	2	4
Other Professions	2	—	2
Industrialists and Businessmen	21	11	33
Journalists and Authors	4	—	4
Trade Union Officials	10	—	10
Married Women	15	1	15
Not known	5	1	6
Other	—	1	1
TOTAL	**150**	**57**	**200**

membership of these two august bodies to which so many of the chosen few belong is conducive to their selection. It is there and at the University Clubs that the selectors and selected meet.[1] No doubt, there are also men at the pinnacle of eminence who can be consulted and who will point out likely candidates in the valleys below them. To be well connected by marriage is also of some benefit to would-be women governors or commissioners. The distinction of quite a few of the women who get there seems above all to be that

[1] Of the élite of the Civil Service analysed in Table III, 8 belonged to the Athenaeum, 15 to the Reform Club and 22 to University Clubs.

M

which accrues to their husbands: their own consists largely of the fact that they are not men.

Kinship, as such, does not seem to be an important factor in the selection of the eminent, but the 'tithe' which the total membership of the three groups pay to Eton (33 of the 335 men and women who held office) is statistically of the highest significance. This applies equally to Winchester or Rugby, each of which account for more than their share of public school membership would warrant.[1] A contributor to a recent symposium on the British Power Élite thought that 'Eton and Winchester sometimes seem to be conspiracies rather than educational establishments'.[2] That the membership of such schools acts as a 'network' whose internal lines of communication are links between men who advise and appoint is a suggestive hypothesis but only inside knowledge could throw fuller light on it.

Even without assuming any conscious preference for the men who can sport an 'old school tie', it is plausible to visualize the road to the heights of power in terms of a step-by-step advance and to imagine that at each point acquired advantages tend to reinforce each other. Among the 339 persons in the three groups of the influential here analysed 151, or 45 per cent, had received their pre-university education in public boarding schools—two-thirds of them in the '20 Major Public Schools' specially investigated. Almost the same number (154), were educated at Oxford or Cambridge. In this sample, as well as throughout the population as a whole, these two factors are correlated to a significant degree. And in the groups here studied, prestigeful educational background and social and educational rank attained are also closely linked. In the social groups from which the *appointed executants of power* are traditionally chosen the correlation between general achievement and original educational or social advantages is already high. My impression is that in the élites themselves it is even higher.

In the socially fairly homogeneous milieu from which, as we saw, the bulk of the members of the major élite groups are recruited,

---

[1] The comparatively poor performance of Harrow is difficult to explain.

[2] A. Hartley: 'Inevitable Oligarchy', *The Twentieth Century*, October 1957, p. 304.

the discovery of fairly minute differences in respect of parental background, education and career becomes increasingly tedious and progressively less illuminating. Morphology and aetiology must give way to topography and functional analysis if our political system is to be more fully understood.

ELITES: STABLE AND IN FLUX

The picture of élite groups presented here has been in the nature of an extended time-exposure. Even a ten-year stretch does not permit us to trace fundamental changes in the internal composition or function. But by following the background of individual members one can relate separate élite groups, institutionalized or transient, to the wider and less mutable social structure. And we have found that the bulk of the membership of individual élites is firmly rooted in the general social élite. Some men have intruded from below, pushed up by sheer ability, their eminence often the result of scientific or academic distinction. Others are selected as representatives of the organization which they serve. Their moves are as gentle and often as little significant as the mantle of knighthood which falls on the shoulders of the successful and acceptable trade union leader.

In the economic élite, too, few men have risen from the lower deck. Among the men in charge of the big industrial corporations and the great banks and commercial institutions of the City of London, 'new men' are possibly rarer than in the political leadership. The managerial ladder helps men to step up, but it rarely extends from the bottom to the board room. A tenth of the three élite groups analysed sat on the boards of the comparatively small number of large and very large industrial enterprises which today dominate British industry.[1] Half of these had been educated in public schools: few appear to have risen from the working class. And such rises as occur are more likely among the giant industrial

[1] Very large Companies are the 100 largest enterprises under the control of their own board listed by the N.I.E.S.R. in their 'Classified List of Large Companies engaged in British Industry'. Their assets range from £14·5m. (Ansells Brewery) to I.C.I. with assets of £438m. Large Companies are the remaining (412) companies with assets of £2·5m. or more, engaged mainly in *industry and trade* in the United Kingdom.

corporation, where advancement proceeds often along Civil Service lines. Three of the leaders of I.C.I. of the immediate past, Lord McGowan, Sir Frederick Bain and Mr John Rogers were all born in close proximity in a Glasgow working-class district.[1] The personal founders or expanders of the great industrial and trading enterprises of the late Victorian or Edwardian period, men like Boot, Burnham, Cowdrey, Furness, Lipton or Swaythling, who often started from very humble beginnings, have by all accounts had comparatively few successors. Lord Nuffield is one of the few contemporary industrialists of that type and his biographers doubt whether it would today still be possible to build up a vast enterprise from small beginnings and to keep it under the personal control of its founder.[2]

There exists today in Britain a 'ruling class', if we mean by it a group which provides the majority of those who occupy positions of power, and who, in their turn, can materially assist *their* sons to reach similar positions. The character and composition of this class has clearly undergone some changes since the middle of the last century. The members of aristocratic families form only a minority in the various élite groups here analysed. Even in the Conservative governments of today, only a quarter are aristocrats of more than two generations' standing. The rest are recruited almost exclusively from the groups of upper-middle-class families. Among the leaders of industry, the aristocrat of ancient lineage is not very prominent. Among his sample of 3,215 directors of Companies, with assets worth £1m. or more, Copeman found that just under 2 per cent were Peers or Baronets and a further 0·5 per cent were sons of Peers.[3] And many of this small group are likely to be men who were themselves ennobled or at the best were the sons of newly created Peers.[4]

The analysis of groups of non-governmental decision-makers, two or three generations ago, would have produced a picture much more closely related to the group of country squires and titled landed magnates and the members of their immediate

[1] R. Lewis and R. Stewart: *The Boss*, 1958, p. 58.
[2] P. S. Andrews and E. Brunner: *The Life of Lord Nuffield*, 1955, p. 342.
[3] Copeman, *op. cit.*, p. 84.
[4] See Chapter V above.

families than their contemporary successors. The wider 'ruling class' of today still includes the descendants of those who formed its predominant element in Victorian times, but new groups have clearly and inevitably come to the fore. A hundred years ago the typical Royal Commissioner was the 'Barrister of six years' standing'.[1] Today lawyers are still among the members of such investigating bodies but more frequently as Chairmen of Committees or Royal Commissions. Five of the sixteen Royal Commissions set up since 1944 were chaired by High Court Judges. Instead of lawyers the academics have come to the fore. Two Vice-Chancellors and five heads of Oxford or Cambridge Colleges chaired seven of the remaining eleven Royal Commissions. Retired Civil Servants or military leaders, too, are increasingly drawn into the sphere of policy-making or are joining the advisory élite. This movement between élite groups with the consequent accretion of responsibility in the hands of a narrowing circle of men, who often make decisions of the utmost gravity, is one of the essential features of the much used and much misused term *Power Élite*. Behind the individuals who make what may appear to themselves and to others merely isolated decisions and 'behind the events of history linking the two, are the major institutions of modern society. The hierarchies of state, and corporation and army constitute the means of power. As such they are now of a consequence not before equalled in human history.' These three institutions interlock 'as decisions tend to be total in their consequences the *leading men in each of the three domains of power tend to gather together to form the power élite.*'[2] So C. Wright Mills writes in the book whose title has produced echoes beyond the confines of the American scene which it analyses and condemns.

The smallness of these Isles, and Britain's relative poverty, makes nonsense of any facile application of Mills's model to the structure of our society and our political system. Nor is Great Britain socially or economically America on a reduced scale. In

---

[1] These were often paid for their labour as commissioners, a feature widely criticized at the time. Paradoxically it seems that one of the bad features of our present system is that it does pay only expenses and costs of maintenance while attending meetings. Membership is thus inevitably restricted to those who can dispose freely of their time.

[2] C. Wright Mills: *The Power Élite*, 1956, pp. 5 and 9 (my italics).

the rigidity of its unwritten constitution, the formal power of the Cabinet and of Parliament seems to me still vastly greater than the relative subordinate position which the proponent of the 'Power Élite' hypothesis assigns to the average American politician, with the exception of the very highest members of the Executive. Although the independent Member of Parliament is nearly extinct, the Government must yet *lead* the House and its followers and must exercise persuasion as well as pressure. Private members, in their turn, can still influence the Executive either on the floor of the House or in the Committee Rooms upstairs. The members of the Government must still rub shoulders with their colleagues on the back-benches of Parliament and, despite the growth of the Cabinet Secretariat, there is as yet nothing at No. 10 Downing Street comparable to the Presidential entourage and the Brains' Trusts of the White House.[1] Nor would it seem to make sense to ascribe to Mr Macmillan's companions on the grouse-moors the same significance which Mills gives to the men with whom President Eisenhower was in the habit of playing golf.[2]

But as we saw already in connection with the evolution of the political élite proper, movement between élite groups has in the course of this century tended to increase. Generals, Civil Servants and high-ranking businessmen have moved into ministerial office with little or no preliminary introduction into the world of Parliament, to which they must still formally belong. Such men have not only moved into the board-rooms of major industrial or commercial corporations; they have also assumed direction of nationalized Railways or Airlines, accepted the Mastership of Oxford Colleges or the Chairmanship of the B.B.C. Sir Oliver Franks has moved from a university Chair to a Civil Service career culminating in the headship of an important Ministry. He returned to the Provostship of an Oxford College, moved to the highest Ambassadorial post (Ambassador to Washington) went from there to the Chairmanship of Lloyd's Bank only to return to academic life twenty years after he left it. Such travels among the peaks of power are exceptions, few have equalled them. But élite groups have not

---

[1] The fact that members of the American Administration do *not* belong to Congress is, of course, important for the understanding of structural differences.
[2] Mills, *op. cit.*, p. 234.

only their internal overlap—most pronounced in the economic directorate. Men move constantly between them, contemporaneously or over a period of time.

This kind of distribution of power position has been plotted for some of the major élite groups.[1] Naturally not all affiliations have been enumerated. It seemed right to concentrate on membership and office holding of groups which rank comparatively high in the exercise of economic or political power or influence, while disregarding positions of mere social prestige, such as leadership in voluntary organizations, charities, professional bodies and the like. Apart from the élite categories enumerated or analysed in Tables III–VII, trade union leadership, Membership of the House of Commons,[2] Peerages and leading positions in party organizations have been counted. Membership of some lesser Government Boards has also been noted. The data on which this analysis has been based are almost entirely taken from *Who's Who* and other biographical reference works and the entries there may be occasionally incomplete. Cross-checking of membership of Royal Commissions and Committees, however, does not suggest that there are significant omissions in those entries which refer to the *cursus honorum* of an individual.

In listing the membership of committees or advisory bodies, only one entry is given in each category. But even without allowing for the membership of a host of committees and advisory bodies— up to ten have been found in quite a few cases—the results suggest that within the group of the 'elect' élite membership is unequally distributed. At the bottom end there are 200-odd (out of a total of over 500) for whom no activity in any other élite group is known. At the other end are the *pluralists of power*, men who over a number of years or occasionally even simultaneously, exert influence through a number of advising or decision-making bodies. Power attracts such men and power breeds more power and influence.

A Minister of Health (Eton and Cambridge) becomes the head of a Cambridge College, a member of an Area Board of a Nationalized Industry, Vice-Chancellor of the University, heads a Departmental Committee, chairs one Royal Commission and later

---

[1] See below, pp. 363–367.
[2] In the case of members of the Government membership of the House of Commons is not specifically mentioned.

another (Sir H. U. Willink). A leading industrialist (Rugby and Cambridge) is not only a Director of the Bank of England, and a President of the Federation of British Industries. He also chairs an advisory Council and a Royal Commission, and no sooner has the work of the latter come to an end than he is invited to head another committee on the future of Broadcasting (Sir Harry Pilkington). The Chairman and Managing Director of one of the largest Industrial Concerns, ranking twentieth place among the 100 giants, (King Edward VI Grammar School, Birmingham, no university) joins within a decade a number of highly important bodies: the Advisory Council of the D.S.I.R., the Atomic Energy Authority, and the Board of Governors of the B.B.C. He becomes a director of the Commonwealth Development Finance Corporation and finally heads a small inquiry into the future of a vast nationalized undertaking. Its report, involving far-reaching changes of organization and policy is accepted by the Government (Sir Ivan Stedeford). A solicitor (Rugby, Oxford) becomes Headmaster of Rugby and later Chairman of the B.B.C. (Sir Arthur Fforde). Another Governor of that body (Eton and Cambridge) is a Peer, nephew of a Prime Minister, a one-time Chairman of the Scottish Division of the National Coal Board (Earl Balfour). The Vice-Chancellor of an English university (Tonbridge School, Oxford—Modern Greats) becomes a Vice-Chairman of the B.B.C. and of the British Council, Chairman of an important Advisory Council. He is a member of a number of other important bodies in the educational field, sits on the General Nursing Council and on the Governing Board of the National Institute for Research in Nuclear Science (Sir Philip Morris).

The reasons for such peregrinations in this penumbra of politics are not quite clear. Is there a shortage of men capable of heading important government missions and willing to do so? Is previous good performance a guarantee for success in very disparate fields, or does public confidence in the work of a committee depend on the renown of the man who heads it? If so, the name is generally not one that has an ancient ring. The reputations come today from the field of industry or science, the universities and Whitehall. Pluralities of power are widely distributed; in interpreting the spread of membership among different élite groups which is summarized in Table VIII we must bear in mind that the picture is inevitably truncated. Not all élites have been included and the net of affiliations is incomplete. The men included are far from having completed their span of influence; if the same groups be examined after another decade the total of affiliations would be larger.

Table VIII gives an indication of the hierarchical structure of power-holding among the members of the various élite groups.

TABLE VIII

Cross Membership of Elite Groups:

Affiliations with other Elite groups	Lab. Gov't, 1945–51	Cons. Gov't, 1951–55	Directorate of Culture	Scientific Directorate	Govern-ment Committee Men
None	56	45	25	26	57
One	36	22	17	25	61
Two	14	15	11	8	47
Three	6	4	8	10	21
Four	1	2	1	2	8
Five or more ..	—	—	3	3	6
TOTAL ..	113	88	65	74	200
Total of Member-ships	86	76	84	100	284

In the Conservative, *as well* as in the Labour Government, half of those who held office are so far without membership in other élite groups. But here the similarity ends. If we compare the pattern of affiliations revealed in the charts at the end of this chapter, quite a different set of configurations emerges. Nearly one-half of those members of the Conservative Administration who have affiliations with other élite groups are connected with the leadership of industry and finance, either as members of the board of industrial giants or as directors of leading banks or insurance companies or as spokesmen of principal economic pressure groups. Among the Labour leadership only a mere handful have joined the boards of either nationalized industries or of large private enterprises. Of the two who have followed a ministerial career with high positions in Industry—Lord Shawcross as a Director of Shell and Lord Wilmot as Director and Deputy Chairman of Boulton

& Paul; one has since severed his connection with the Labour Party. Labour ministers, on the other hand, have been active on Government Committees and Royal Commissions to a much greater extent than their opposite numbers.

The membership of the other three élite groups does not only present a greater degree of involvement in other élite positions but the diagrams show the power and the weight of some of these affiliations. The 57 Chairmen of Government Committees do not only hold another 126 élite positions, but these include 13 Peerages, 13 directorships in Banks, Insurance Companies, large industrial undertakings and boards of nationalized industries. None of them had held extremely high positions in the Civil Service at home and abroad and eleven belonged to the upper levels of the Judiciary.

DIAGRAM E: AFFILIATIONS OF MEMBERS OF THE LABOUR
GOVERNMENT, 1945–51, WITH OTHER ÉLITE GROUPS

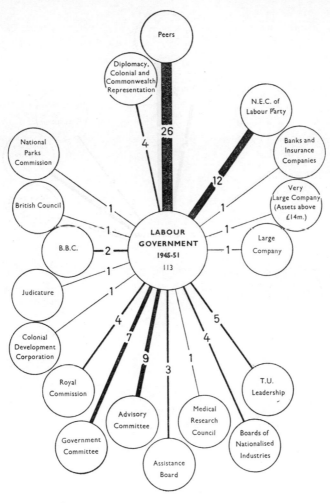

No. of Members	113
Members without Affiliations with other Élite Groups.. ..	56
Members with Affiliations with other Élite Groups	57
Total of Affiliations	86
No. of Affiliations per Member	1·5

DIAGRAM F: AFFILIATIONS OF MEMBERS OF THE
CONSERVATIVE GOVERNMENT, 1951–55, WITH OTHER
ELITE GROUPS

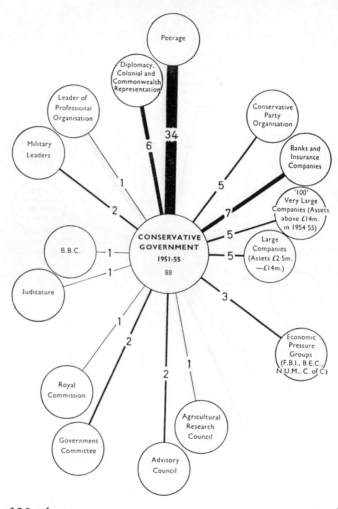

No. of Members		88
Members without Affiliations with other Elite Groups.. ..		45
Members with Affiliations with other Elite Groups		43
Total of Affiliations		76
No. of Affiliations per Member involved		1·8

DIAGRAM G: AFFILIATIONS OF MEMBERS OF THE 'CULTURAL DIRECTORATE' WITH OTHER ELITE GROUPS

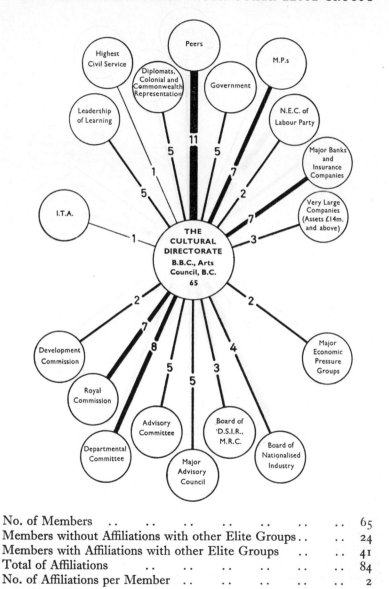

No. of Members	..	..	..	..	..	65
Members without Affiliations with other Elite Groups..					..	24
Members with Affiliations with other Elite Groups			..		..	41
Total of Affiliations	..	..	..	..	..	84
No. of Affiliations per Member	..	..	..	..		2

DIAGRAM H: AFFILIATIONS OF MEMBERS OF THE 'SCIENTIFIC DIRECTORATE' WITH OTHER ELITE GROUPS

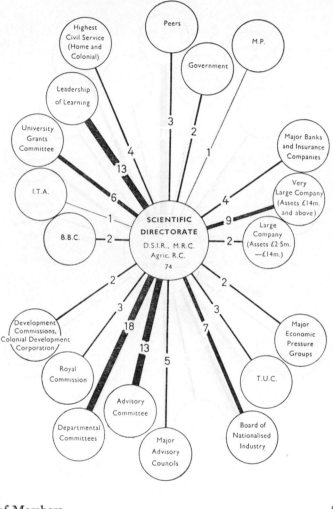

No. of Members 84
Members without Affiliations with other Elite Groups.. .. 26
Members with Affiliations with other Elite Groups 48
Total of Affiliations 100
No. of Affiliations per Member involved 4

DIAGRAM I: AFFILIATIONS OF ROYAL COMMISSIONERS
AND CHAIRMEN OF COMMITTEES WITH OTHER ELITE
GROUPS

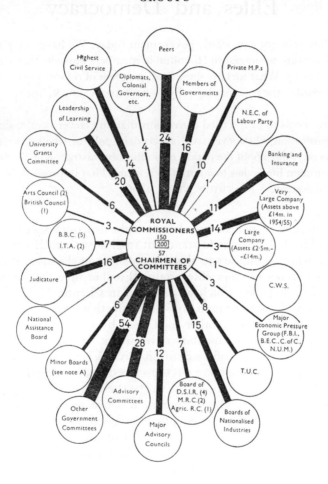

No. of Members	..	..	..	..	..	..	200
Members without Affiliations with other Elite Groups..					..		57
Members with Affiliations with other Elite Groups			..		..		143
Total of Affiliations		..	..	..	..	..	291
No. of Affiliations per Member involved				..	..	..	2

CHAPTER XII

Elites and Democracy

'We have not got democratic government today. We have never had it and I venture to suggest to Honourable members opposite that we shall never have it. What we have done in all progress of reform and evolution is to broaden the basis of oligarchy.'—ANTHONY EDEN, 1928.

'There seems to be a settled conviction that any clever man, trained in any profession whatsoever, will succeed in politics whether or no he knows anything about the details of public administration or the facts of the common life he has to attempt to reform. That impression we must seek to destroy.'—BEATRICE WEBB, 1896.

THE process of our analysis has brought us from a society where the political élite seems to stand out in almost singular eminence, to one where it appears to share its position at the apex of power with a number of other élite groups. Further investigation of the Victorian oligarchy, which was studied in Chapter II, would undoubtedly show the extent to which effective power over public affairs was enjoyed by other men than by those engaged in the actual process of parliamentary government. We know little as yet about the power and influence of the Civil Service at that time. Its rôle was on the whole more circumscribed than today; this was an age when ministers frequently wrote their own letters and dispatches. Yet during the temporary absence of the Secretary of State Mr 'Over-Secretary' Stephens 'reigned over our colonies in solitary grandeur'.[1] And as the century advanced more high-ranking Civil Servants achieved positions of similar influence. Large territorial Lords enjoyed great influence over parts of the country and through it they could exercise effective political power. Such was the position of the Stanleys in Lancashire. 'The adherence

---

[1] From a letter to his wife, September 1838 quoted in C. E. Stephens (ed.): *Sir James Stephens, Letters with biographical notes*, 1906, p. 56.

of Lord Derby to the Liberal cause', Harcourt wrote to Hartington, 'would be the gain of half the country'.[1] Great Victorian hostesses exercised power through their 'salons' and a man like Delane, the autocratic editor of *The Times*, was consulted by Prime Ministers.

But however diversified, the mid-nineteenth century élite had its focus undoubtedly in the two Houses of Parliament and in the style of life and common educational background to which all but few of its members belonged.

By contrast, the contemporary élite, analysed in the previous chapter, appears at first sight disparate and lacking unity. As the result of changes in the relative social position of different groups of the population, élite position, conceived in terms of power, no longer corresponds as closely to high rank as measured in terms of income or social prestige, as it did a hundred years ago. Considerable power can be combined with a relatively low salary—as in the case of some Trade Union leaders—while the much talked about speculator or the possessor of some freak talent might possess great wealth and display an ostentatious style of life without enjoying much power. Indeed real power may be almost inversely related to publicity. Information about some of the men at its apex is sparse; their names are hardly known to more than a small group.[2] We know far less about what goes on in the Board Rooms of I.C.I. or English Electric than about the private meeting of back-bench M.P.s in the Committee Rooms of the House of Commons.

The movement between élite groups which has been sketched, the reliance of governments on men with a ready-made reputation, real or alleged, or on those with exceptional experience outside politics, suggest equally that no hierarchy of élite groups is clearly evident. Indeed, the host of committees which surround the government—fact finding, advising, policy-devising—and the

---

[1] B. Holland: *Life of the Duke of Devonshire*, 2 vols., 1911 vol. I, p. 255. Power of this kind has largely disappeared although this particular influence lingered on. The 17th Earl declared in 1924 that he was paying the expenses of three candidates and was also subscribing largely in five other seats. If he had any standing in Lancashire, he wrote at the time, it was because he had 'always done many things which might come under the heading of "the daily round, the trivial task".' Churchill *op. cit.*, p. 576.

[2] *Who's Who* does not contain the biographies of all members of the boards of even the largest companies.

N

emergence of a race of perennial chairmen, the 'patron saints of the establishment' raises even the spectre of political decisions passing from government and Parliament.

Such a view neglects an important and indeed crucial aspect of the distribution of power: the supremacy of the government in and through parliament as a law-making and law-enforcing body. Because of this the political élite occupies a special position among the élites. Collectively it can, in the last resort, give orders to those who occupy the commanding heights in the economic and social sphere, and it enjoys this power because its organization is even more comprehensive than that of the largest body outside the political field and because it has the means of enforcing its policy.[1]

The superior position of the *political* élite is thus no longer primarily due to the high rank, social influence or economic wealth of its members. The majority of them do not even enjoy particularly great *personal* power. Those who do seek the latter will generally find more opportunity to exercise it as top executives in the great corporate organizations rather than in Parliament or in all but the highest government offices. Indeed, such power may occasionally come to men, who are formally lowly placed, but who occupy a strategic office which either gives them intimate access to a powerful individual—such as the office of Principal Private Secretary to a high-ranking Minister—or one that permits them independent action through the accumulation of know-how and experience of a special kind.[2] If we are to rank élites today it would be rather in a hierarchy in terms of the sanctions which each group can impose on those who fail to submit to its power.[3] And here the political élite, acting through the institutions of the government, still holds a position of unrivalled eminence. The quality of those who belong to it is therefore still of crucial importance for the well-being of society. The processes of election, selection and promotion by

[1] *cf.* S. F. Nadel: 'The Concept of Social Élites', *International Social Science Bulletin*, vol. VIII, p. 421.

[2] An example of the latter is the career of Sir Ralph Furse who, while occupying a position of comparatively minor rank in the Civil Service, undertook for a generation almost single-handed the selection of entrants into the Colonial Service. See his autobiography, *Aucuparius*, 1962.

[3] 'Power is any opportunity within a social system to impose one's will on others even against opposition'. Max Weber, *op. cit.*, p. 28.

which political leadership emerges are still important for the working of parliamentary democracy.

With the growth of political democracy the choice of representatives became gradually subject to popular control, but it would be fallacious to conclude from this that those who emerge as victors in the internal battles of the modern democratic state are inevitably or by definition the men best suited to govern us. We saw that in the struggle for place and position some are heavily handicapped and that on the long road to eminence others found the barriers down against them. Institutional forces, prejudice and inertia prevented the free flow of talent even into the lower ranges of the political hierarchy and the conditions under which politicians perform their duties will also determine the character and the qualifications of the men who will come forward.

The analysis of the *cursus honorum* in the political élite showed how a good and early start, material independence, rank and relatives helped men to rise in politics. The delay between the entry of the entrepreneurial and professional middle classes into the House of Commons and their arrival at the top of the political ladder is largely due to the working of these hidden factors. In this sense the process of élite formation can affect adversely the working of a democratic political system. The nearer we get to the apex of political decision-making the more 'closed' the circle of the men who participate in it. And the prestige of the men at the top as well as the limitations on effective intra-party democracy help to sustain the power of this small group. This is so in the party of tradition, but similar forces are at work in the party which advocates radical changes in society.

At the same time gradual changes in the process of parliamentary government and in the formation of public opinion have tended to increase the power of the upper echelons of politics, compared with those of the rank and file politicians. Today it is probable that even the Cabinet has lost some of its former status and that vital policies are in effect decided on by an inner circle comprising perhaps a mere handful of senior ministers, if not by the Prime Minister himself.

These two tendencies have gone on apace and they have mutually reinforced each other. They are found at work in Parliament and in the two major political parties. Fifty years ago A. L. Lowell observed that the membership of the House of Commons and of the national government in general was still in the hands of the upper class and he noted that the effects of this were reinforced by the fact that the Cabinet, in which the governing class was most strongly entrenched, was 'gaining in political weight at the expense of the House of Commons'. He added that 'all the prophecies of the levelling effects of democracy in Great Britain have so far proved fallacious. *Where political class jealousy is weak, social ambition and social cohesion are among the strongest forces in human nature,* and in a society as centralized and powerfully constructed as that of England they are not likely to fade quickly into the background.'[1]

Since then the balance of political forces has altered. The Labour Party has become a considerable political force and men who started from the very bottom of British Society have reached the highest rungs of the political ladder. Yet Lowell's conclusions have not lost their significance even for the 1960's. In the interplay of social classes, political parties and mores of government which determine the character and composition of the political élite, the strength and power of the British upper class has largely persisted. Two generations and two World Wars after Lowell, another sympathetic foreign observer described Britain's political system as an 'aristo-democracy'. He was not seeking to imply that Britain was ruled by a fossilized and antiquated class of noblemen but rather that 'England remained an aristocratic state in the sense not of rule by the closed shop of a hereditary oligarchy, but of rule by the class whose members . . . had carried away the biggest prizes in the struggle for existence'.[2]

In reminding us of the relative absence of class-antagonism, of the continued self-assertion on the part of an old ruling class and of the desire on the part of the middle-class politicians to emulate their 'betters', Lowell underlined an important factor which made for the stability of the political leadership. In the development of the party system of parliamentary government in the second half of the nineteenth century the ties of kinship and friendship which united the leading members of the 'ins' and 'outs', helped to keep political strife within reasonable bounds. Even the rise of organized Labour and its growing representation in Parliament only rarely brought

[1] A. L. Lowell: *The Government of England*, 2 vols., 1908, vol. II, p. 513 (my italics).
[2] J. H. Huizinga: *Confessions of a European in England*, 1958, p. 105.

sounds of violent class-conflict into the parliamentary arena. Whatever might have been said on the platform about fundamental dissensions in British society was re-echoed much more faintly in the chamber of the House of Commons. Labour's political representation worked within the established framework of parliamentary institutions. We saw that it accepted the mores and forms of political life at Westminster and that it did not shut itself off from the members of the party opposite. Although the Parliamentary Labour Party contained the only sizeable segment of M.P.s with a working-class background, Labour politicians have, in the course of their rise in the governing hierarchy, tended to become absorbed in the wider political ruling class.

If the political system is more representative today than it was a hundred years ago, this is due to the democratic character of the processes by which M.P.s are selected rather than to the wide range in the social background of the men chosen. Entry into politics has been made easier, the party organizations are more powerful and more democratic than in the days of the caucus, and talent is no longer barred from a political career, unless flanked by wealth. Yet the House of Commons is today anything but a microcosm of the nation.

I do not mean to imply that a socially broadly based representation is either a symptom or a pre-condition of an effective democratic system but I think it would contribute to it by enabling the House of Commons to draw on a wide range of experience. It is strange that the availability of so many different types of specialists has generally been praised as a valuable feature of the membership of the House of Lords rather than of the elected chamber.

It will be obvious from the facts and figures presented earlier that the meshes of the selection net spread out by the two parties and the character of parliamentary activity as such favour certain types of candidates and inhibit others. Among the active politicians, businessmen, lawyers, teachers, miners and journalists abound but scientists, clerks, housewives, agricultural workers or former civil servants or local government officers, to name only a few groups, are much less well represented in the House of Commons. Even industrial workers enter it usually only via the corridors of a Trade Union office.

If the range of occupational experience of Parliament is narrow, the educational background of Parliament, as we saw, is lopsided in the extreme. Given the gulf between the private and the public sector in education, the fact that nearly the whole of the membership of one party and a significant minority of the other were educated in fee-paying boarding schools means that a majority of the membership of the House of Commons lacked during some of the most formative years of their lives any contact with those outside the circle of the upper or the upper middle class. And except for such periods of social upheaval as occur in times of war, the initial gulf must of necessity widen during the years of adulthood, and the natural distance between M.P.s and electors is bound to heighten it. This distance will, in turn, affect the quality of the dialogue between the ordinary men and their elected representatives and act as a barrier to democracy.[1]

The age structure of the House of Commons can hardly be expected to be a replica of that of the adult population as a whole and it is probably to the benefit of Parliament that men no longer seek to enter it on the very threshold of adulthood. But it seems equally undesirable that others should enter it when they are on the verge of retirement, as happens today. Such men will often lack the adaptability necessary to learn the ways of the House of Commons or the energy and open-mindedness to acquire new knowledge. And if they succeed in making the transition, 'old age is upon them'. Few men who have entered the House of Commons in their late fifties or sixties have made a mark there, except in special circumstances. It would be invidious to fix a maximum age of entry into Parliament but there should clearly be an incentive for M.P.s to retire at an age when in other occupations men leave their posts. As things stand, they often fail to do so. Vanity plays a part here, so does fear of poverty. The superannuated Trade Union official turned M.P., whose pension is small and who may be plagued by ill-health, probably does not find it easy to exchange a parliamentary salary for honourable but ill-paid retirement.[2] He ought not to be called upon to face such an alternative.

The quality of the nation's elected representatives and their

---

[1] cf. R. H. Tawney: 'The Problem of the Public Schools', *Political Quarterly*, 1943, pp. 117–49.

[2] At present M.P.s are entitled to a pension from the Members' fund to which they contribute £12 p.a. if they have served for ten years. The maximum

ability to carry out their duties is clearly related to their economic position and to the status and scope of the job. Yet the conditions under which the M.P. carries out his work do not easily permit the development and display of 'judgment and industry' which in Burke's famous phrase is the duty which an M.P. owes to his constituents. To be a professional politician *ought* to be a full-time job. It cannot be so if the income which he receives for performing his duties is inadequate and insufficient. In 1953, when the parliamentary salary was only £1,000, a 'considerable number of Members made it clear beyond any doubt that they can not (out of this) afford the expenses which they deem necessary for carrying out their parliamentary duties efficiently and, at the same time, maintain a reasonable standard of living for themselves and their families'.[1] A Parliamentary salary should be large enough to give an adequate income to men from all sections of the populations and not only to those who can combine it comparatively easily with their occupation. M.P.s ought not to be faced with the choice of either devoting part of their time to other activities or of being content with a comparatively low standard of living and an uncertain material future.

The report of the Parliamentary Select Committee quoted above recognized this. It would deplore it if Parliament were composed of 'full-time politicians in the sense of men and women cut off from any practical share in the work of the nation' but it added that it would be no less damaging to the country if the House of Commons were to become a place where members 'could not give of their best because of a dominating need to escape from financial pressure.'[2]

How to fix the remuneration of M.P.s and maintain it at an adequate level and allow for inflation and the rise in real incomes is a secondary and technical consideration.[3] What is essential, is to find a sum, which would not be a positive disincentive to the man who

[1] *Report of the Select Committee of the House of Commons on Members' expenses* 1953 para. 27 (B.P.P. 1953–54, vol. VII).

[2] *ibid*. para. 54.

[3] To tie it to a grade in the Civil Service, such as Assistant Secretary, as has frequently been suggested, would be a simple device.

---

pension is £500 provided that the total income will not exceed £650. The figures for widows are £500 and £450 respectively.

wished to devote part of his life to politics while at the same time discouraging those who would merely seek cash and kudos.

The arguments which apply to the payment of politicians apply with equal force to his 'pension'. If being a 'Parliament-Man' is a full-time job, it ought not to be exercised by men for whom it has become too onerous. 'The miserable nature of the Members (Pension) Fund', a recent critic has written 'would alone be good reason (for the professional politician) for changing jobs—or emigrating to Canada'.[1] The retirement arrangements ought to enable a politician to face resignation with equanimity, and enable constituency organizations to encourage him to do so without feeling that they may inflict undue hardship upon him.

All this will not necessarily bring men from all walks of life into Parliament, nor is it likely to produce a Parliament of supermen. It is only a pre-condition for treating full-time political activity as a profession. There is little danger that this will either turn politics into a 'job' or transform the politician into an unscrupulous careerist. In any case those who select M.P.s can be generally trusted to weed out the possible financial adventurer. What is needed are improvements in the procedures used for the selection of parliamentary candidates, making them more democratic and more efficient.[2]

Nor is the argument convincing that M.P.s ought to have another job so as to carry out their political duties better. No doubt the atmosphere at Westminster is artificial and there is a danger that members may lose touch with reality in their daily round of Chamber, Smoking-Room, Restaurant, Library and Lobby. To overcome this members need outside *interests* and the time to pursue them. A more rational time-table, perhaps a four-day week accompanied by shorter recesses, might help members to make a substantial contribution to politics without losing their natural place in society.

---

[1] cf. B. R. Crick: *Reform of the Commons*, 1959, p. 8.

[2] We should recognize, however, that in the last resort the choice will rest with a comparatively small number of individuals using their senses and their intelligence. I don't think that the institution of a 'primary' on the American model would be an improvement of existing procedures or that selectors would be helped by the results of proficiency tests of prospective Parliamentary candidates as J. F. S. Ross has suggested in his *Parliamentary Representation* (p. 230).

For what are the alternatives? Parliamentary activity would be restricted to a new rentier class, men and women of independent means who would engage in the 'game of politics' as an earlier generation had done. Bearing in mind the seriousness with which the Victorian governing class approached its task, such a solution might present some outward attractions. One cannot withhold a certain admiration for the Country Gentlemen who a hundred years ago were prepared to spend much time, energy and money on parliamentary activities and public service in general. They were frequently men of limited intellectual endowments, their minds were robust rather than subtle, and they were greatly handicapped in their task by the limited and narrowly circumscribed training which they had received in their youth. But they were generally conscientious men with a highly developed code of honour and feeling of loyalty. Given their upbringing it is hardly surprising that many identified the good of the nation with the interests of the group to which they belonged; it seems more significant that in their approach to politics so many transcended narrow class issues.

There is little likelihood that a similar type of politician would evolve today; the character of the community and the social climate in which these men functioned are no more. By occupation, possession and family tradition the Victorian politician was much more firmly rooted in local society than his contemporary successor who must of necessity range himself in the serried ranks of his party and who will tend to identify himself with national rather than local issues. When the change occurred and politicians became more dependent on a wider public, Ostrogorski noted that the choice of men by the 'caucus' 'left much less to natural selection determined by the spontaneous play of social forces'. Political leadership, he thought, was bound to become much more manufactured and consequently much less responsible.[1]

I think that Ostrogorski was mistaken in this latter view but the danger that politicians might approach their daily task with an insufficient sense of duty is ever present. It would be a likely consequence of any lowering of the status and position of private Members of Parliament.

[1] *cf. op. cit.*, vol. I, p. 592.

Failure to recognize parliamentary activity as a profession might well cause an increasing number of M.P.s to concentrate on other affairs than the business of the House of Commons, except when issues of first rate importance or matters of private concern were being discussed. Politics would then become a game in which the gentlemen and players of the government side would be ranked against a similarly composed team on the opposition benches. There would be some sixty hard-working members of the government and a somewhat smaller number of shadow-ministers. The vital political decisions would be made every five years or so when the electorate would select the captain of the ship of state and some of his principal lieutenants and would determine the general course which he was to follow. In the years between elections the policy of Government or Opposition would be decided by the Prime Minister or the leaders of the Opposition in consultation with a small number of very senior colleagues. A disciplined army of back-benchers would flock to Westminster for important debates and divisions, leaving the ordinary routine work of Parliament and the debating of less important measures to a stage-army of 'little men . . . desperately fighting over things that do not matter.'[1]

And all this whilst the real battles are decided elsewhere? This is so crucial a question that it ought to be discussed at some length. The political élite, while retaining the power of ultimate sanction, may lose the opportunity of decisive action through the progressive lengthening of the processes of control and command. This development affects not only the range of democratic decisions but it also has repercussions on the character of the representation. For the quality of the politicians may be closely linked to their power—or the lack of it—as to their selection and the general purpose of their careers. Will men who are willing to devote a critical intelligence, expertise and initiative to the furtherance of some public goal or the realization of a political programme, continue to find a satisfying outlet for their abilities in parliamentary politics? Will they choose a political career even under better material conditions if their opportunities to influence decisions as back-benchers continue to decline?

---

[1] As quoted by Crick from a leading article of *The Times* of December 23, 1957 (*op. cit.*, p. 5).

That there has already been such a decline, few will doubt. Its symptoms have been frequently discussed in terms of the decrease in private members' time, the growing party discipline and the general lack of opportunity to investigate government policy in detail. It might also be considered in relation to the rise in the number of non-representative bodies which administer public funds or which are either implementing government policy laid down in broad outlines or propose new departures on matters of public concern. There is a danger that what are virtually political decisions are 'pre-empted' by a host of 'part-time' governors: unknown, unrepresentative but influential.[1]

It is in the nature of such committees and advisory bodies that they should work in comparative privacy. Even where the examination of witnesses takes place in public, and where the minutes of evidence are published, the committee-room is not conceived as a debating chamber. The underlying assumption is that they should be non-partisan in character and that a small number of men—and generally one or two women—intelligent, articulate and broad-minded—will through investigation and deliberation arrive at a unanimous, fair and balanced solution to the problem posed. Whether discussion can really achieve this kind of unanimity of views unless it already existed from the beginning, seems doubtful and if a resulting agreement is only due to the strong pressure exercised by a few powerful individuals, it will be spurious. But the underlying premise seems to me equally question-begging. Why should a committee be regarded as more effective and useful if it produces a unanimous report; why should non-partisanship at the same time mean lack of representativeness?

We have seen that the élites which surround the political élite proper are composed to an excess of the members of the well-to-do, well-educated and presumably well-meaning upper and middle classes. The good are generally great and the great are expected to be good. Advisers, Governors and Committeemen are normally laden with experience and heavy with the duties of office. They are mostly men in their fifties and frequently in their sixties who will

---

[1] The latest example of this tendency is the creation in 1962 of a National Incomes Commission, charged with far-reaching investigatory and advisory functions over the whole field of incomes and salaries.

have achieved the zenith of success and who will feel the weight of responsibility press on their shoulders. Their names spell solidity and their distinction will reassure.

There are exceptions to this. Men and women of another mould and stamp do occasionally enter the outer world of politics like the working-class housewife on a Royal Commission. But they stand generally on the periphery. On the whole, the picture which emerged from the analysis in the last chapter suggests a very lopsided distribution of ability in Britain. Is it really rational to assume that talent in our society is distributed in the ratio of *two* to *three* between those who were privately and those who were publicly educated, as the tables on pp. 346–353 suggest, or that industrialists are inherently more able than Trade Union leaders. And why should men be thought to be so much more competent to decide on matters affecting education and the social services than women? This curious imbalance is further enhanced by the peregrinations of some men between committees, boards and the like and by the general move between leading positions in industry, science, the universities and Whitehall.

I believe it is inevitable that non-elected bodies, composed of experts, administrators and men, who probe existing conditions and formulate new policies, will flank the world of politics proper. And like their counterparts in the administration they will frequently make quasi-political decisions. A House of Commons composed of professional politicians, and making wider use of the committee system, would have more time and opportunity to undertake some of the controlling and enquiring at present undertaken by the world of the committee, but it cannot act as a substitute for them.

It would seem desirable therefore that the membership of such bodies should be much more broadly based and that those who sit around the polished horseshoe tables should be genuinely representative of thought and feeling of wide sections of the population. There should be men on the make as well as those who have already arrived, junior managers as well as company directors, younger lecturers as well as professors near the retiring age. Recruitment should be from the unknown as well as from the distinguished, from working men as well as from men who have no need to work. This would undoubtedly mean that members of investigating bodies should be paid for their services if these cause them to forgo earnings, but this is a small price to pay for their greater representativeness.

We might go further and question the value of Royal Commissions and similar bodies as *investigating* bodies as such. It is true that the great Commissions of Inquiry of the nineteenth and early twentieth century threw a strong light on hidden corners of social life and collected data hitherto unknown and often unsuspected. Their greatness lay in their use of techniques of social investigation initiated or directed by a Charles Booth, Edwin Chadwick or Beatrice Webb.

Recent Royal Commissions have been more reluctant to probe deeply into the fundamental issues which they were set up to investigate. A Commission on Divorce which did not investigate the social aspects of family life is only one instance of this.[1] It is moreover doubtful whether even these élites of the investigating bodies are still suited to their tasks. Their basic techniques—the interrogation of witnesses and the perusal of memoranda—are probably no longer adequate for the examination of the more subtle and more complex social and economic problems which present themselves today. These require the application of modern methods of social research and protracted investigation and study. Provisions in this field, although increasing are as yet woefully inadequate. Forty years ago the Haldane Committee on the Machinery of Government urged the establishment of facilities for 'inquiry, research and reflection before policy is defined and put into operation' and concluded that 'a Cabinet with such knowledge at its disposal would be in a position to devolve with greater freedom the duties of administration and even of legislation'.[2]

Much has already been achieved in this direction but there seems no reason why *all* the facts needed for the execution of social and economic policy should not be provided by the government either directly under departmental auspices or through sponsored investigations at universities or research institutes.[3] Thus the

---

[1] *cf.* O. R. McGregor: 'The Morton Commission; A Commentary'. *British Journal of Sociology*, 1956, pp. 171–93.

[2] *loc. cit.*, para. 12–17.

[3] *cf.* A. P. Herbert: *Anything but Action*, 1961.

findings of social scientists should eventually prove more useful than many deliberations by commissions of inquiry.[1]

We saw in the last chapter, that the 'penumbra of politics' of which the world of committees is a part is still comparatively large and diffuse. But we also noted that parallel with the concentration of power in the economic field there has been some multiplication and interlocking of power-holding in the circle of government-appointed advisers and directors. This movement has so far been comparatively small and democracy may as yet not suffer unduly from the extent to which these positions are held in plurality.[2]

However, it should not be allowed to spread; we may even ask whether there is really any need to burden even a small number of men with a multiplicity of governing tasks? They can hardly give an alert mind and vigorous thought to each and all of the duties with which they are charged, and the government, by shunting one set of men from one body to another, probably deprives itself of the services of other men with fresh minds and new ideas. It ought perhaps be regarded as a maxim of good government that positions of responsibility should be shared out as widely as possible. By doing so we should be able to bring the maximum amount of talent to the service of the community. And talent may produce ideas. Boldness, Tocqueville wrote, is a smaller danger to democratic society than the mediocrity of desires.[3]

For our complex modern society to function efficiently talent and élite position ought to be closely linked. Indeed, the road towards social as well as political democracy might be measured by the milestones which mark the removal of barriers to the exercise of ability. Yet the advance has not been rapid or equally marked on all fronts. And almost everywhere we find that élite positions have been less 'open' than career grades. It seems, that having eased the

---

[1] cf. D. V. Glass: 'The Application of Social Research' (Inaugural Lecture) *British Journal of Sociology*, 1950, pp. 17–30.

[2] The contemporaneous overlapping of élite groups membership occurs largely in respect of the formal representation of powerful organizations like the British Employers' Confederation, the Federation of British Industries or the T.U.C. on government bodies and the like. cf. P. E. P.: *Government and Industry*, pp. 130–2.

[3] Quoted by J. Lively: *The Social and Political Thought of Alexis de Tocqueville*, 1962. p. 162.

steps by which successive generations can attain the bottom rungs of career ladders, we fail to ensure that talent, once found, is always adequately utilized.

Even in the Civil Service, where the maxim of 'la carrière ouverte aux talents' has been longest at work, mobility has not been perfect; the higher grades of the administrative class tend to be recruited from men with a more exclusive social and educational background than the lower ones.[1]

In the political élite proper we found equally that the difference in the background between the rank and file politician and those who reach the leadership strata was pronounced and significant. The social gap between back-benchers and the men who obtain office has slowly become narrower but at the same time it seems that the original drive towards a widening of the field of recruitment has lost its impetus. In the selection of politicians as candidates for parliament and elsewhere a middle- or upper-class social and educational background appears to be of increasing importance.

It is, however, in the economic field that the entry into top positions seems most restricted. Although the entrepreneurial road to success has largely been replaced by the management ladder it is difficult to feel convinced that only objective criteria are used in the process of selection and promotion. Would the latter really bring about a managerial hierarchy where greater responsibility and higher social background are fairly closely related?[2] This and the persistence of public school men in the Company Directorate or the family ramifications in the City—a new cousinhood paralleling in the world of finance an older political kinship network—all suggest that 'connections', ownership and wealth weigh at least as much as ability.[3]

The reinforcing of initial material advantages by a restrictive and exclusive educational system and the selective social ties which may be formed in the 'old school' or an Oxbridge Junior Common Room is probably more than anything else responsible for the 'closed' character of British élite groups. Lord Maugham, a former Lord Chancellor, who had only been to a minor public school, thought

---

[1] See above, pp. 330–31.
[2] See above, pp. 333–37.
[3] cf. Lupton and Wilson, loc. cit.

that men who had been educated at one of the well known institutions had gained no advantage over him except one, but one which was very important. 'Wherever they go they find friends, probably wearing the same "school tie" to give them a helping hand; and in many cases their kindly words spoken in time, may make all the difference between success and failure.'[1]

Today it is the educational system which largely regulates social and occupational opportunities and through these the entry into the élite proper. Those who pass through the public schools or through the universities, acquire a passport for entry into the professions, administration and business. The boys and girls, who leave the grammar schools with the General Certificate of Education in their pockets, form the rear. The great 'silent social revolution' occurred at the entry into the grammar schools. The chances of someone who had started his schooling in a public elementary school to get to a grammar school are today more than fifty times as great as at the end of the last century. There has been no corresponding expansion of the higher stages of the scholastic ladder. Equality of educational opportunity has been defined as 'an equal chance to reveal differences which may be superiorities'.[2] Given the unequal distribution of ability and intelligence it is obvious that the shape of the educational hierarchy must resemble a stepped pyramid. There seems, however, no inherent reason why the slope of the pyramid should be as steep as it is or that talent and ability should be wasted at each step.

The reasons for this waste lie partly in the educational system and partly in the material environment and social climate in which schools and universities work. At present all these factors combine to tilt the balance of educational success at each stage in favour of the middle class. At that critical date, half-way between birth and marriage, the *eleven-plus* examination, the educational chances of the middle-class boy or girl are greater than those of the working-class child. Their parents can let him opt out of the competition and give them a chance to obtain his secondary schooling in the private sector. The middle-class child may thus obtain a grammar school

---

[1] Lord Maugham: *At the End of the Day*, 1954, p. 14.
[2] T. H. Marshall: 'Social Selections in the Welfare State', *Eugenics Review*, 1953, pp. 81–93.

type of education even if his level of ability would otherwise put him into the secondary modern school. In the examination itself we find that at the borderline, where other factors than mere performance in the test may be decisive, a higher class background and the chances of obtaining a grammar school place are to some extent correlated.[1]

From the threshold of the grammar school onwards environmental factors affect performance. Educational attainment and scholastic success will be influenced not only by the material conditions of the home but also, more subtly, by the aspirations which parents have for their children and by the importance which they attach to education.[2] While the middle-class parent has grasped the importance of the educational ladder for the material prospects of their children, and is using it to the fullest, this is much less so in the working-class milieu.

The extent of this wasting of talent shows itself at the second hurdle of the educational system: the entry into the universities. The preponderance of middle-class children among university students compared with its share among the thirteen-year-olds, who can be found at state-supported grammar schools or in 'efficient' independent schools, shows that a significant proportion of children from working-class homes have either left the grammar schools before reaching the sixth form or have chosen not to proceed to college.[3] There is no bias on the part of selectors but there is also no climate of opinion which makes study at universities or colleges the obvious and natural goal of all those who could profit from it. If higher education was accorded the same importance as is currently given to it in the United States, or in Canada, society would look with dismay at our apparent failure to develop fully the talents of over half of those who on the basis of innate

---

[1] cf. D. V. Glass, *Differential Fertility, Ability and Educational Opportunity* (Godfrey Thomson Lecture, 1961, p. 21, reporting an as yet unpublished investigation).

[2] The two latter factors are closely linked to the educational attainments of the parents themselves. cf. E. Fraser: *Home Environment and the School*, 1959, J. Floud *et al.*: *Social Class and Educational Opportunity*, 1956.

[3] On the social background of students see R. K. Kelsall: *Applications for Admission to British Universities* published by the Association of Universities of the British Commonwealth, 1957.

ability would be able to benefit from education at the university level.[1]

Such an imbalance in the opportunity pattern will limit social mobility and must, eventually, affect the entry into élite positions. We do not know the extent of the wastage among the men and women of very high intellectual calibre, but even if it is small the efficacy of selection will at each level depend on the pool of trained intelligence from which it may draw.

To enlarge the reservoir of well-educated men and women demands a new approach to education and probably also a widening of the meshes of the educational net at all levels, even at the risk of increasing the numbers of those who will fail to make the grade, be it at the stage of secondary or higher education. It might also mean that some will receive 'more' education than they might need for their occupational activities—as many women do today without this causing great consternation.

The democratic view of the ideal working of the educational system has long been opposed by an 'élitist' concept of scholastic training whose aim is the breeding of a cadre of prospective national leaders. It found its clearest expression in the public school system whose ethos, as we saw, appealed to loyalty, responsibility and the spirit of service. And although its appeal was restricted to a tiny section of society the effectiveness of its tenets for the formation of the Victorian ruling class was marked. This seems to be no longer so today. According to an internal observer the appeal to leadership and service counts for little. The majority of the boys 'regard their privileges . . . as the natural and proper prerogative of the class to which their parents belong.'[2]

In order to counter this and to keep in step with the more widespread egalitarian feeling of the twentieth century it has been suggested that the area of recruitment of the public schools should be widened and that they might even become entirely the training

---

[1] Of all National Service recruits called up between 1956–58, who after testing were put in the topmost of ten ability groups, 59 per cent had left school before the age of eighteen. Among the sons of manual workers in that category 76 per cent did so. cf. Central Advisory Council for Education: 15 to 18, 2 vols., 1959–60.

[2] John Wilson; Public Schools and Private Practice, 1962, p. 120 (the author is a Senior Master at a Public School).

places of the 'natural' leaders of the nation without any reference to social origin or ability to pay.[1]

This might effectively destroy the present link between family background, educational career and subsequent high office but by concentrating on the advancement of individuals we might easily neglect an important aspect of the educational system: the raising of the general level of ability, understanding and judgment throughout the population. It is this which presents, in the long run, the best guarantee for an effective link between élite and democracy and between the increasingly complicated policy issues which confront the administrators and their popular control.

When, in 1867, the first bases for a democratic franchise were laid, Robert Lowe, one of the most forceful and outright opponents of the measure, expressed the conviction that it 'will be absolutely necessary that you shall prevail on our future masters to learn their letters'. Education, he went on, 'has become paramount to every other question that has been brought before us. From the moment that you entrust the masses with power their education becomes an absolute necessity'.[2]

Compared with a hundred years ago the issues which confront us today are vastly more complicated and the choices which politicians are asked to make may have much more far-reaching and possibly fatal consequences than those which confronted their predecessors in the middle years of the Victorian era. Throughout this book attention has been paid to the way in which the changing character of the executive function has influenced the type of politician who emerges and achieves office. At the same time failures and shortcomings have been stressed and some of the imperative changes in the selection process and working-conditions of élite groups have been discussed in this chapter. To adjust the élites to the needs of the time is, however, only one of the important problems. It is equally necessary to reduce the distance between rulers and ruled. To do this we must provide a general level of education which is as much above the three R's aimed at after 1867 as the degree of complexity of our policies today is above those of a century ago.

---

[1] cf. Wilson, op. cit. and R. P. Williams: *Whose Public Schools?*, 1957.

[2] Hansard, 3rd series, vol. 188, c.1549.

To pin one's hope for the future on a new mental approach and a changed intellectual outlook by those who are at the centre of things seems to me insufficient. I find it difficult to believe that 'Britain's malaise . . . is . . . a malaise among the few thousand managers of our society who have failed to absorb and communicate new challenges and new ideas'.[1] I think that the problems of democratic government and of the responsible exercise of power in Britain today are in part at least structural problems. We must face squarely such issues as the selection of potential rulers, the control of the leadership, the widening scope for talent, the turnover of élites, the development of ability and the fostering of critical understanding throughout the population.

[1] A. Sampson: *Anatomy of Britain*, 1962, p. 638.

Index

INDEX